D0562704

Requiem of the Rose King

7

AYA KANNO

Based on *Henry VI* and *Richard III*
by William Shakespeare

Story Thus Far

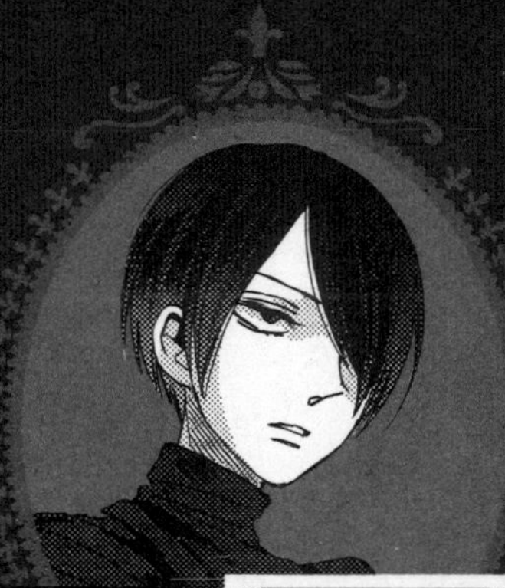

WHITE ROSE

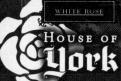

House of York

RICHARD

The third son of York, he has been shunned by his mother since childhood.

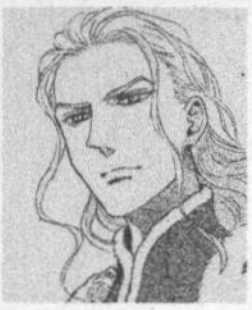

Richard, Duke of York

Father of Richard. He was the light of hope for Richard, but he was killed by Lancaster.

Cecily

Mother of Richard. She despises him.

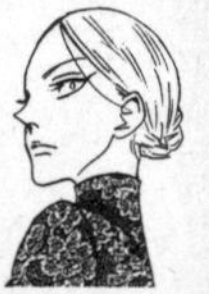

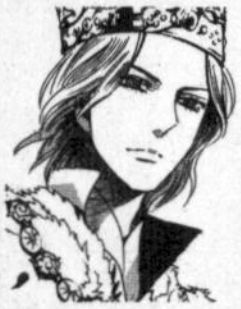

Edward

The oldest son of the House of York who is maneuvering to get the throne back. He's inordinately fond of women.

George

The second son of the House of York. He joined forces with Warwick to incite a rebellion but has now rejoined his brothers.

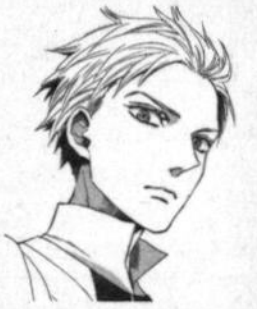

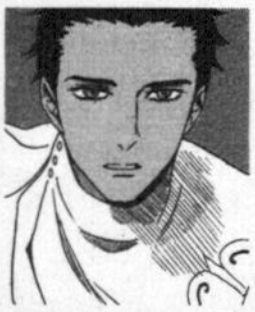

Catesby

Richard's attendant since childhood. He knows Richard's secret.

House of Nevills

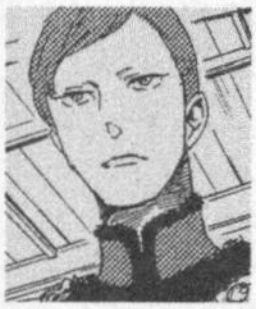

Earl of Warwick

He betrayed the House of York and joined the Lancasters. He was struck down by Buckingham.

Anne

She liked Richard but became the wife of Edward of Lancaster in a strategic marriage.

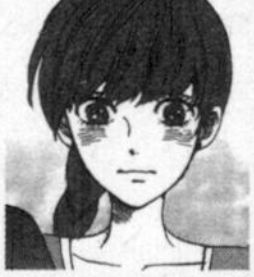

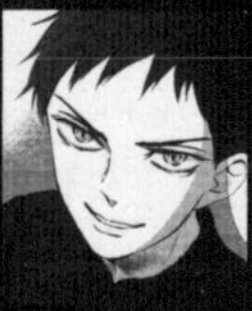

Buckingham

Very ambitious. He has come forward and named himself Richard's kingmaker.

Elizabeth

Married Edward of York and is now queen. She lost her husband in the war and harbors a grudge against the House of York.

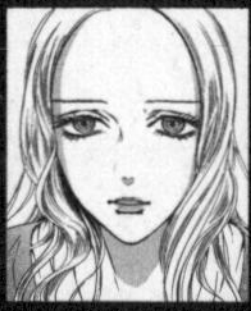

Characters &

RED ROSE

House of Lancaster

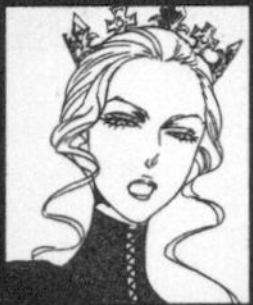

Margaret

She is Henry's wife, but she feels little love for him. Her goal is the restoration of the Lancasters.

Edward

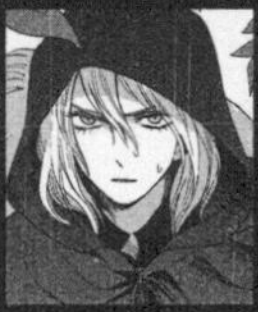

Son of Henry. Strong willed. He is in love with Richard.

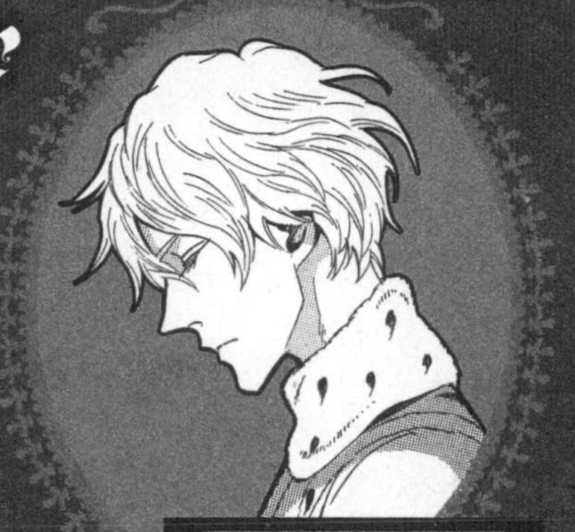

HENRY THE SIXTH

King once more. He's very pious and hates fighting. Occasionally, he disguises himself as a shepherd and meets up incognito with Richard.

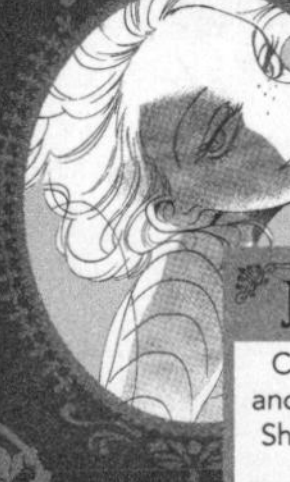

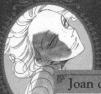

Joan of Arc

Called a French witch and burned at the stake. She appears to Richard as a ghost.

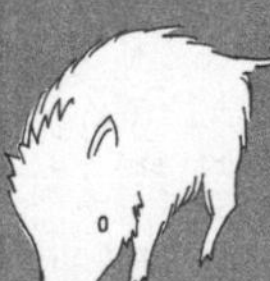

White boar

Saved by Richard when it was injured. The boar is very close to Richard.

Story thus far...

ENGLAND, THE MIDDLE AGES.

The two houses of York and Lancaster are caught in repeated royal contest, the age of the War of the Roses.

King Edward welcomes Elizabeth as his queen, without discussing it with his retainers. Furious at the king's selfish behavior, Warwick incites a rebellion with George. When Warwick joins forces with Margaret to restore Henry to the throne, he becomes regent, gaining power equivalent to that of the king.

Having set off to win back George on his brother Edward's orders, Richard happens to meet Henry along the way. When they spend time alone together, Richard realizes that he's in love with Henry, but Henry says he can never love anyone. Richard locks those feelings away in his heart, but the two swear they'll meet again.

Richard brings George over to the York side and, with his quick wit, leads their army to victory on the battlefield. York crushes Lancaster, and with his back against the wall, Warwick tries a temporary retreat in order to regroup. However, he is cut down by Buckingham, who is strategically disguised as Richard. Margaret arrives at the port leading reinforcement troops, and they charge toward the battlefield knowing nothing of the current situation.

In the midst of all this, Richard, seeking to take the life of King Henry in order to avenge his father, finally comes face-to-face with Henry, who is hiding near the battlefield...

Requiem of the Rose King

Contents

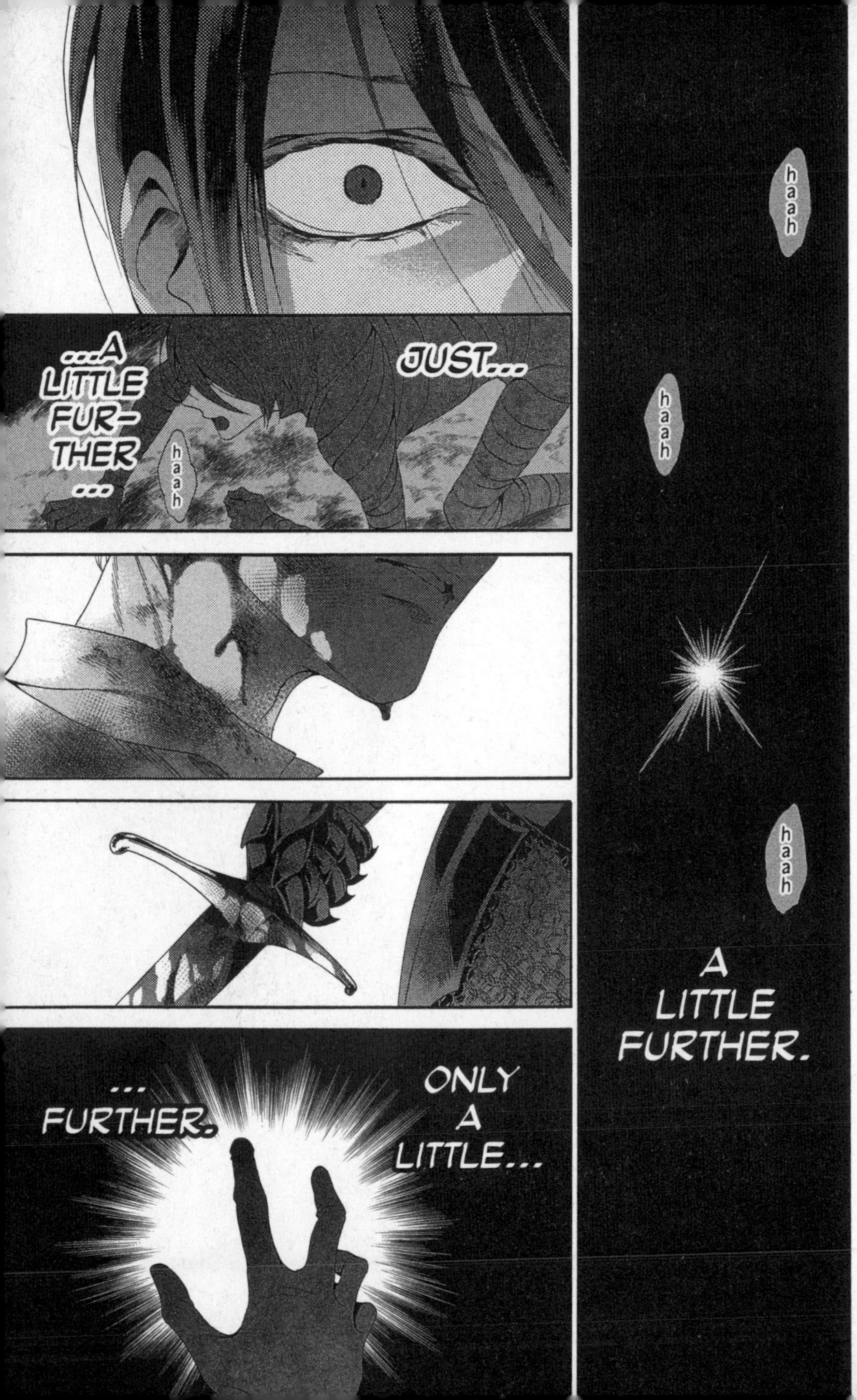
haah
haah
haah
A LITTLE FURTHER.
JUST...
...A LITTLE FUR-THER...
haah
ONLY A LITTLE...
...FURTHER.

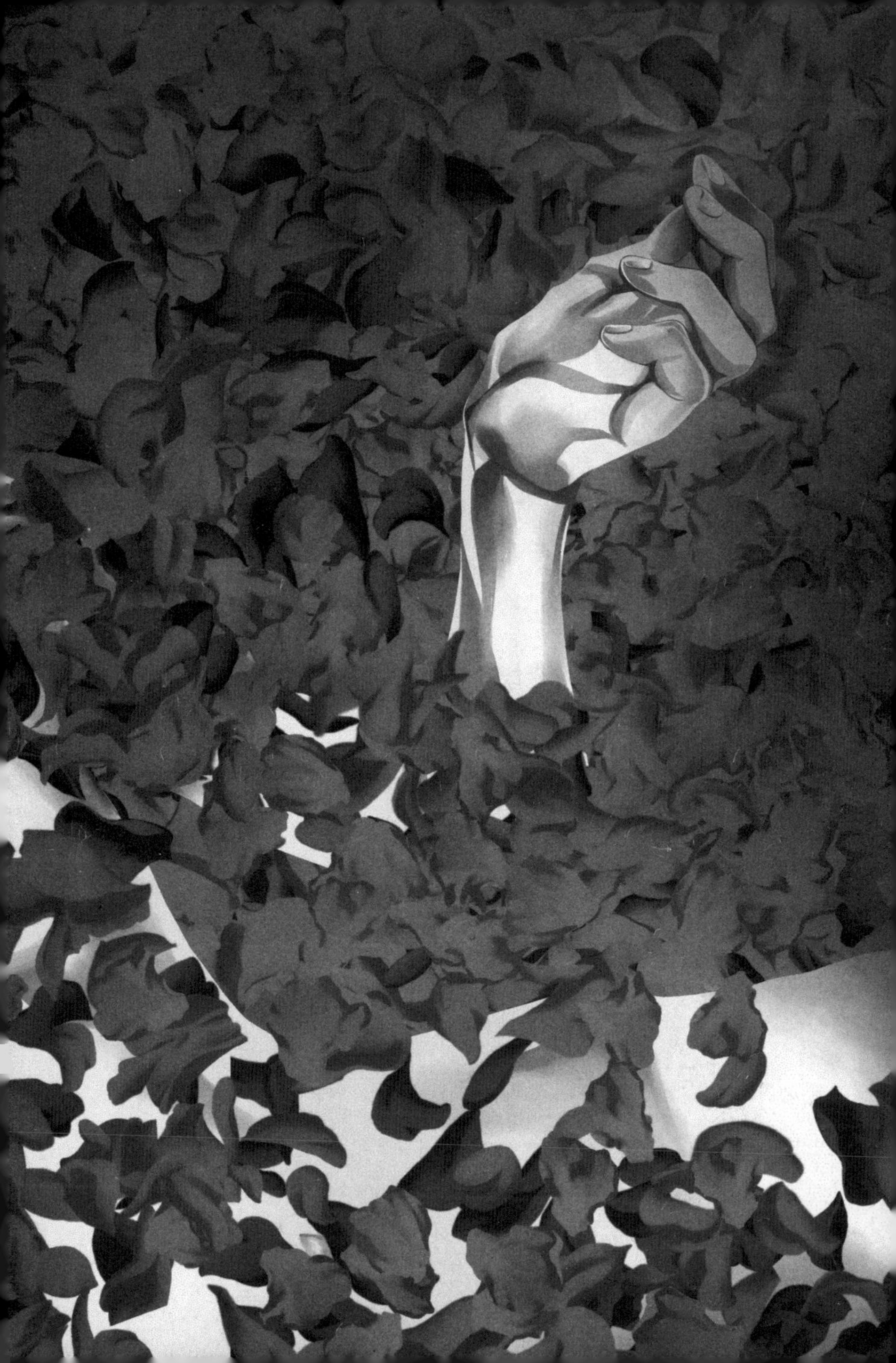

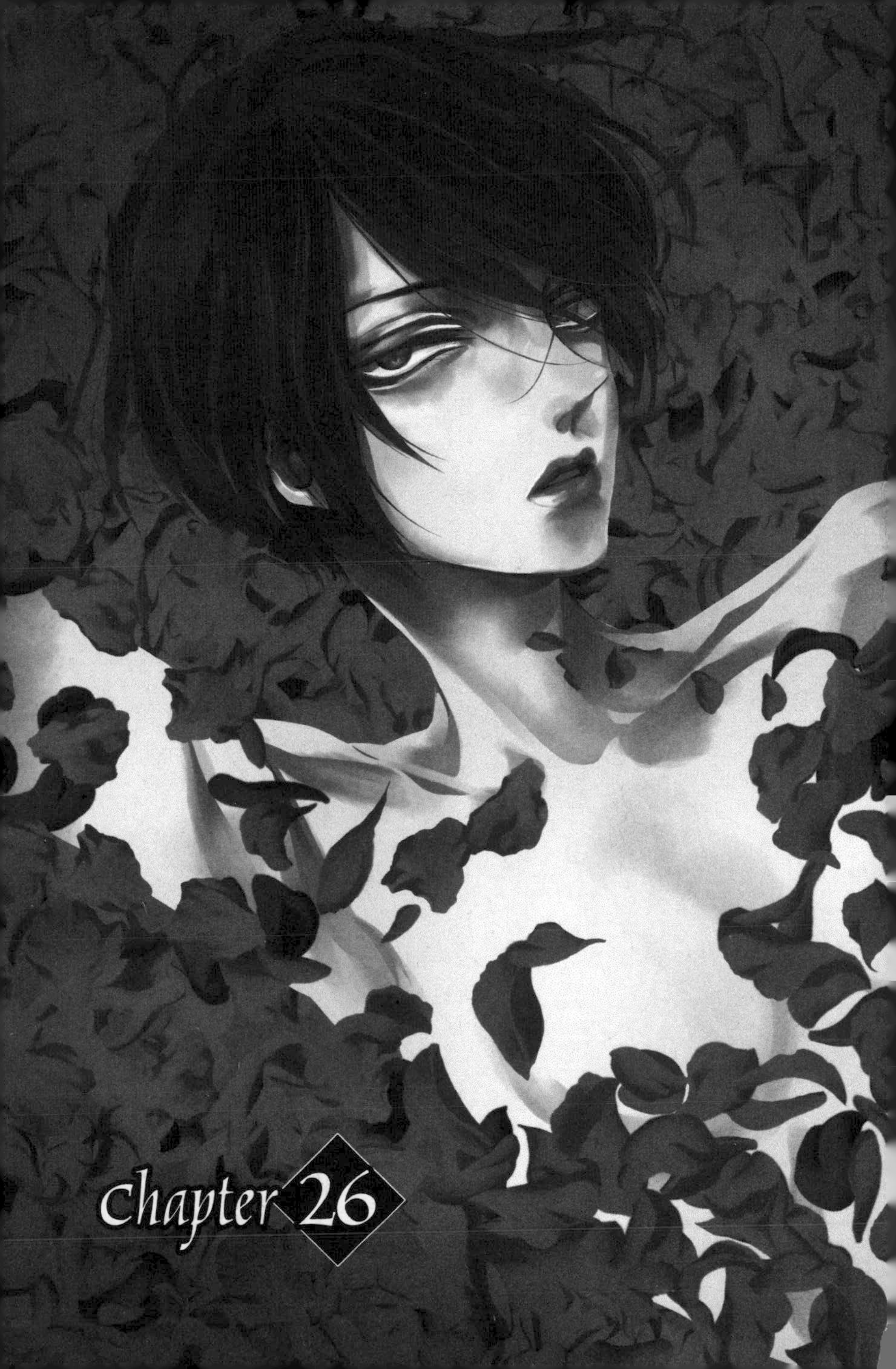
Chapter 26

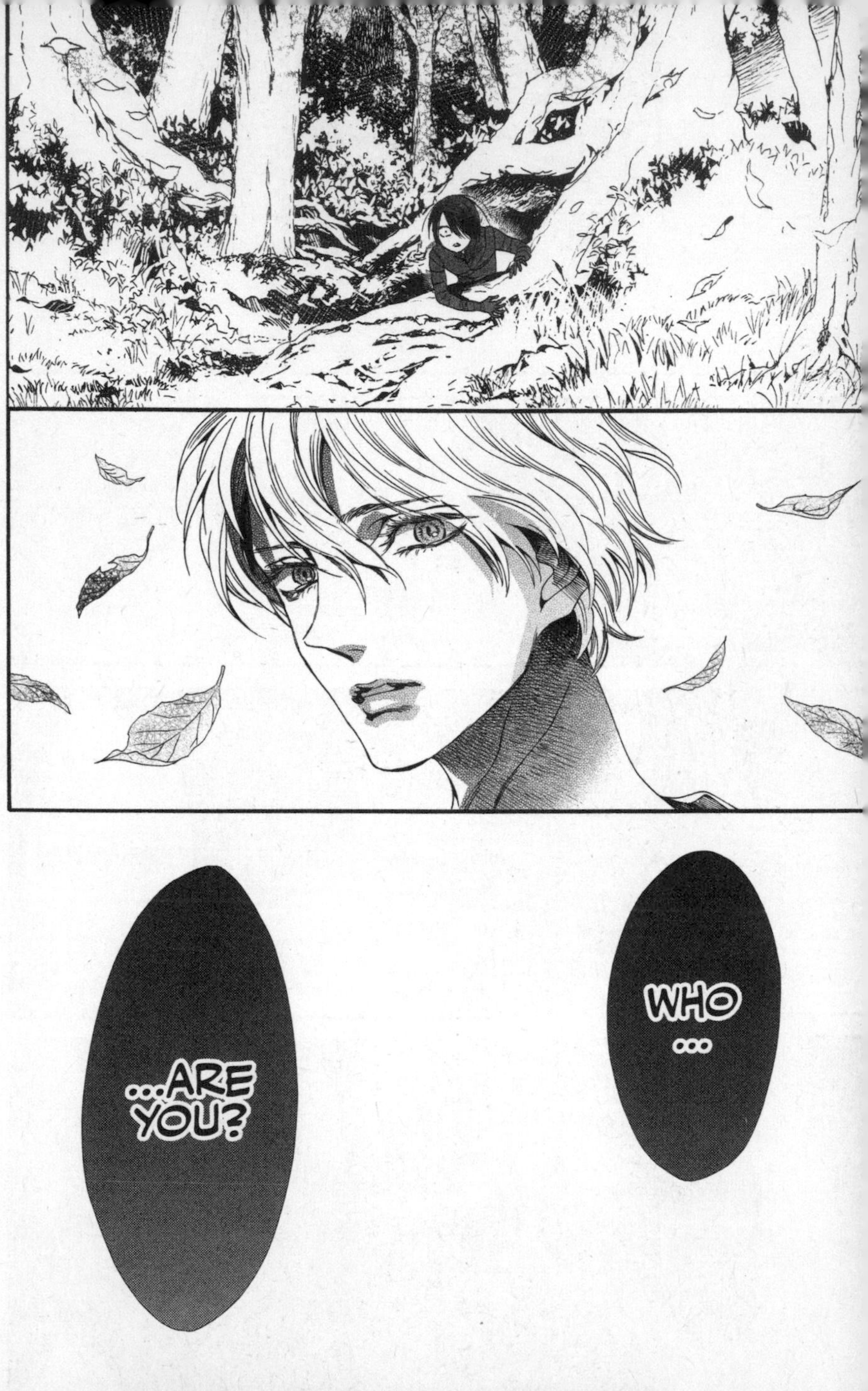
WHO ...
...ARE YOU?

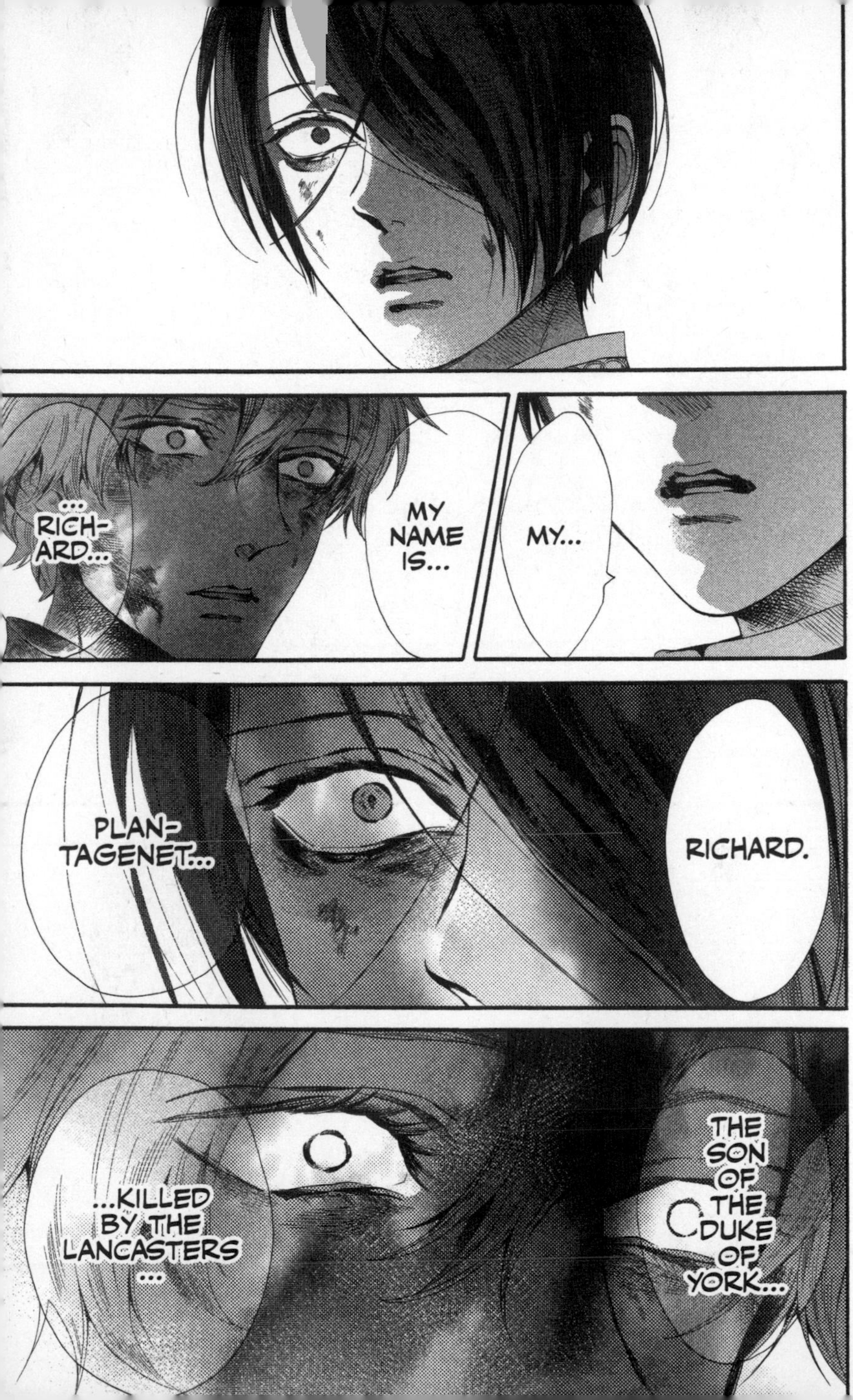
MY...
MY NAME IS...
...RICHARD...
RICHARD.
PLANTAGENET...
THE SON OF THE DUKE OF YORK...
...KILLED BY THE LANCASTERS...

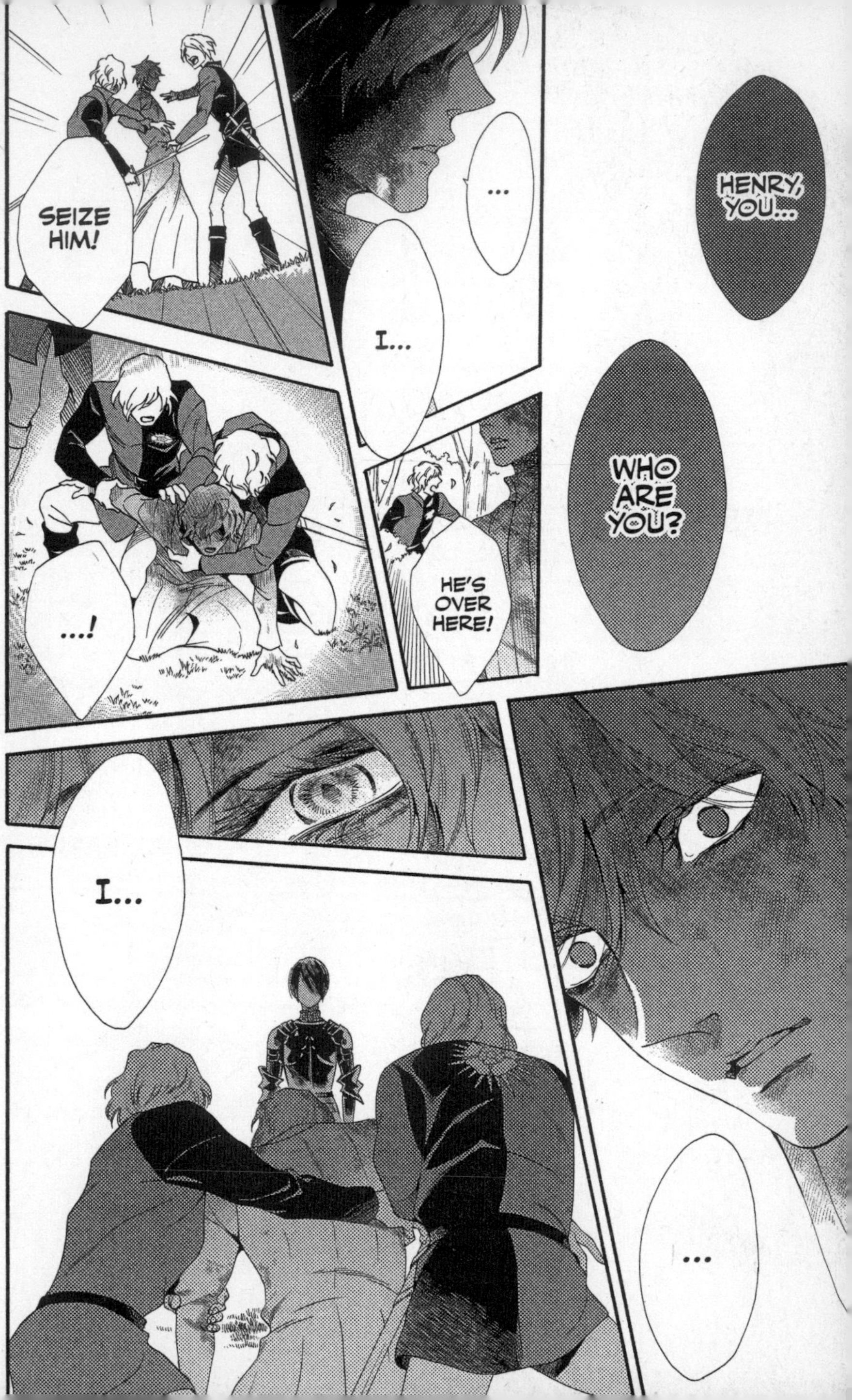
HENRY, YOU...
WHO ARE YOU?
...
I...
SEIZE HIM!
HE'S OVER HERE!
...!
...
I...

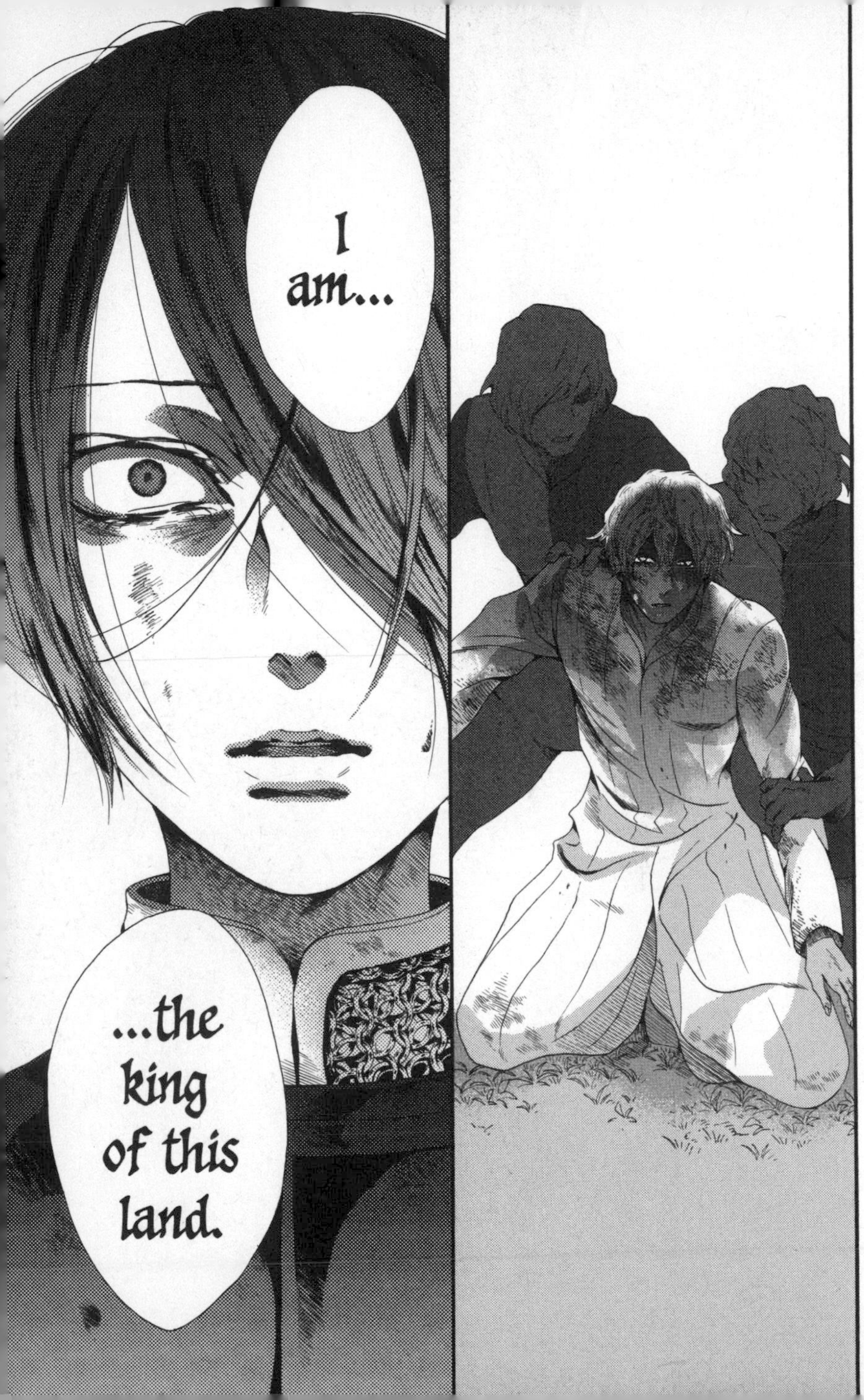
I am...
...the king of this land.

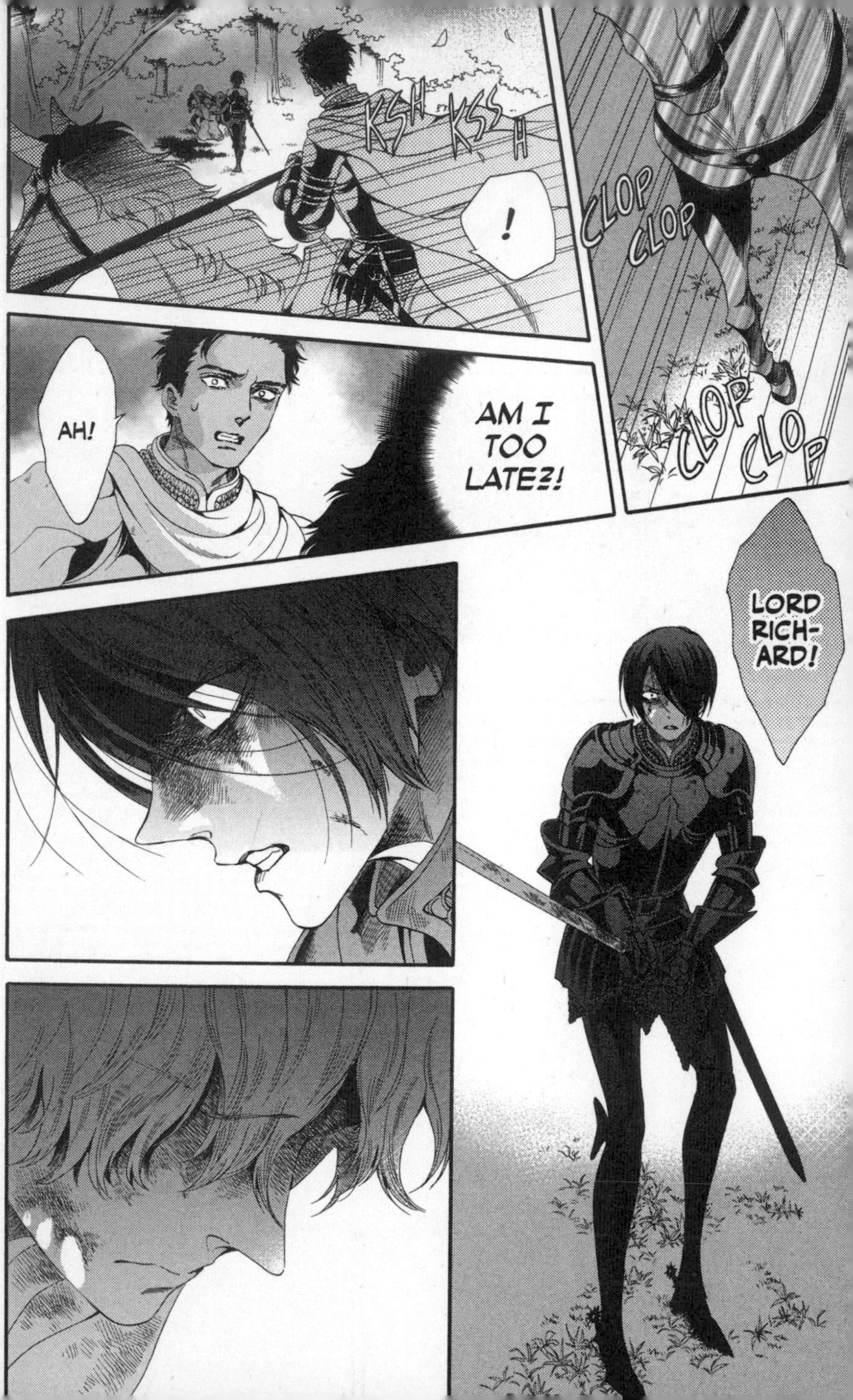
CLOP CLOP
CLOP CLOP
KSH KSSH
!
AM I TOO LATE?!
AH!
LORD RICH-ARD!

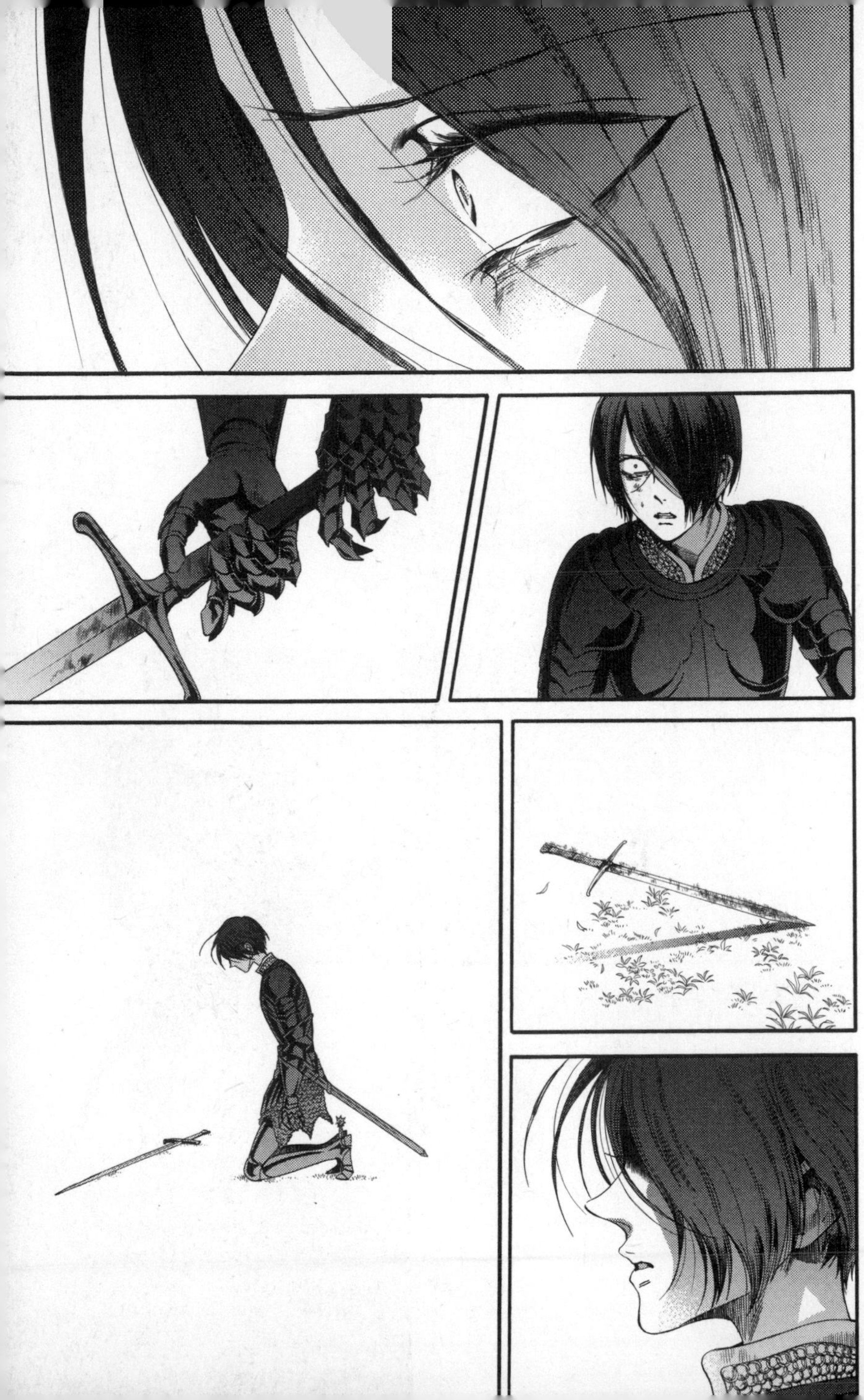

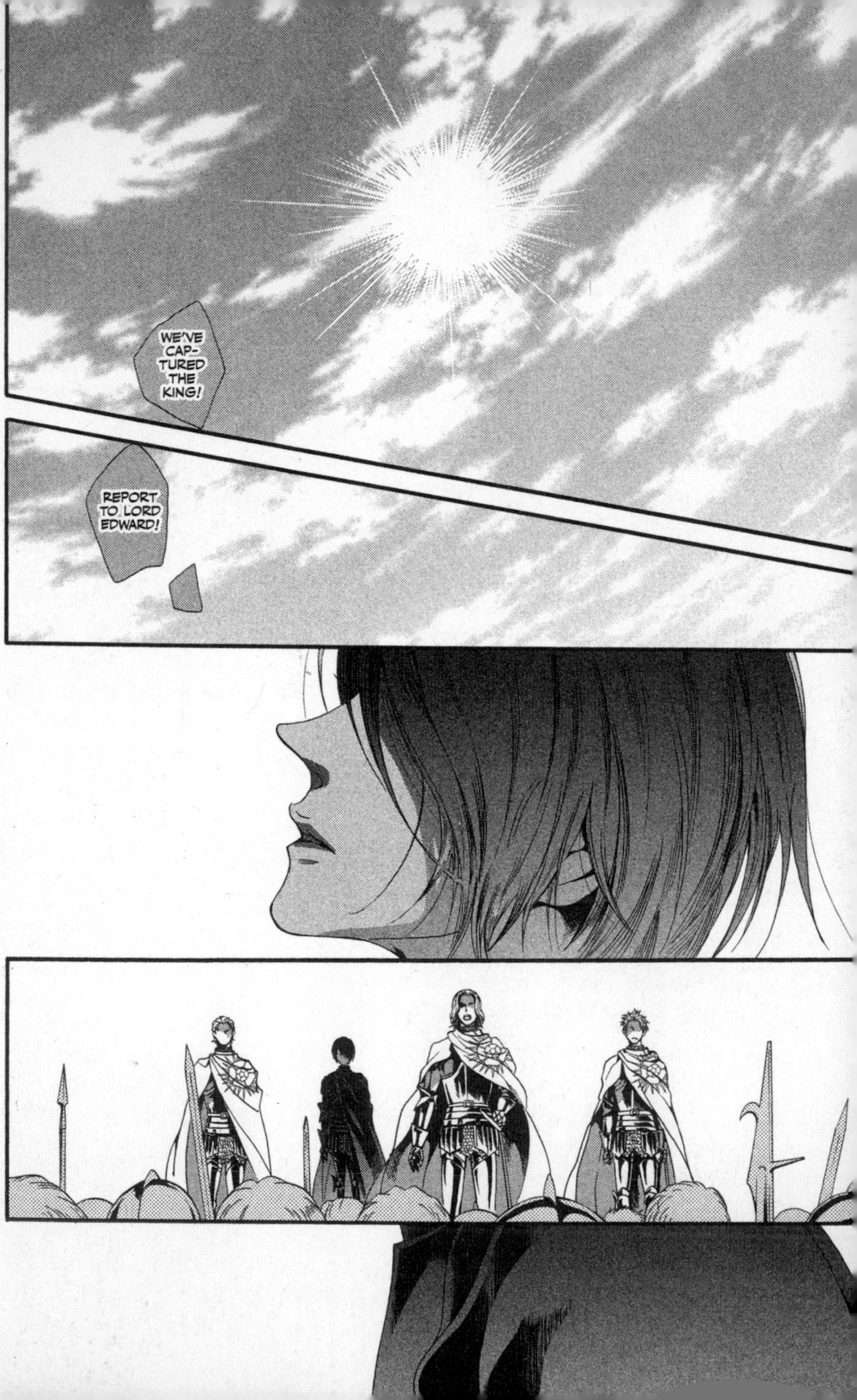
WE'VE CAP-TURED THE KING!
REPORT TO LORD EDWARD!

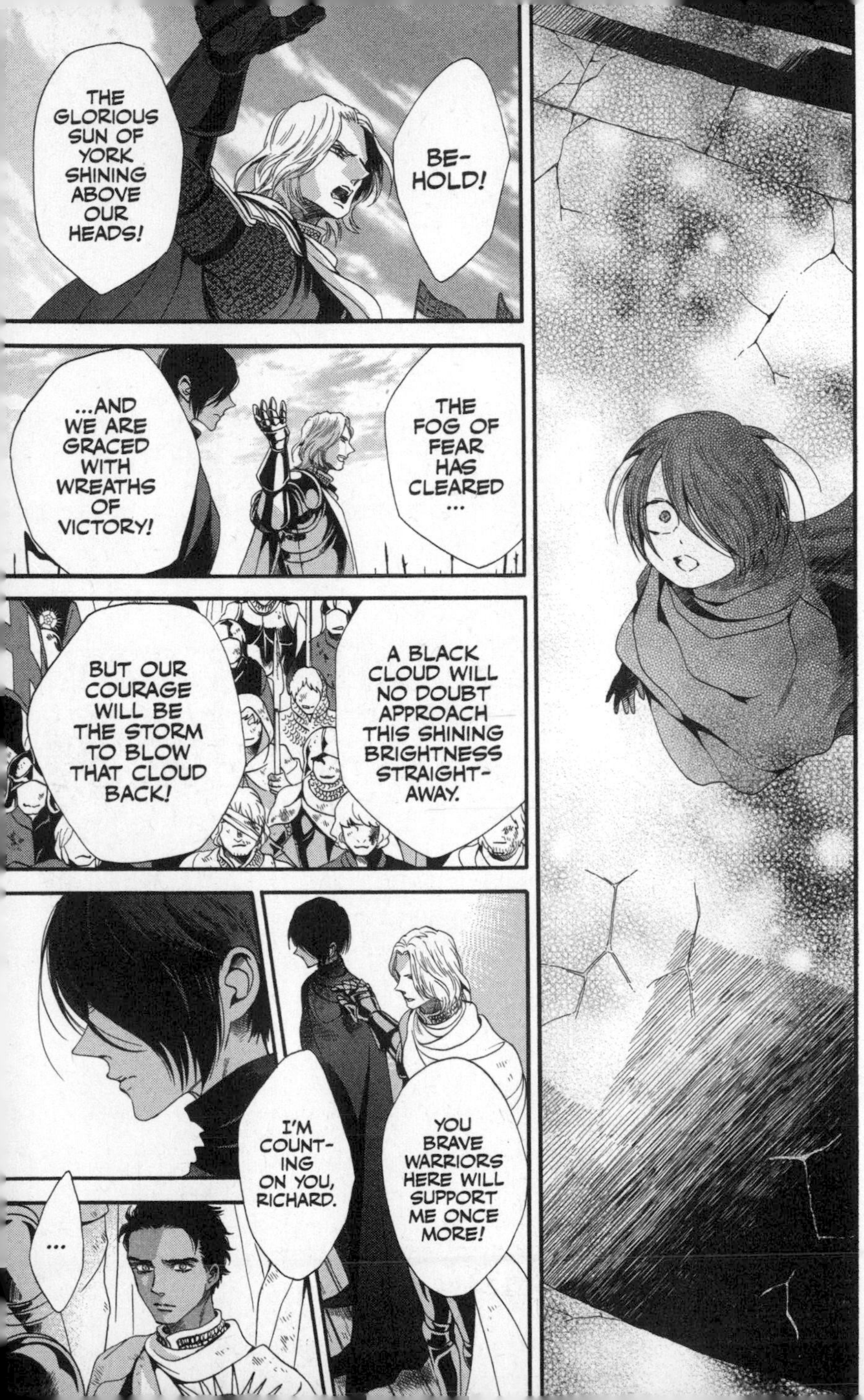
BE-HOLD!
THE GLORIOUS SUN OF YORK SHINING ABOVE OUR HEADS!
THE FOG OF FEAR HAS CLEARED...
...AND WE ARE GRACED WITH WREATHS OF VICTORY!
A BLACK CLOUD WILL NO DOUBT APPROACH THIS SHINING BRIGHTNESS STRAIGHT-AWAY.
BUT OUR COURAGE WILL BE THE STORM TO BLOW THAT CLOUD BACK!
YOU BRAVE WARRIORS HERE WILL SUPPORT ME ONCE MORE!
I'M COUNTING-ING ON YOU, RICHARD.
...

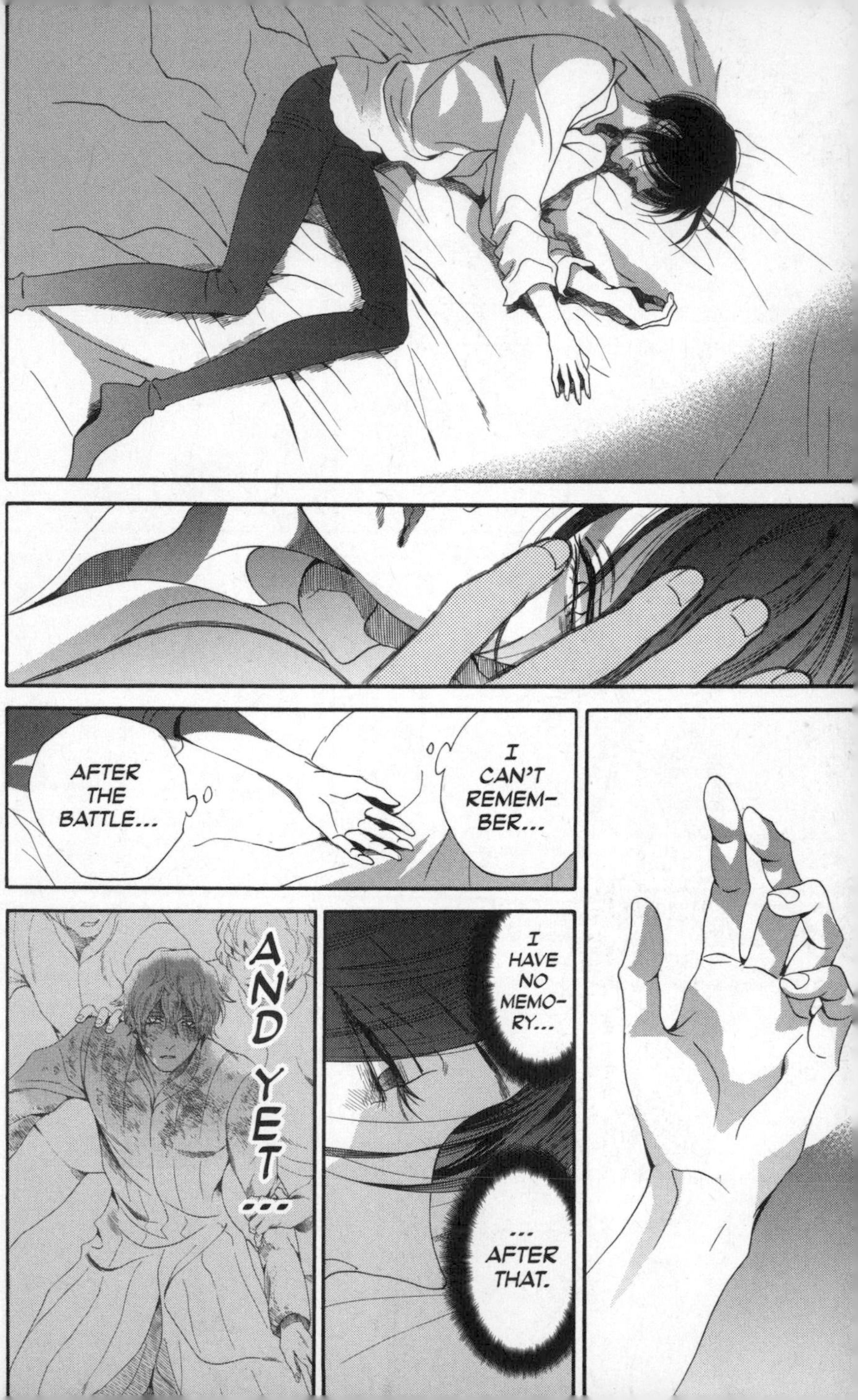
I CAN'T REMEMBER...
AFTER THE BATTLE...
I HAVE NO MEMORY...
...AFTER THAT.
AND YET...

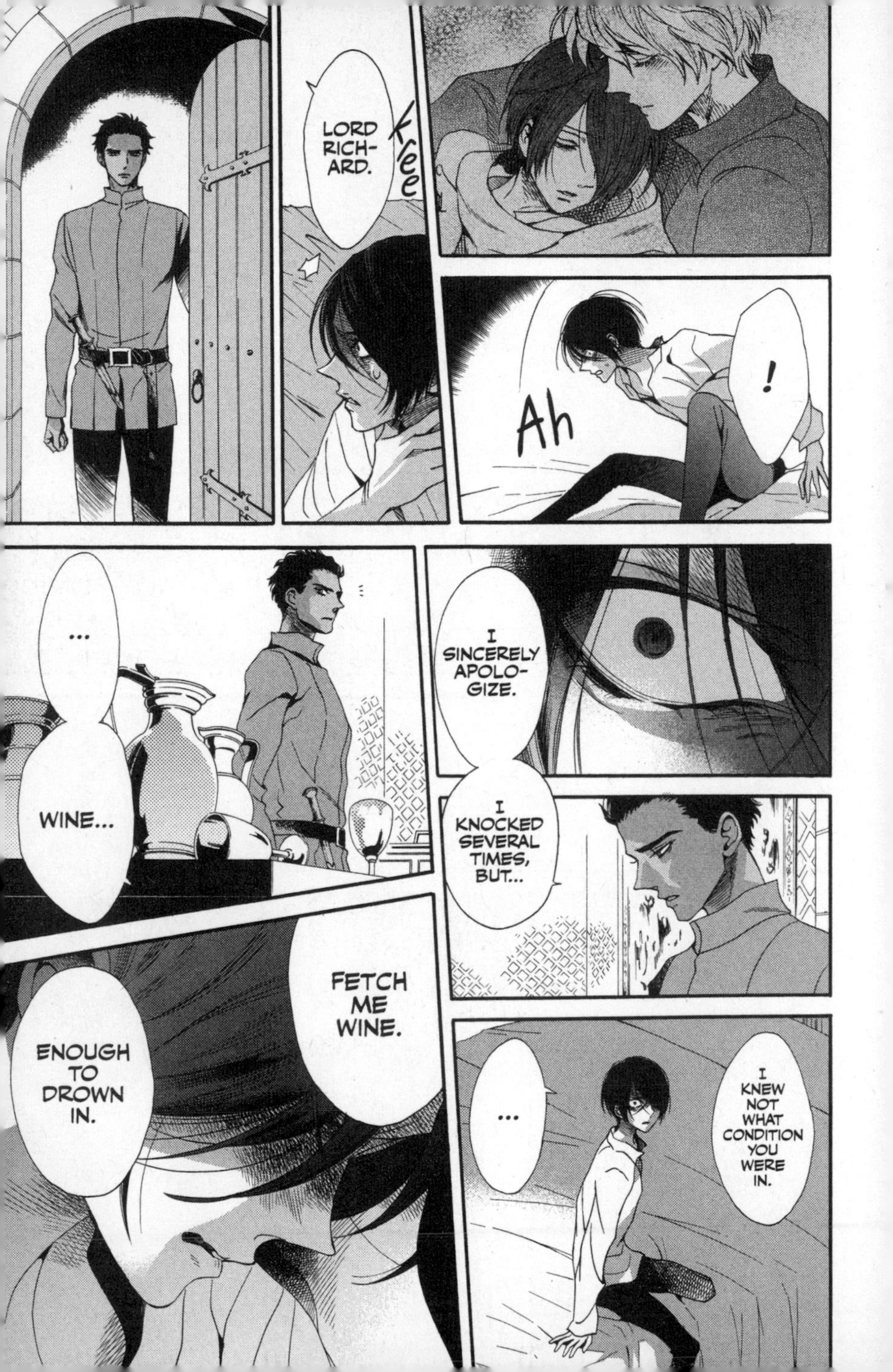

!
Ah
LORD RICH-ARD.
kree
I SINCERELY APOLO-GIZE.
I KNOCKED SEVERAL TIMES, BUT...
...
WINE...
I KNEW NOT WHAT CONDITION YOU WERE IN.
...
FETCH ME WINE.
ENOUGH TO DROWN IN.

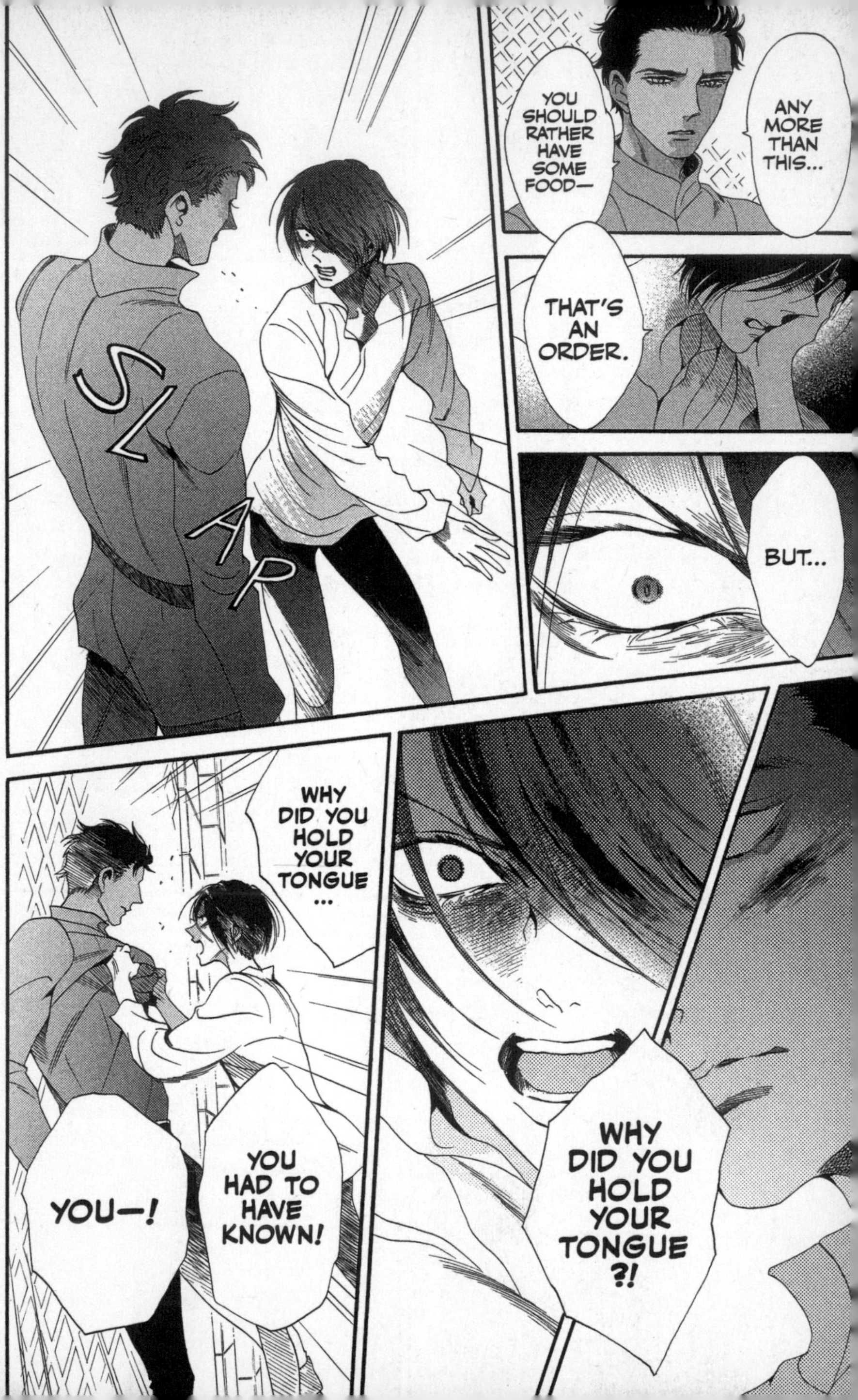
ANY MORE THAN THIS...
YOU SHOULD RATHER HAVE SOME FOOD—
THAT'S AN ORDER.
BUT...
SLAP
WHY DID YOU HOLD YOUR TONGUE?!
WHY DID YOU HOLD YOUR TONGUE...
YOU HAD TO HAVE KNOWN!
YOU—!

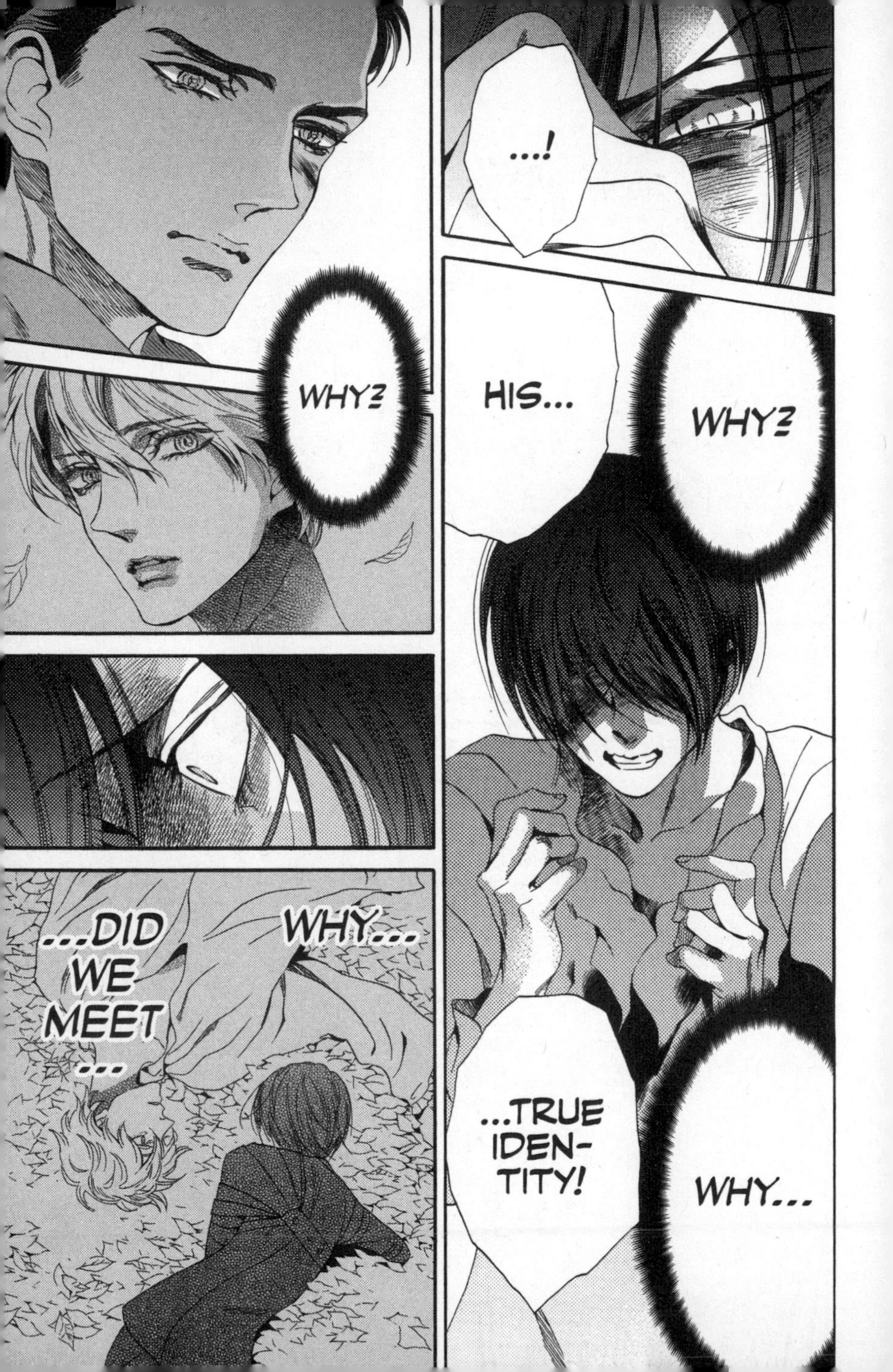
...!
HIS...
WHY?
...TRUE IDENTITY!
WHY...
WHY?
WHY...
...DID WE MEET ...

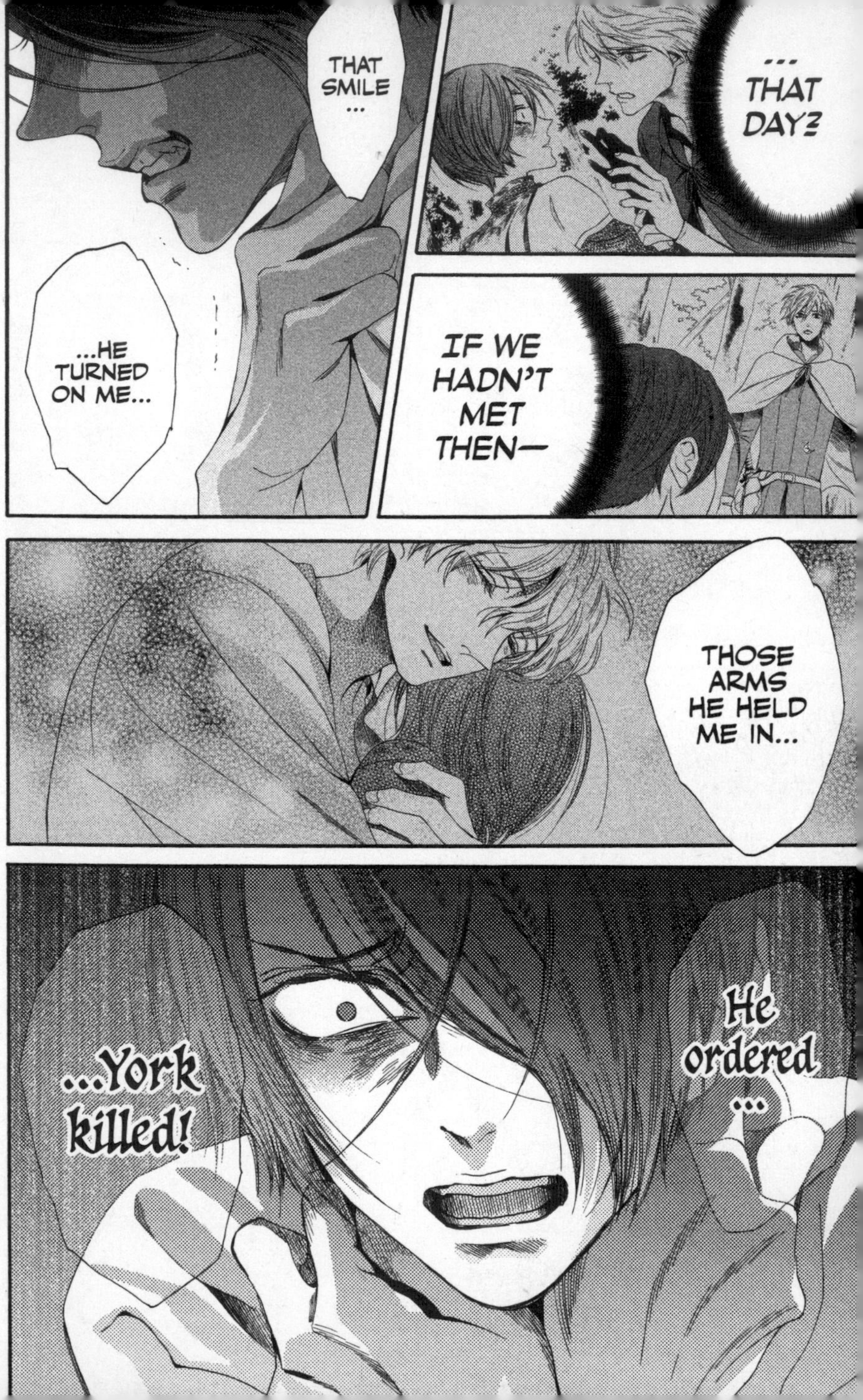
...THAT DAY?
IF WE HADN'T MET THEN—
THAT SMILE...
...HE TURNED ON ME...
THOSE ARMS HE HELD ME IN...
He ordered...
...York killed!

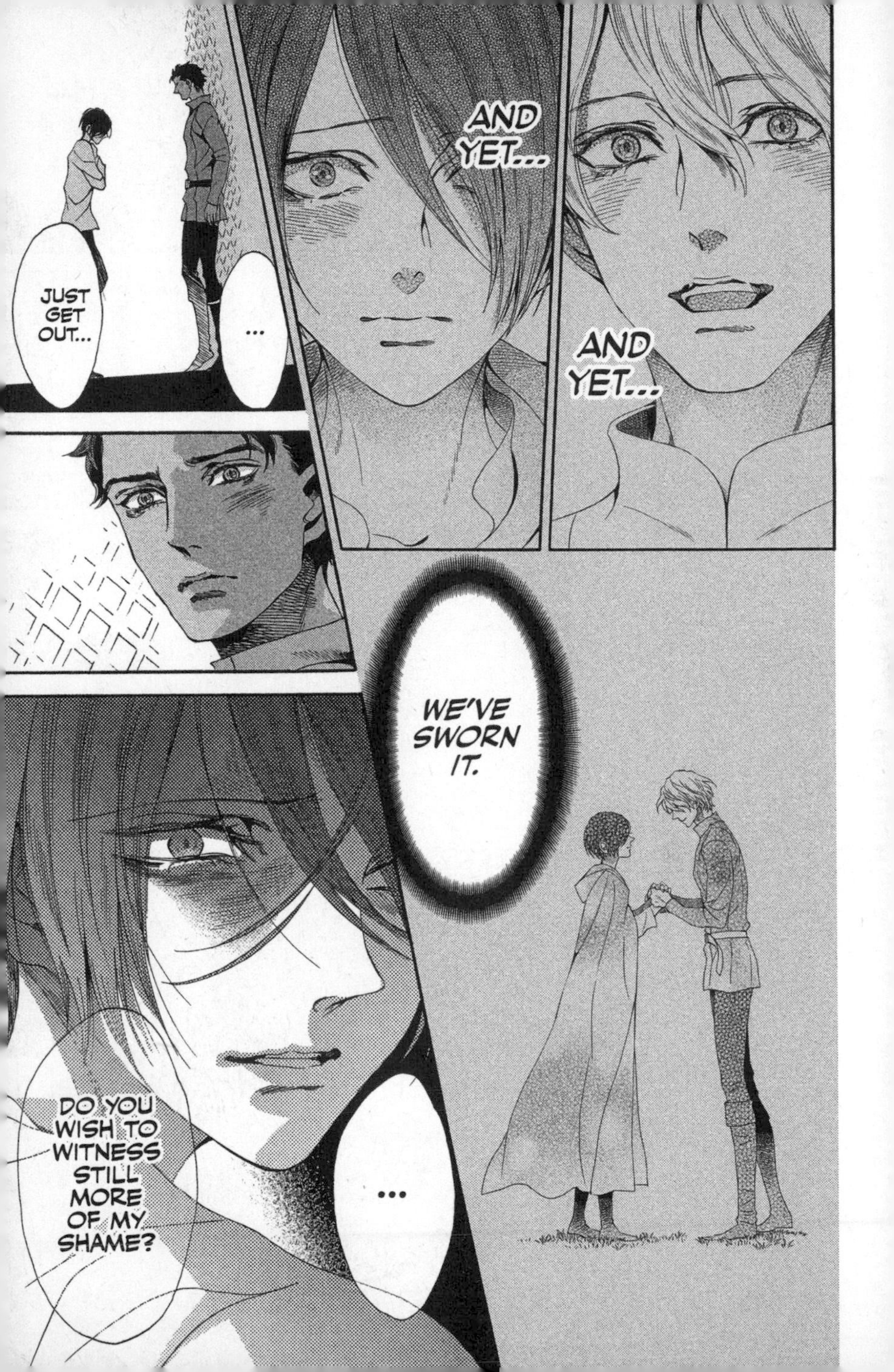
AND YET...
AND YET...
...
JUST GET OUT...
WE'VE SWORN IT.
...
DO YOU WISH TO WITNESS STILL MORE OF MY SHAME?

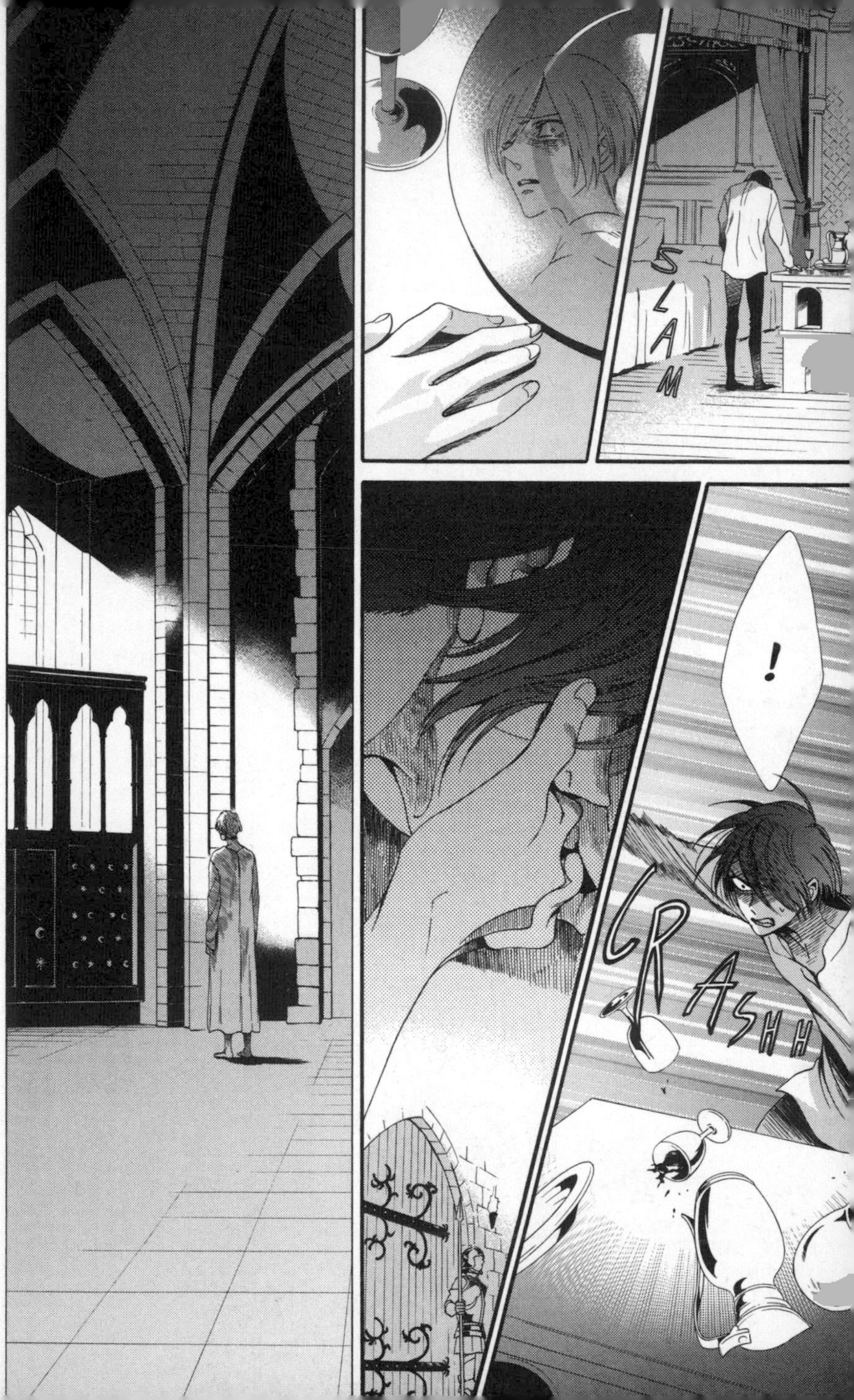
SLAM
!
CRASHH

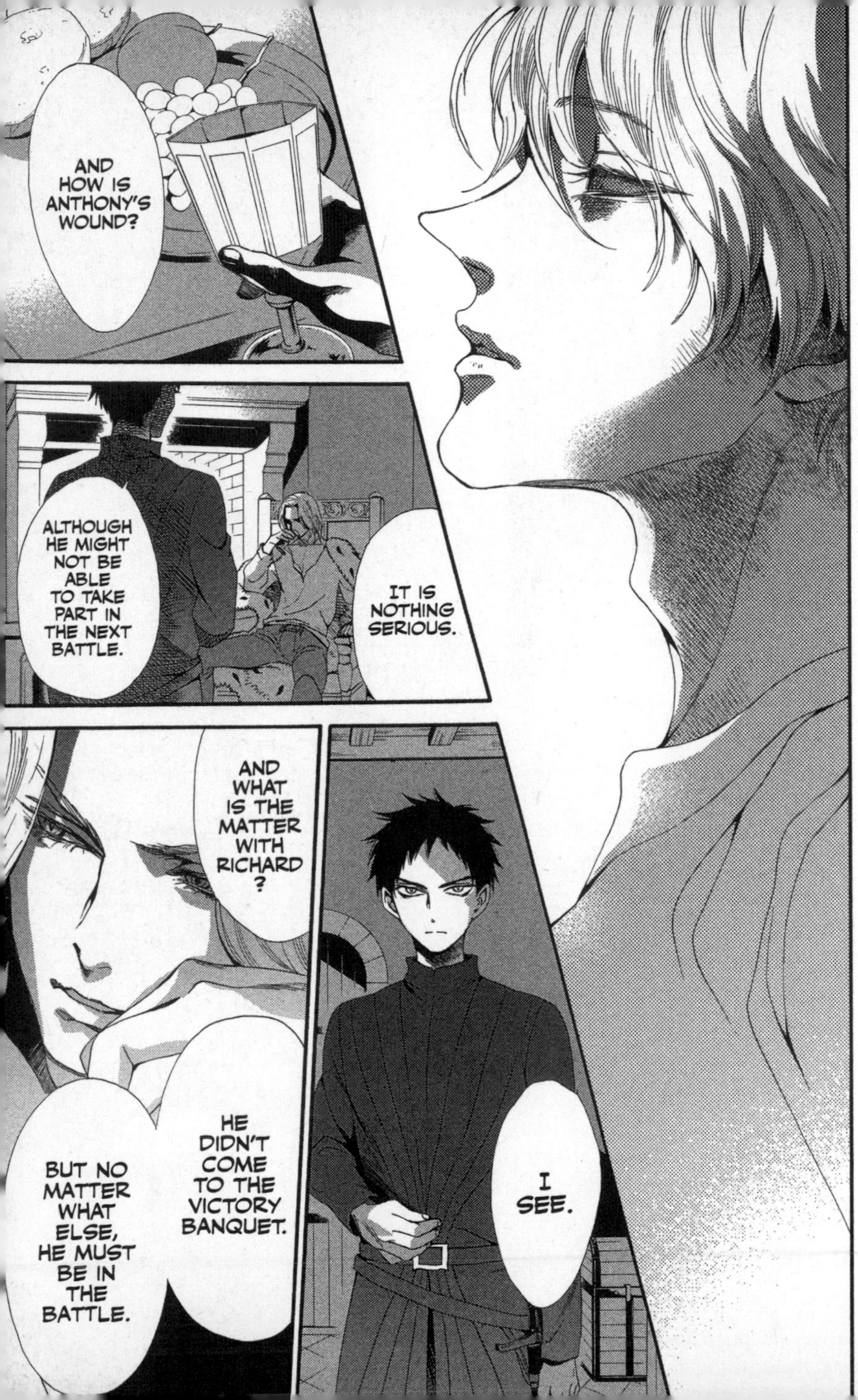
AND HOW IS ANTHONY'S WOUND?
IT IS NOTHING SERIOUS.
ALTHOUGH HE MIGHT NOT BE ABLE TO TAKE PART IN THE NEXT BATTLE.
I SEE.
AND WHAT IS THE MATTER WITH RICHARD?
HE DIDN'T COME TO THE VICTORY BANQUET.
BUT NO MATTER WHAT ELSE, HE MUST BE IN THE BATTLE.

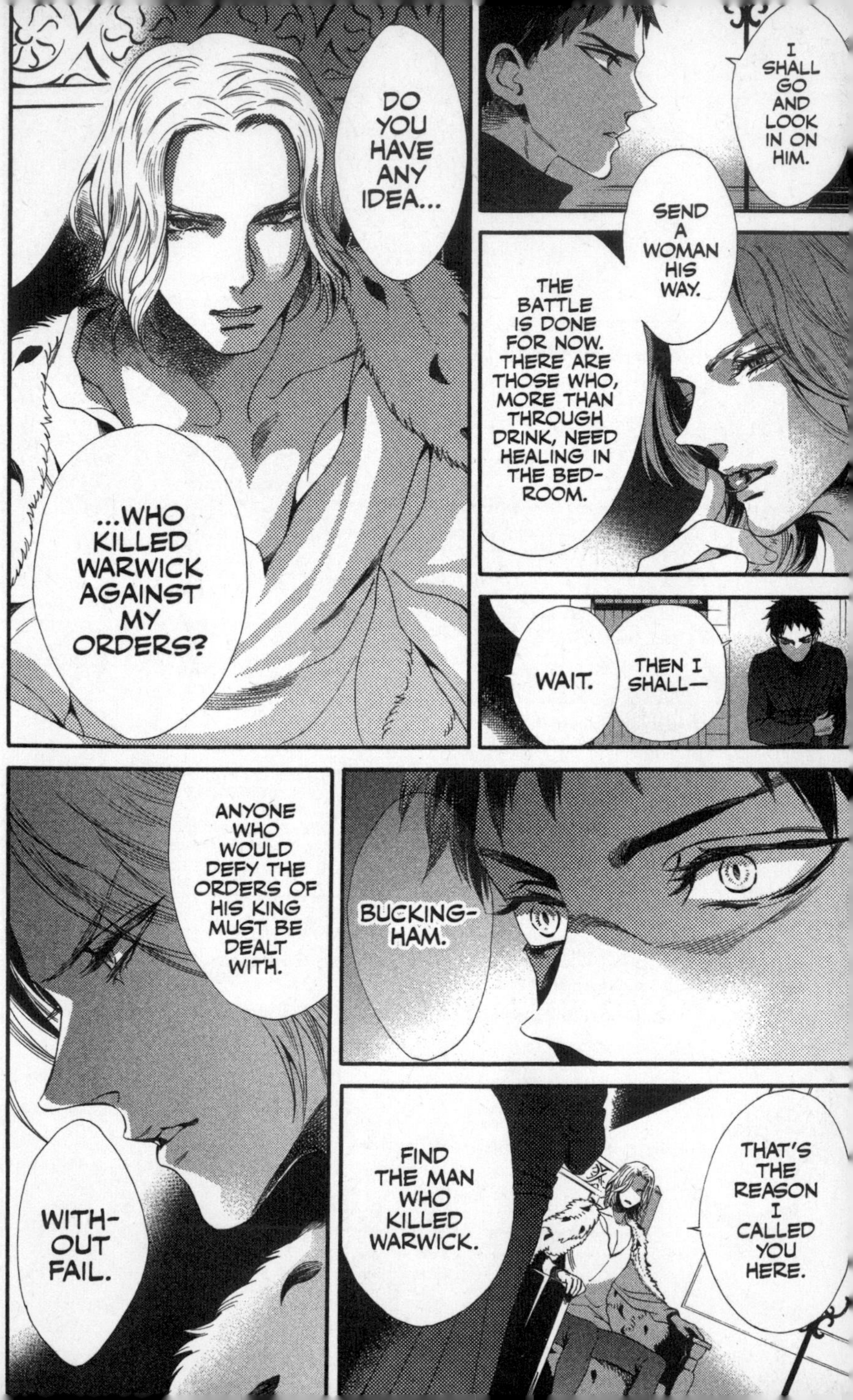
I SHALL GO AND LOOK IN ON HIM.
SEND A WOMAN HIS WAY.
THE BATTLE IS DONE FOR NOW. THERE ARE THOSE WHO, MORE THAN THROUGH DRINK, NEED HEALING IN THE BED-ROOM.
THEN I SHALL—
WAIT.
DO YOU HAVE ANY IDEA...
...WHO KILLED WARWICK AGAINST MY ORDERS?
BUCKING-HAM.
THAT'S THE REASON I CALLED YOU HERE.
FIND THE MAN WHO KILLED WARWICK.
ANYONE WHO WOULD DEFY THE ORDERS OF HIS KING MUST BE DEALT WITH.
WITH-OUT FAIL.

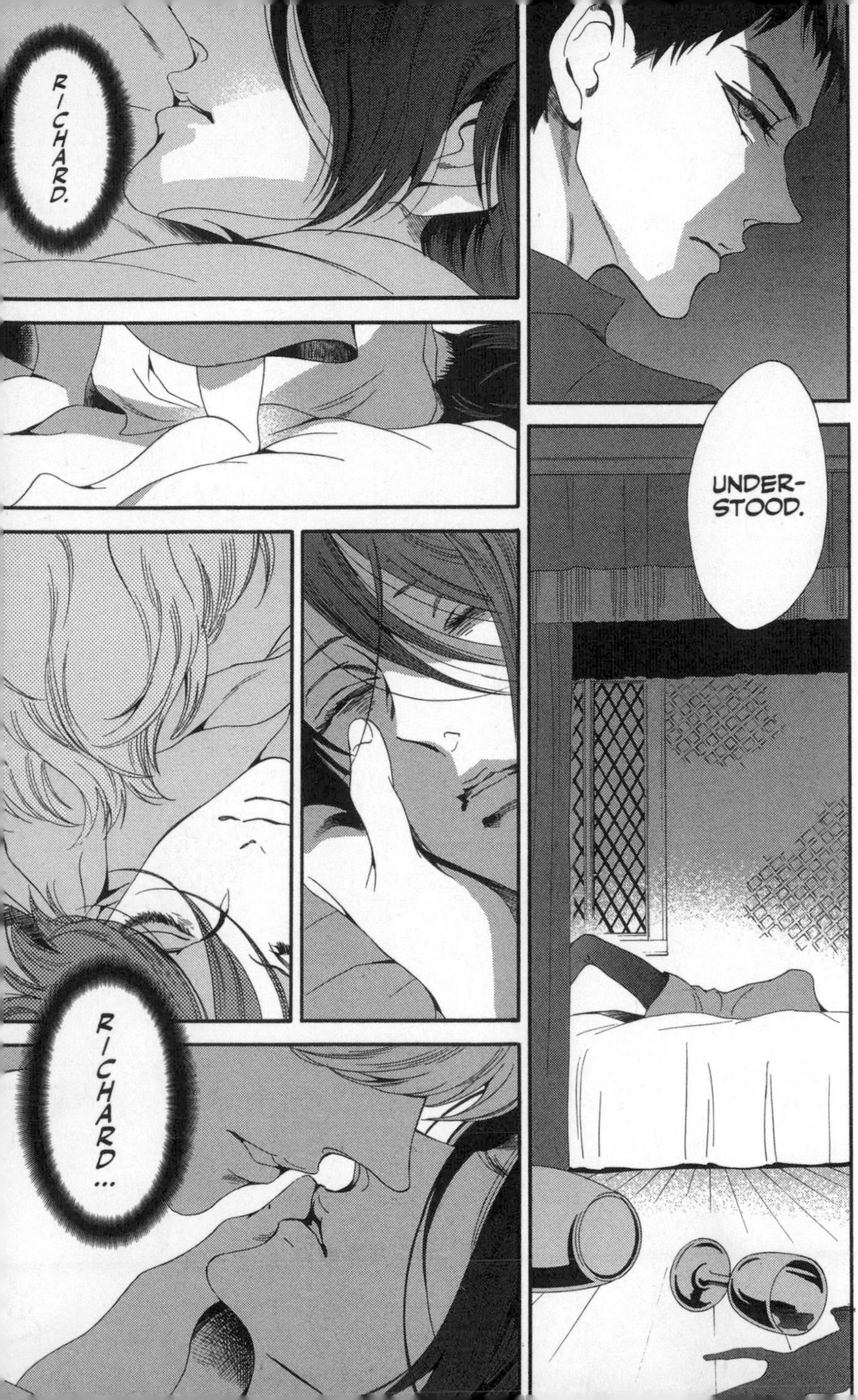
UNDER-
STOOD.
RICHARD.
RICHARD...

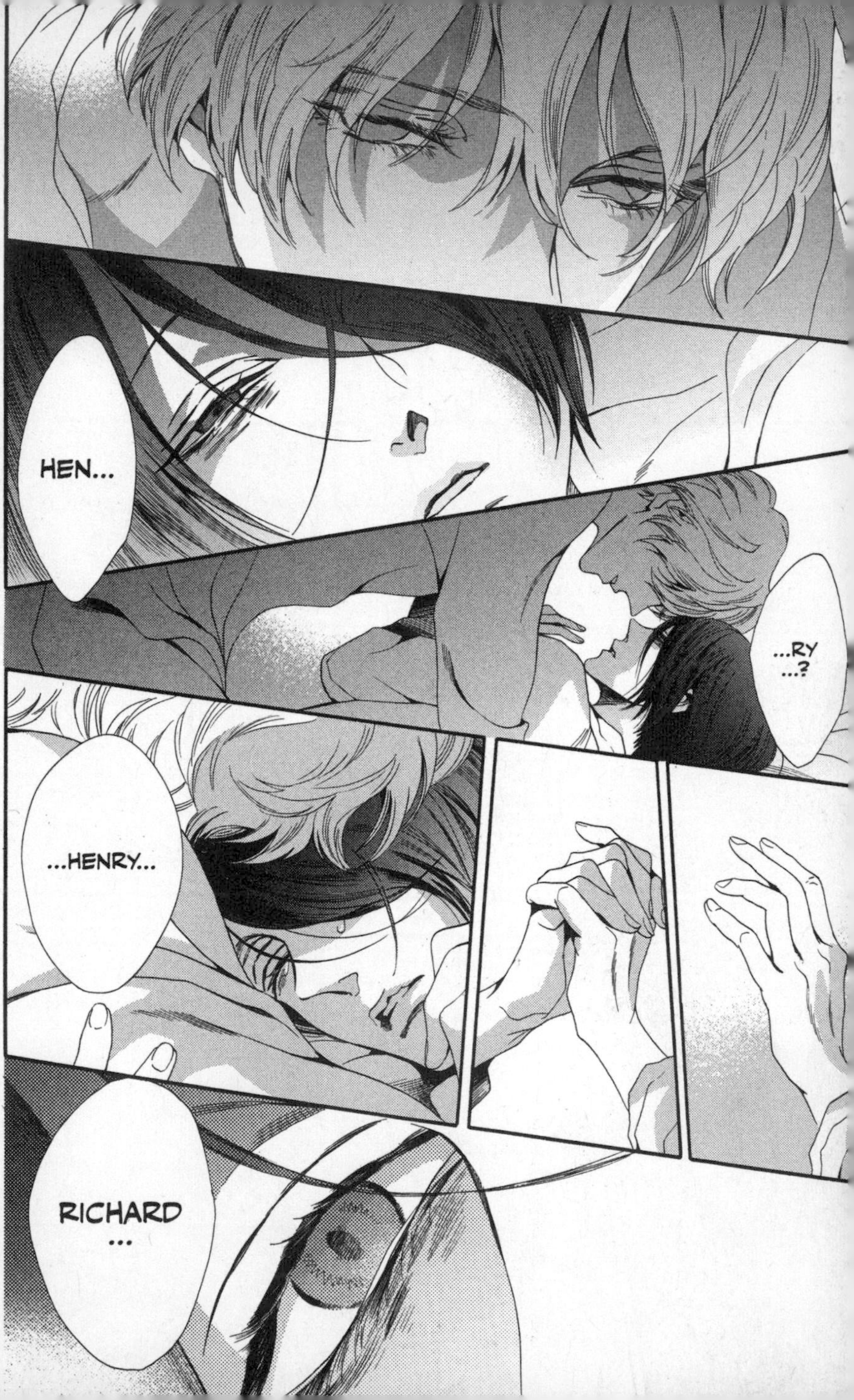
HEN...
...RY ...?
...HENRY...
RICHARD ...

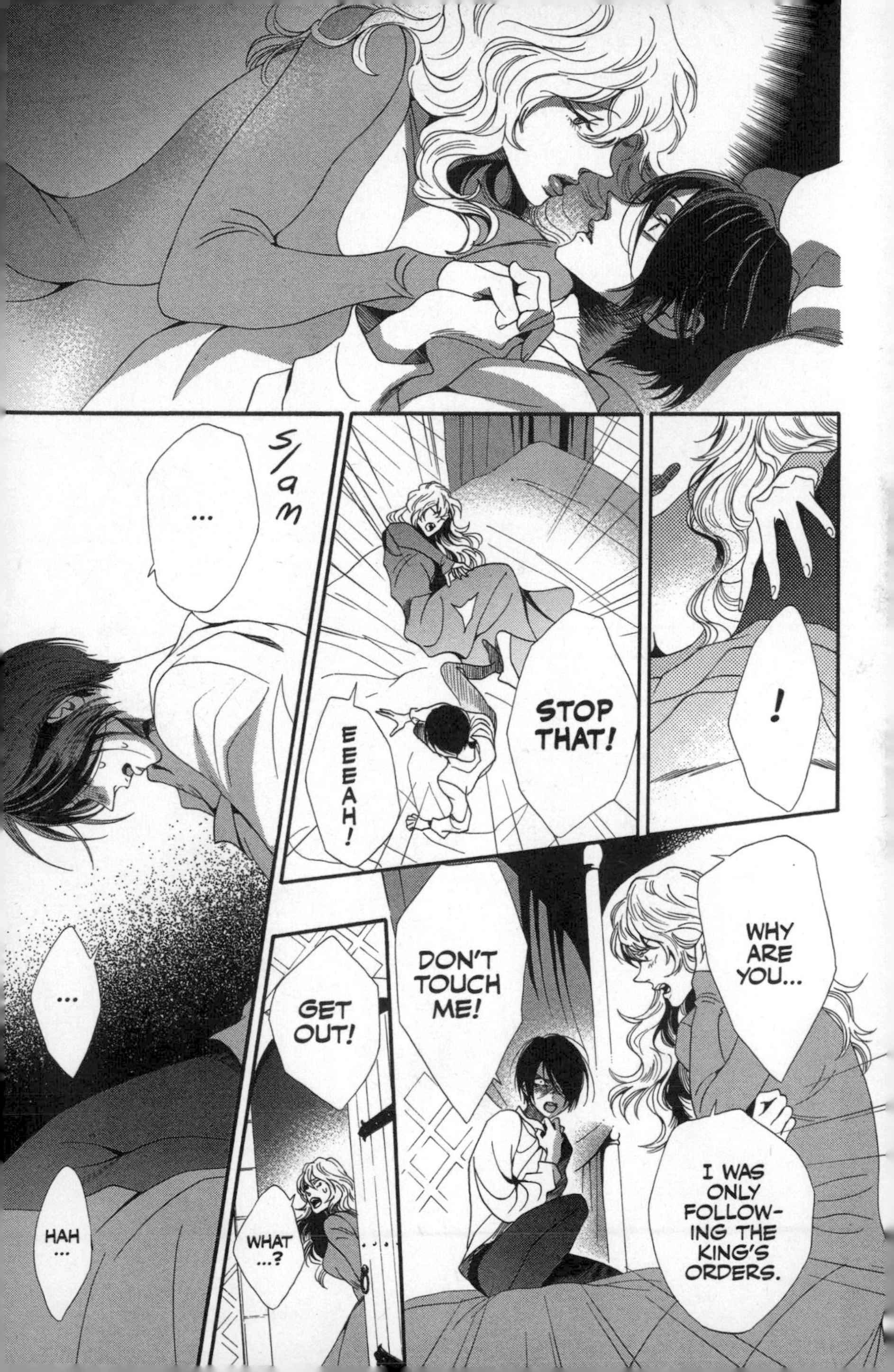

!
STOP THAT!
EEEEAH!
WHY ARE YOU...
I WAS ONLY FOLLOWING THE KING'S ORDERS.
DON'T TOUCH ME!
GET OUT!
WHAT...?
Slam
...
...
HAH...

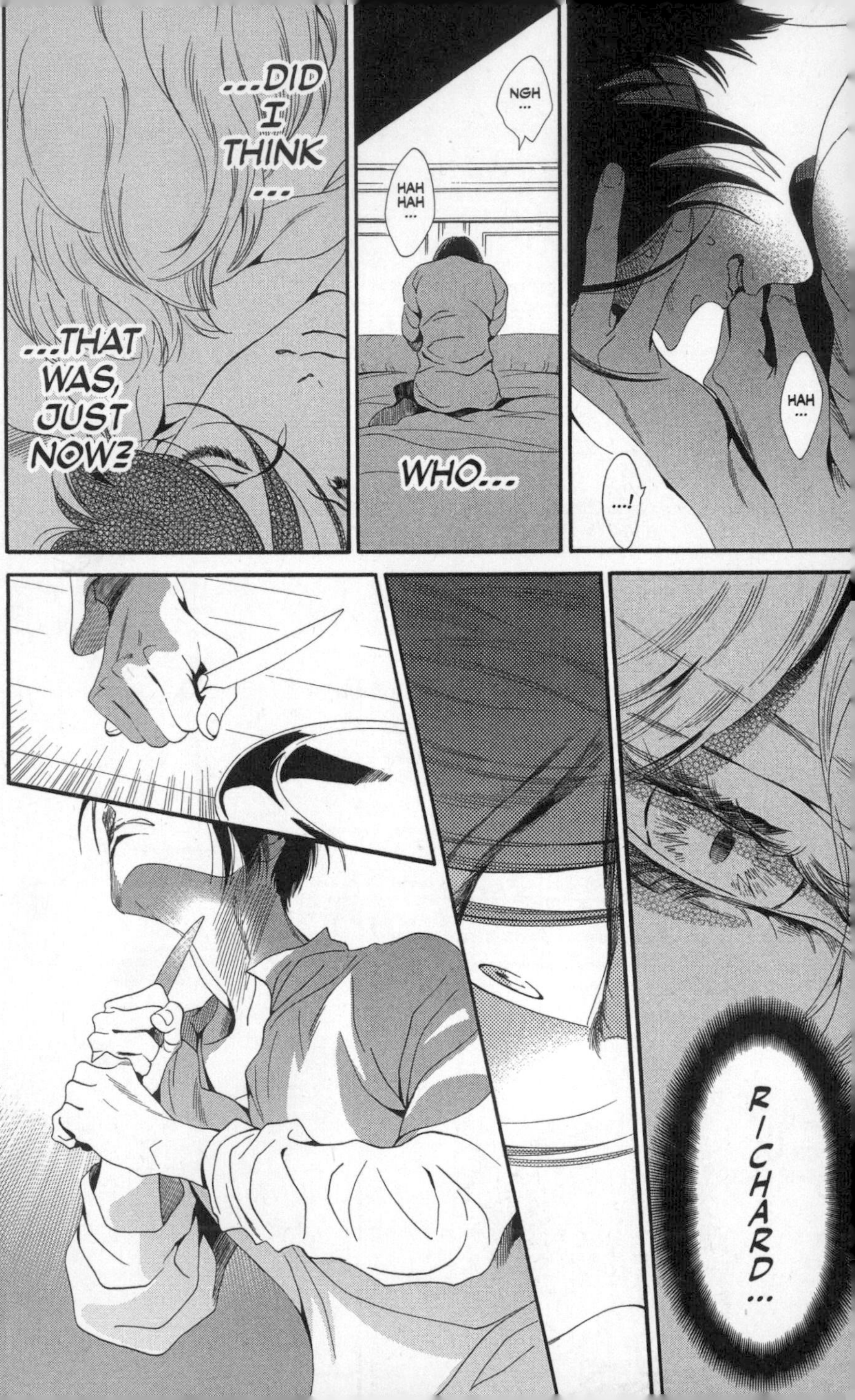
HAH...
...!
NGH...
HAH HAH...
WHO...
...DID I THINK...
...THAT WAS, JUST NOW?
RICHARD...

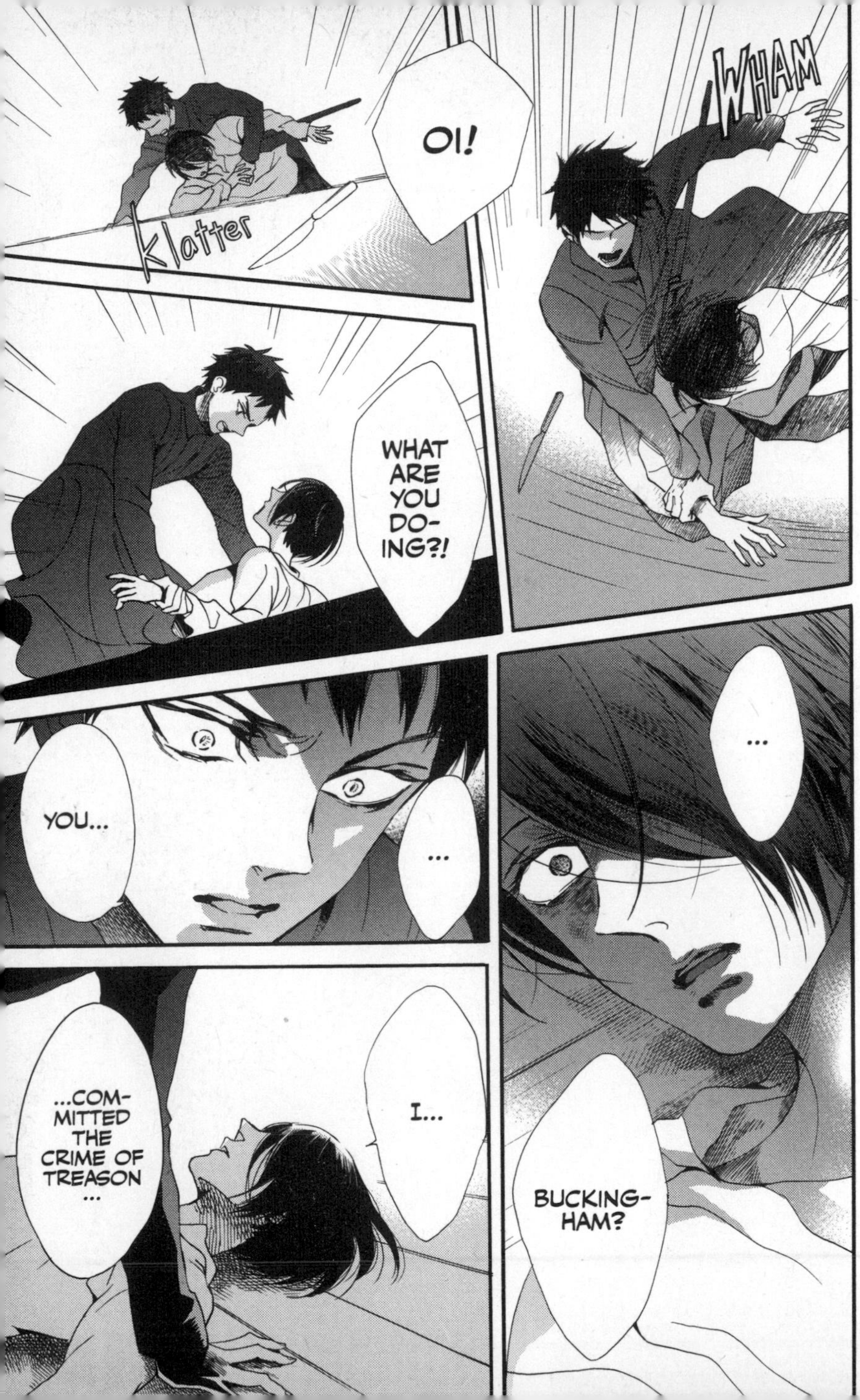
WHAM
OI!
klatter
WHAT ARE YOU DO-ING?!
...
BUCKING-HAM?
...
YOU...
I...
...COM-MITTED THE CRIME OF TREASON ...

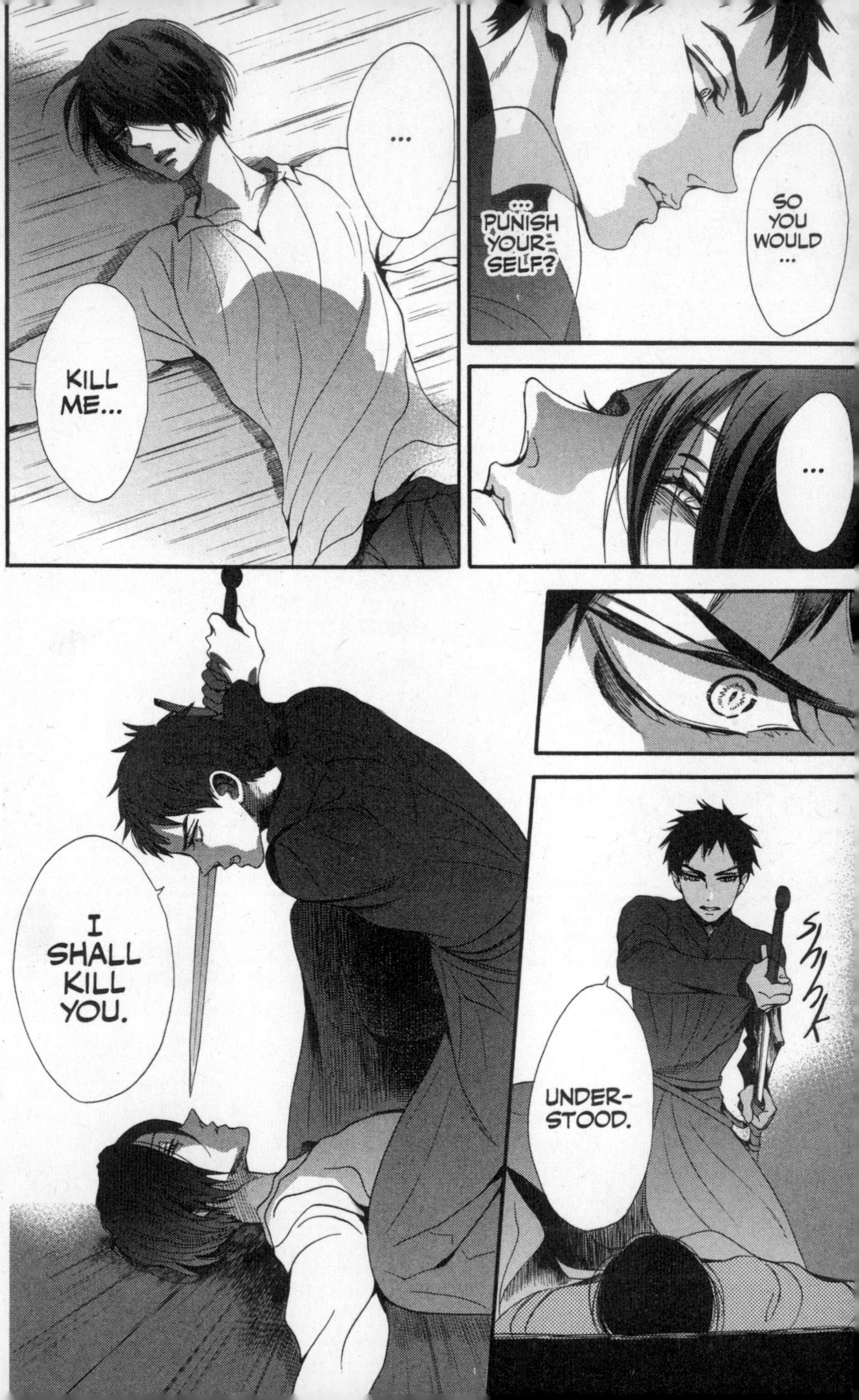
SO YOU WOULD ...
...PUNISH YOUR-SELF?
...
...
KILL ME...
UNDER-STOOD.
SHINK
I SHALL KILL YOU.

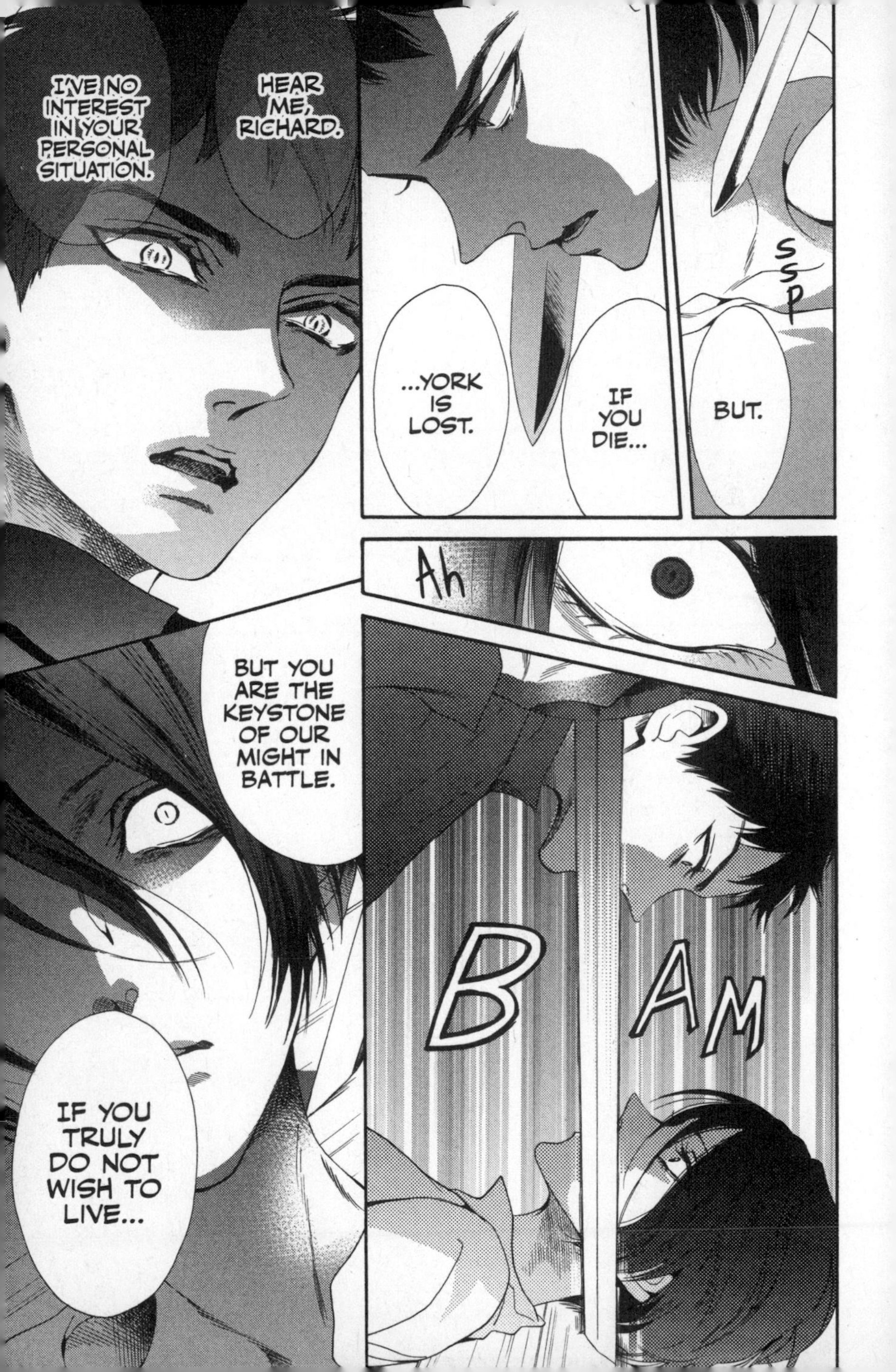
SSP
BUT.
IF YOU DIE...
...YORK IS LOST.
Ah
BAM
HEAR ME, RICHARD.
I'VE NO INTEREST IN YOUR PERSONAL SITUATION.
BUT YOU ARE THE KEYSTONE OF OUR MIGHT IN BATTLE.
IF YOU TRULY DO NOT WISH TO LIVE...

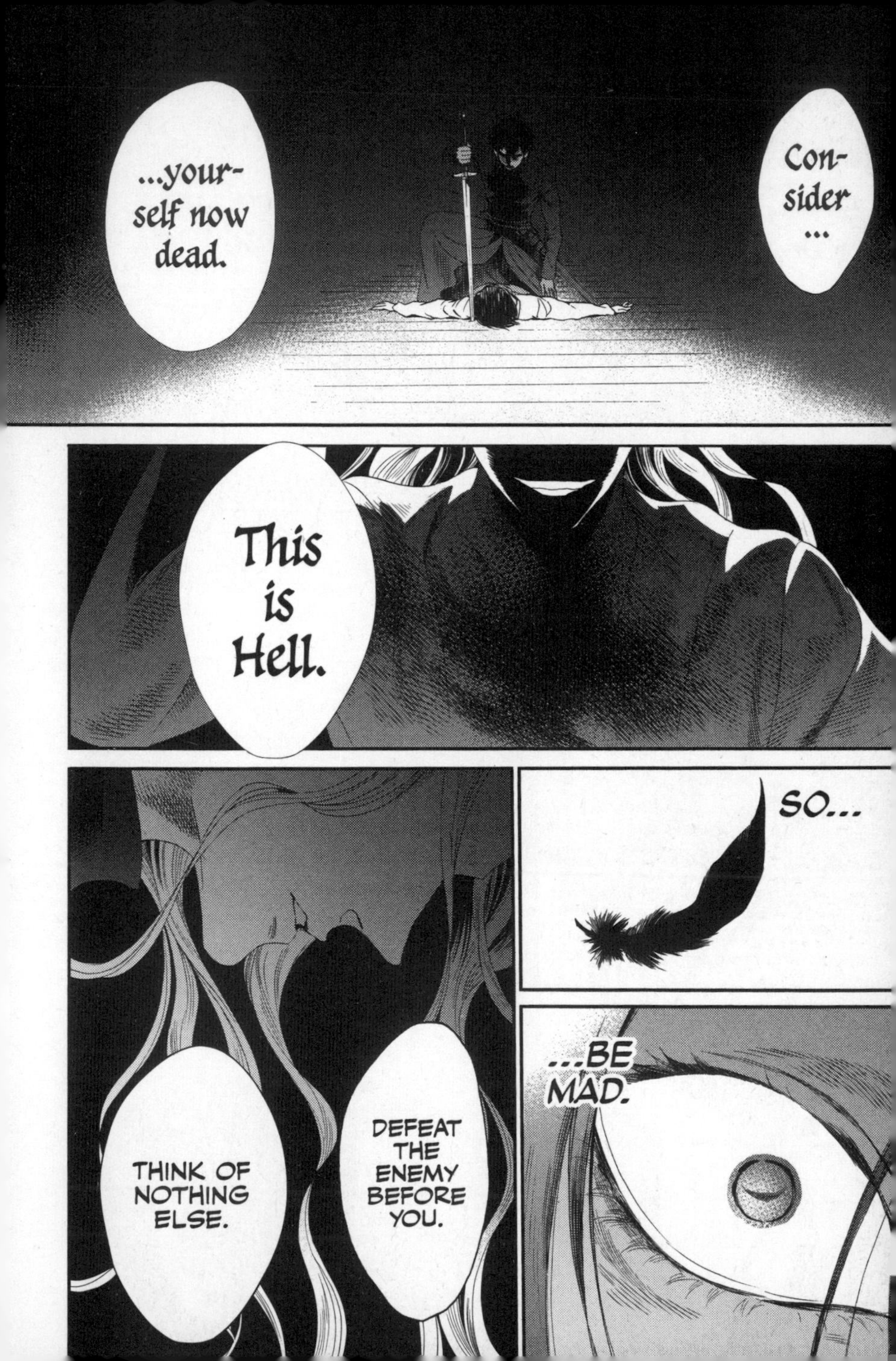
Con-sider...
...your-self now dead.
This is Hell.
SO...
...BE MAD.
DEFEAT THE ENEMY BEFORE YOU.
THINK OF NOTHING ELSE.

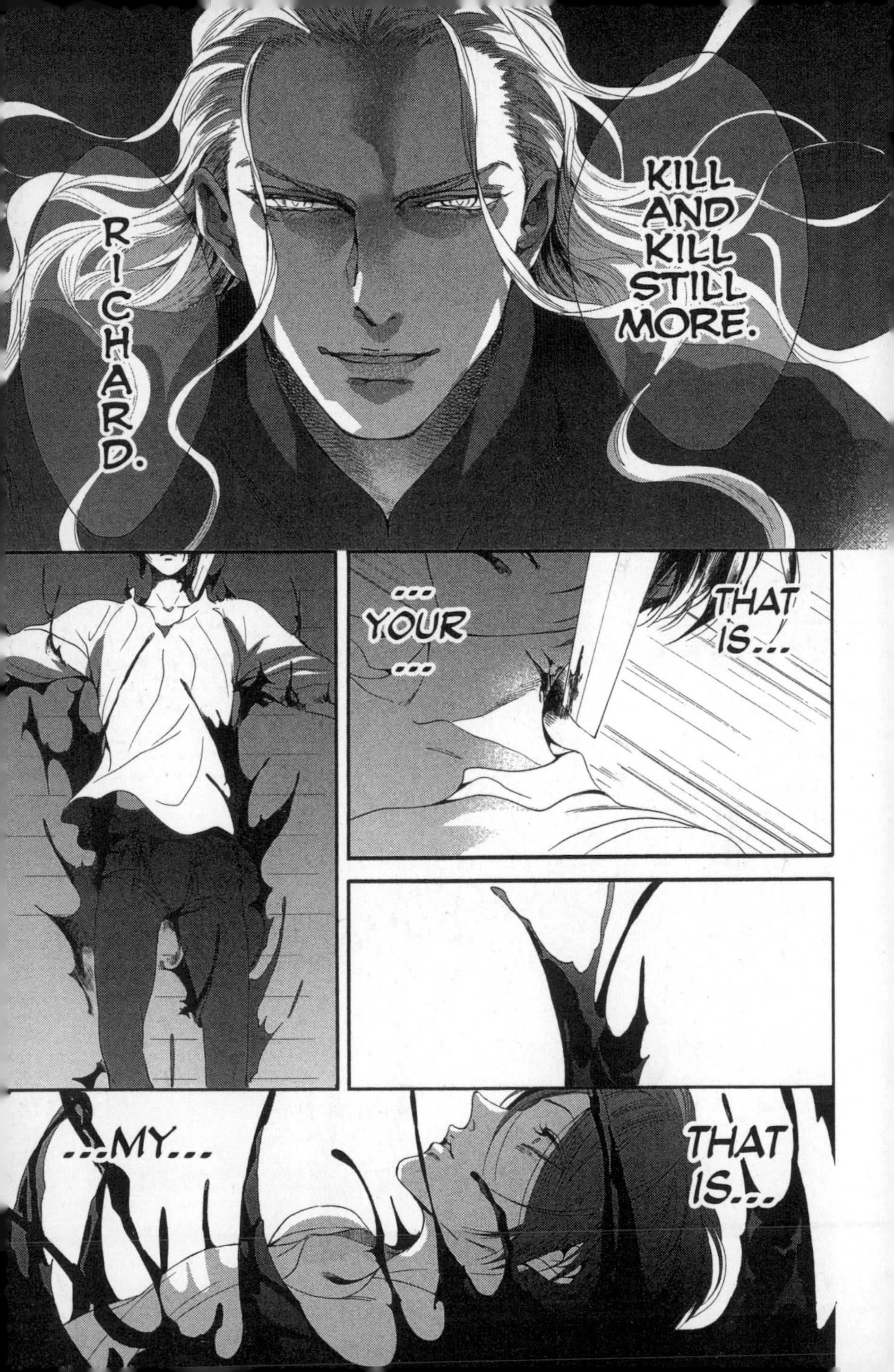
KILL AND KILL STILL MORE.
RICHARD.
THAT IS...
...YOUR...
THAT IS...
...MY...

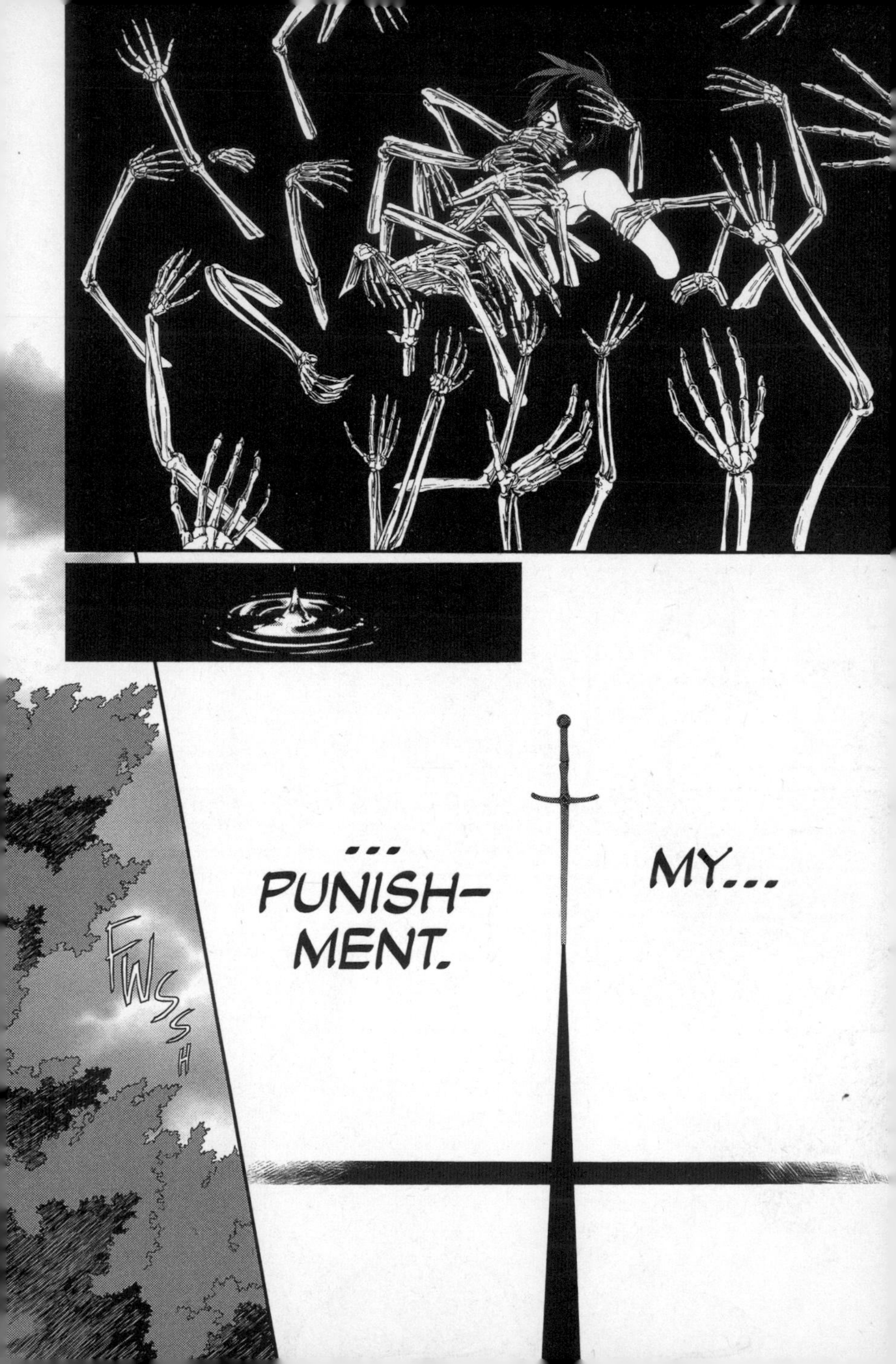
MY...
...PUNISH-MENT.
FWSSH

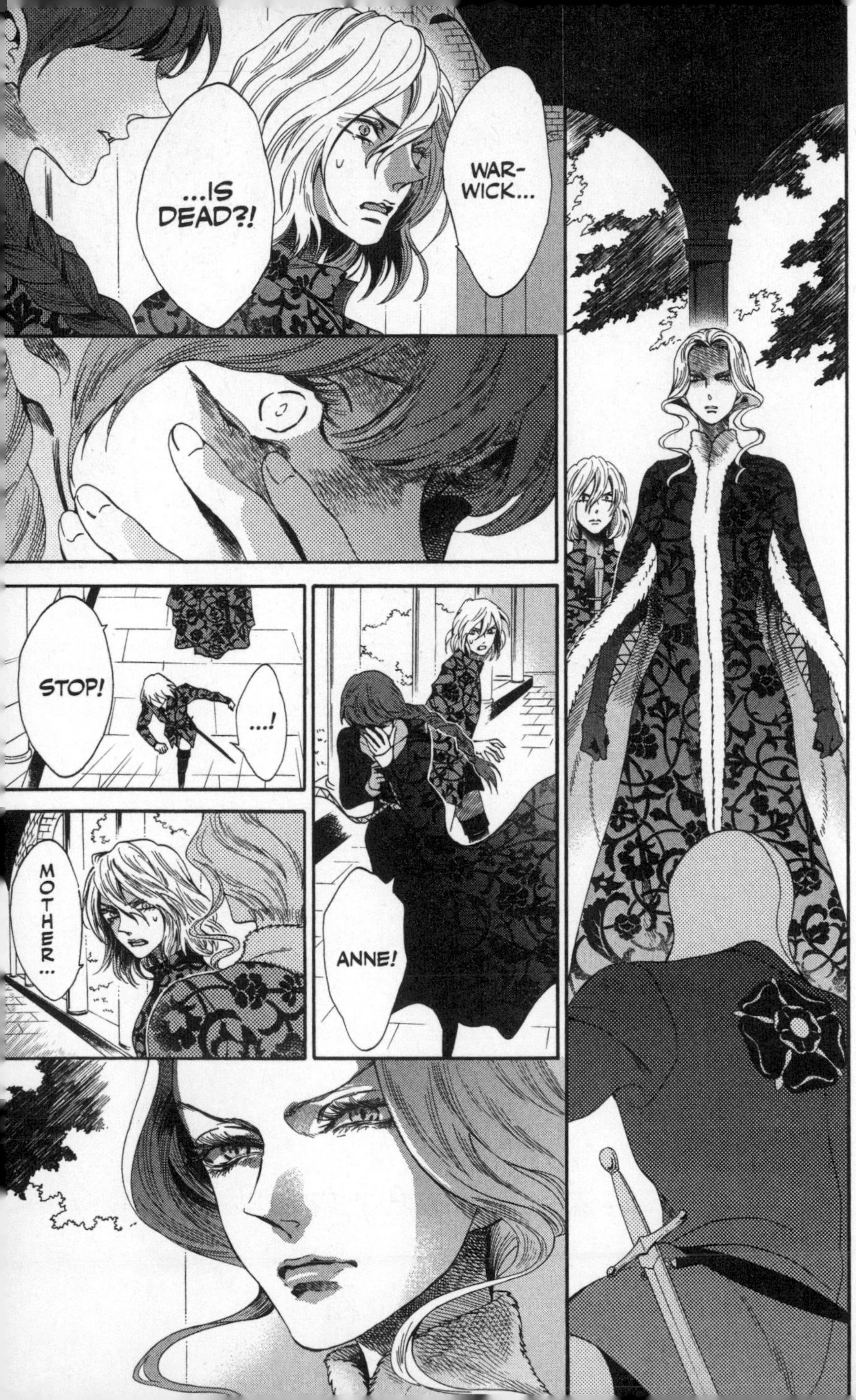
WAR-WICK...
...IS DEAD?!
ANNE!
STOP!
...!
MOTHER...

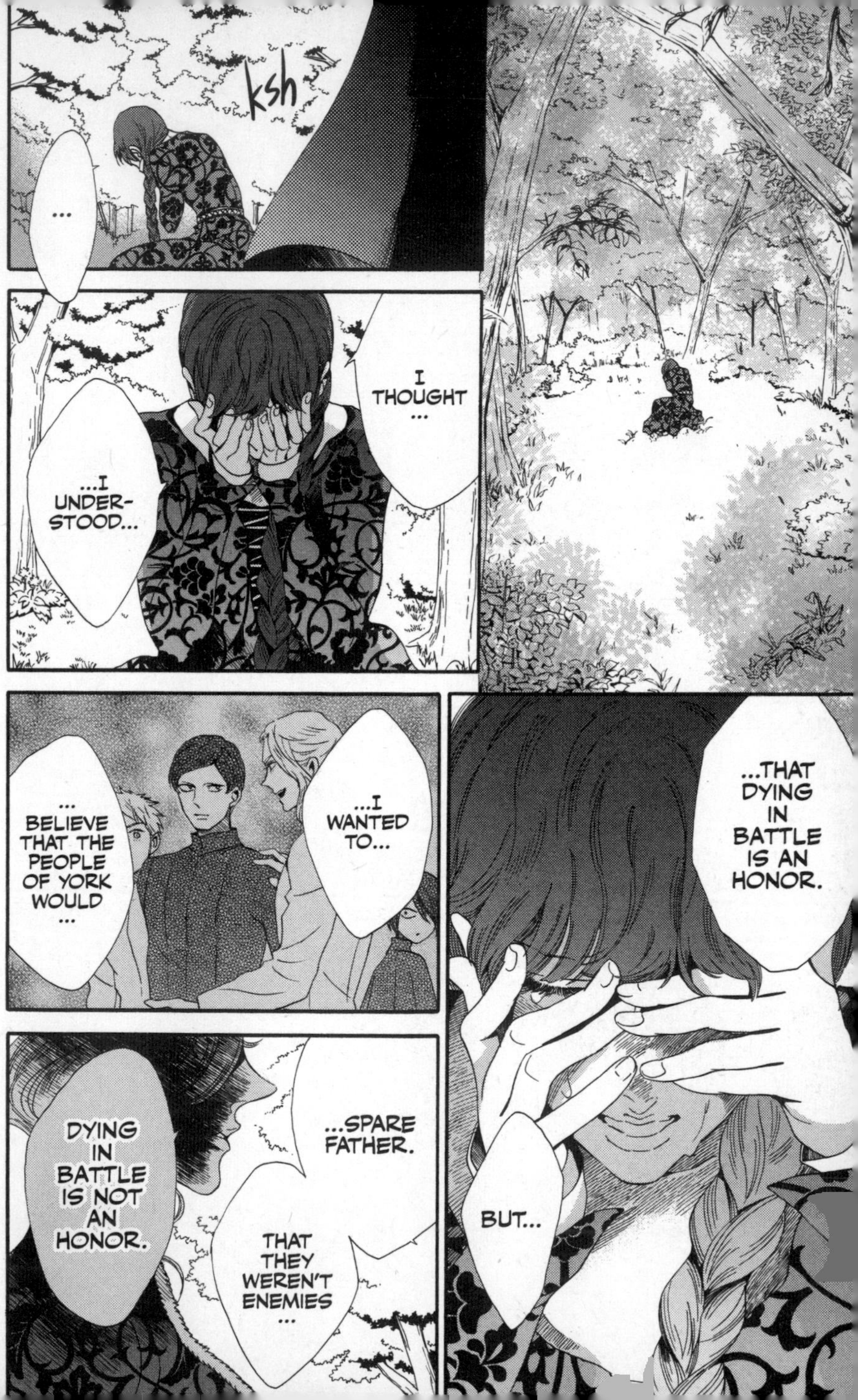
ksh
...
I THOUGHT...
...I UNDERSTOOD...
...THAT DYING IN BATTLE IS AN HONOR.
BUT...
...I WANTED TO...
...BELIEVE THAT THE PEOPLE OF YORK WOULD...
...SPARE FATHER.
THAT THEY WEREN'T ENEMIES...
DYING IN BATTLE IS NOT AN HONOR.

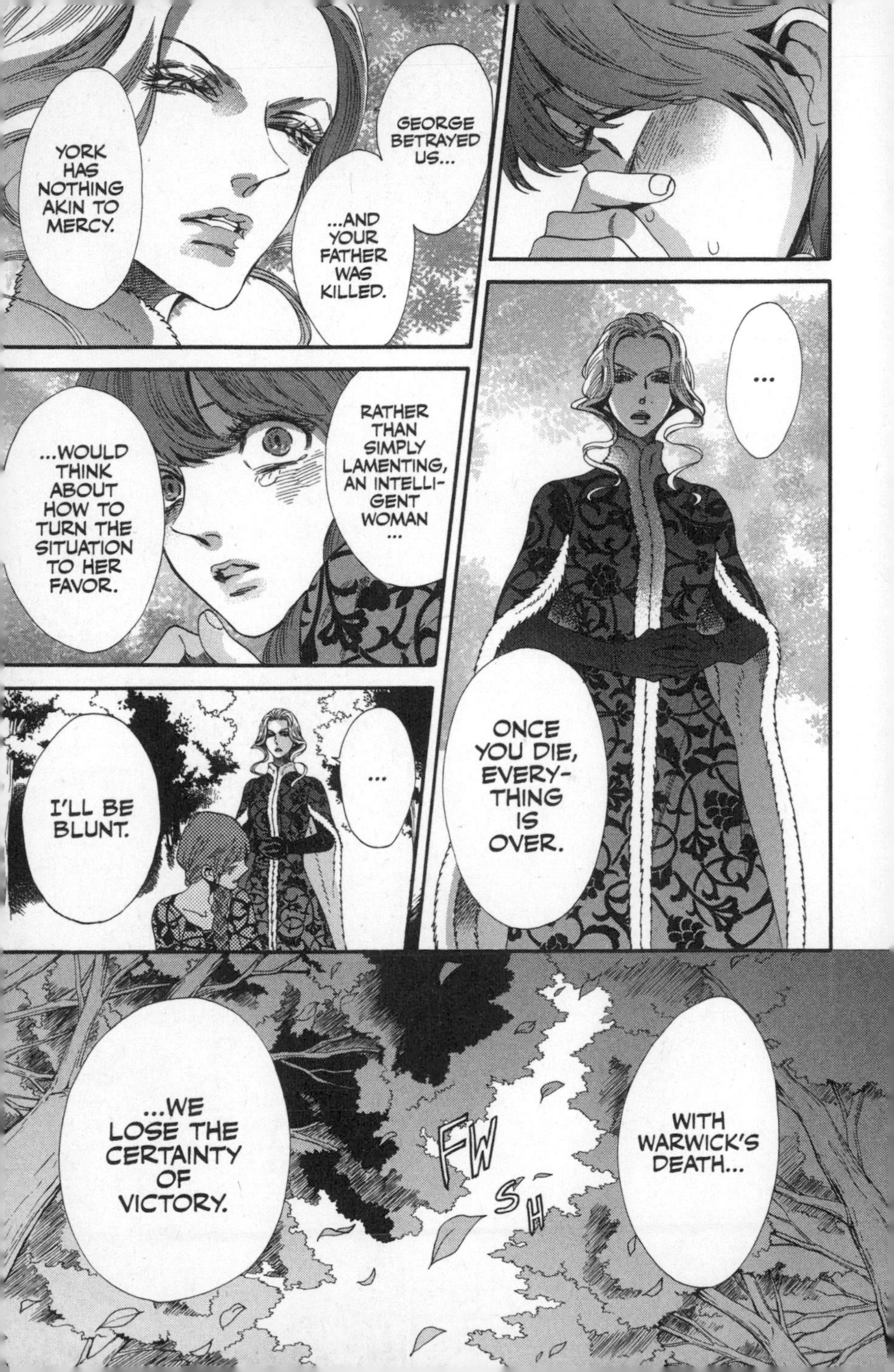
GEORGE BETRAYED US...
...AND YOUR FATHER WAS KILLED.
YORK HAS NOTHING AKIN TO MERCY.
...
ONCE YOU DIE, EVERY-THING IS OVER.
RATHER THAN SIMPLY LAMENTING, AN INTELLI-GENT WOMAN ...
...WOULD THINK ABOUT HOW TO TURN THE SITUATION TO HER FAVOR.
...
I'LL BE BLUNT.
WITH WARWICK'S DEATH...
FWSH
...WE LOSE THE CERTAINTY OF VICTORY.

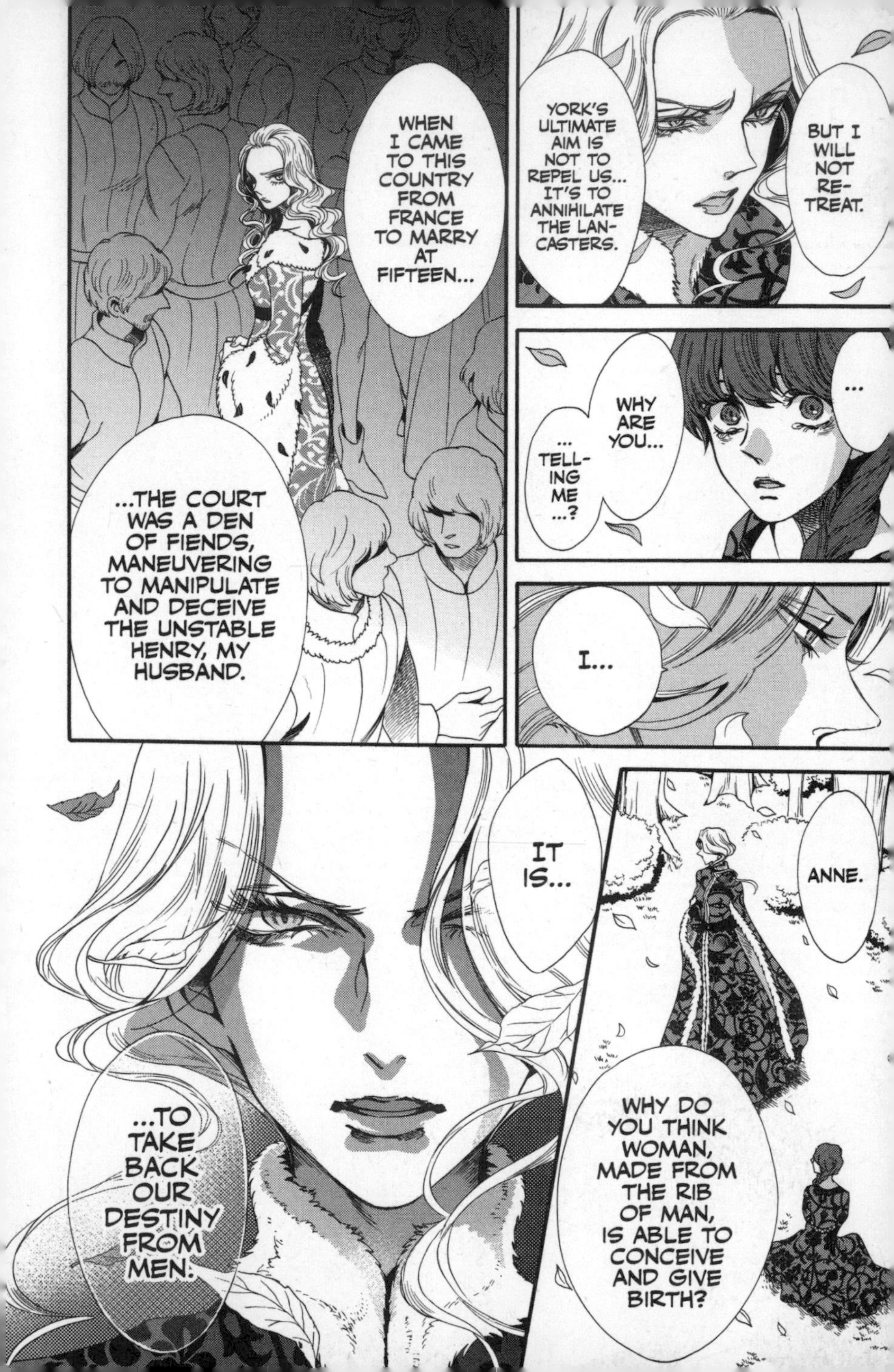
BUT I WILL NOT RE-TREAT.
YORK'S ULTIMATE AIM IS NOT TO REPEL US... IT'S TO ANNIHILATE THE LAN-CASTERS.
...
WHY ARE YOU...
... TELL-ING ME ...?
I...
WHEN I CAME TO THIS COUNTRY FROM FRANCE TO MARRY AT FIFTEEN...
...THE COURT WAS A DEN OF FIENDS, MANEUVERING TO MANIPULATE AND DECEIVE THE UNSTABLE HENRY, MY HUSBAND.
ANNE.
WHY DO YOU THINK WOMAN, MADE FROM THE RIB OF MAN, IS ABLE TO CONCEIVE AND GIVE BIRTH?
IT IS...
...TO TAKE BACK OUR DESTINY FROM MEN.

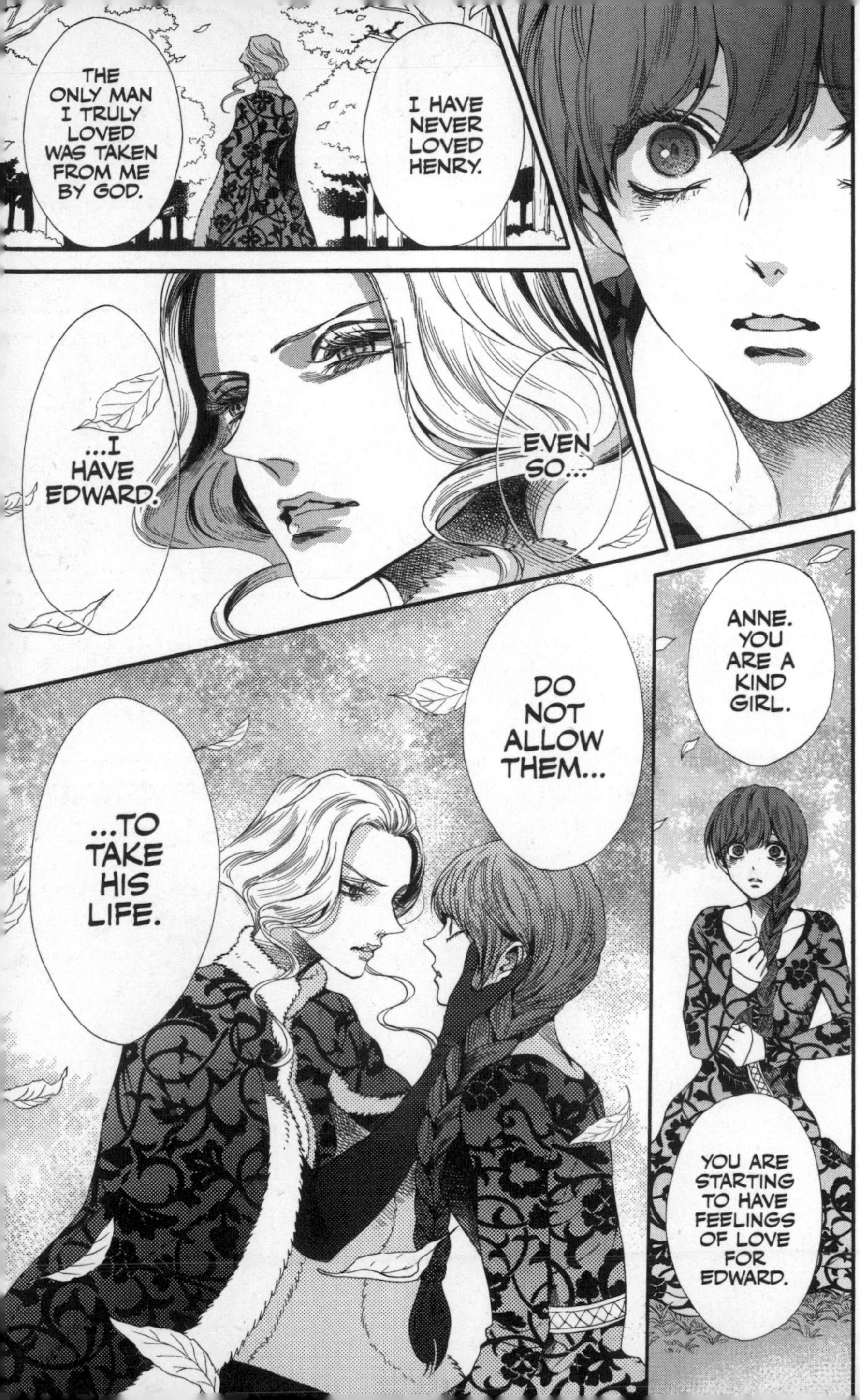
I HAVE NEVER LOVED HENRY.
THE ONLY MAN I TRULY LOVED WAS TAKEN FROM ME BY GOD.
EVEN SO...
...I HAVE EDWARD.
ANNE. YOU ARE A KIND GIRL.
YOU ARE STARTING TO HAVE FEELINGS OF LOVE FOR EDWARD.
DO NOT ALLOW THEM...
...TO TAKE HIS LIFE.

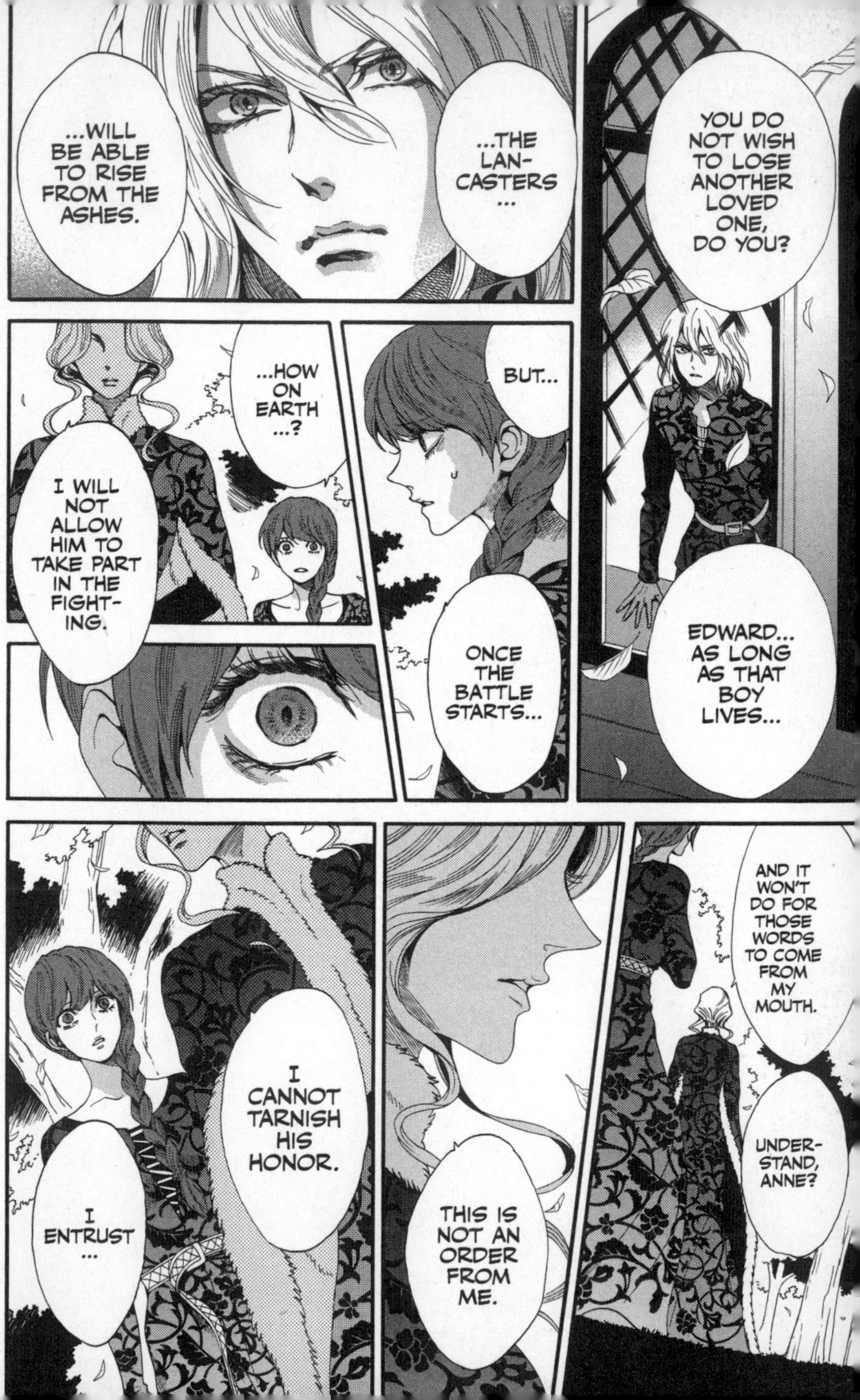
YOU DO NOT WISH TO LOSE ANOTHER LOVED ONE, DO YOU?
EDWARD... AS LONG AS THAT BOY LIVES...
...THE LAN-CASTERS ...
...WILL BE ABLE TO RISE FROM THE ASHES.
BUT...
ONCE THE BATTLE STARTS...
...HOW ON EARTH ...?
I WILL NOT ALLOW HIM TO TAKE PART IN THE FIGHT-ING.
AND IT WON'T DO FOR THOSE WORDS TO COME FROM MY MOUTH.
UNDER-STAND, ANNE?
THIS IS NOT AN ORDER FROM ME.
I CANNOT TARNISH HIS HONOR.
I ENTRUST ...

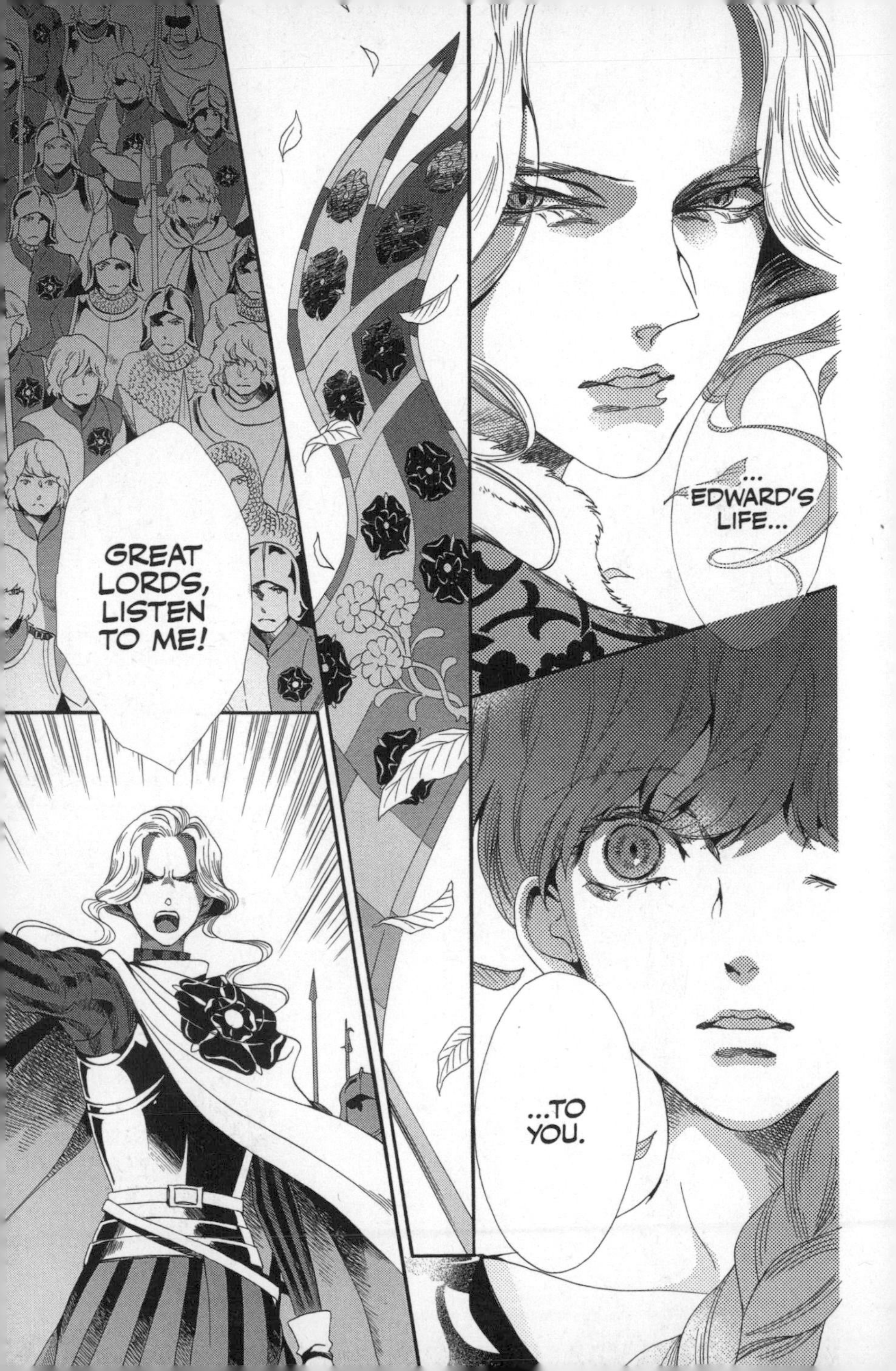
...EDWARD'S LIFE...
...TO YOU.
GREAT LORDS, LISTEN TO ME!

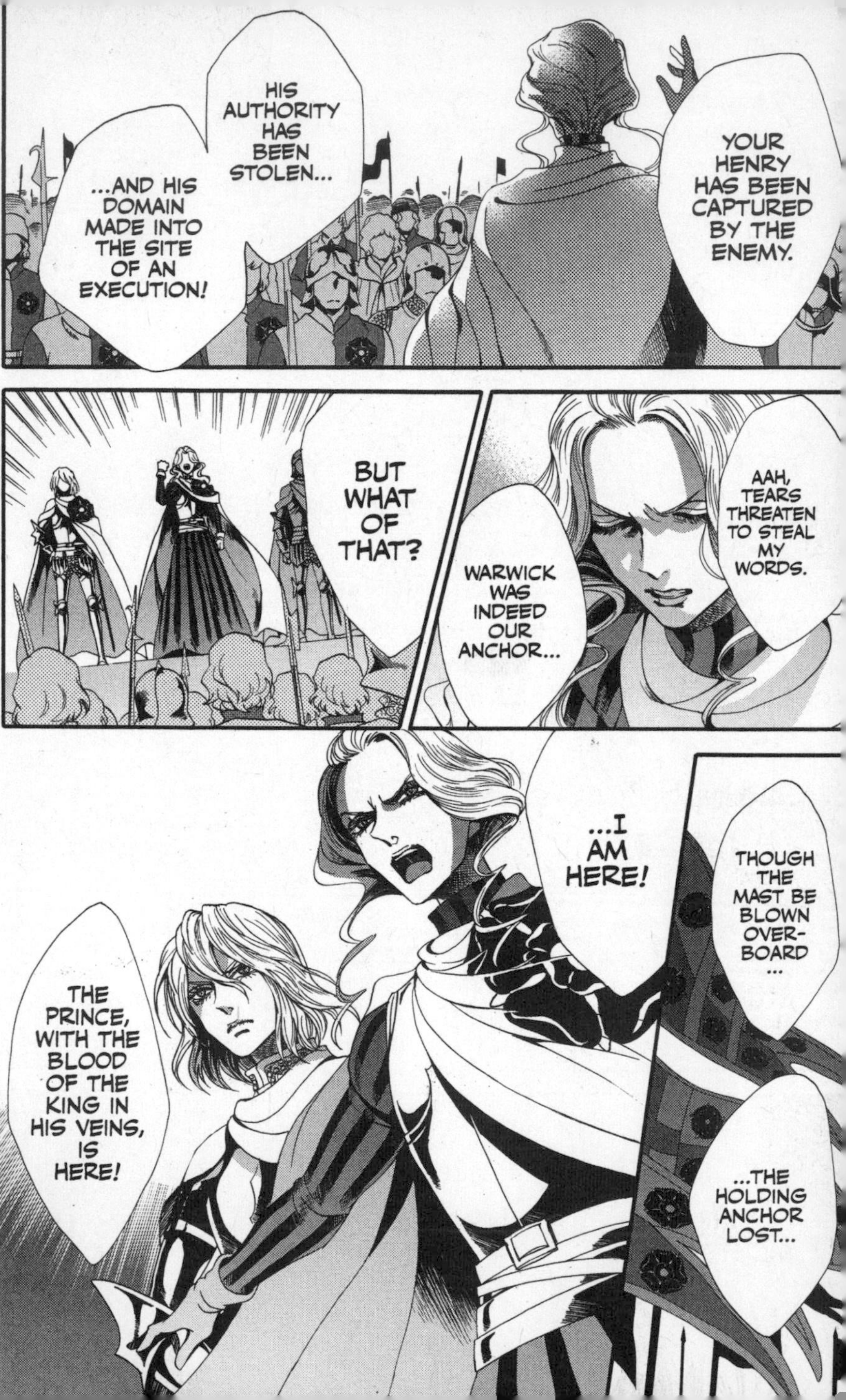
YOUR HENRY HAS BEEN CAPTURED BY THE ENEMY.
HIS AUTHORITY HAS BEEN STOLEN...
...AND HIS DOMAIN MADE INTO THE SITE OF AN EXECUTION!
AAH, TEARS THREATEN TO STEAL MY WORDS.
WARWICK WAS INDEED OUR ANCHOR...
BUT WHAT OF THAT?
THOUGH THE MAST BE BLOWN OVER-BOARD...
...THE HOLDING ANCHOR LOST...
...I AM HERE!
THE PRINCE, WITH THE BLOOD OF THE KING IN HIS VEINS, IS HERE!

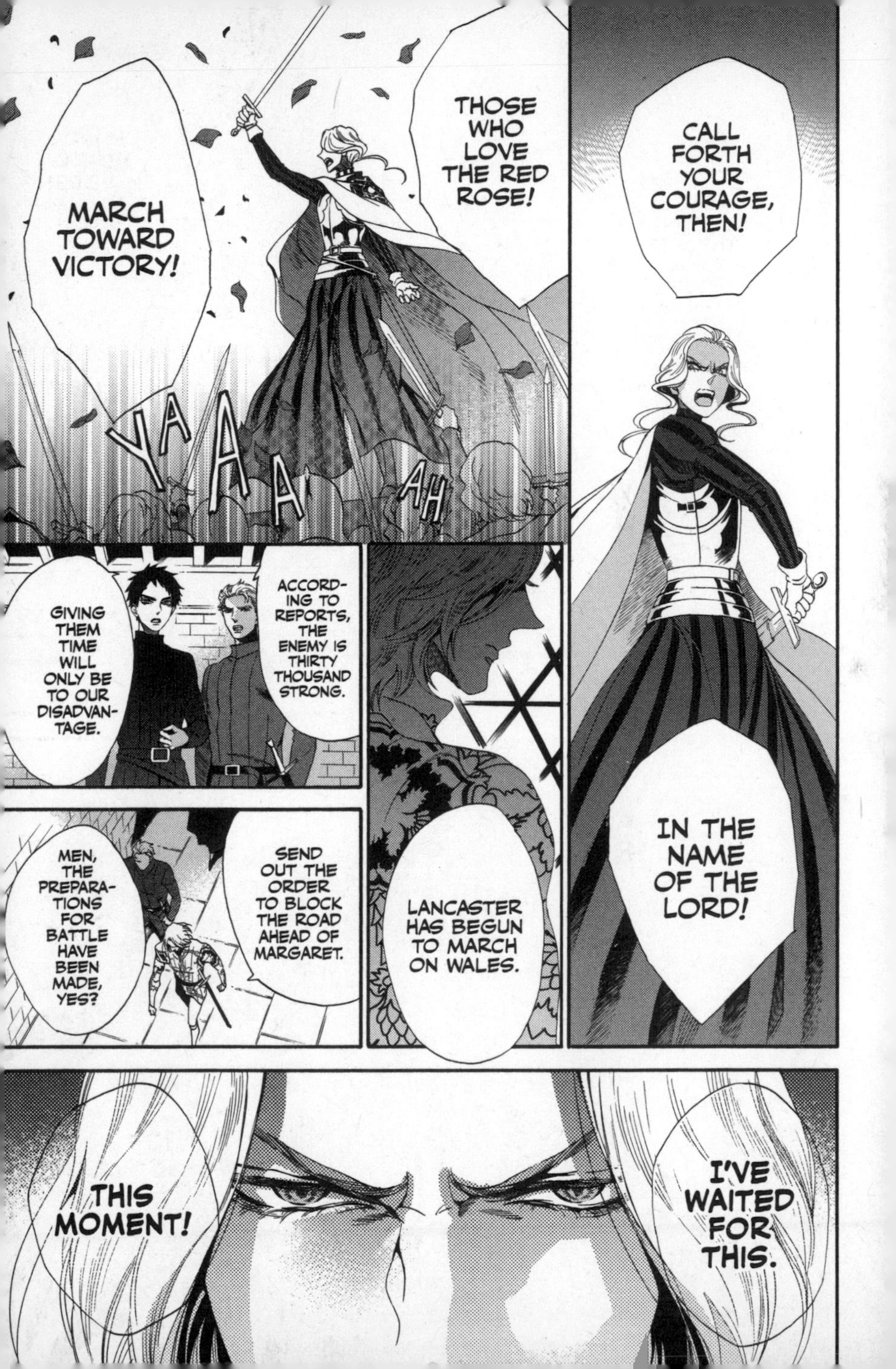
CALL FORTH YOUR COURAGE, THEN!
IN THE NAME OF THE LORD!
THOSE WHO LOVE THE RED ROSE!
MARCH TOWARD VICTORY!
YAAAAH
LANCASTER HAS BEGUN TO MARCH ON WALES.
ACCORDING TO REPORTS, THE ENEMY IS THIRTY THOUSAND STRONG.
GIVING THEM TIME WILL ONLY BE TO OUR DISADVANTAGE.
SEND OUT THE ORDER TO BLOCK THE ROAD AHEAD OF MARGARET.
MEN, THE PREPARATIONS FOR BATTLE HAVE BEEN MADE, YES?
I'VE WAITED FOR THIS.
THIS MOMENT!

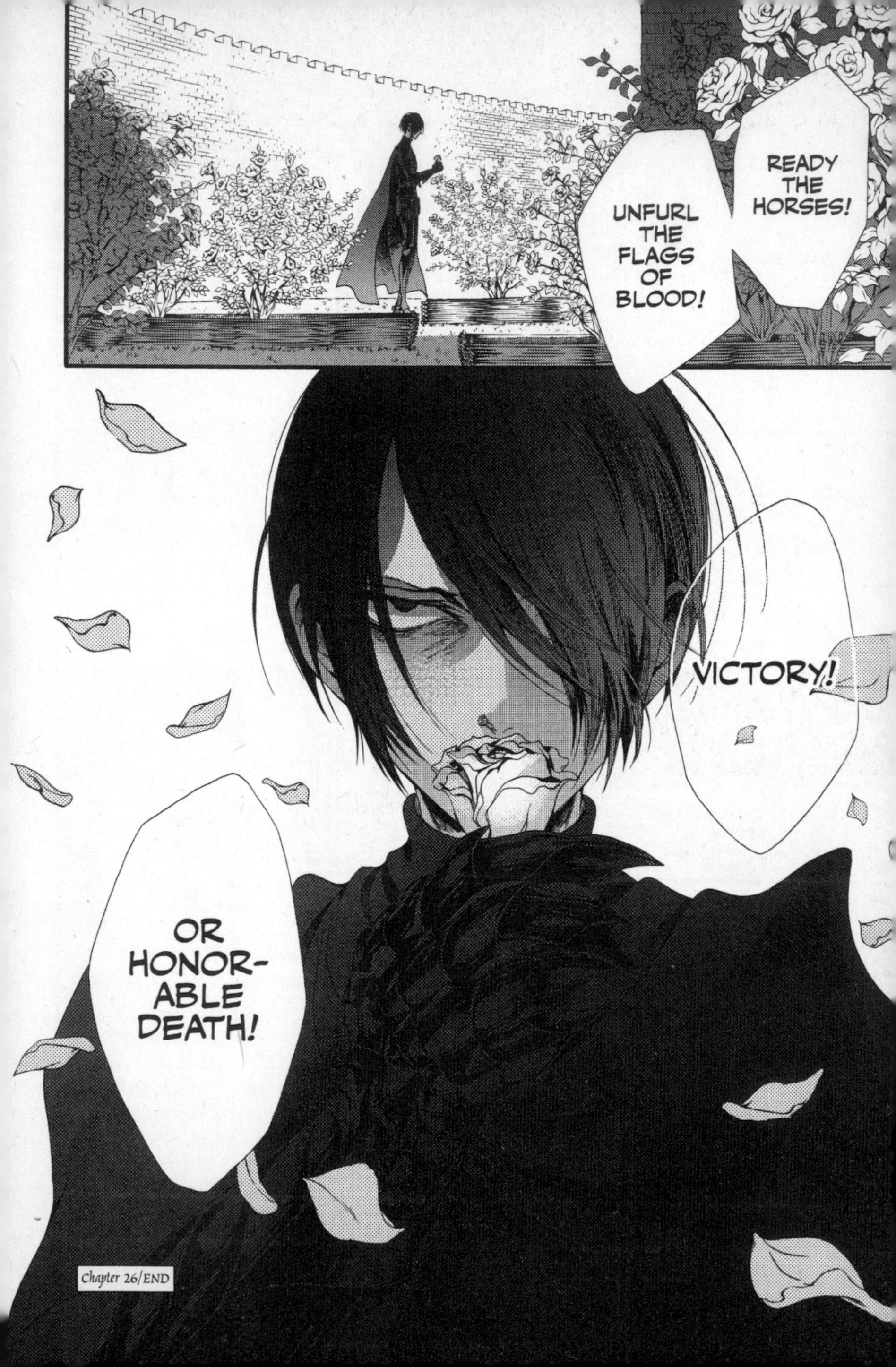
READY THE HORSES!
UNFURL THE FLAGS OF BLOOD!
VICTORY!
OR HONOR-ABLE DEATH!
Chapter 26/END

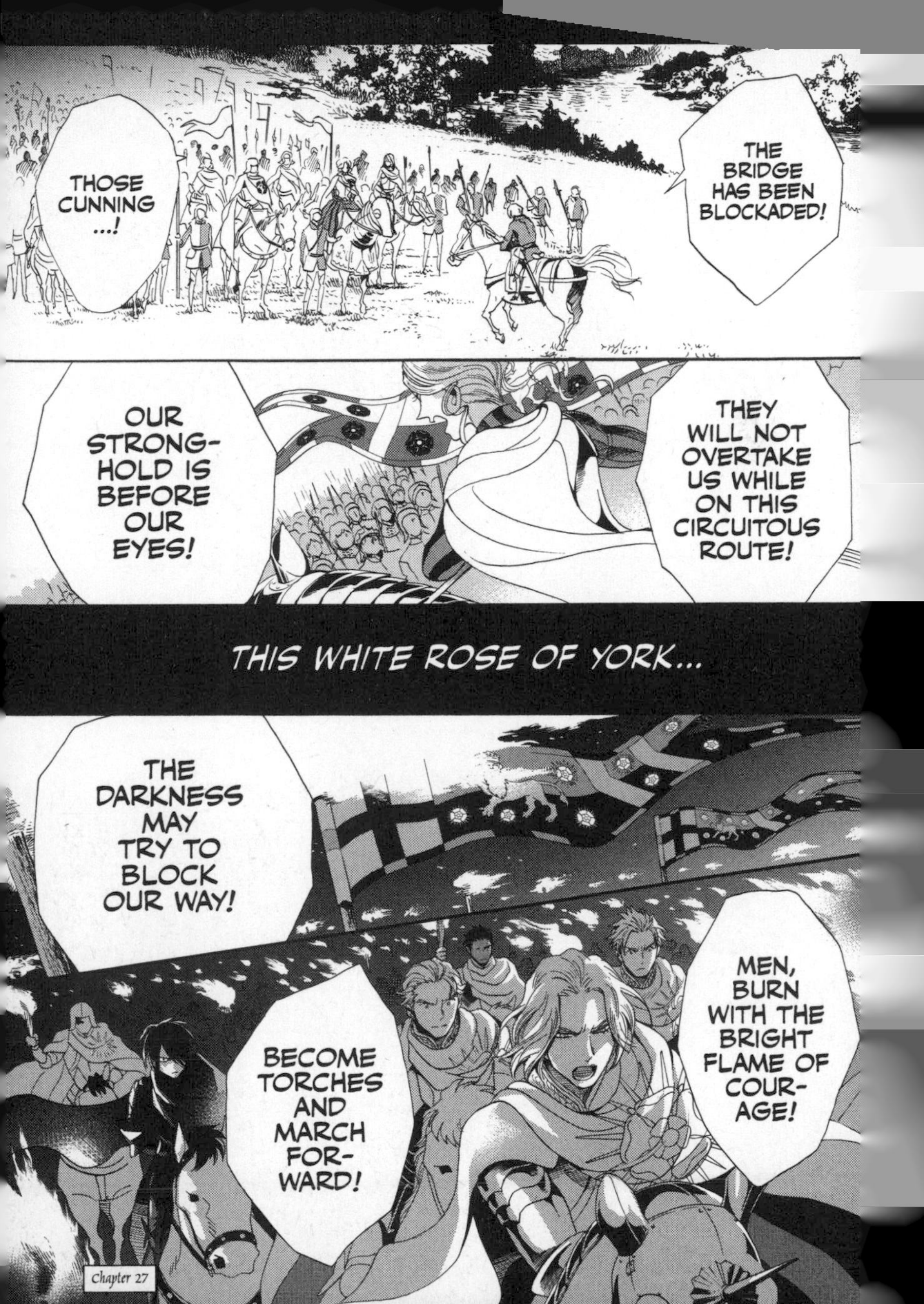
THE BRIDGE HAS BEEN BLOCKADED!
THOSE CUNNING...!
THEY WILL NOT OVERTAKE US WHILE ON THIS CIRCUITOUS ROUTE!
OUR STRONGHOLD IS BEFORE OUR EYES!
THIS WHITE ROSE OF YORK...
THE DARKNESS MAY TRY TO BLOCK OUR WAY!
MEN, BURN WITH THE BRIGHT FLAME OF COURAGE!
BECOME TORCHES AND MARCH FORWARD!
Chapter 27

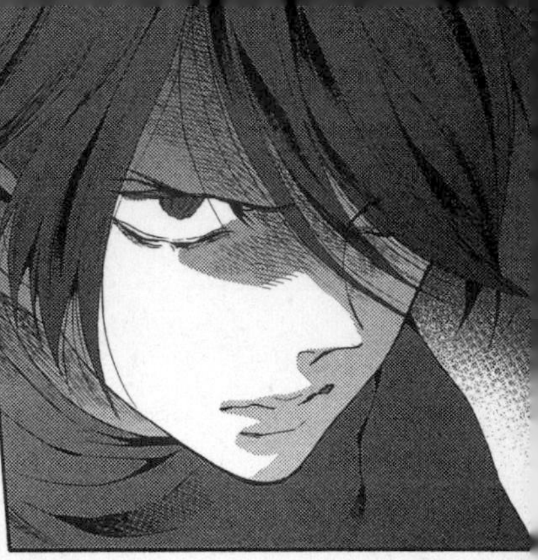

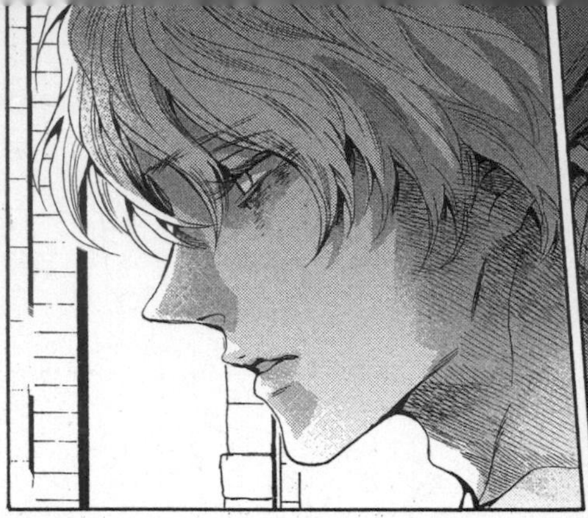

THEY SHALL BE THE SYMBOLS OF MUTUAL ENEMIES.

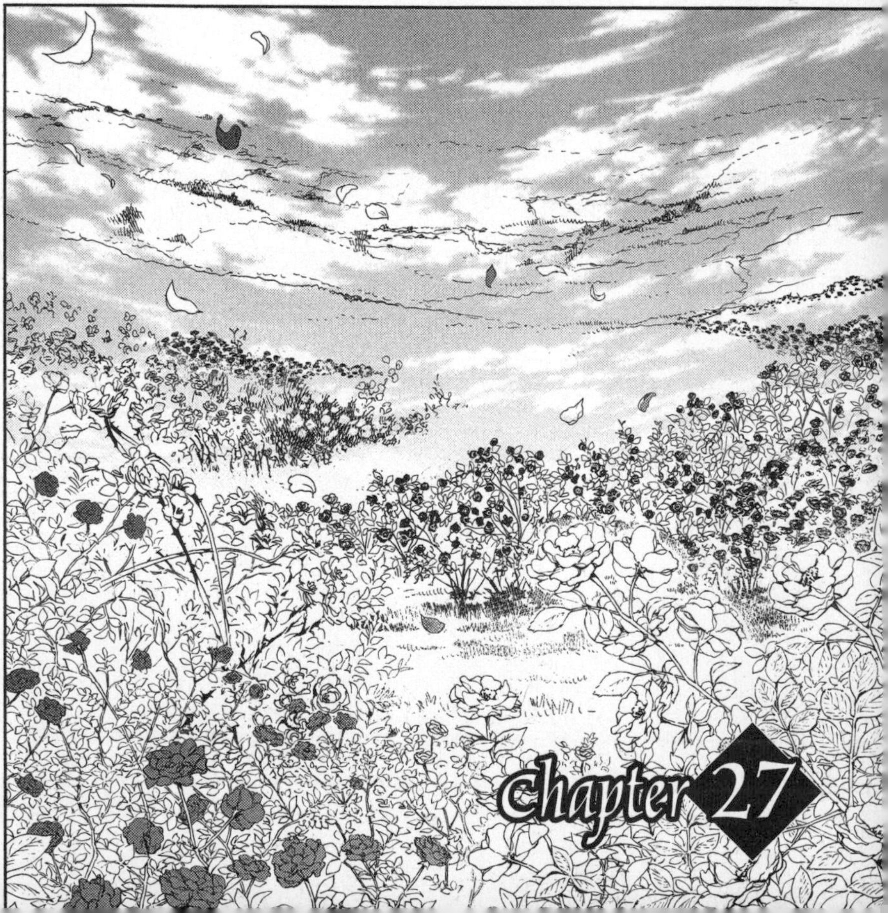
Chapter 27

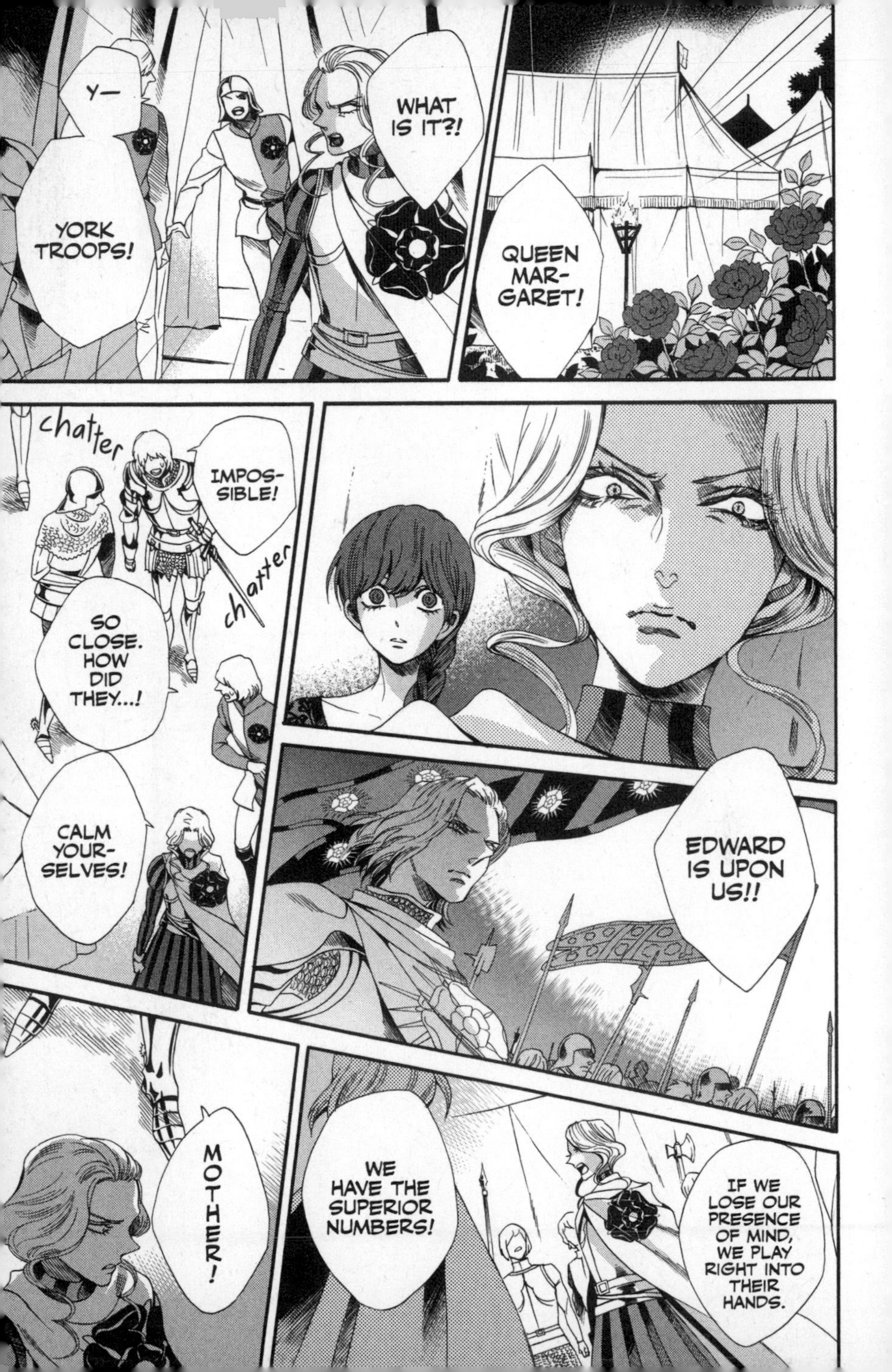
QUEEN MARGARET!
WHAT IS IT?!
Y—
YORK TROOPS!
EDWARD IS UPON US!!
IMPOSSIBLE!
chatter
chatter
SO CLOSE. HOW DID THEY...!
CALM YOURSELVES!
IF WE LOSE OUR PRESENCE OF MIND, WE PLAY RIGHT INTO THEIR HANDS.
WE HAVE THE SUPERIOR NUMBERS!
MOTHER!

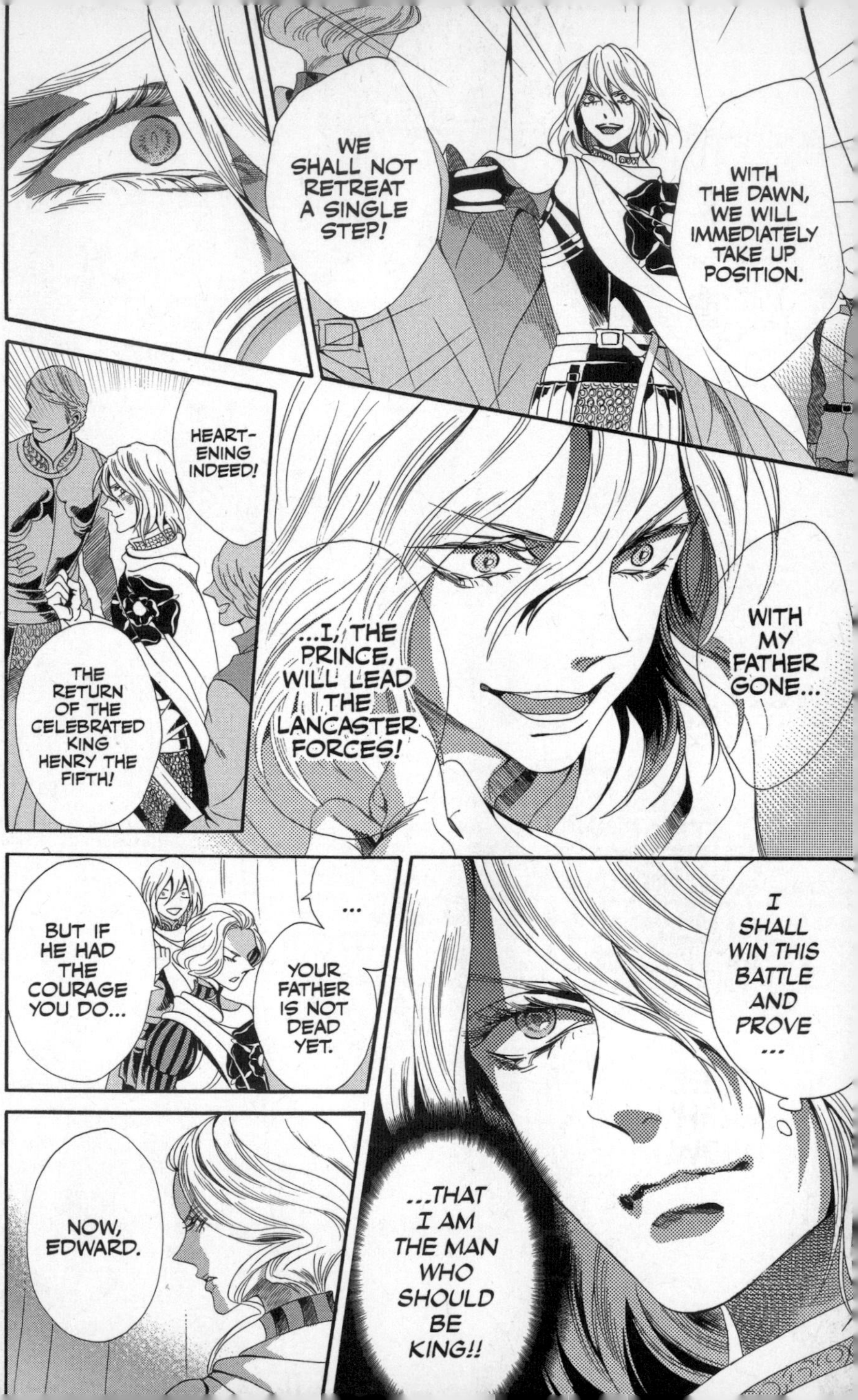
WITH THE DAWN, WE WILL IMMEDIATELY TAKE UP POSITION.
WE SHALL NOT RETREAT A SINGLE STEP!
WITH MY FATHER GONE...
...I, THE PRINCE, WILL LEAD THE LANCASTER FORCES!
HEART-ENING INDEED!
THE RETURN OF THE CELEBRATED KING HENRY THE FIFTH!
I SHALL WIN THIS BATTLE AND PROVE...
...THAT I AM THE MAN WHO SHOULD BE KING!!
...
YOUR FATHER IS NOT DEAD YET.
BUT IF HE HAD THE COURAGE YOU DO...
NOW, EDWARD.

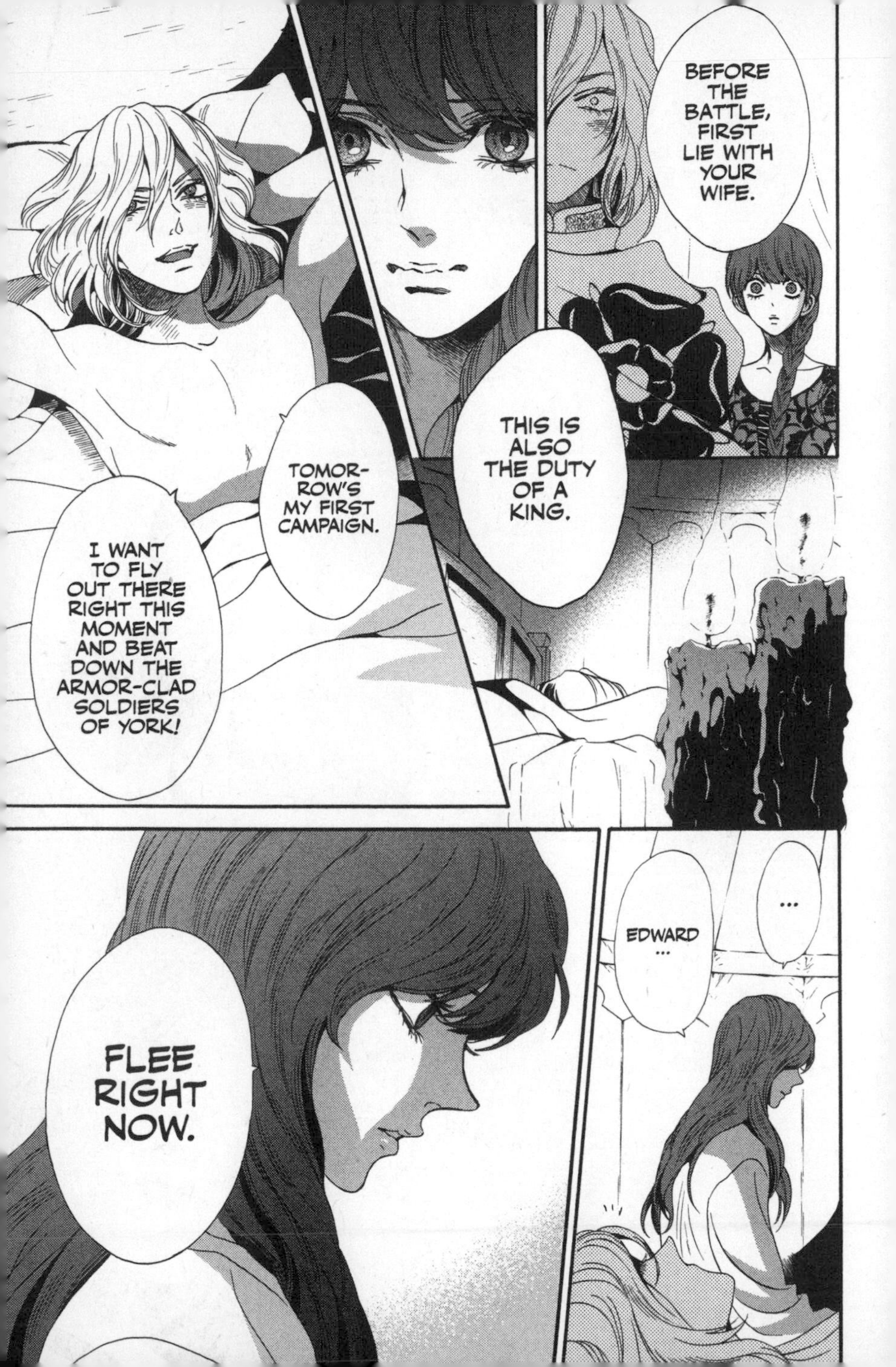
BEFORE THE BATTLE, FIRST LIE WITH YOUR WIFE.
THIS IS ALSO THE DUTY OF A KING.
TOMOR-ROW'S MY FIRST CAMPAIGN.
I WANT TO FLY OUT THERE RIGHT THIS MOMENT AND BEAT DOWN THE ARMOR-CLAD SOLDIERS OF YORK!
...
EDWARD ...
FLEE RIGHT NOW.

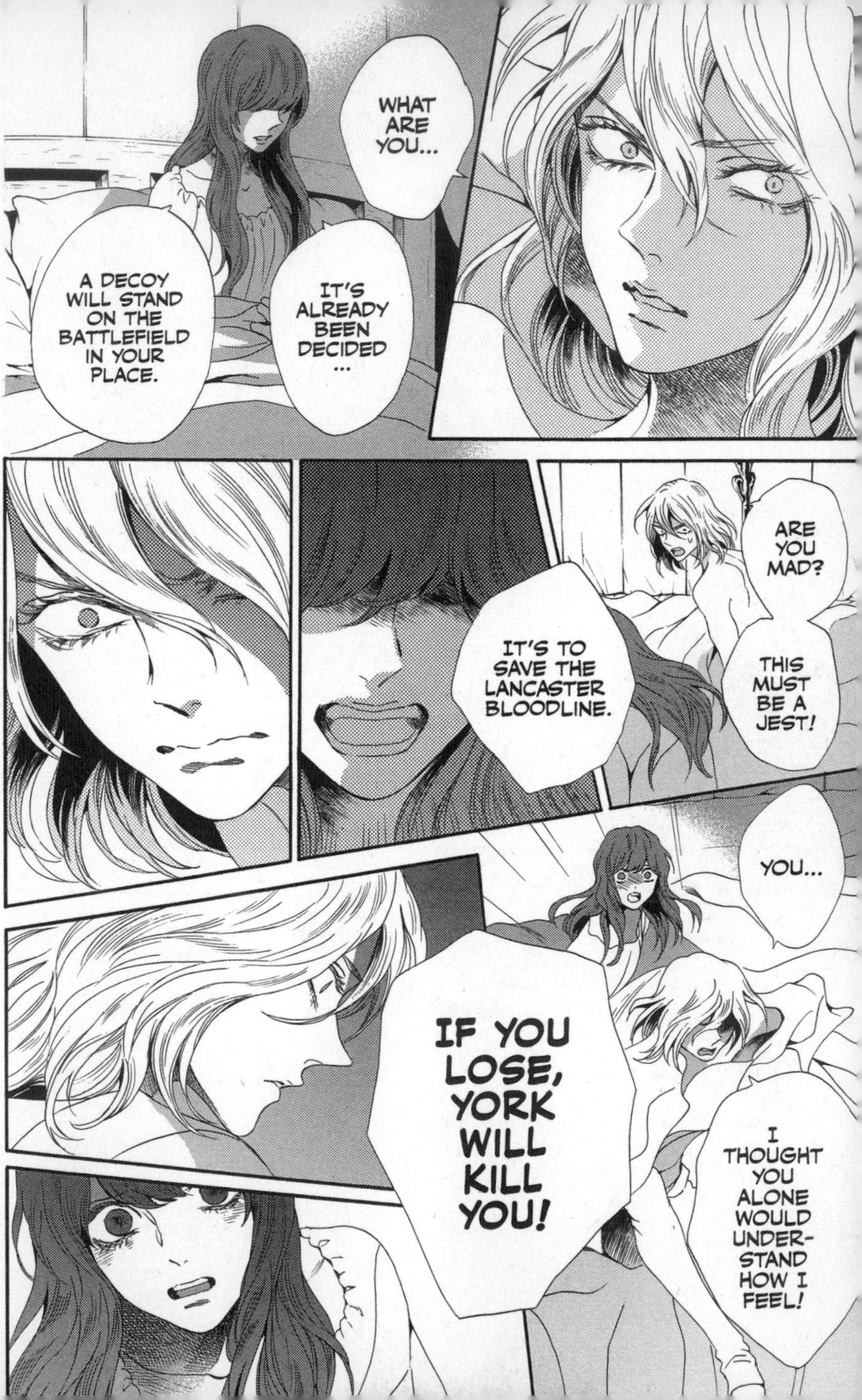
WHAT ARE YOU...
IT'S ALREADY BEEN DECIDED...
A DECOY WILL STAND ON THE BATTLEFIELD IN YOUR PLACE.
ARE YOU MAD?
THIS MUST BE A JEST!
IT'S TO SAVE THE LANCASTER BLOODLINE.
YOU...
I THOUGHT YOU ALONE WOULD UNDER-STAND HOW I FEEL!
IF YOU LOSE, YORK WILL KILL YOU!

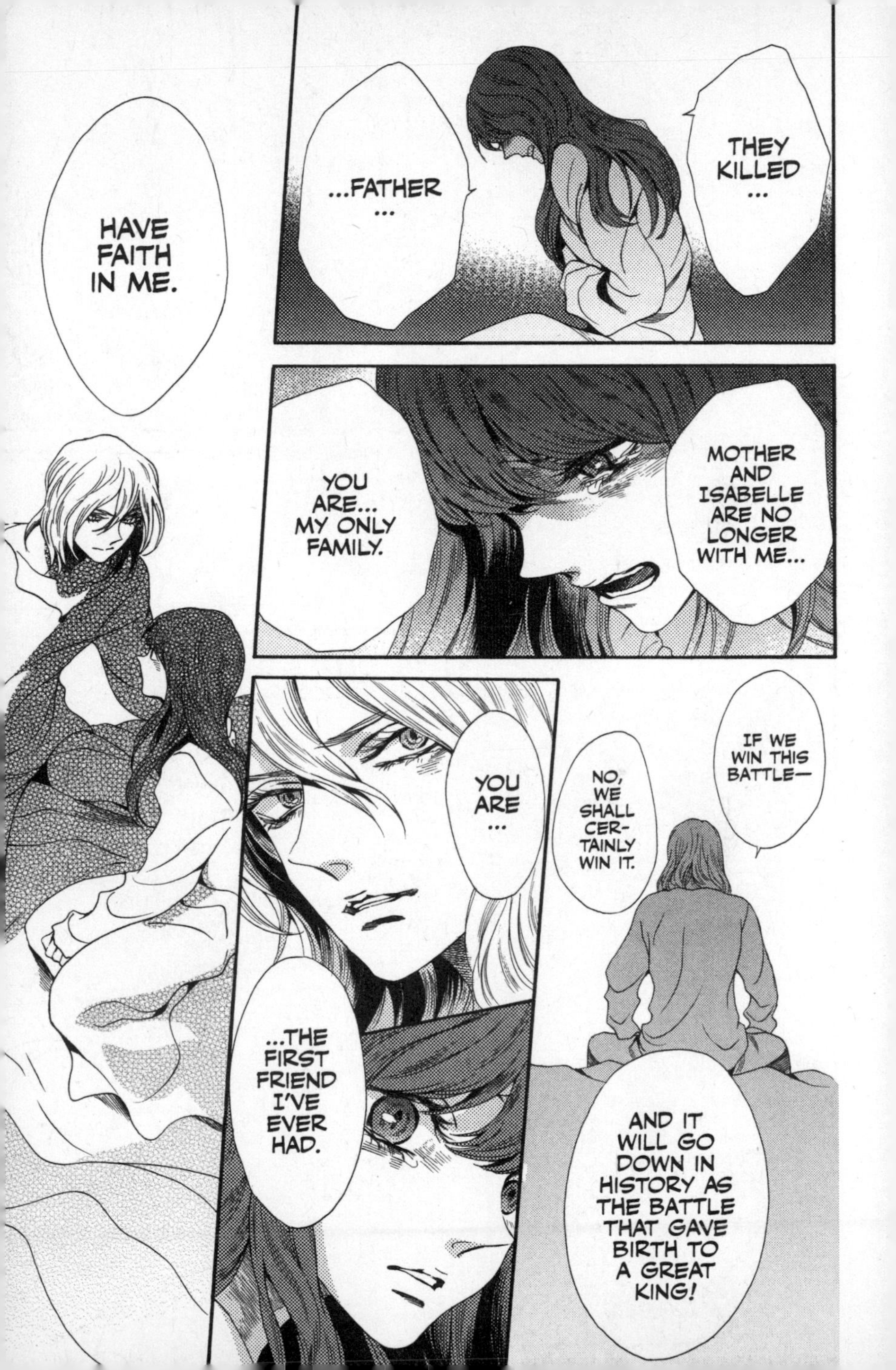
THEY KILLED ...
...FATHER ...
MOTHER AND ISABELLE ARE NO LONGER WITH ME...
YOU ARE... MY ONLY FAMILY.
HAVE FAITH IN ME.
IF WE WIN THIS BATTLE—
NO, WE SHALL CER-TAINLY WIN IT.
AND IT WILL GO DOWN IN HISTORY AS THE BATTLE THAT GAVE BIRTH TO A GREAT KING!
YOU ARE ...
...THE FIRST FRIEND I'VE EVER HAD.

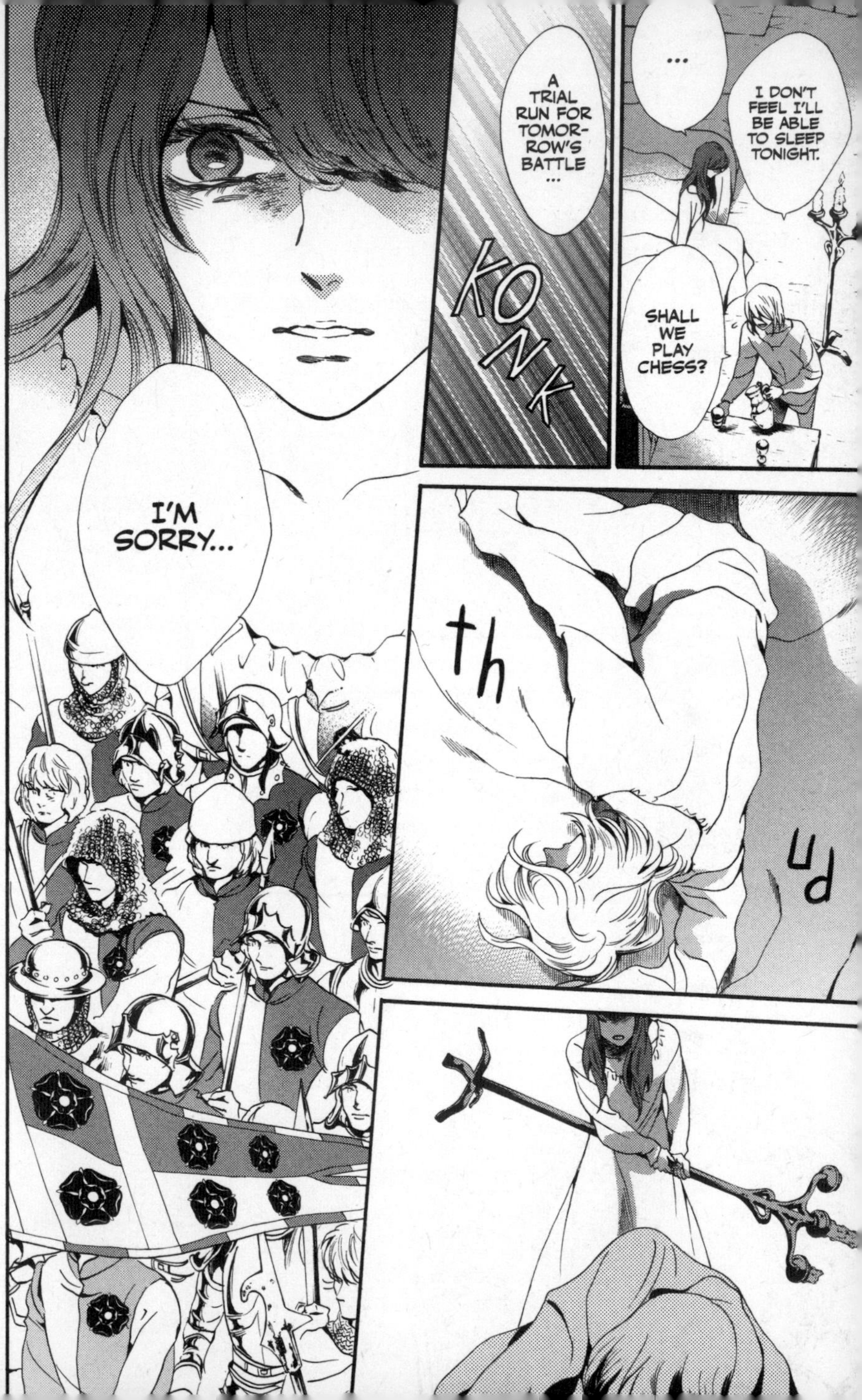
I DON'T FEEL I'LL BE ABLE TO SLEEP TONIGHT.
...
SHALL WE PLAY CHESS?
A TRIAL RUN FOR TOMORROW'S BATTLE...
KONK
thud
I'M SORRY...

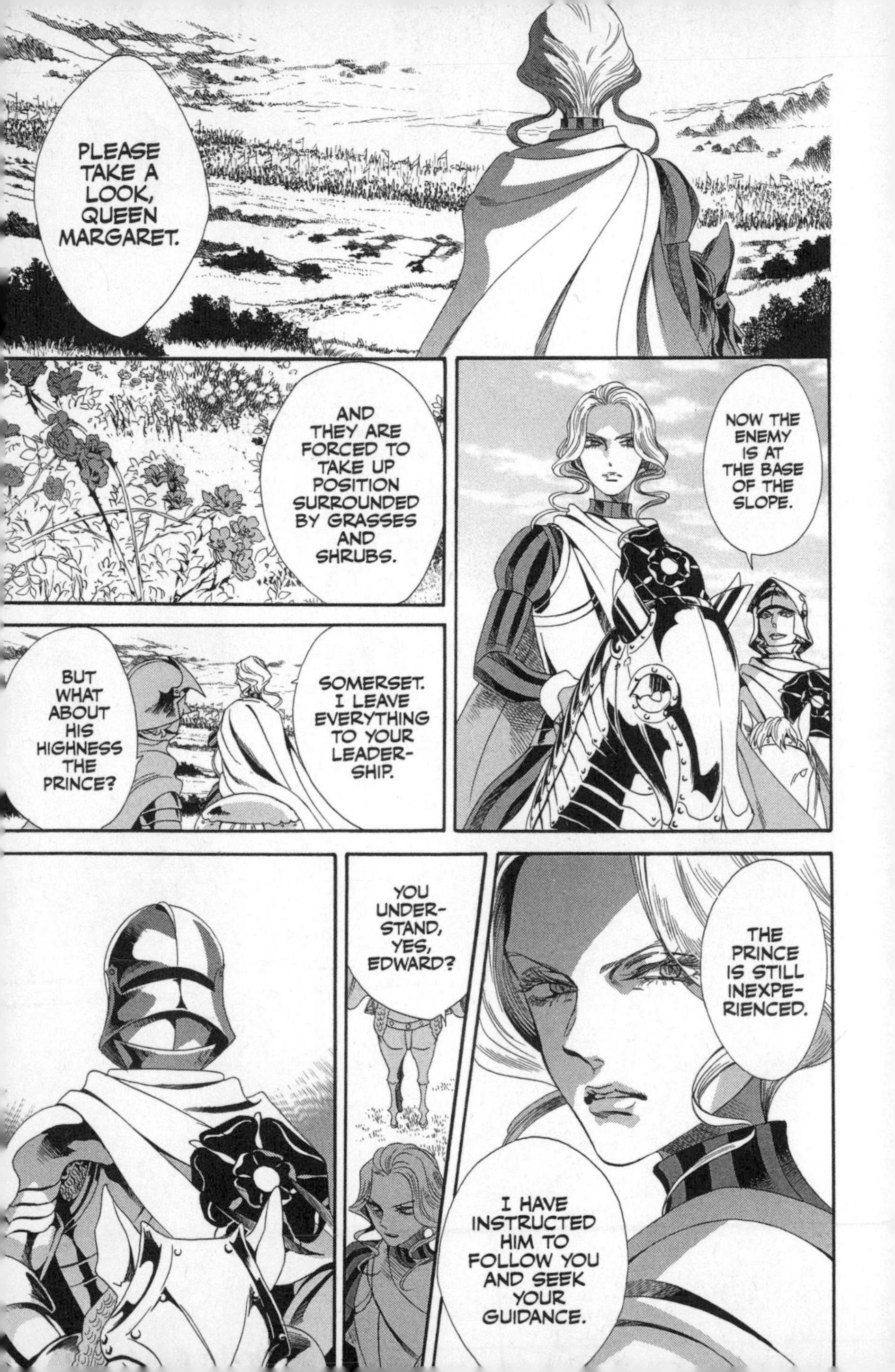
PLEASE TAKE A LOOK, QUEEN MARGARET.
NOW THE ENEMY IS AT THE BASE OF THE SLOPE.
AND THEY ARE FORCED TO TAKE UP POSITION SURROUNDED BY GRASSES AND SHRUBS.
SOMERSET. I LEAVE EVERYTHING TO YOUR LEADER-SHIP.
BUT WHAT ABOUT HIS HIGHNESS THE PRINCE?
THE PRINCE IS STILL INEXPE-RIENCED.
I HAVE INSTRUCTED HIM TO FOLLOW YOU AND SEEK YOUR GUIDANCE.
YOU UNDER-STAND, YES, EDWARD?

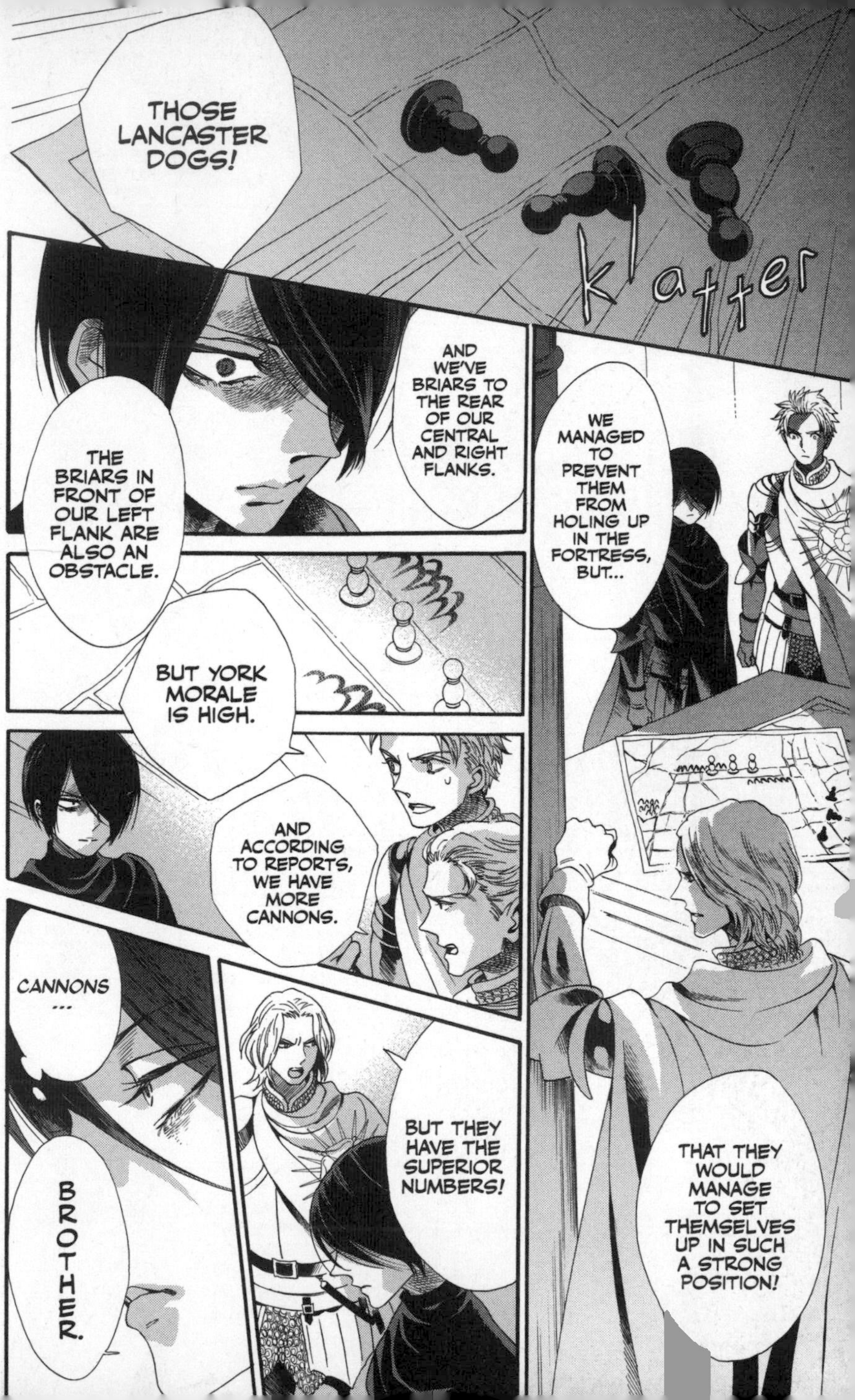
THOSE LANCASTER DOGS!
klatter
WE MANAGED TO PREVENT THEM FROM HOLING UP IN THE FORTRESS, BUT...
THAT THEY WOULD MANAGE TO SET THEMSELVES UP IN SUCH A STRONG POSITION!
AND WE'VE BRIARS TO THE REAR OF OUR CENTRAL AND RIGHT FLANKS.
THE BRIARS IN FRONT OF OUR LEFT FLANK ARE ALSO AN OBSTACLE.
BUT YORK MORALE IS HIGH.
AND ACCORDING TO REPORTS, WE HAVE MORE CANNONS.
BUT THEY HAVE THE SUPERIOR NUMBERS!
CANNONS...
BROTHER.

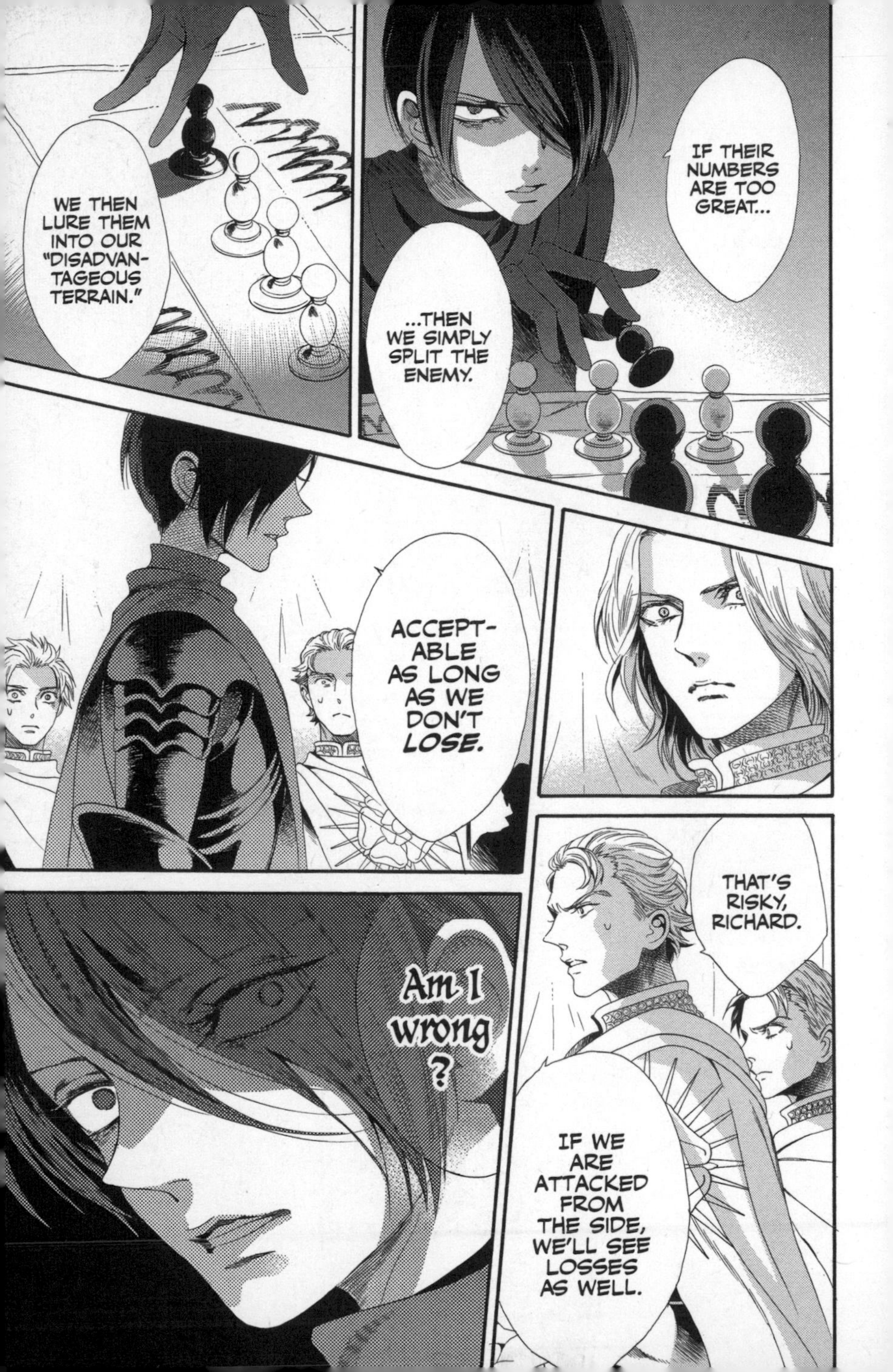
IF THEIR NUMBERS ARE TOO GREAT...
...THEN WE SIMPLY SPLIT THE ENEMY.
WE THEN LURE THEM INTO OUR "DISADVANTAGEOUS TERRAIN."
ACCEPTABLE AS LONG AS WE DON'T *LOSE.*
THAT'S RISKY, RICHARD.
IF WE ARE ATTACKED FROM THE SIDE, WE'LL SEE LOSSES AS WELL.
Am I wrong?

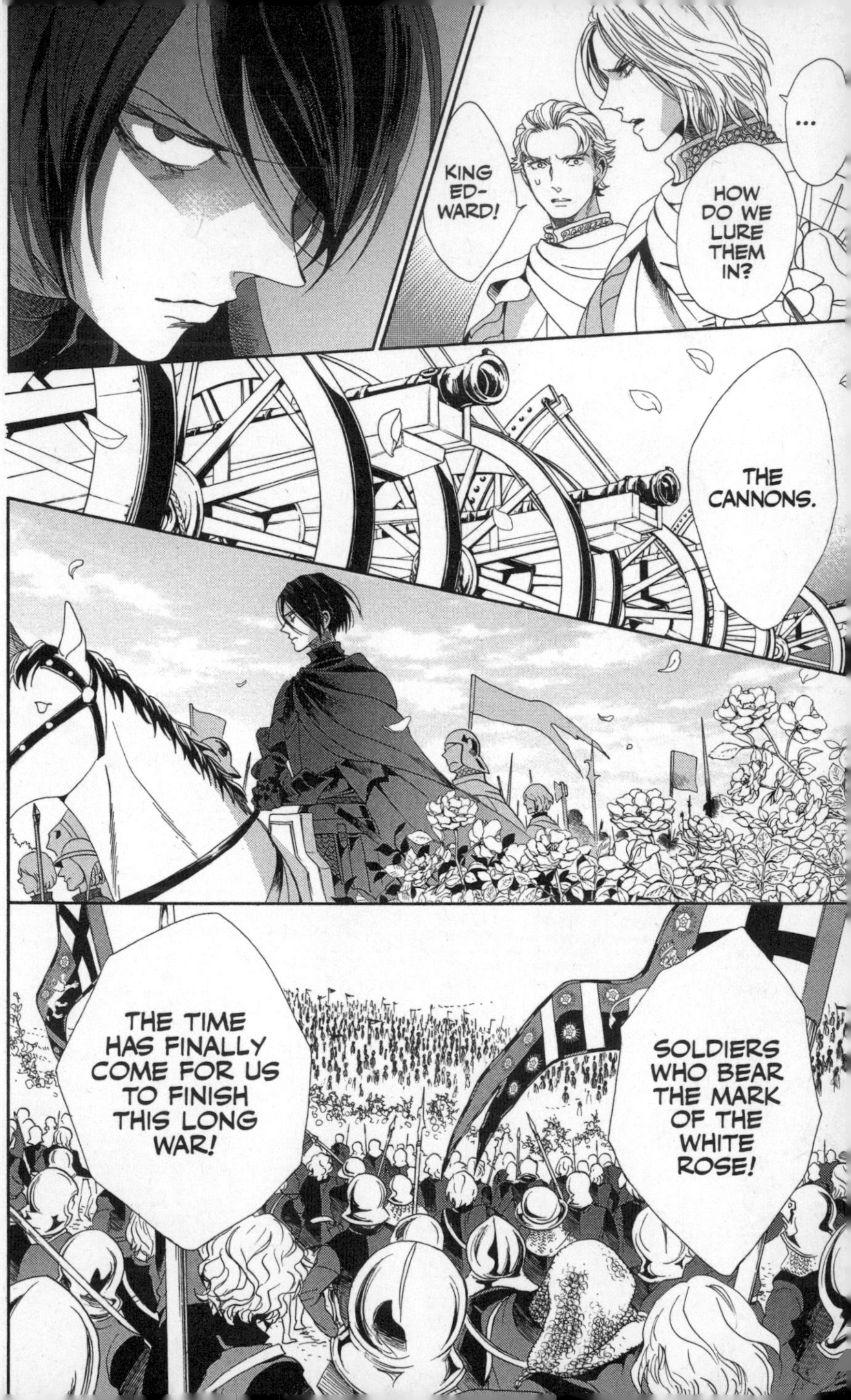
...
HOW DO WE LURE THEM IN?
KING ED-WARD!
THE CANNONS.
SOLDIERS WHO BEAR THE MARK OF THE WHITE ROSE!
THE TIME HAS FINALLY COME FOR US TO FINISH THIS LONG WAR!

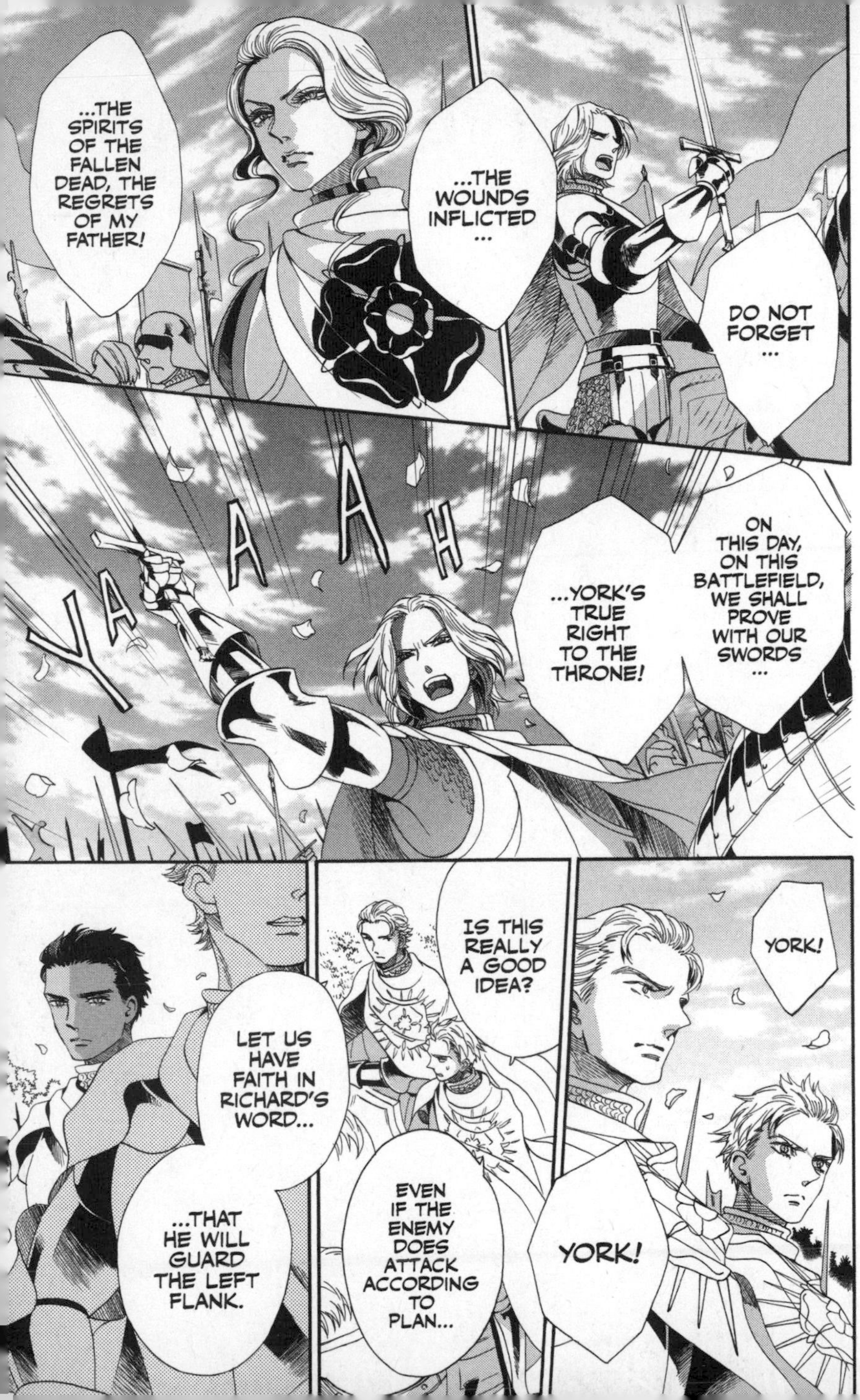
DO NOT FORGET ...
...THE WOUNDS INFLICTED ...
...THE SPIRITS OF THE FALLEN DEAD, THE REGRETS OF MY FATHER!
ON THIS DAY, ON THIS BATTLEFIELD, WE SHALL PROVE WITH OUR SWORDS ...
...YORK'S TRUE RIGHT TO THE THRONE!
YAAAH
YORK!
YORK!
IS THIS REALLY A GOOD IDEA?
EVEN IF THE ENEMY DOES ATTACK ACCORDING TO PLAN...
LET US HAVE FAITH IN RICHARD'S WORD...
...THAT HE WILL GUARD THE LEFT FLANK.

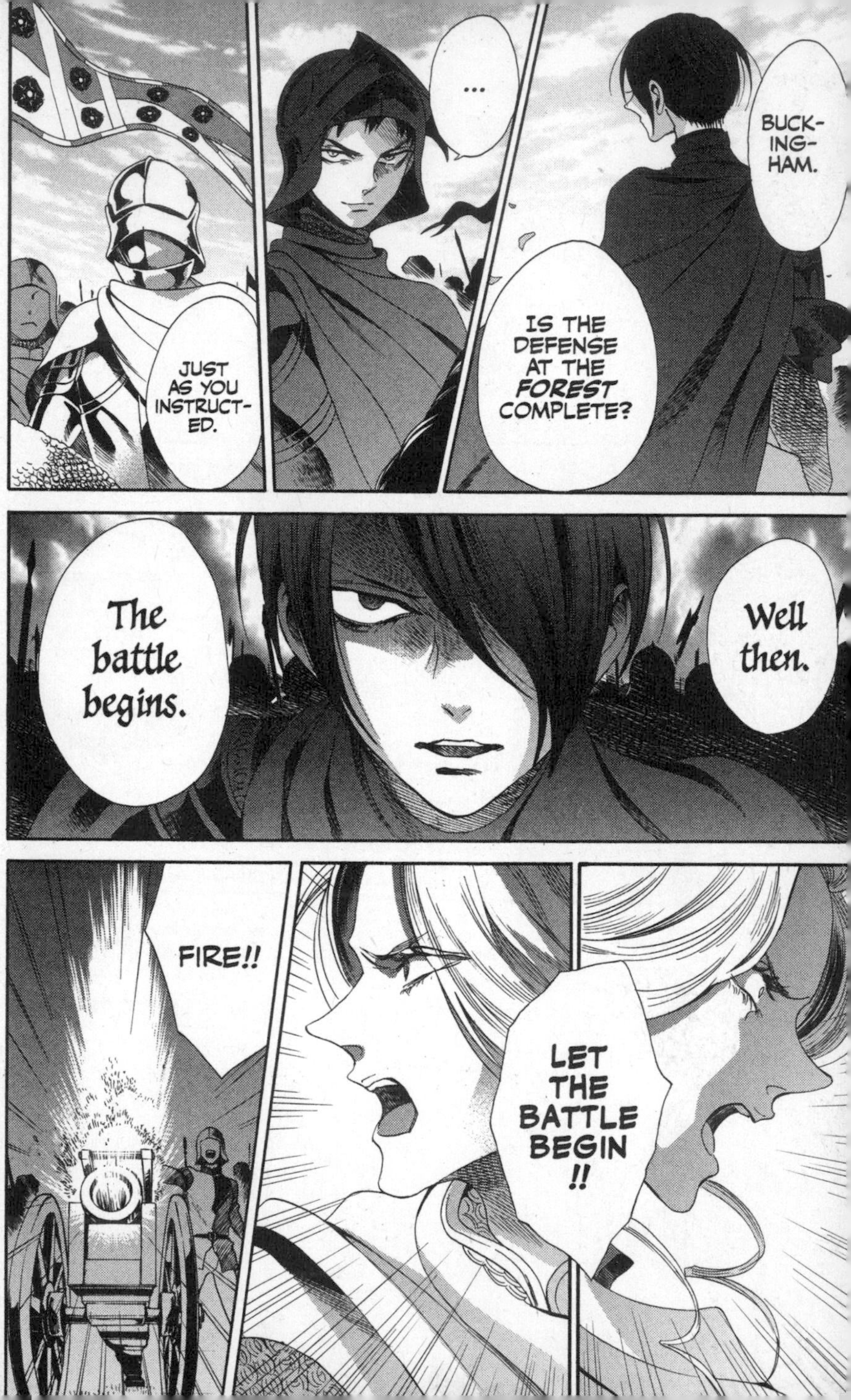
BUCKINGHAM.
IS THE DEFENSE AT THE *FOREST* COMPLETE?
...
JUST AS YOU INSTRUCTED.
Well then.
The battle begins.
LET THE BATTLE BEGIN!!
FIRE!!

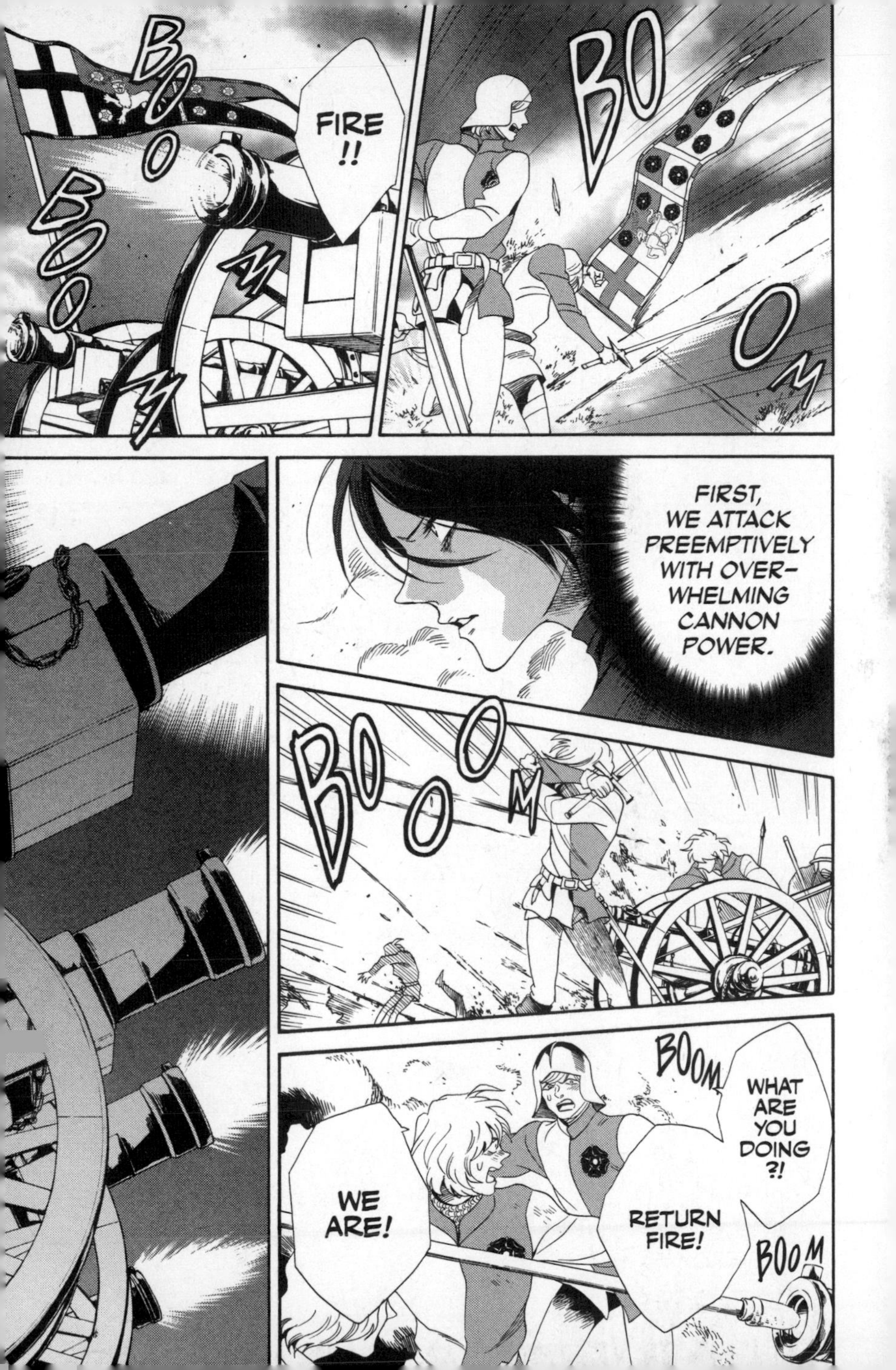

BO
OM
FIRE !!
BOOO
BOOOOM
FIRST, WE ATTACK PREEMPTIVELY WITH OVER-WHELMING CANNON POWER.
BOOOOM
BOOM
WHAT ARE YOU DOING ?!
RETURN FIRE!
WE ARE!
BOOM

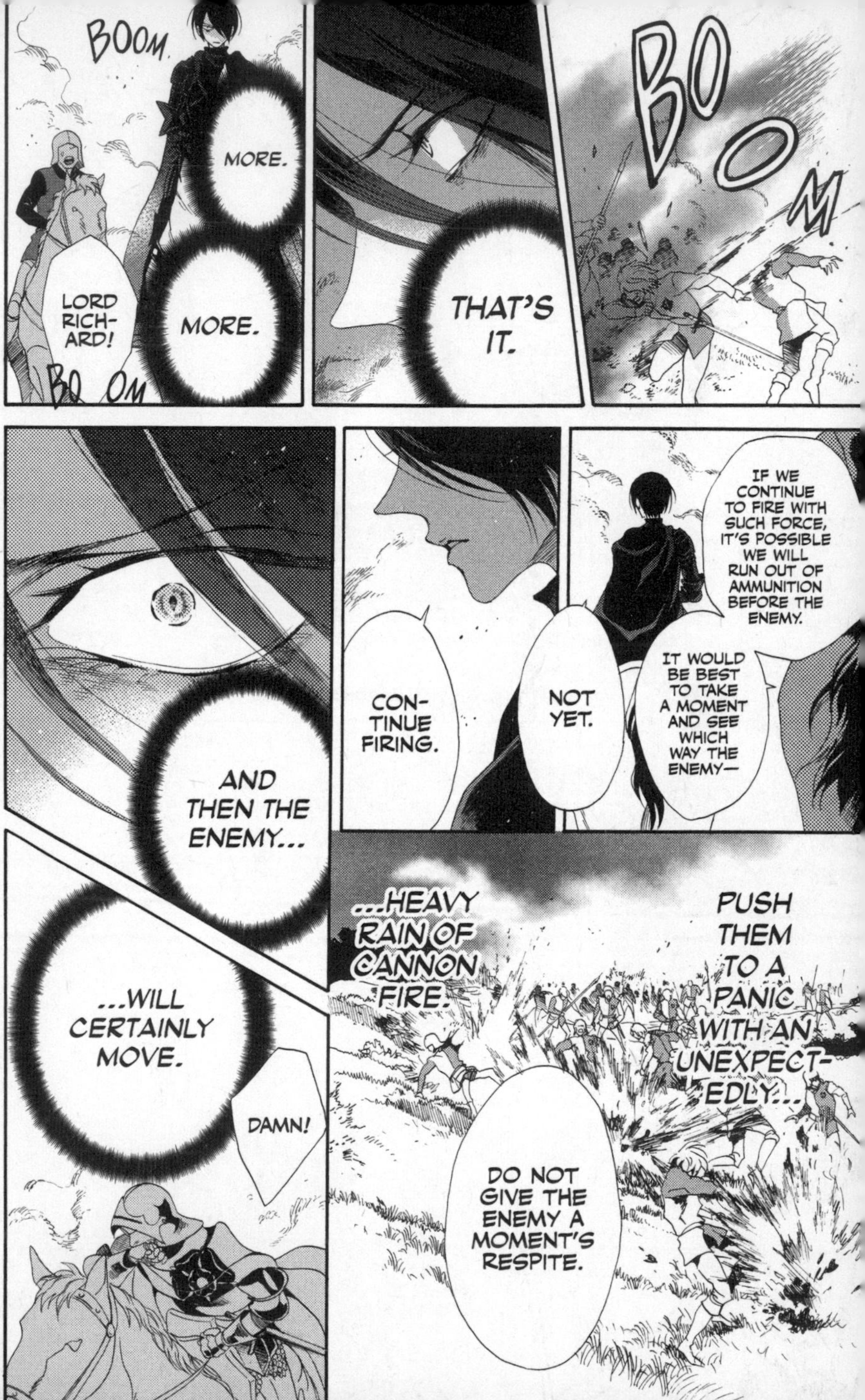
BOOM
THAT'S IT.
BOOM
MORE.
MORE.
LORD RICH-ARD!
BO OM
IF WE CONTINUE TO FIRE WITH SUCH FORCE, IT'S POSSIBLE WE WILL RUN OUT OF AMMUNITION BEFORE THE ENEMY.
IT WOULD BE BEST TO TAKE A MOMENT AND SEE WHICH WAY THE ENEMY—
NOT YET.
CON-TINUE FIRING.
AND THEN THE ENEMY...
PUSH THEM TO A PANIC WITH AN UNEXPECT-EDLY...
...HEAVY RAIN OF CANNON FIRE.
DO NOT GIVE THE ENEMY A MOMENT'S RESPITE.
...WILL CERTAINLY MOVE.
DAMN!

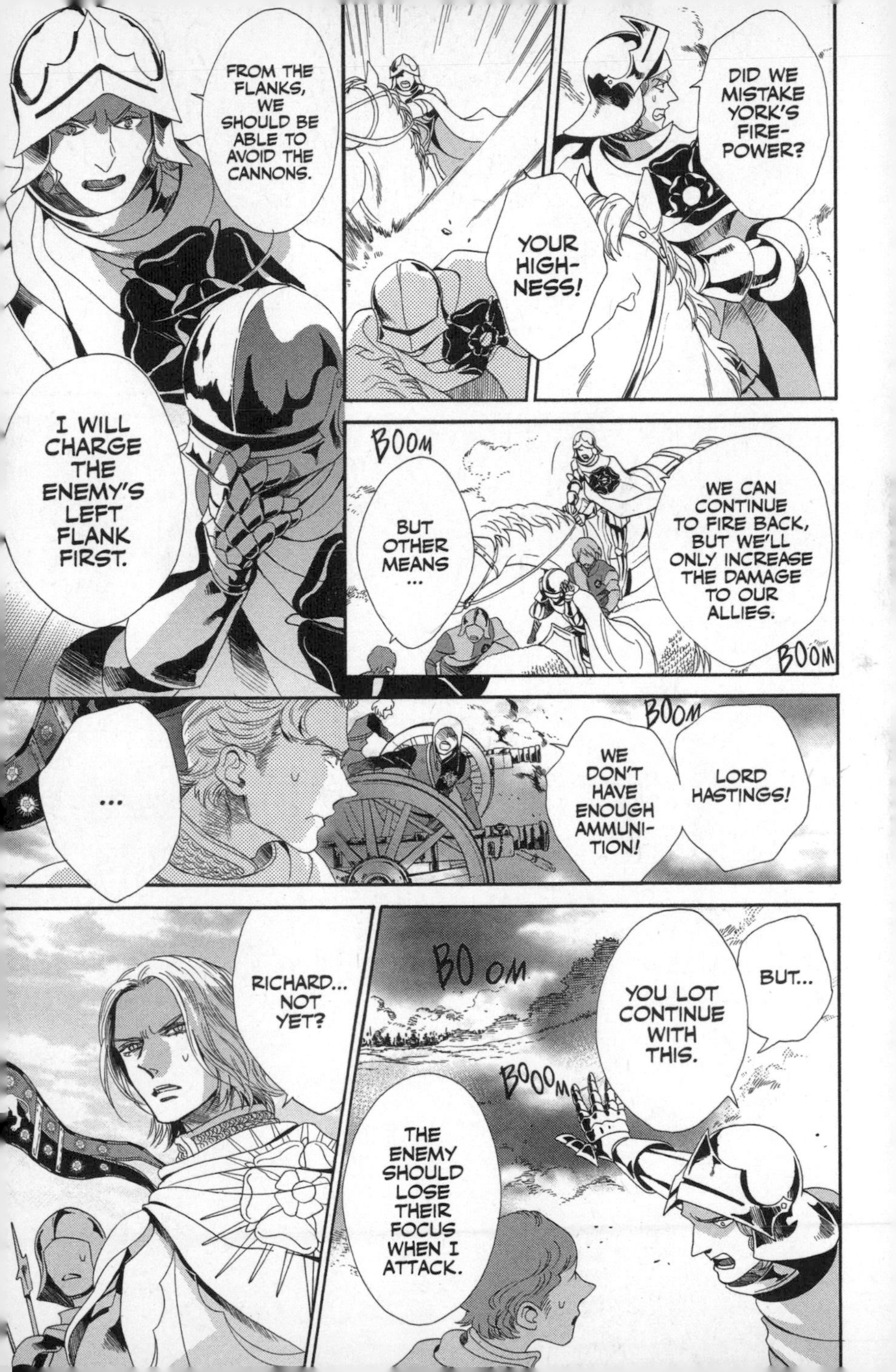
DID WE MISTAKE YORK'S FIRE-POWER?
YOUR HIGHNESS!
BOOM
WE CAN CONTINUE TO FIRE BACK, BUT WE'LL ONLY INCREASE THE DAMAGE TO OUR ALLIES.
BOOM
BUT OTHER MEANS...
FROM THE FLANKS, WE SHOULD BE ABLE TO AVOID THE CANNONS.
I WILL CHARGE THE ENEMY'S LEFT FLANK FIRST.
LORD HASTINGS!
BOOM
WE DON'T HAVE ENOUGH AMMUNITION!
...
BUT...
YOU LOT CONTINUE WITH THIS.
BOOOM
THE ENEMY SHOULD LOSE THEIR FOCUS WHEN I ATTACK.
BO OM
RICHARD... NOT YET?

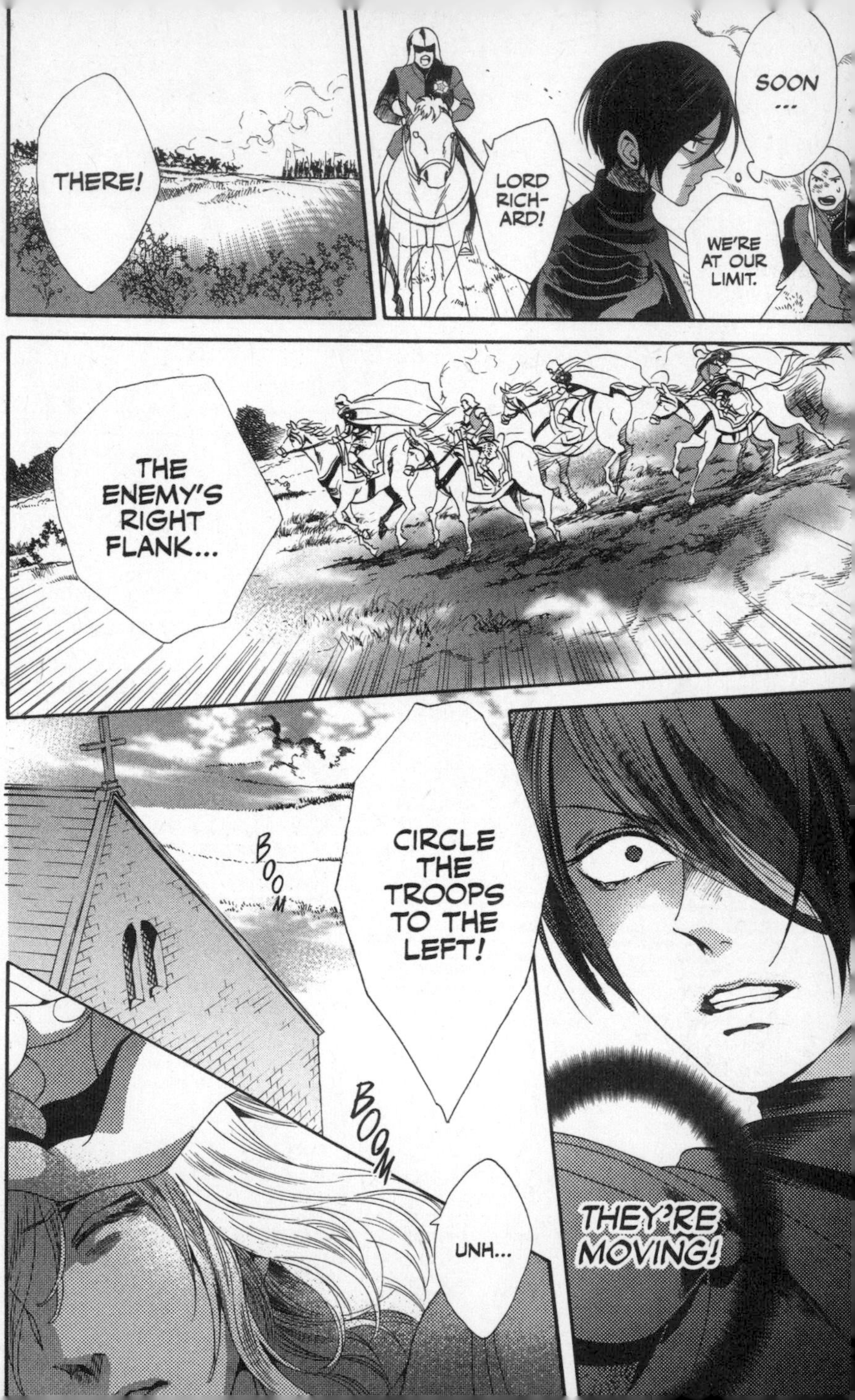
SOON ...
LORD RICH-ARD!
WE'RE AT OUR LIMIT.
THERE!
THE ENEMY'S RIGHT FLANK...
CIRCLE THE TROOPS TO THE LEFT!
BOOM
BOOM
THEY'RE MOVING!
UNH...

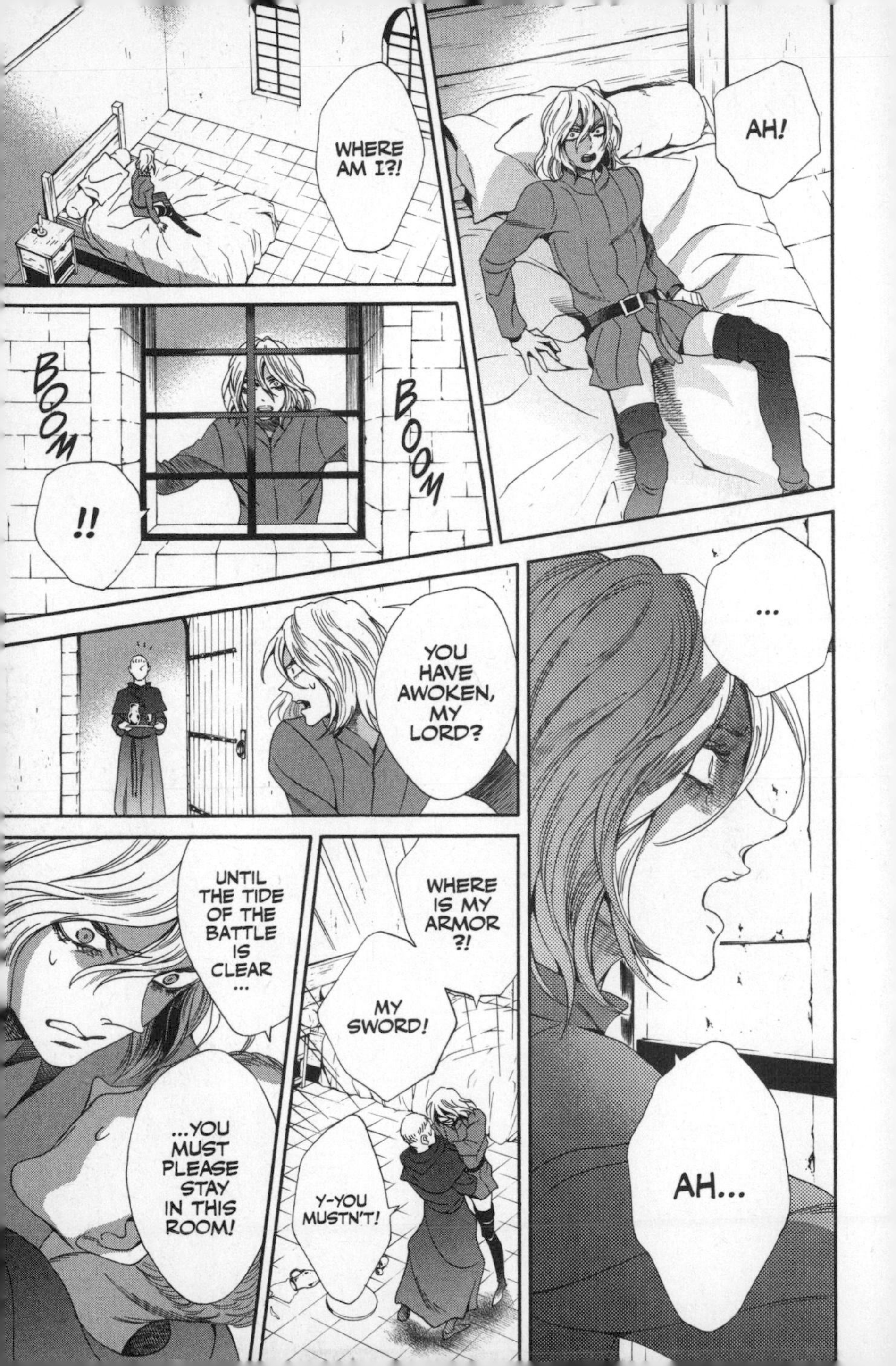
AH!
WHERE AM I?!
BOOM
BOOM
!!
...
AH...
YOU HAVE AWOKEN, MY LORD?
WHERE IS MY ARMOR?!
MY SWORD!
Y-YOU MUSTN'T!
UNTIL THE TIDE OF THE BATTLE IS CLEAR...
...YOU MUST PLEASE STAY IN THIS ROOM!

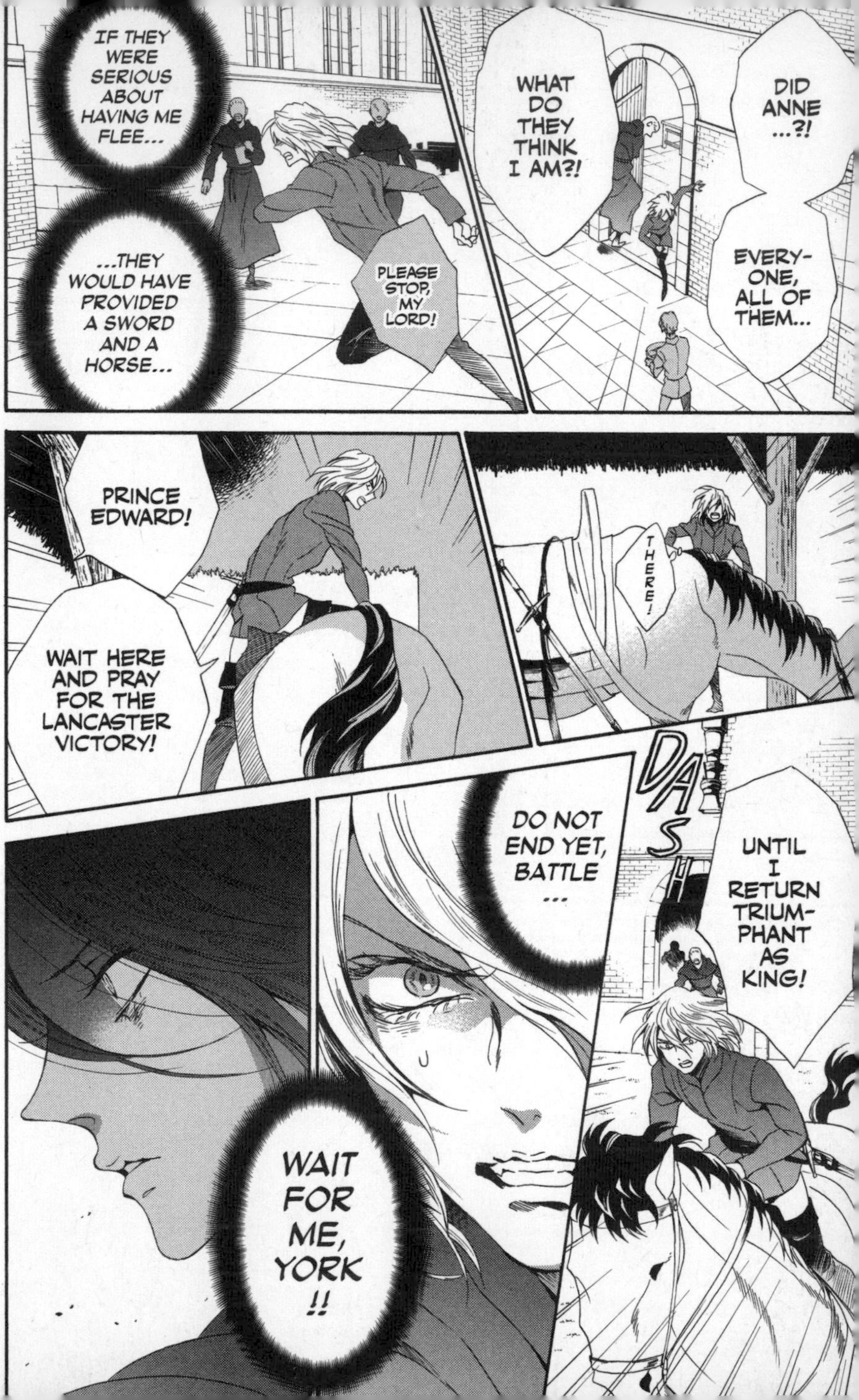
DID ANNE ...?!
EVERY-ONE, ALL OF THEM...
WHAT DO THEY THINK I AM?!
IF THEY WERE SERIOUS ABOUT HAVING ME FLEE...
...THEY WOULD HAVE PROVIDED A SWORD AND A HORSE...
PLEASE STOP, MY LORD!
THERE!
PRINCE EDWARD!
WAIT HERE AND PRAY FOR THE LANCASTER VICTORY!
DASH
UNTIL I RETURN TRIUMPHANT AS KING!
DO NOT END YET, BATTLE...
WAIT FOR ME, YORK!!

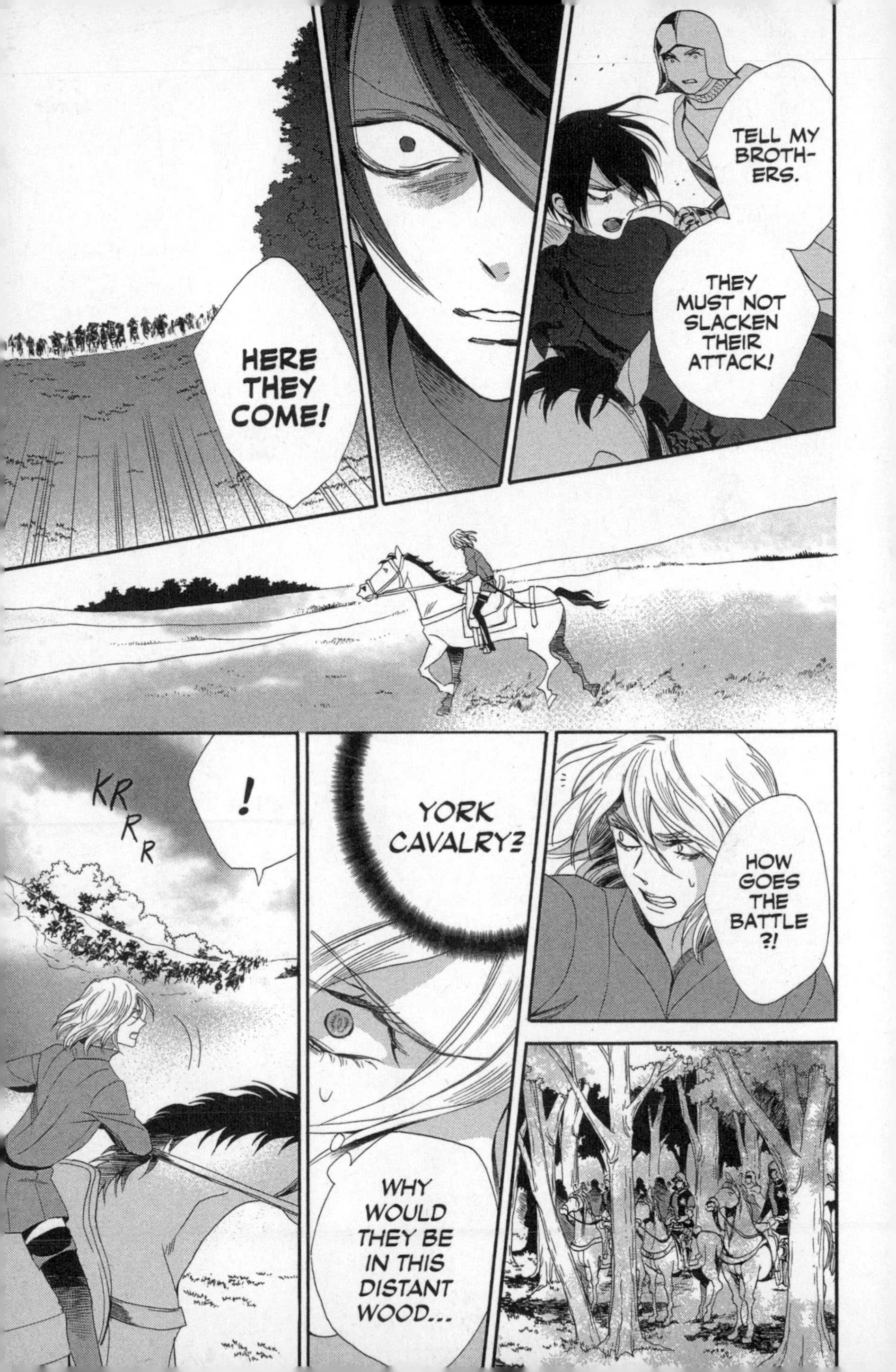
TELL MY BROTHERS.
THEY MUST NOT SLACKEN THEIR ATTACK!
HERE THEY COME!
HOW GOES THE BATTLE?!
YORK CAVALRY?!
WHY WOULD THEY BE IN THIS DISTANT WOOD...
!
KRRR

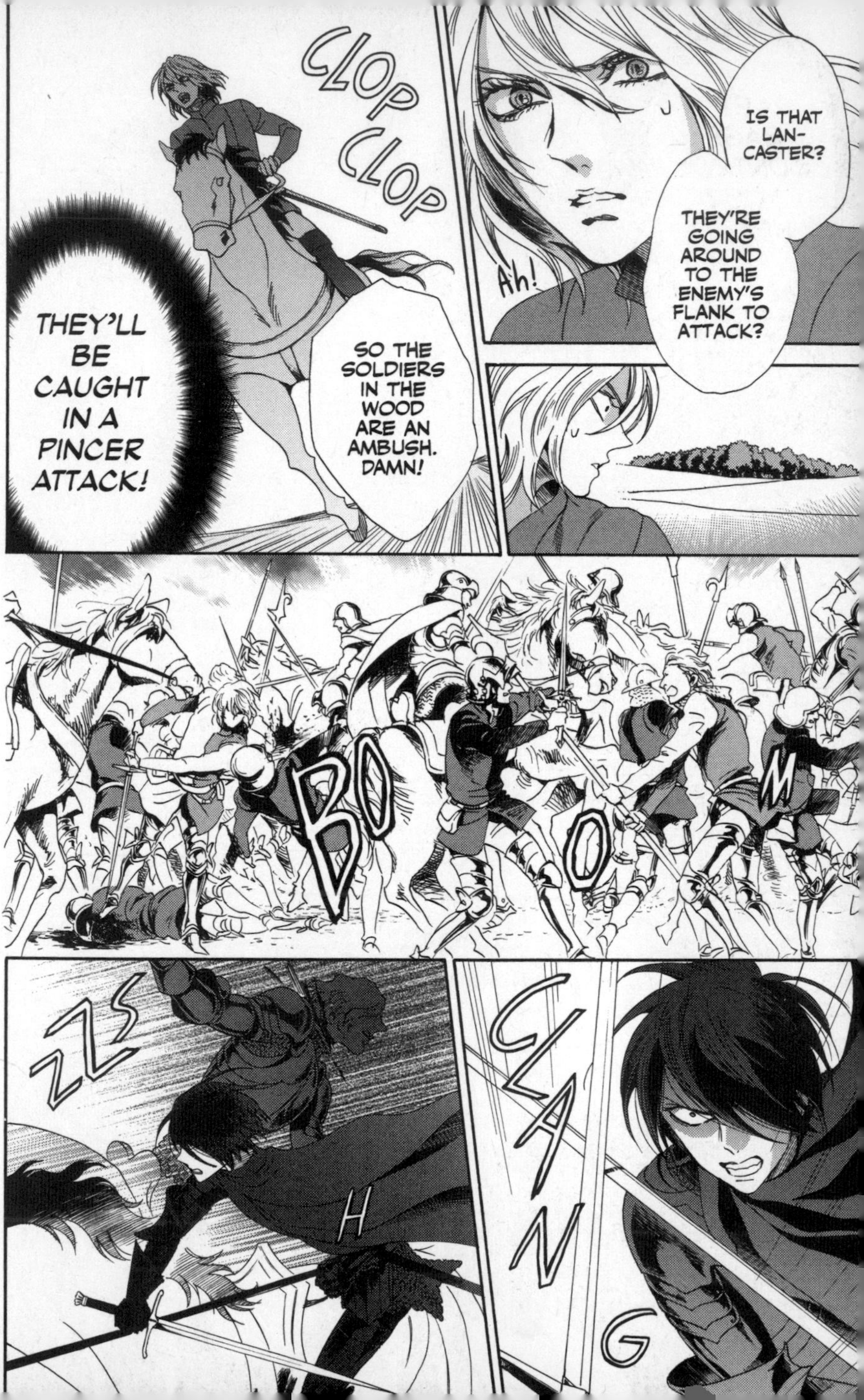
Ah!
IS THAT LAN-CASTER?
THEY'RE GOING AROUND TO THE ENEMY'S FLANK TO ATTACK?
CLOP CLOP
SO THE SOLDIERS IN THE WOOD ARE AN AMBUSH. DAMN!
THEY'LL BE CAUGHT IN A PINCER ATTACK!
BOOM
CLANG
ZZS
H

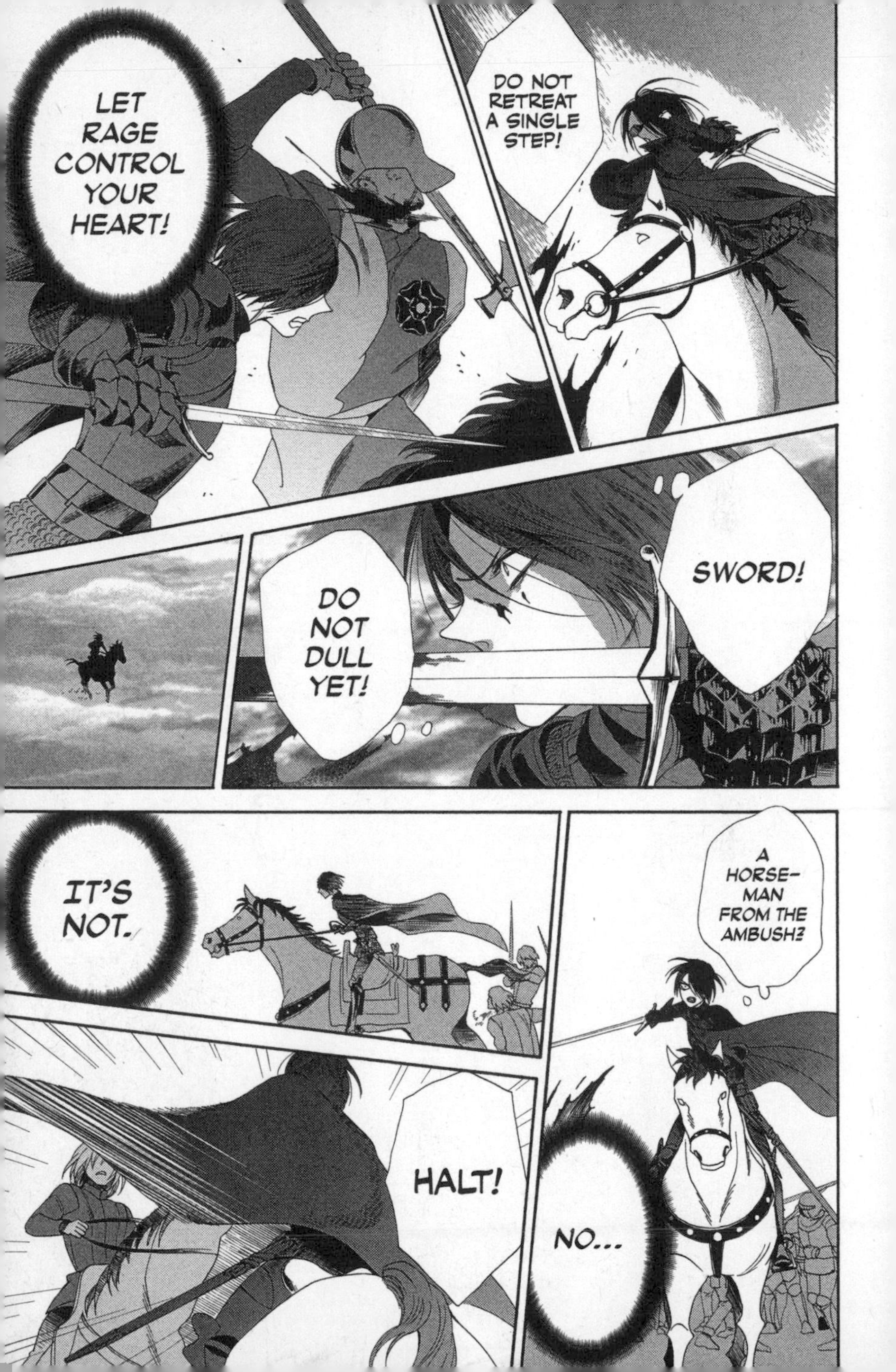
DO NOT RETREAT A SINGLE STEP!
LET RAGE CONTROL YOUR HEART!
SWORD!
DO NOT DULL YET!
A HORSE-MAN FROM THE AMBUSH?
NO...
IT'S NOT.
HALT!

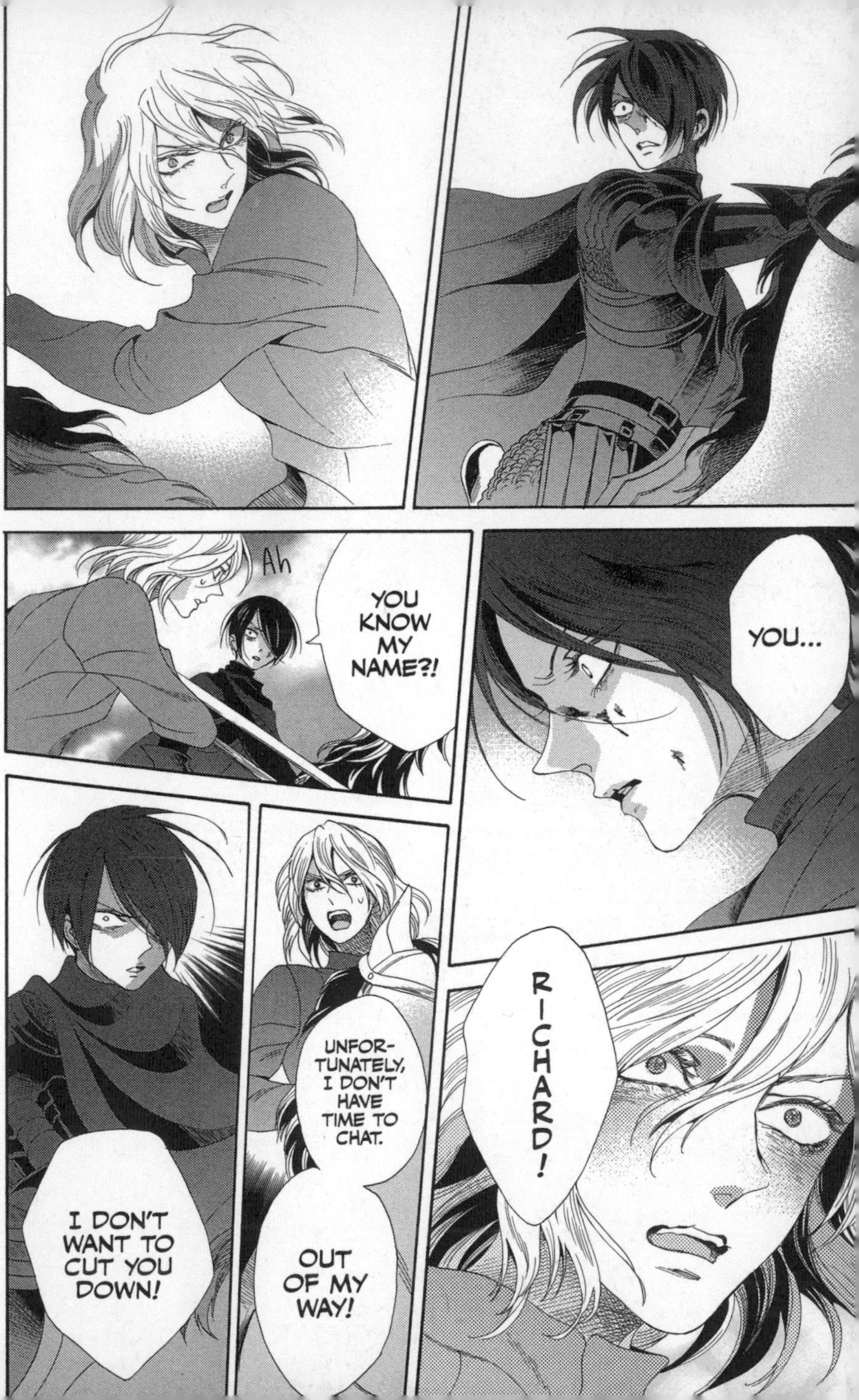
YOU...
RICHARD!
Ah
YOU KNOW MY NAME?!
UNFOR-TUNATELY, I DON'T HAVE TIME TO CHAT.
OUT OF MY WAY!
I DON'T WANT TO CUT YOU DOWN!

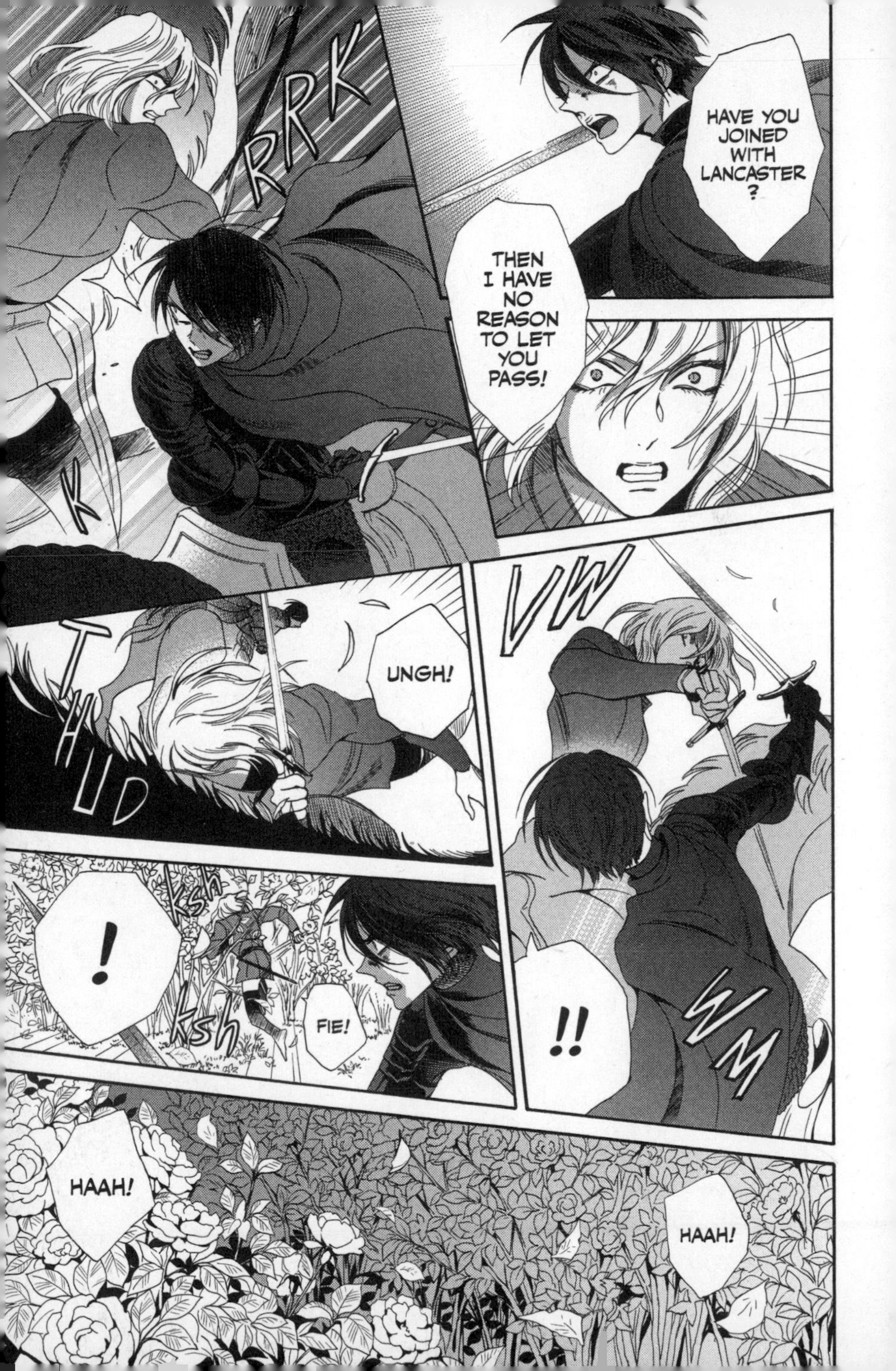
HAVE YOU JOINED WITH LANCASTER?
THEN I HAVE NO REASON TO LET YOU PASS!
RRK
K
VW
!!
WM
UNGH!
THUD
ksh
!
ksh
FIE!
HAAH!
HAAH!

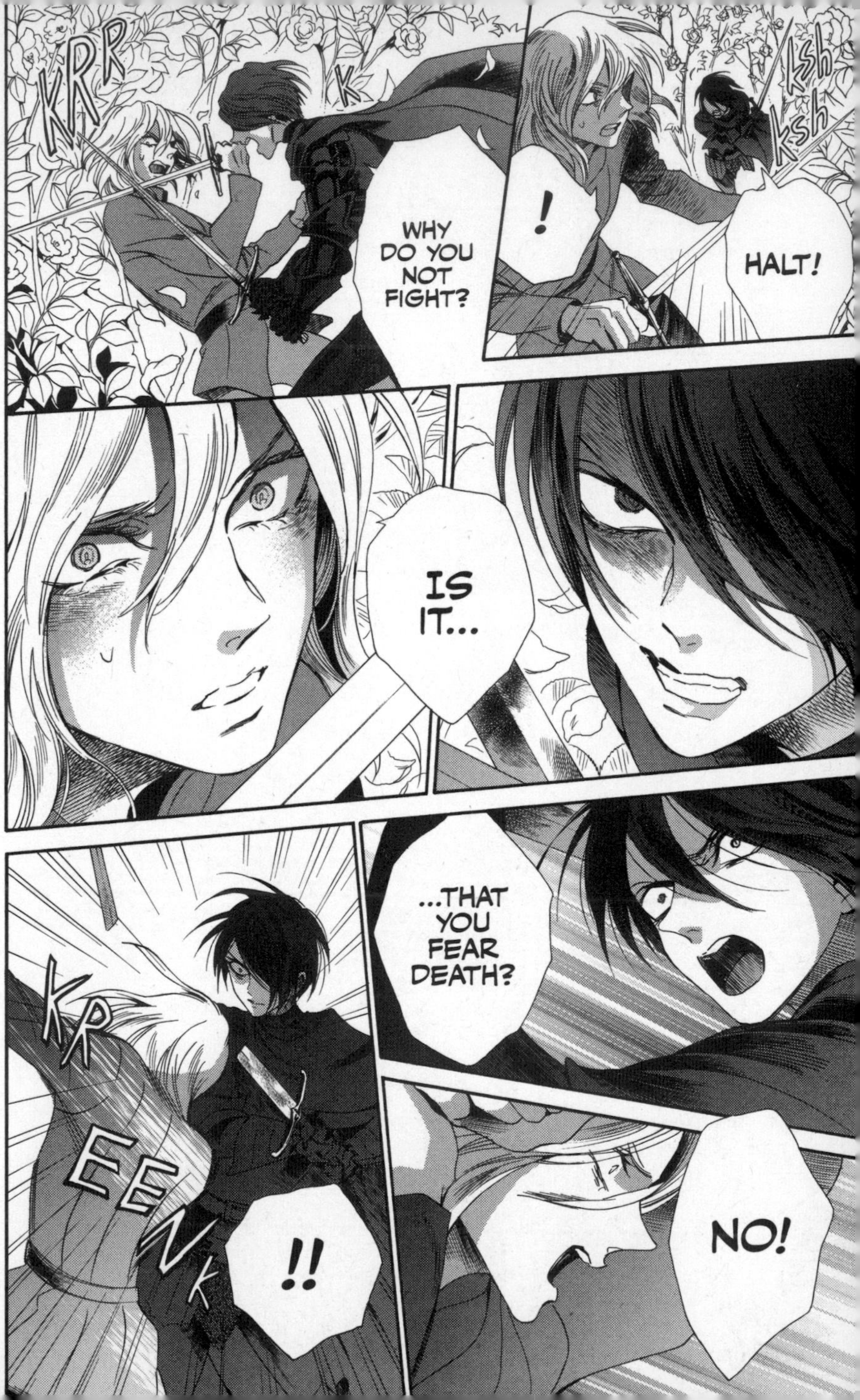

ksh
ksh
HALT!
!
K
KRR
WHY DO YOU NOT FIGHT?
IS IT...
...THAT YOU FEAR DEATH?
NO!
KR
EEENK
!!

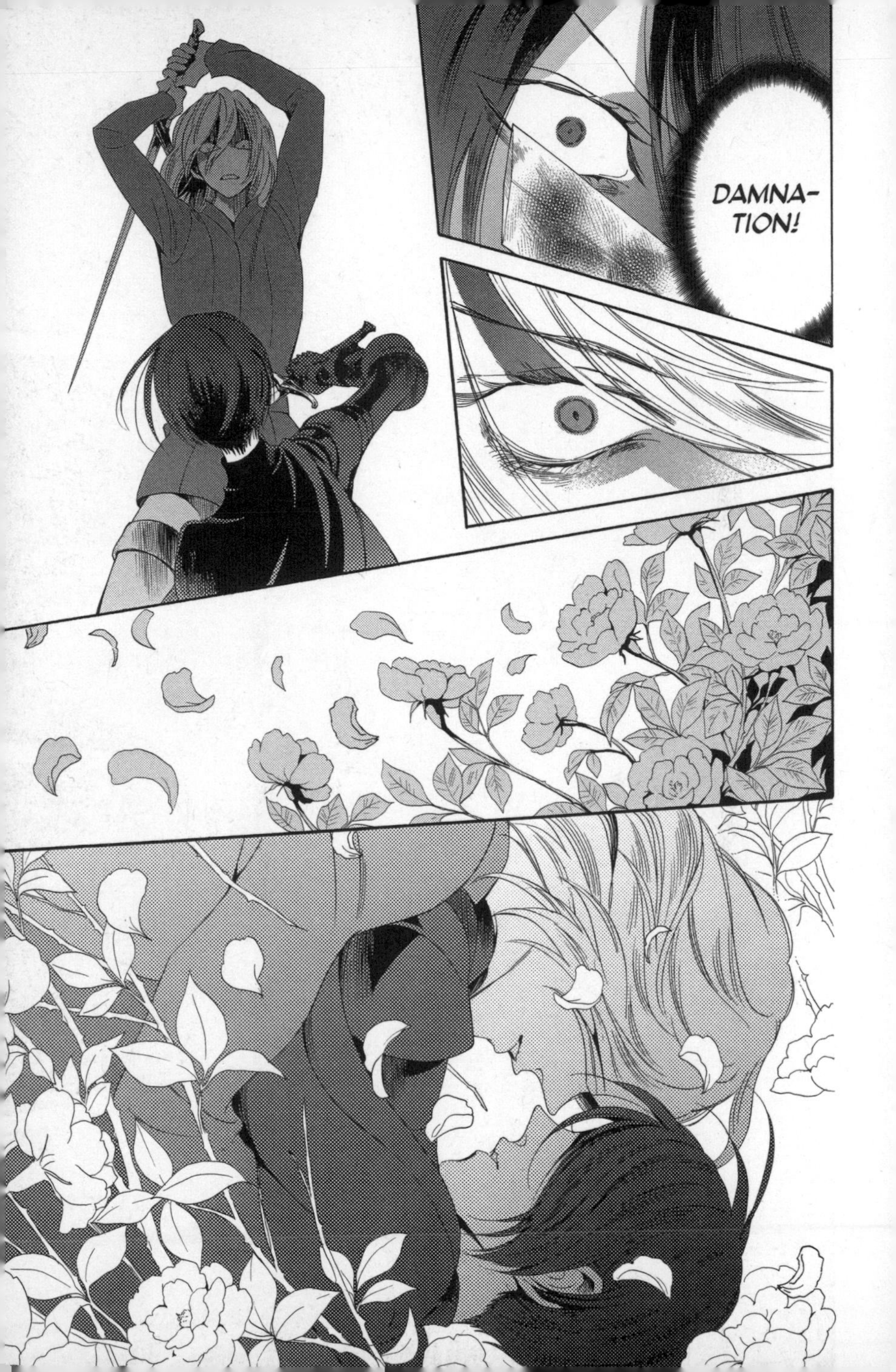
DAMNA-
TION!

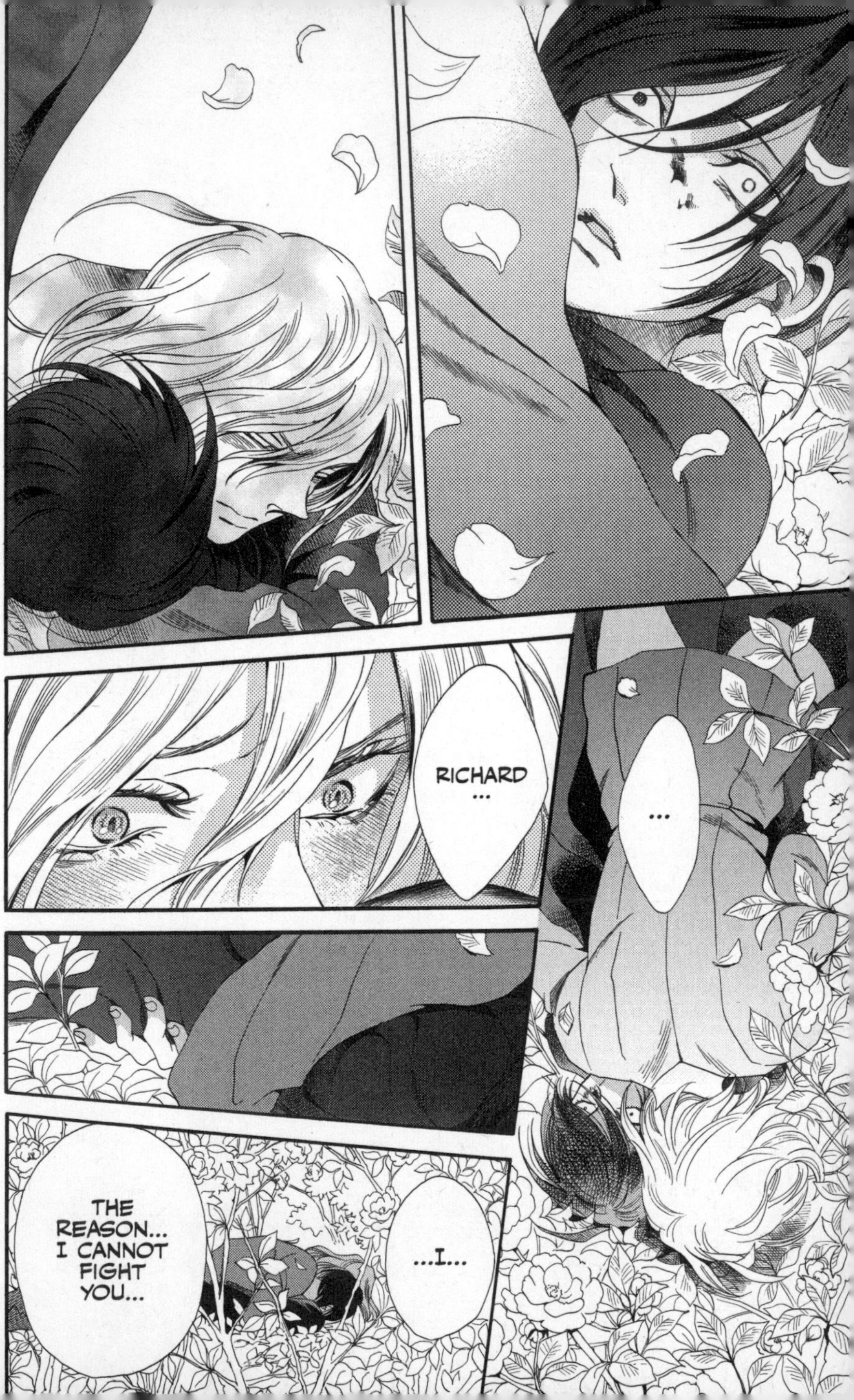
...
RICHARD ...
...I...
THE REASON... I CANNOT FIGHT YOU...

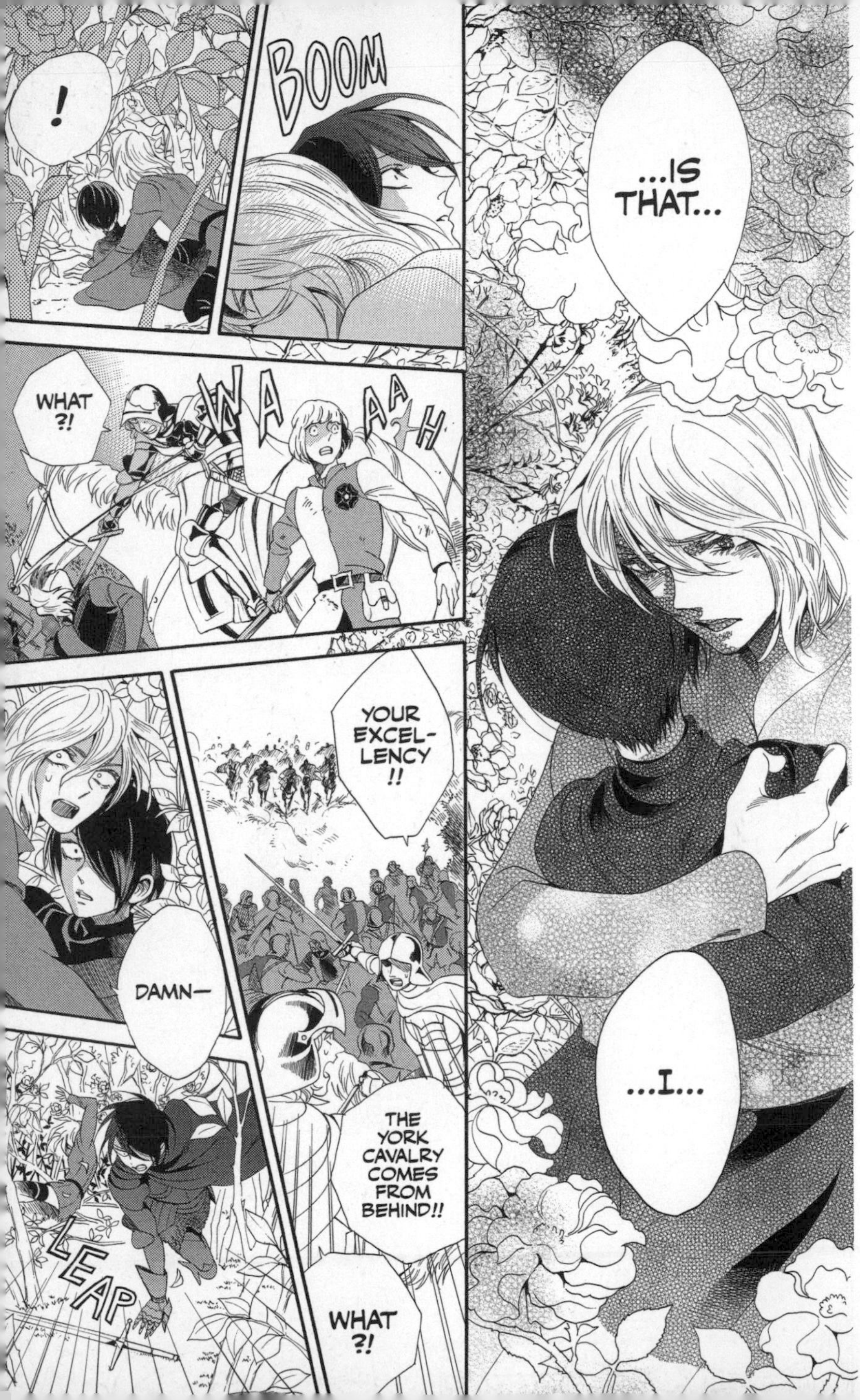
...IS THAT...
...I...
BOOM
!
WAAAH
WHAT ?!
YOUR EXCEL-LENCY !!
DAMN—
THE YORK CAVALRY COMES FROM BEHIND!!
WHAT ?!
LEAP

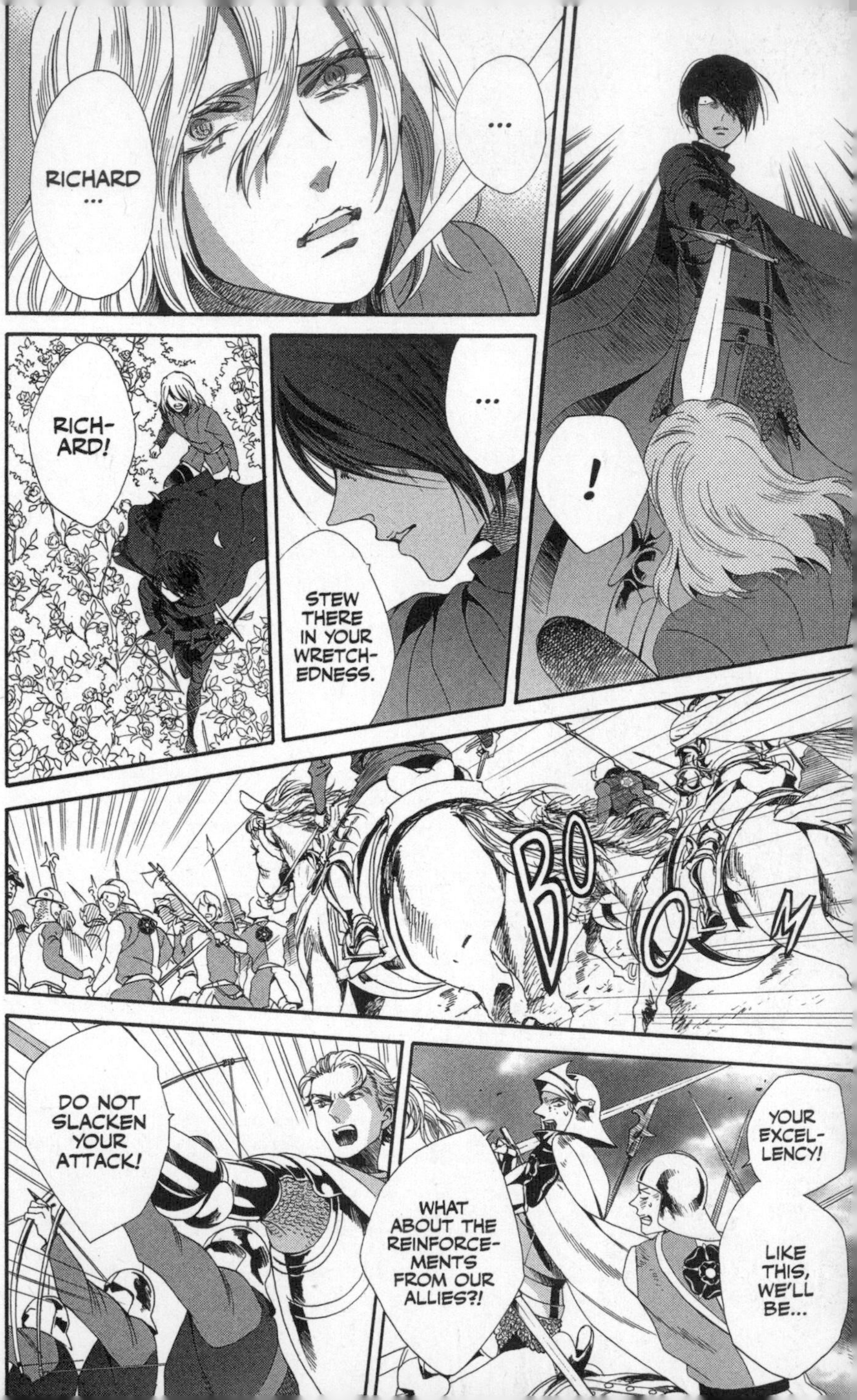
!
...
RICHARD ...
...
STEW THERE IN YOUR WRETCHEDNESS.
RICHARD!
BOOOM
YOUR EXCELLENCY!
WHAT ABOUT THE REINFORCEMENTS FROM OUR ALLIES?!
LIKE THIS, WE'LL BE...
DO NOT SLACKEN YOUR ATTACK!

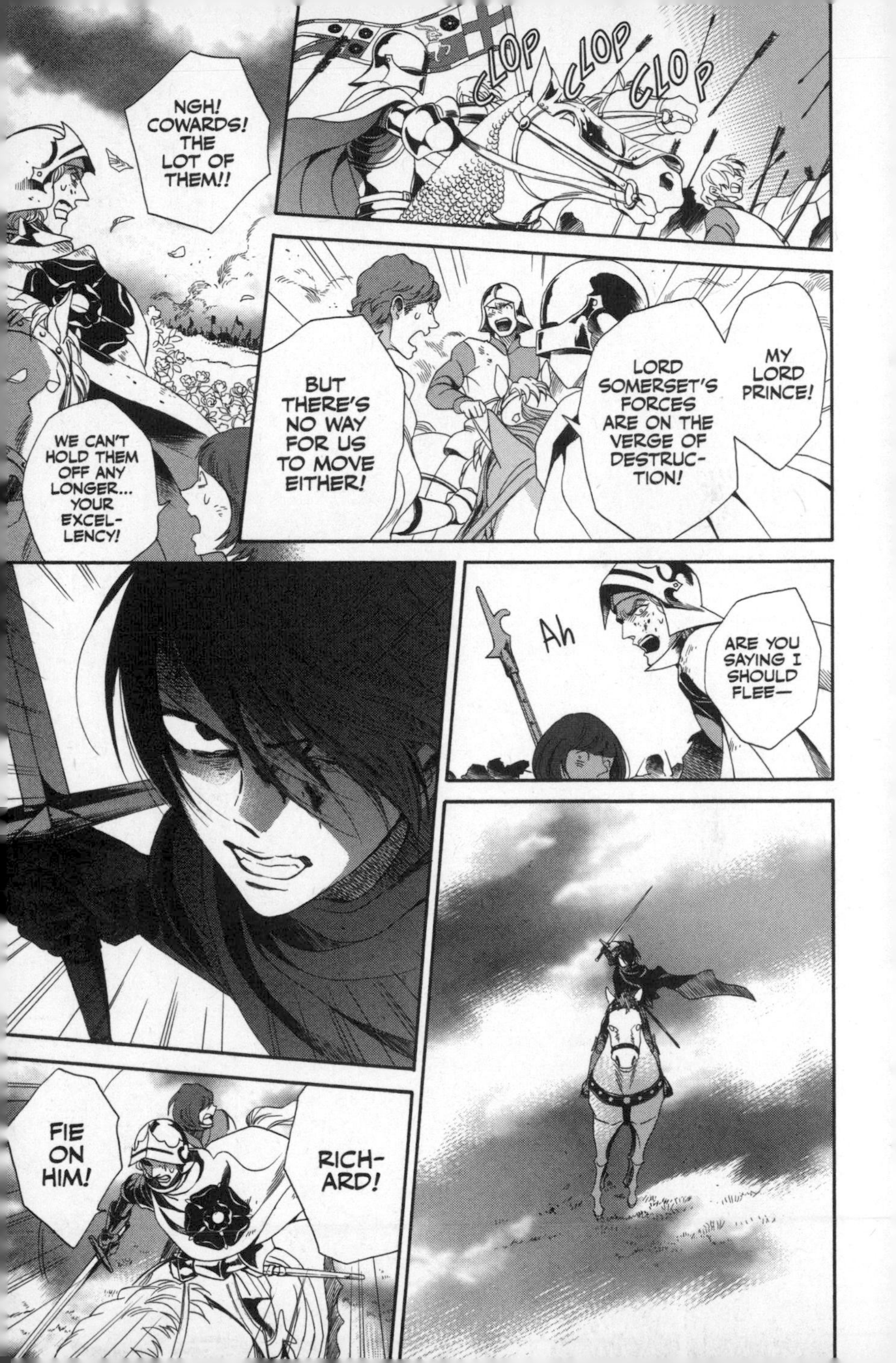
CLOP CLOP CLOP
MY LORD PRINCE!
LORD SOMERSET'S FORCES ARE ON THE VERGE OF DESTRUC-TION!
BUT THERE'S NO WAY FOR US TO MOVE EITHER!
NGH! COWARDS! THE LOT OF THEM!!
WE CAN'T HOLD THEM OFF ANY LONGER... YOUR EXCEL-LENCY!
ARE YOU SAYING I SHOULD FLEE—
Ah
RICH-ARD!
FIE ON HIM!

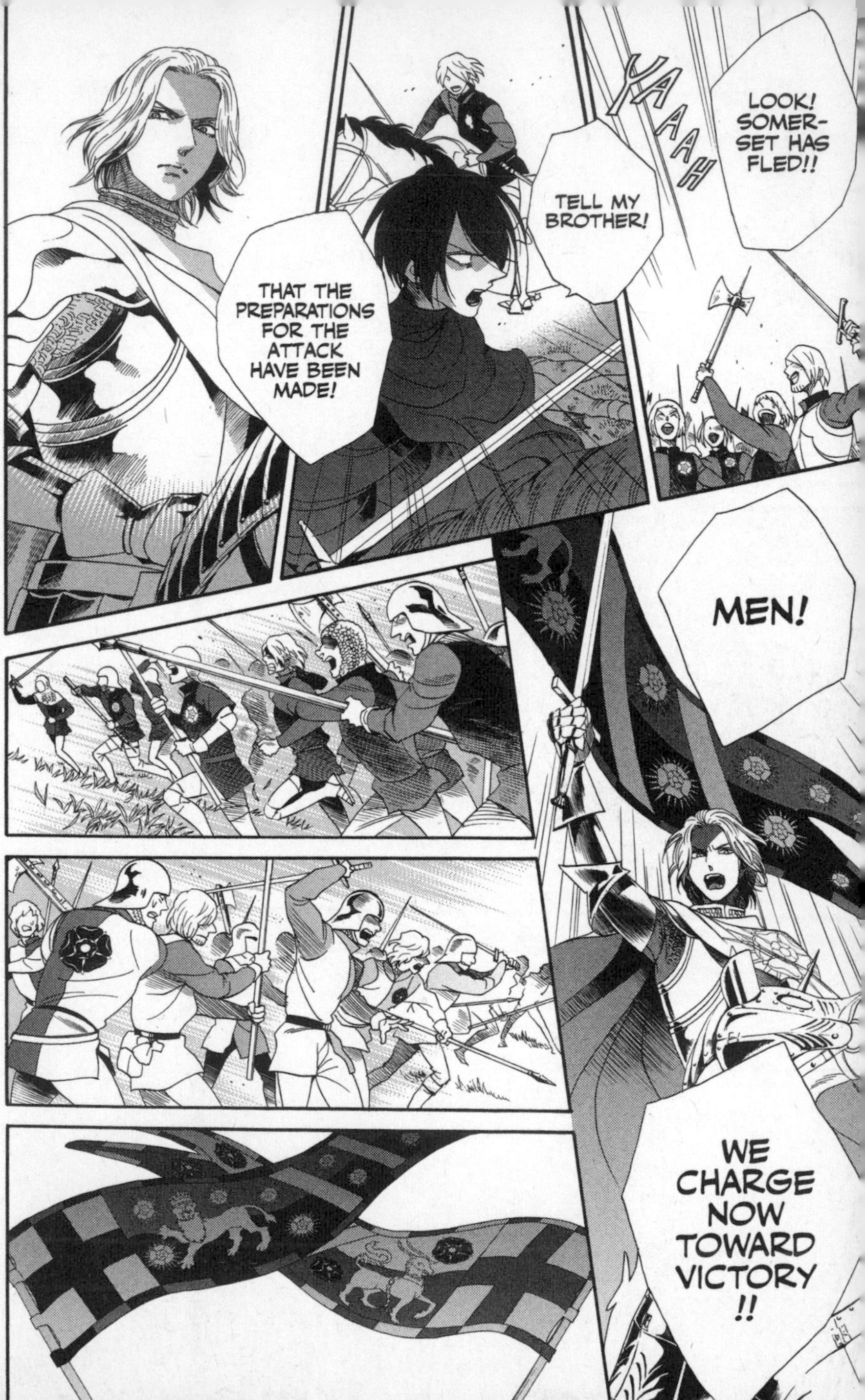
LOOK! SOMER-SET HAS FLED!!
YAAAH
TELL MY BROTHER!
THAT THE PREPARATIONS FOR THE ATTACK HAVE BEEN MADE!
MEN!
WE CHARGE NOW TOWARD VICTORY!!

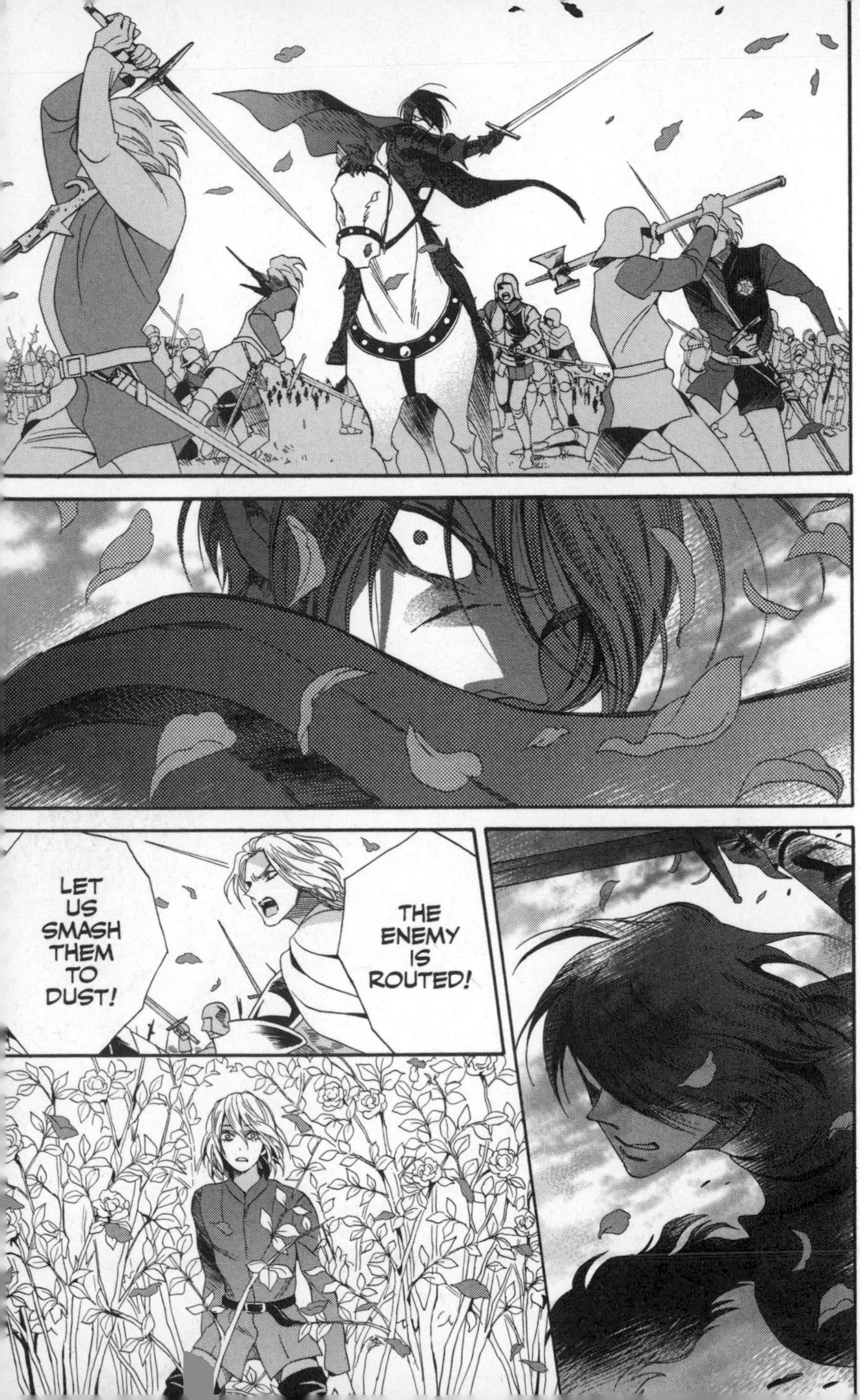
THE ENEMY IS ROUTED!
LET US SMASH THEM TO DUST!

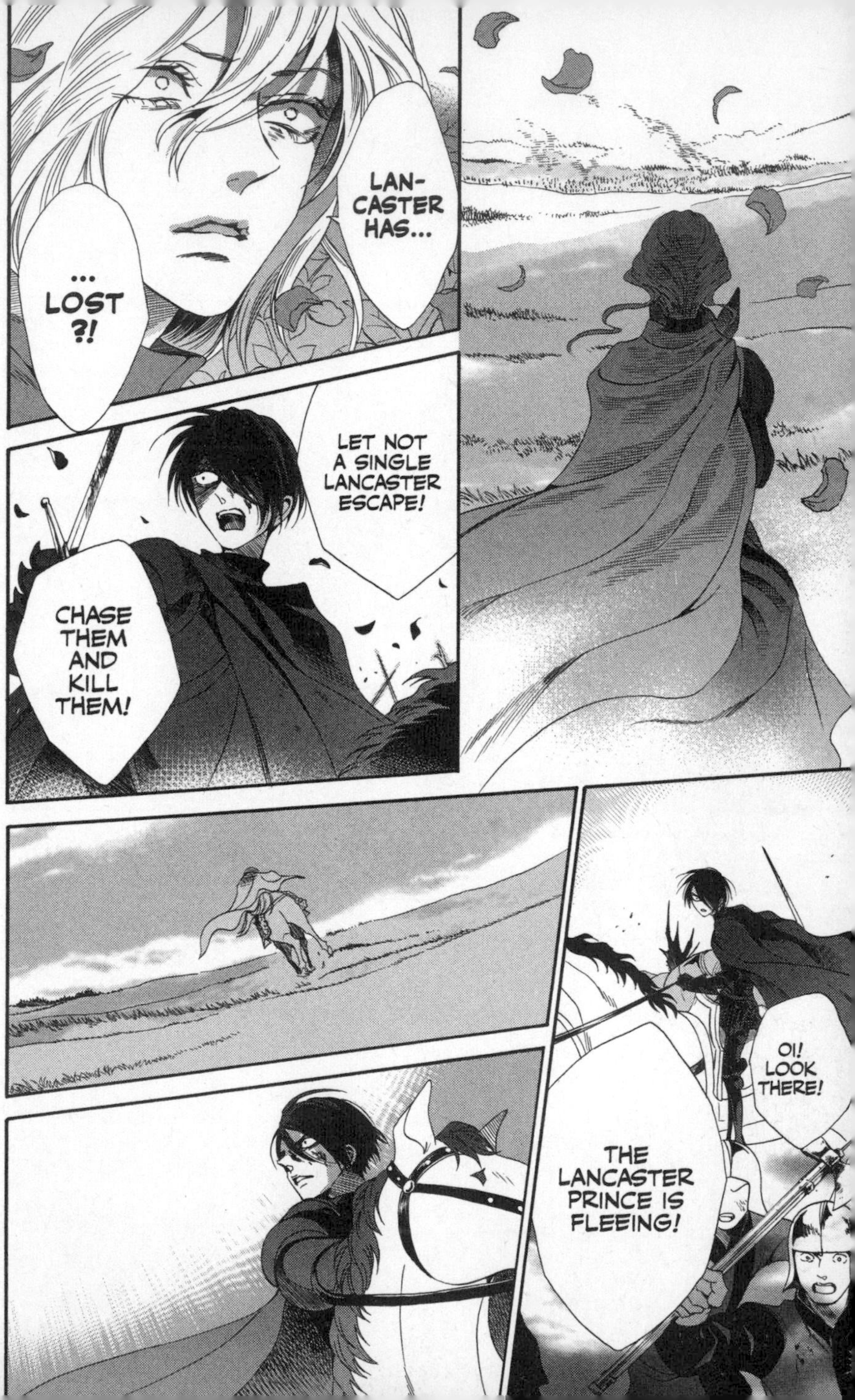
LAN-CASTER HAS...
... LOST ?!
LET NOT A SINGLE LANCASTER ESCAPE!
CHASE THEM AND KILL THEM!
OI! LOOK THERE!
THE LANCASTER PRINCE IS FLEEING!

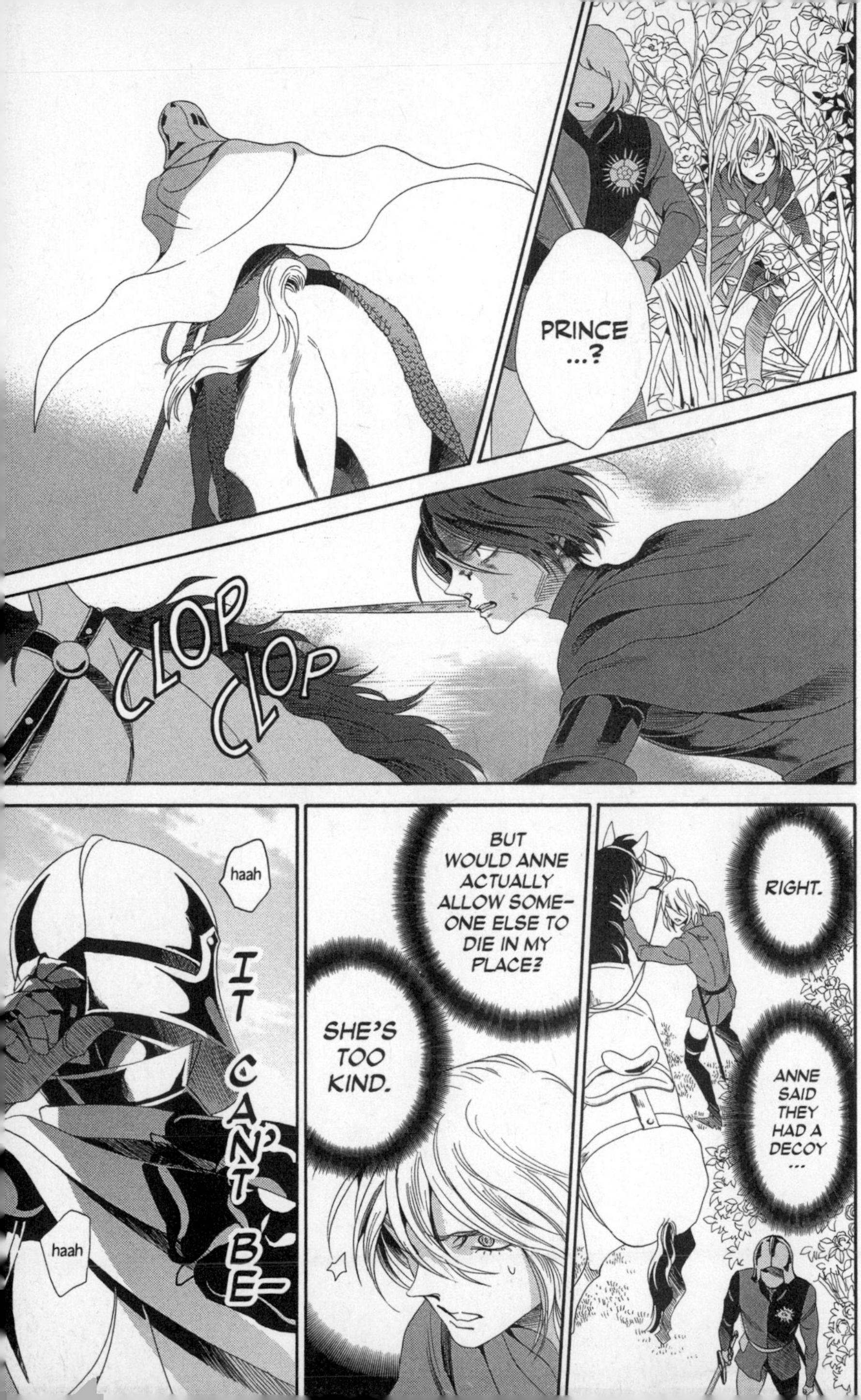
PRINCE ...?
CLOP CLOP
RIGHT.
ANNE SAID THEY HAD A DECOY ...
BUT WOULD ANNE ACTUALLY ALLOW SOME-ONE ELSE TO DIE IN MY PLACE?
SHE'S TOO KIND.
haah
IT CAN'T BE—
haah

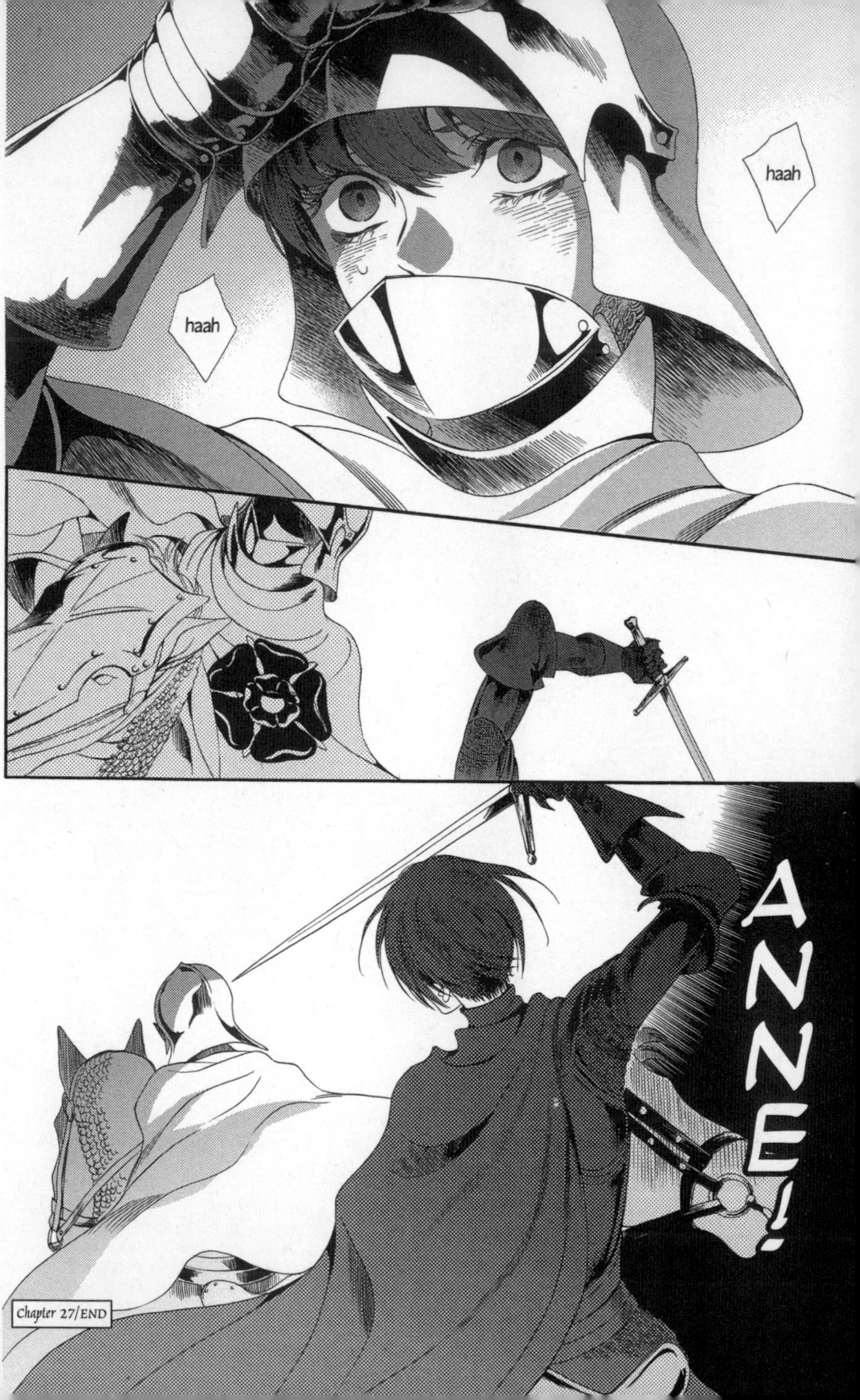
haah
haah
ANNE!!
Chapter 27/END

Chapter 28

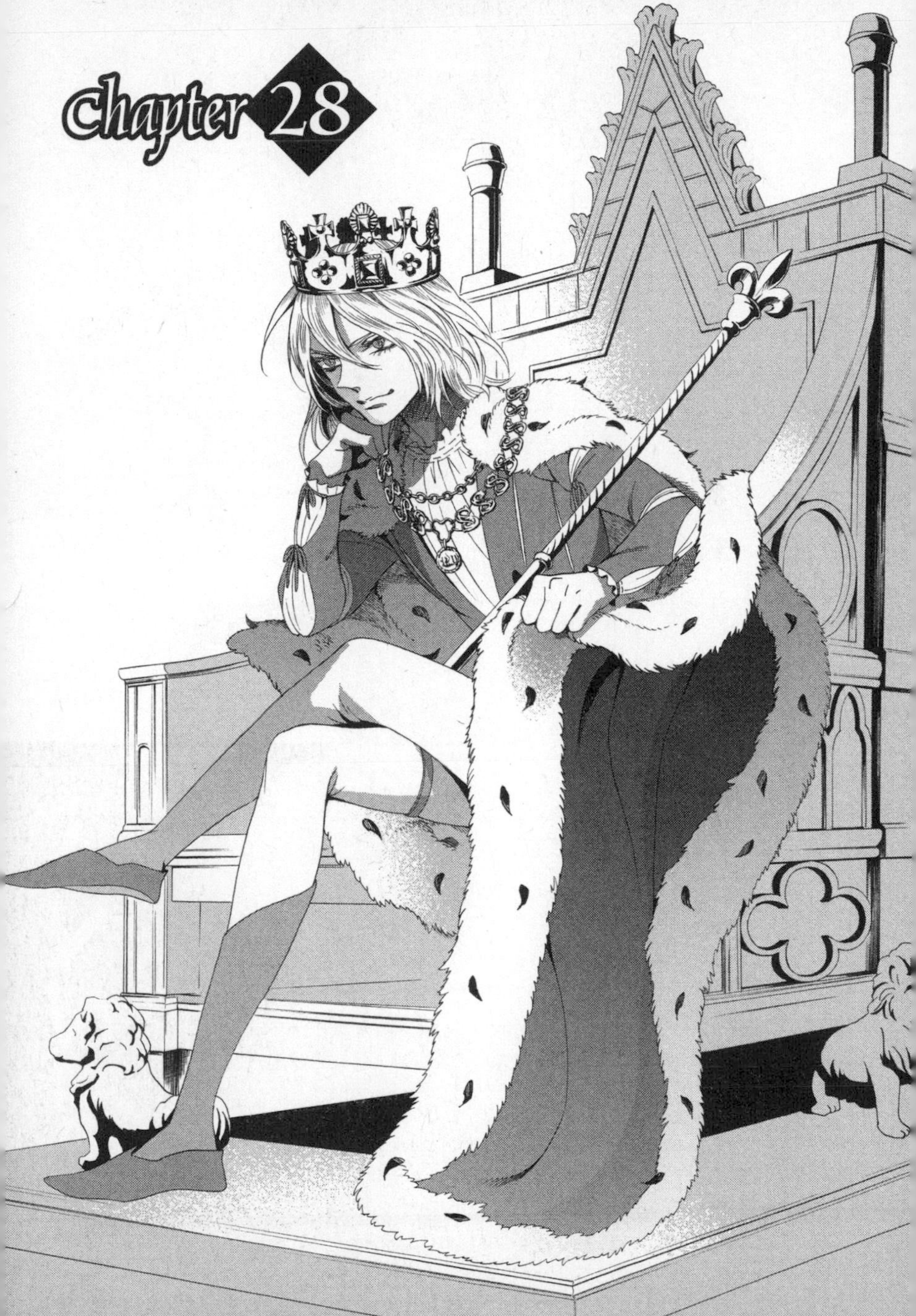

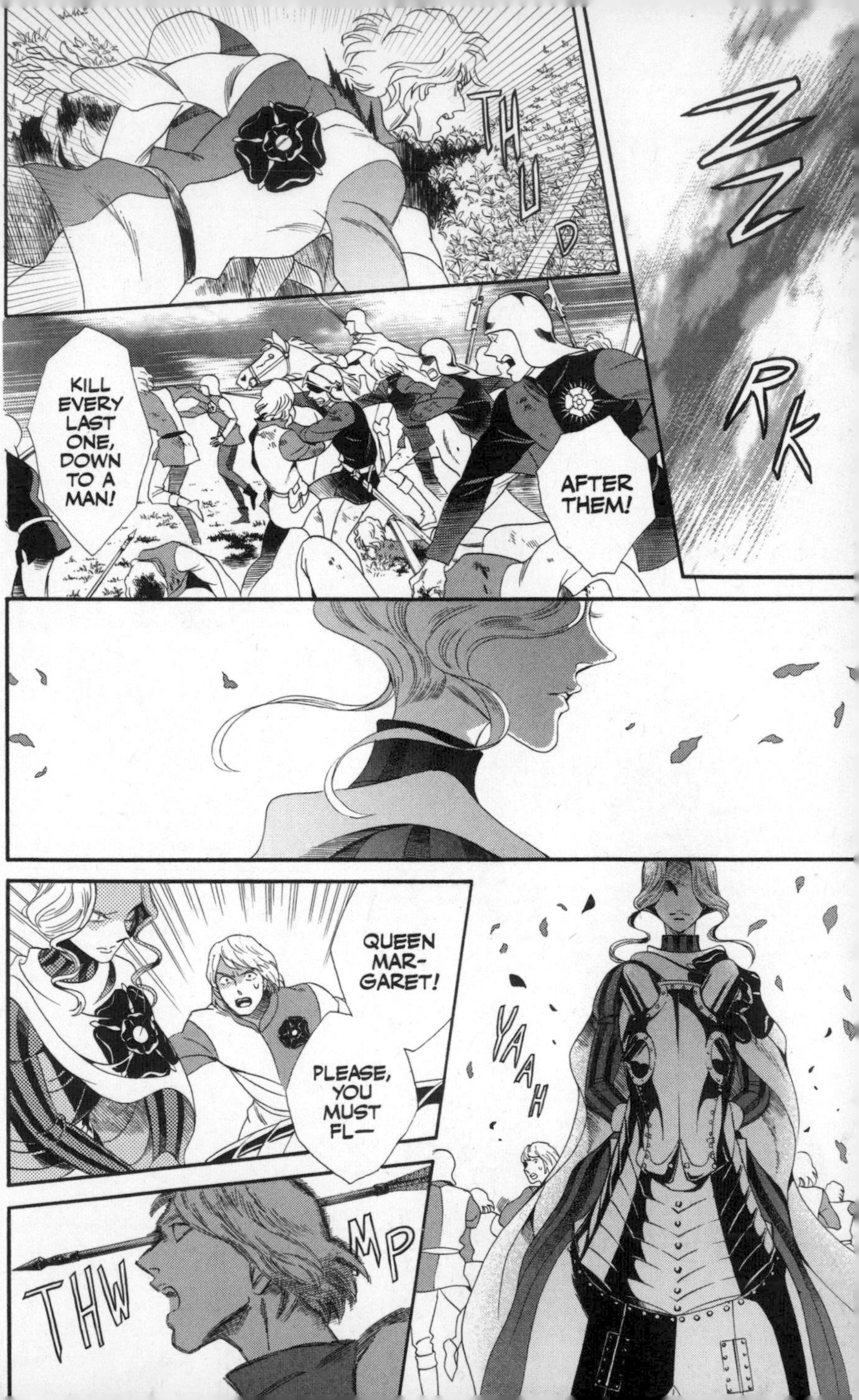
ZZRK
THUD
AFTER THEM!
KILL EVERY LAST ONE, DOWN TO A MAN!
YAAH
QUEEN MAR-GARET!
PLEASE, YOU MUST FL—
THWMP

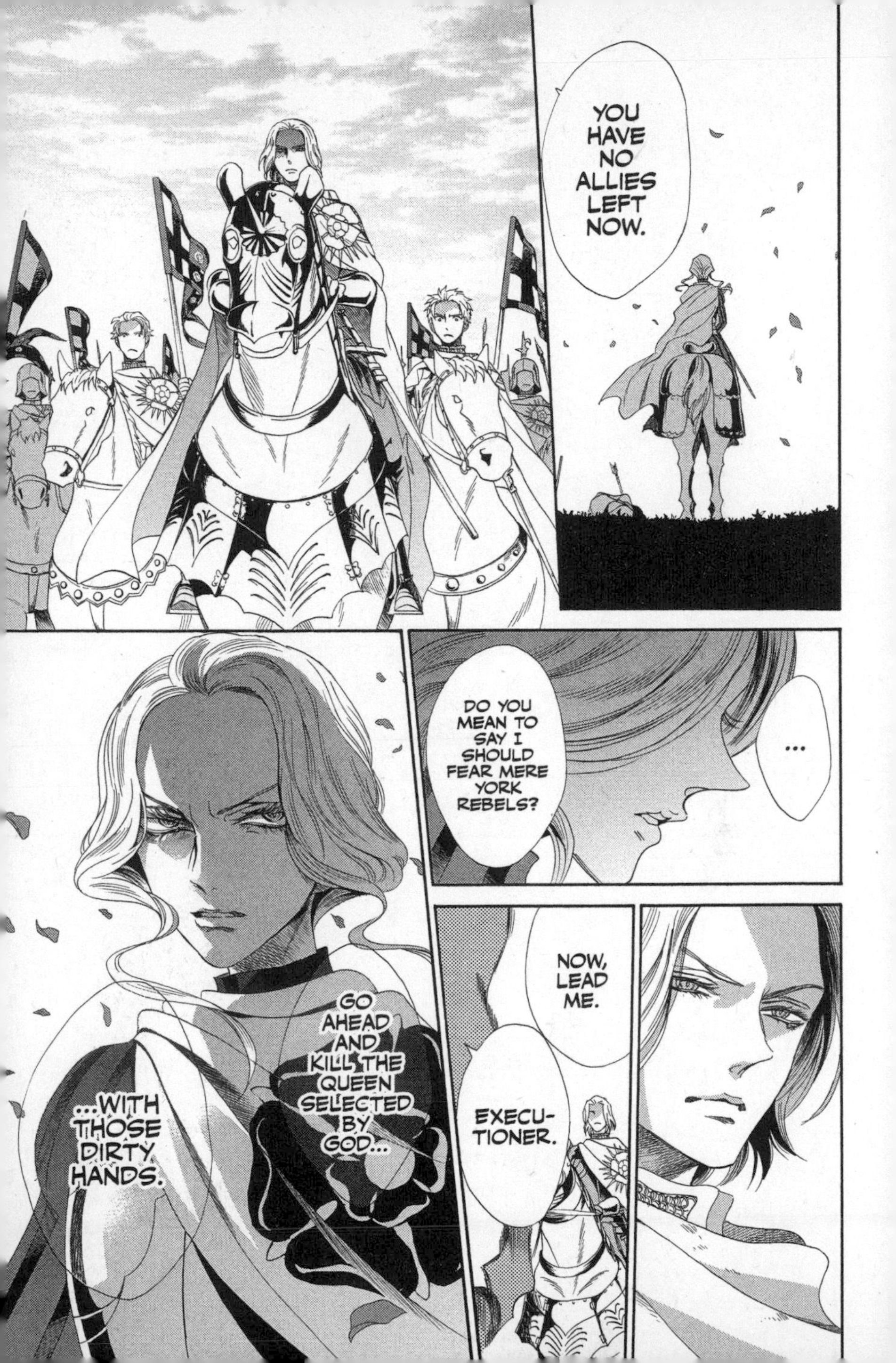
YOU HAVE NO ALLIES LEFT NOW.
...
DO YOU MEAN TO SAY I SHOULD FEAR MERE YORK REBELS?
NOW, LEAD ME.
EXECUTIONER.
GO AHEAD AND KILL THE QUEEN SELECTED BY GOD...
...WITH THOSE DIRTY HANDS.

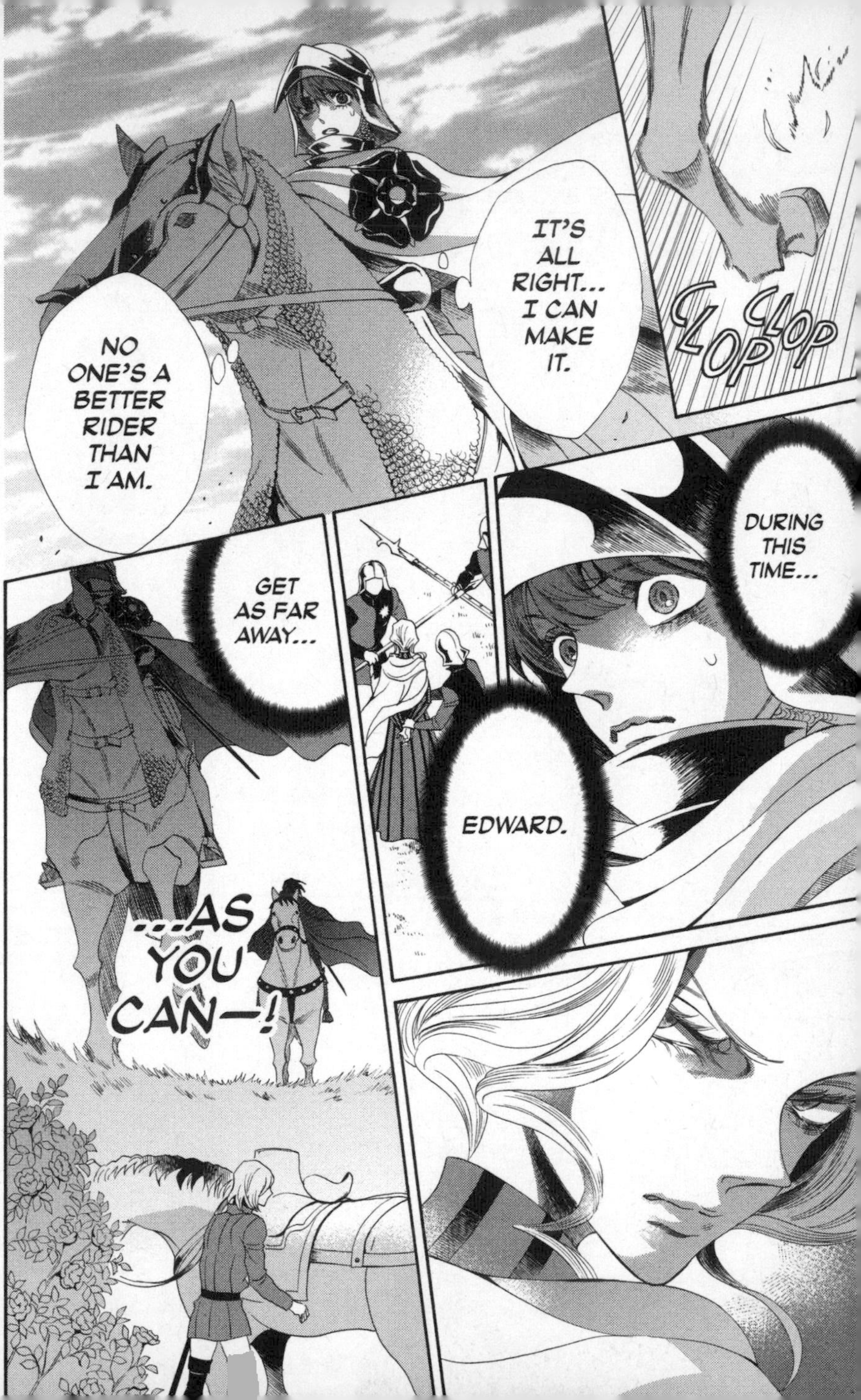
CLOP CLOP
IT'S ALL RIGHT... I CAN MAKE IT.
NO ONE'S A BETTER RIDER THAN I AM.
DURING THIS TIME...
EDWARD.
GET AS FAR AWAY...
...AS YOU CAN—!

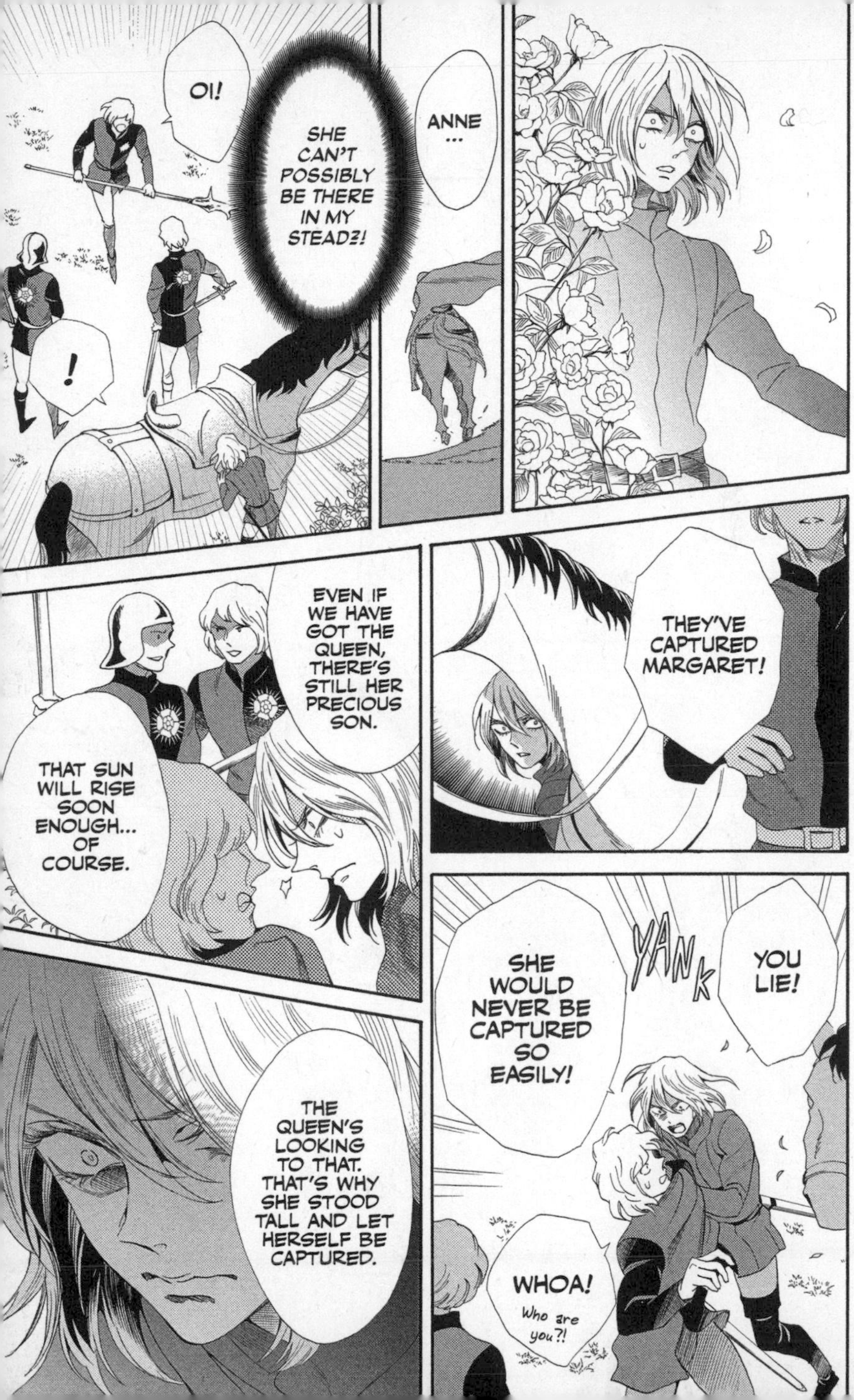
ANNE ...
SHE CAN'T POSSIBLY BE THERE IN MY STEAD?!
OI!
!
THEY'VE CAPTURED MARGARET!
YOU LIE!
SHE WOULD NEVER BE CAPTURED SO EASILY!
YANK
WHOA!
Who are you?!
EVEN IF WE HAVE GOT THE QUEEN, THERE'S STILL HER PRECIOUS SON.
THAT SUN WILL RISE SOON ENOUGH... OF COURSE.
THE QUEEN'S LOOKING TO THAT. THAT'S WHY SHE STOOD TALL AND LET HERSELF BE CAPTURED.

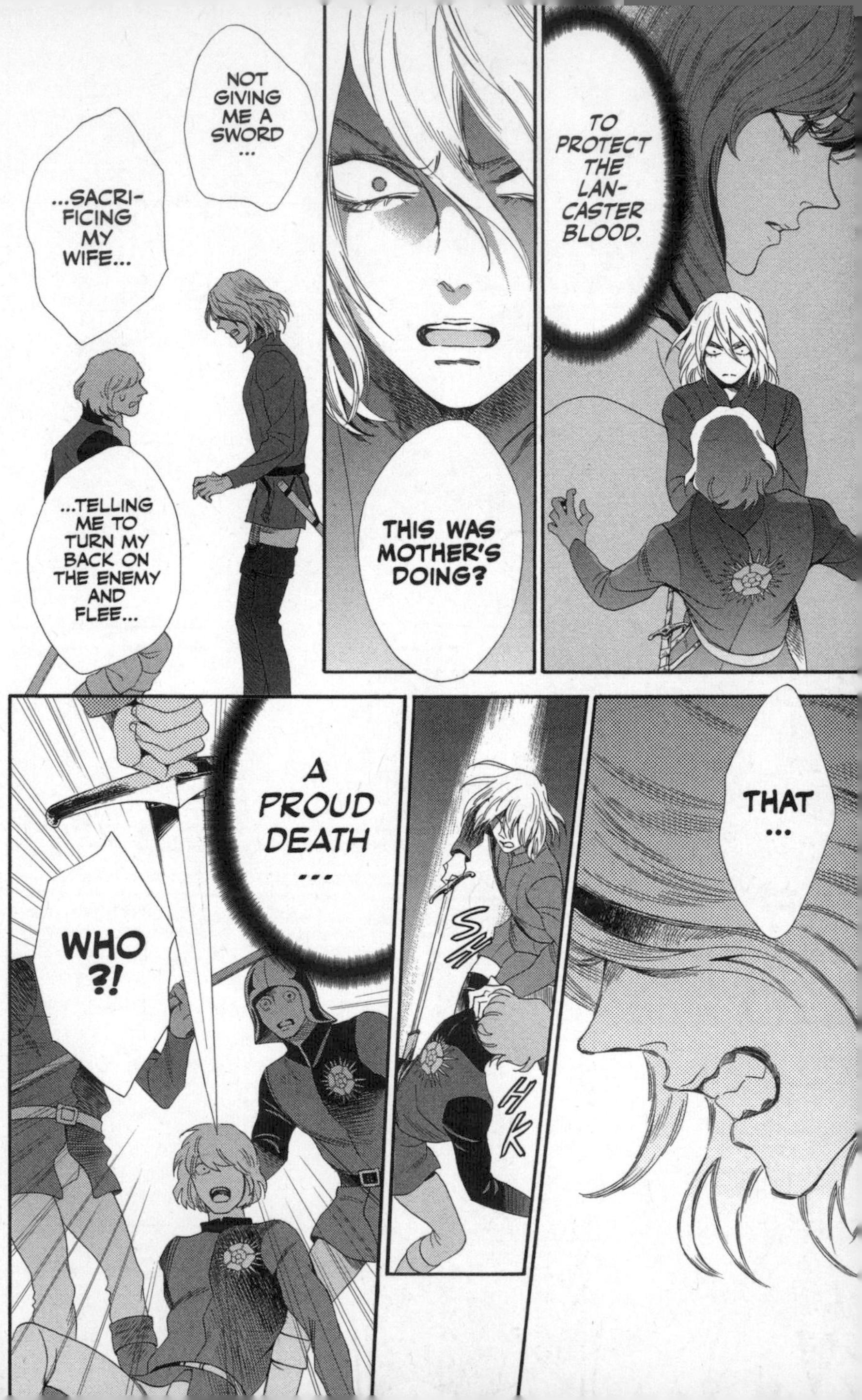
TO PROTECT THE LAN-CASTER BLOOD.
THIS WAS MOTHER'S DOING?
NOT GIVING ME A SWORD ...
...SACRI-FICING MY WIFE...
...TELLING ME TO TURN MY BACK ON THE ENEMY AND FLEE...
THAT ...
A PROUD DEATH ...
SHH
HK
WHO ?!

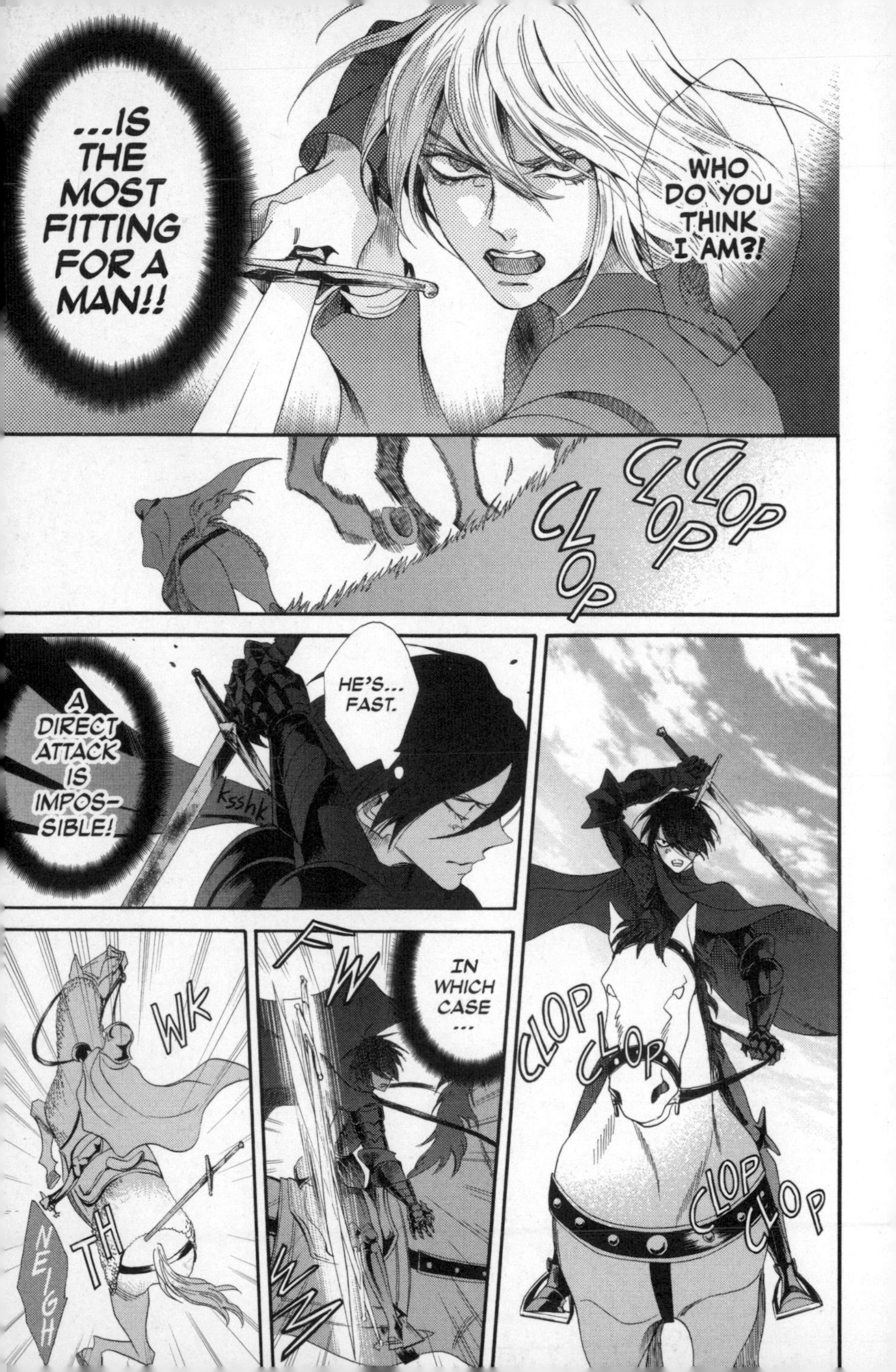
...IS THE MOST FITTING FOR A MAN!!
WHO DO YOU THINK I AM?!
CLOP CLOP CLOP
CLOP CLOP
CLOP CLOP
HE'S... FAST.
ksshk
A DIRECT ATTACK IS IMPOSSIBLE!
FW
IN WHICH CASE...
WM
WK
TH
NEIGH

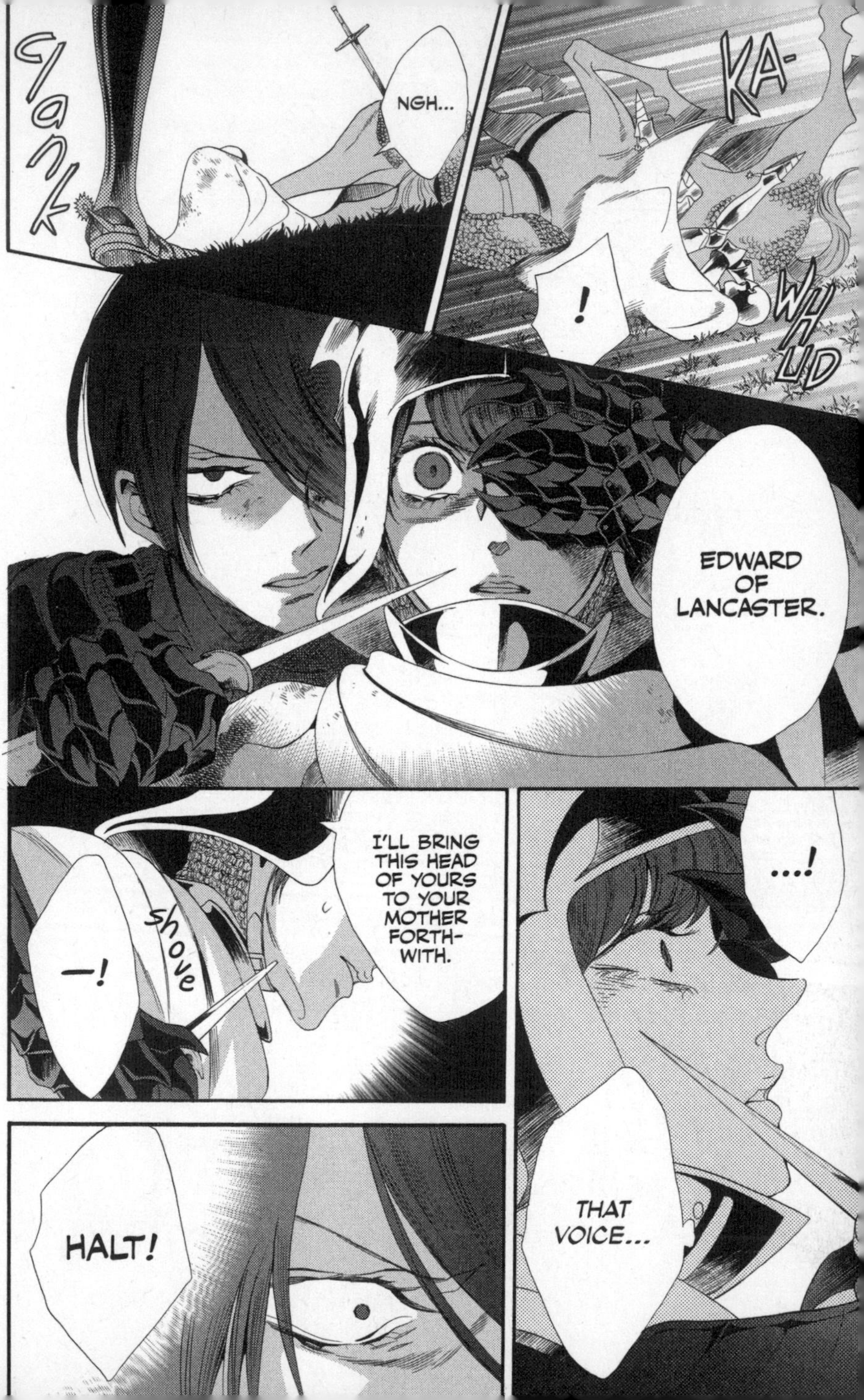
KA-
!
WHUD
clank
NGH...
EDWARD OF LANCASTER.
...!
THAT VOICE...
I'LL BRING THIS HEAD OF YOURS TO YOUR MOTHER FORTH-WITH.
shove
—!
HALT!

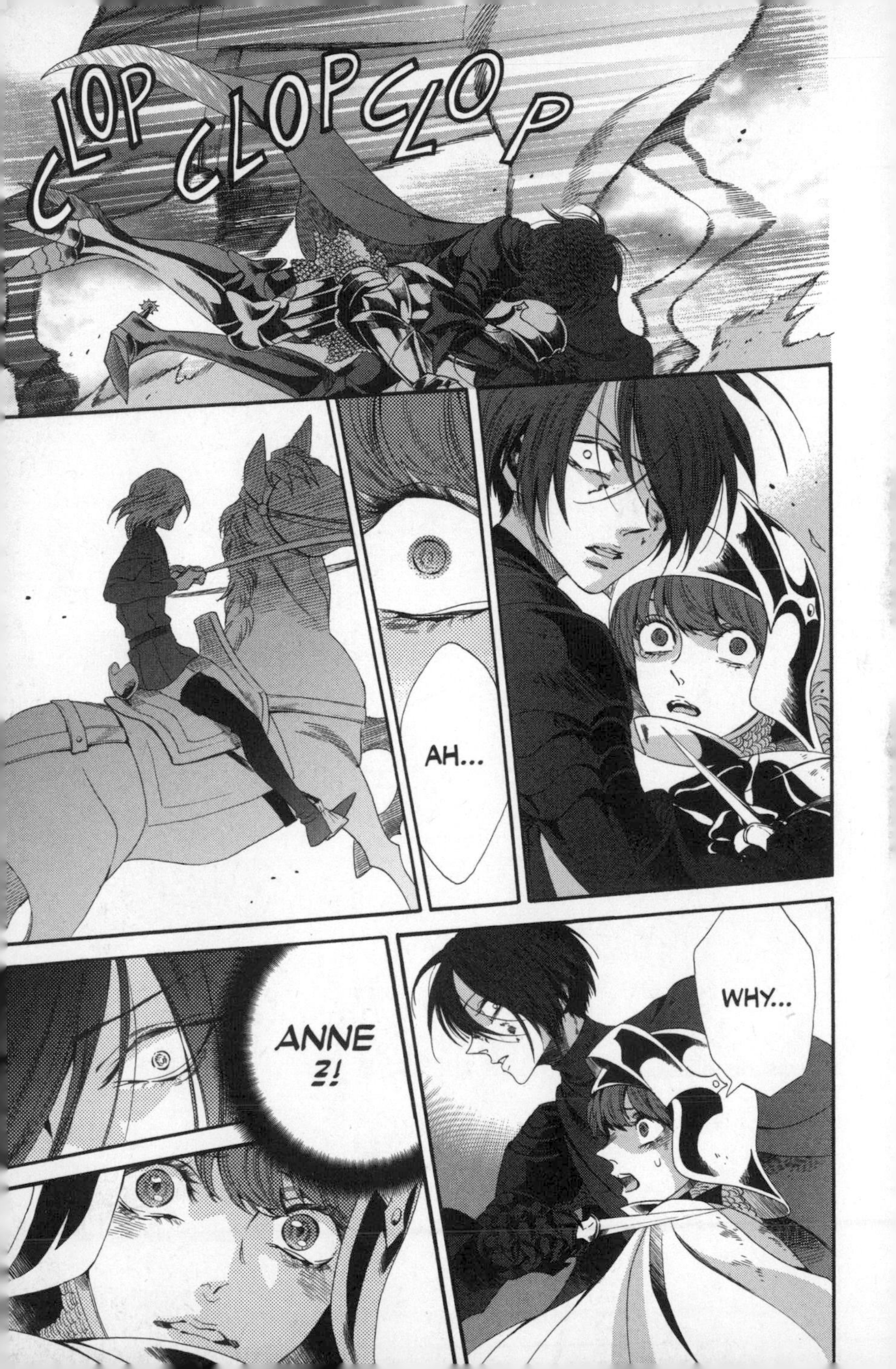
CLOP CLOP CLOP
AH...
WHY...
ANNE ?!

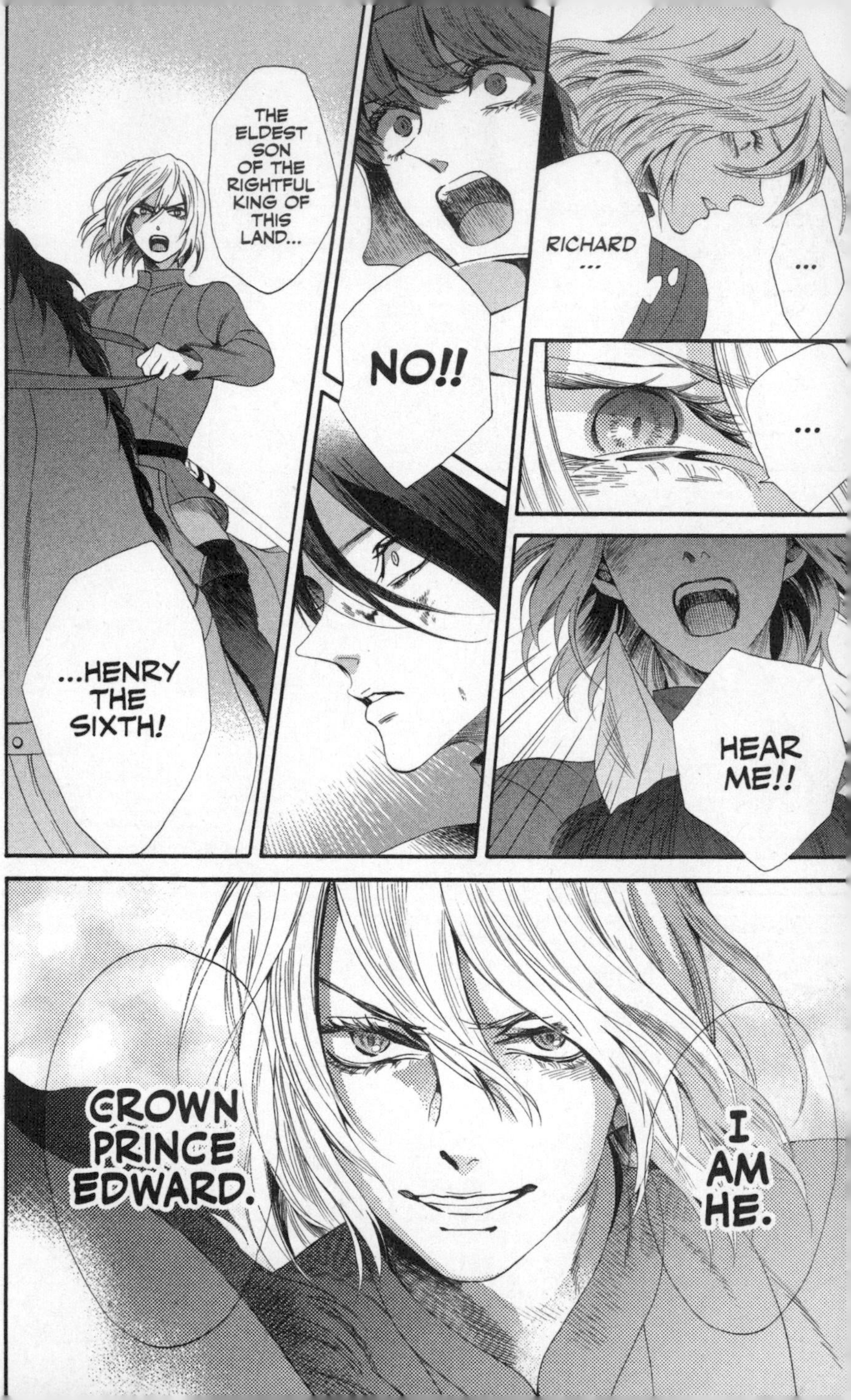
...
RICHARD ...
...
HEAR ME!!
NO!!
THE ELDEST SON OF THE RIGHTFUL KING OF THIS LAND...
...HENRY THE SIXTH!
I AM HE.
CROWN PRINCE EDWARD.

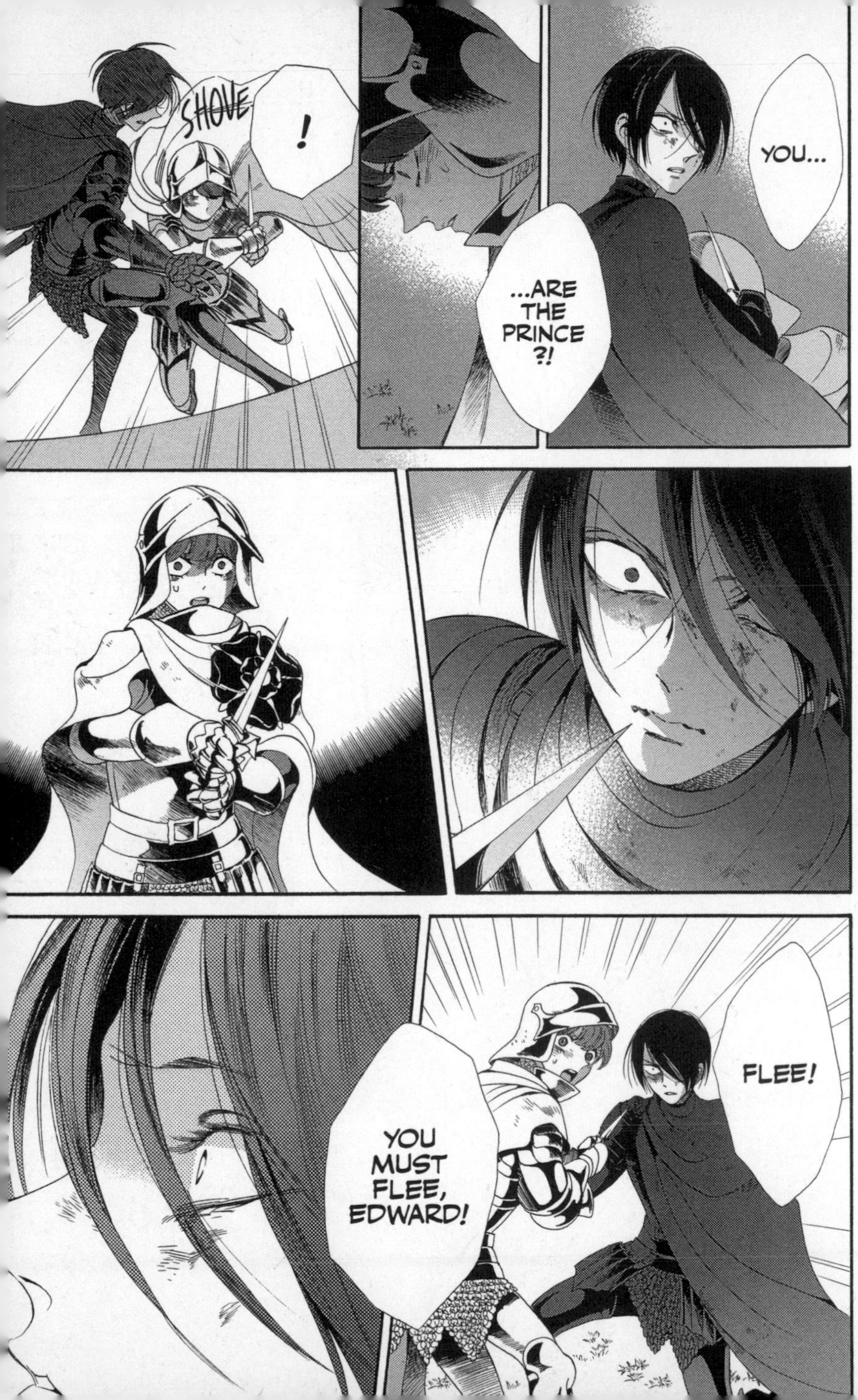
YOU...
...ARE THE PRINCE ?!
!
SHOVE
FLEE!
YOU MUST FLEE, EDWARD!

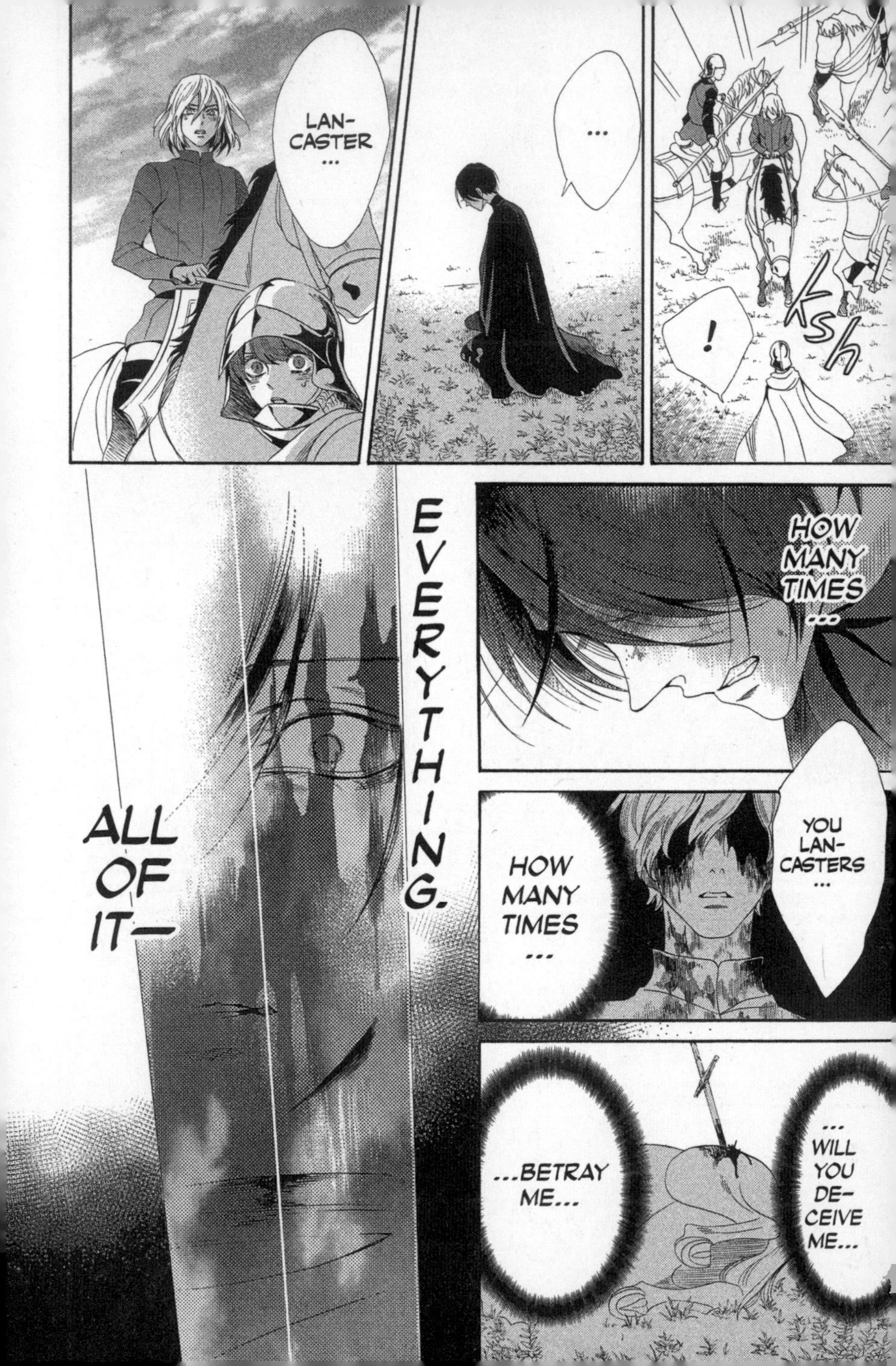
KSH
!
...
LAN-CASTER...
HOW MANY TIMES...
YOU LAN-CASTERS...
HOW MANY TIMES...
...WILL YOU DE-CEIVE ME...
...BETRAY ME...
EVERYTHING.
ALL OF IT—

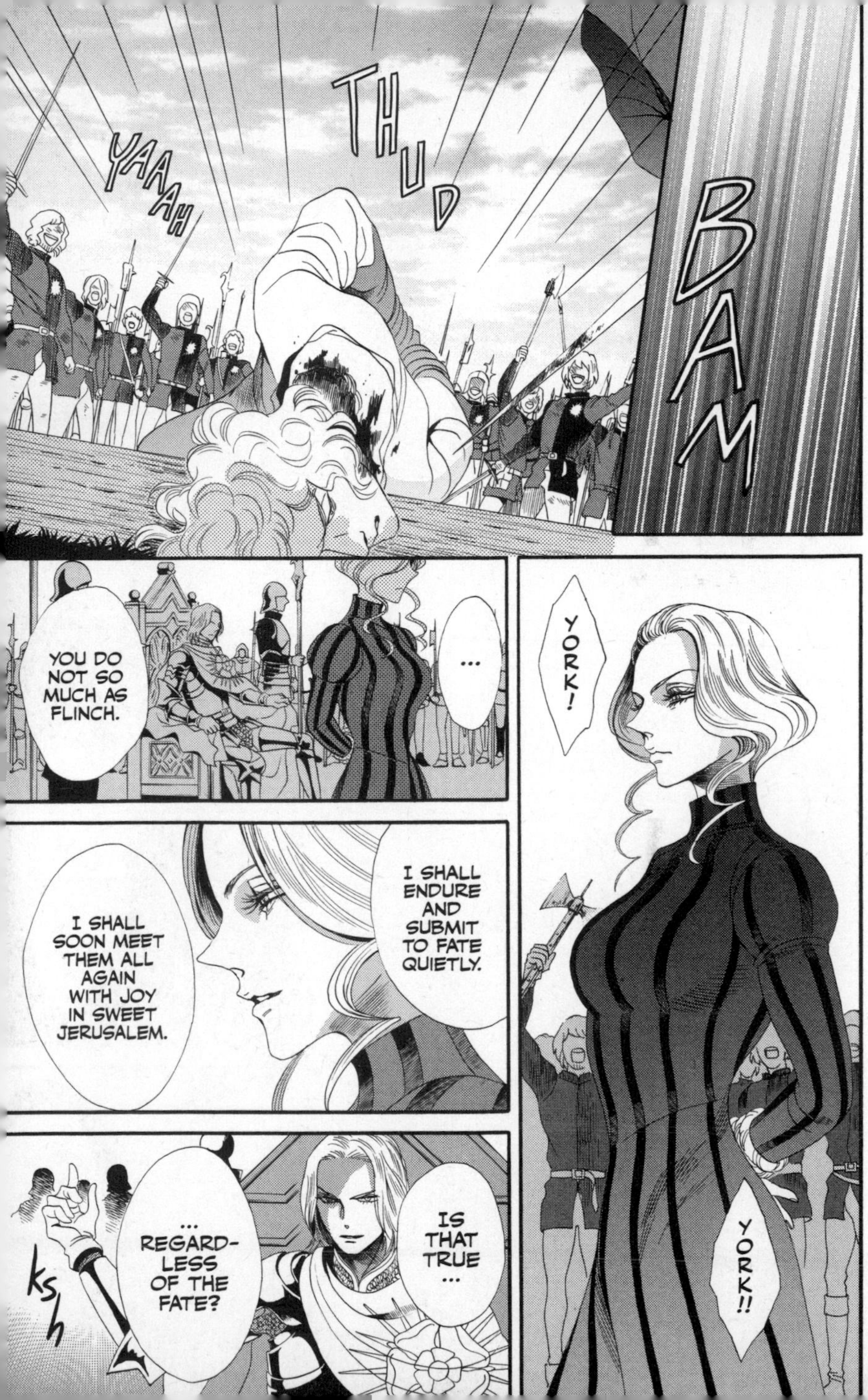
BAM
THUD
YAAAAH
YORK!
YORK!!
...
YOU DO NOT SO MUCH AS FLINCH.
I SHALL ENDURE AND SUBMIT TO FATE QUIETLY.
I SHALL SOON MEET THEM ALL AGAIN WITH JOY IN SWEET JERUSALEM.
IS THAT TRUE ...
... REGARDLESS OF THE FATE?
ksh

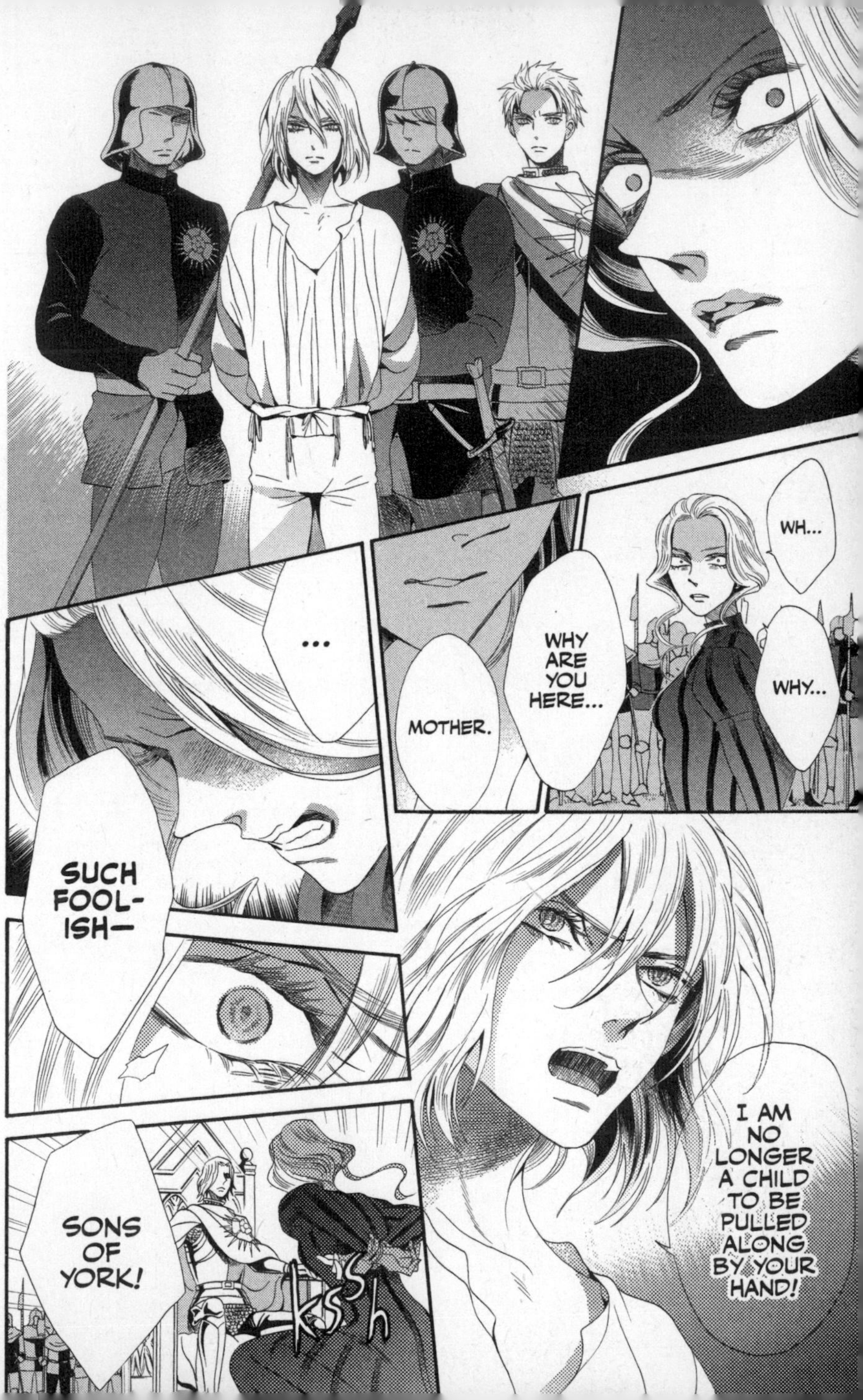
WH...
WHY...
WHY ARE YOU HERE...
MOTHER.
...
SUCH FOOL-ISH—
I AM NO LONGER A CHILD TO BE PULLED ALONG BY YOUR HAND!
SONS OF YORK!
KSSH

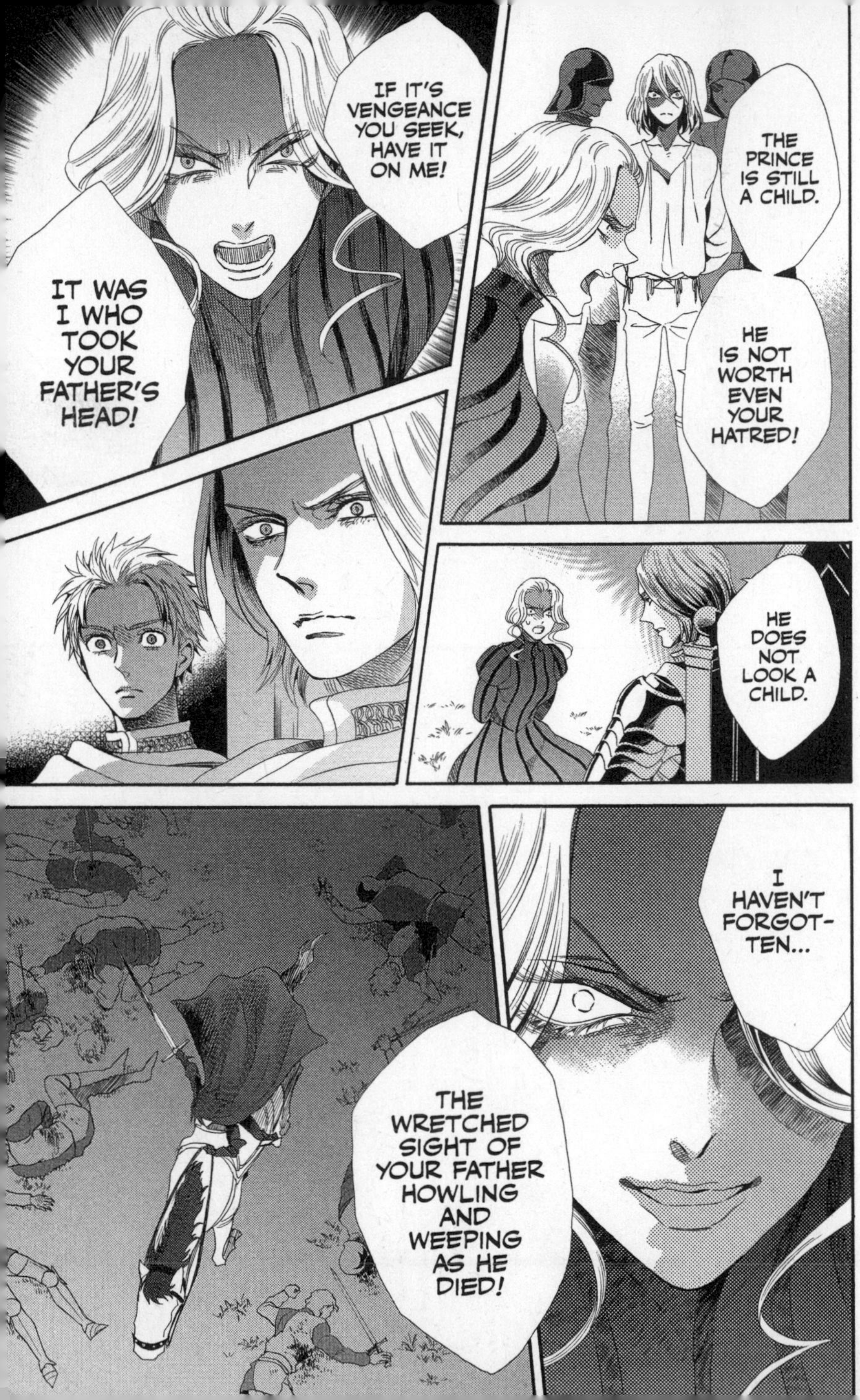
THE PRINCE IS STILL A CHILD.
HE IS NOT WORTH EVEN YOUR HATRED!
IF IT'S VENGEANCE YOU SEEK, HAVE IT ON ME!
IT WAS I WHO TOOK YOUR FATHER'S HEAD!
HE DOES NOT LOOK A CHILD.
I HAVEN'T FORGOT-TEN...
THE WRETCHED SIGHT OF YOUR FATHER HOWLING AND WEEPING AS HE DIED!

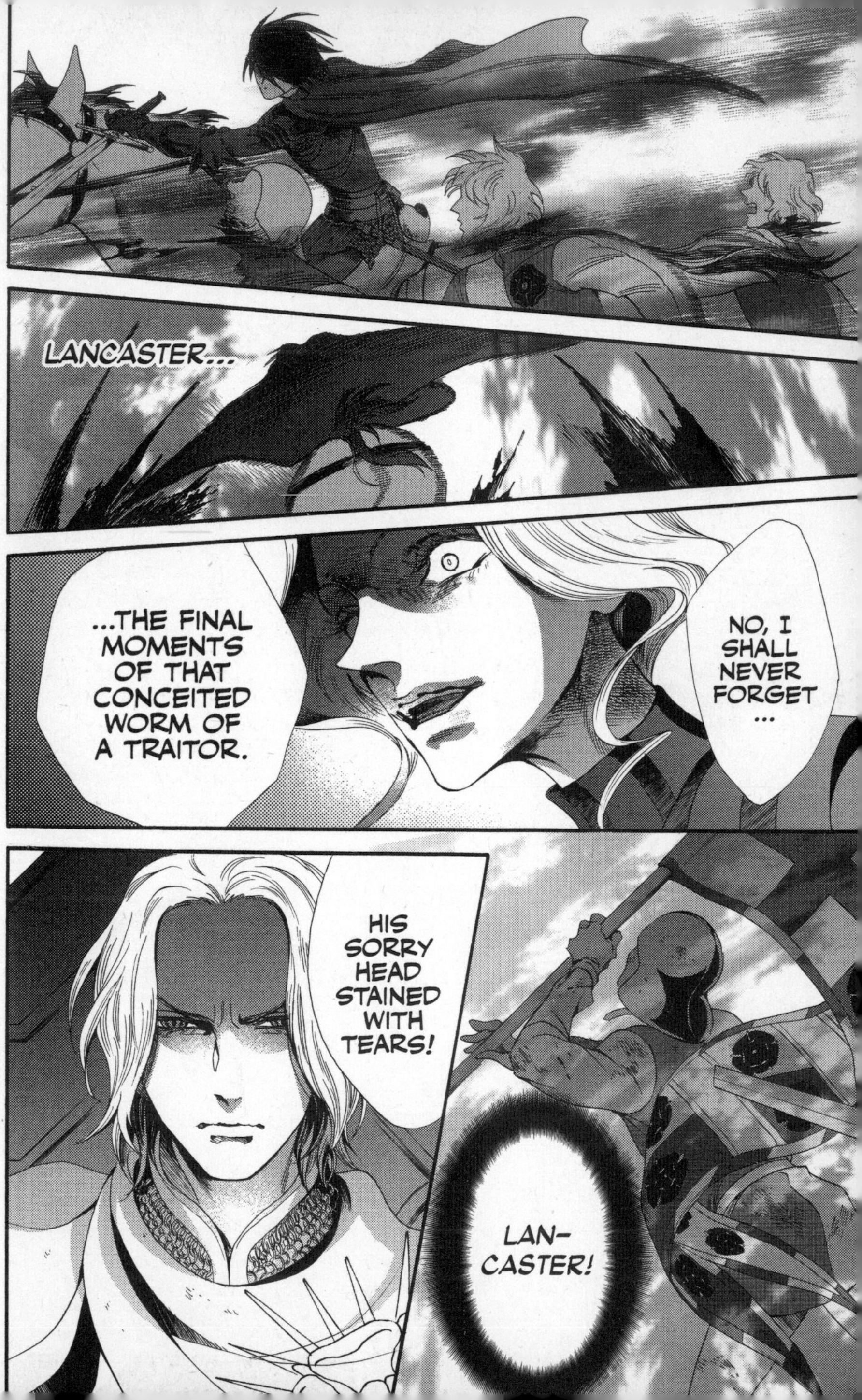
LANCASTER...
NO, I SHALL NEVER FORGET ...
...THE FINAL MOMENTS OF THAT CONCEITED WORM OF A TRAITOR.
LAN-CASTER!
HIS SORRY HEAD STAINED WITH TEARS!

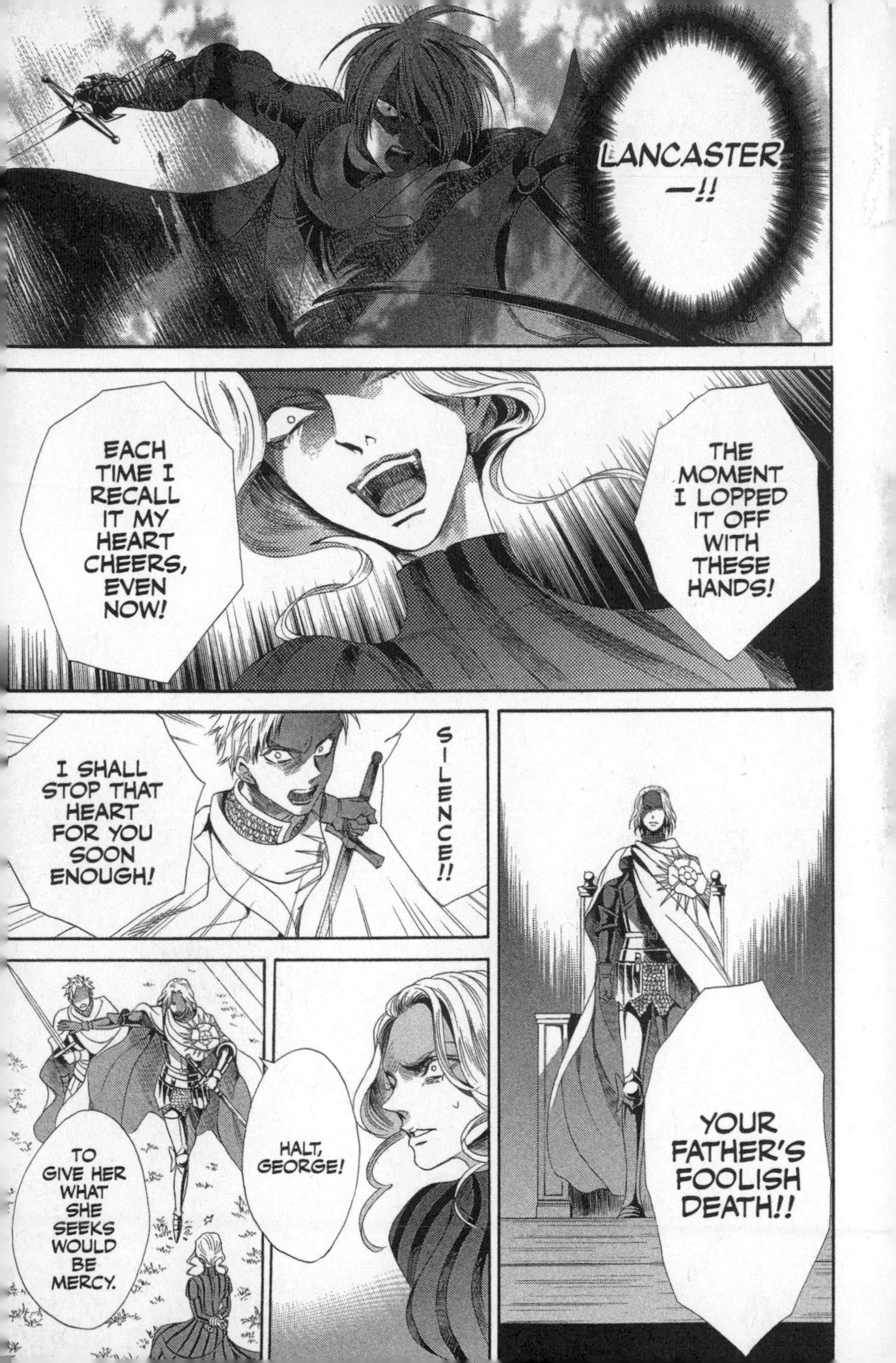
LANCASTER—!!
THE MOMENT I LOPPED IT OFF WITH THESE HANDS!
EACH TIME I RECALL IT MY HEART CHEERS, EVEN NOW!
YOUR FATHER'S FOOLISH DEATH!!
SILENCE!!
I SHALL STOP THAT HEART FOR YOU SOON ENOUGH!
HALT, GEORGE!
TO GIVE HER WHAT SHE SEEKS WOULD BE MERCY.

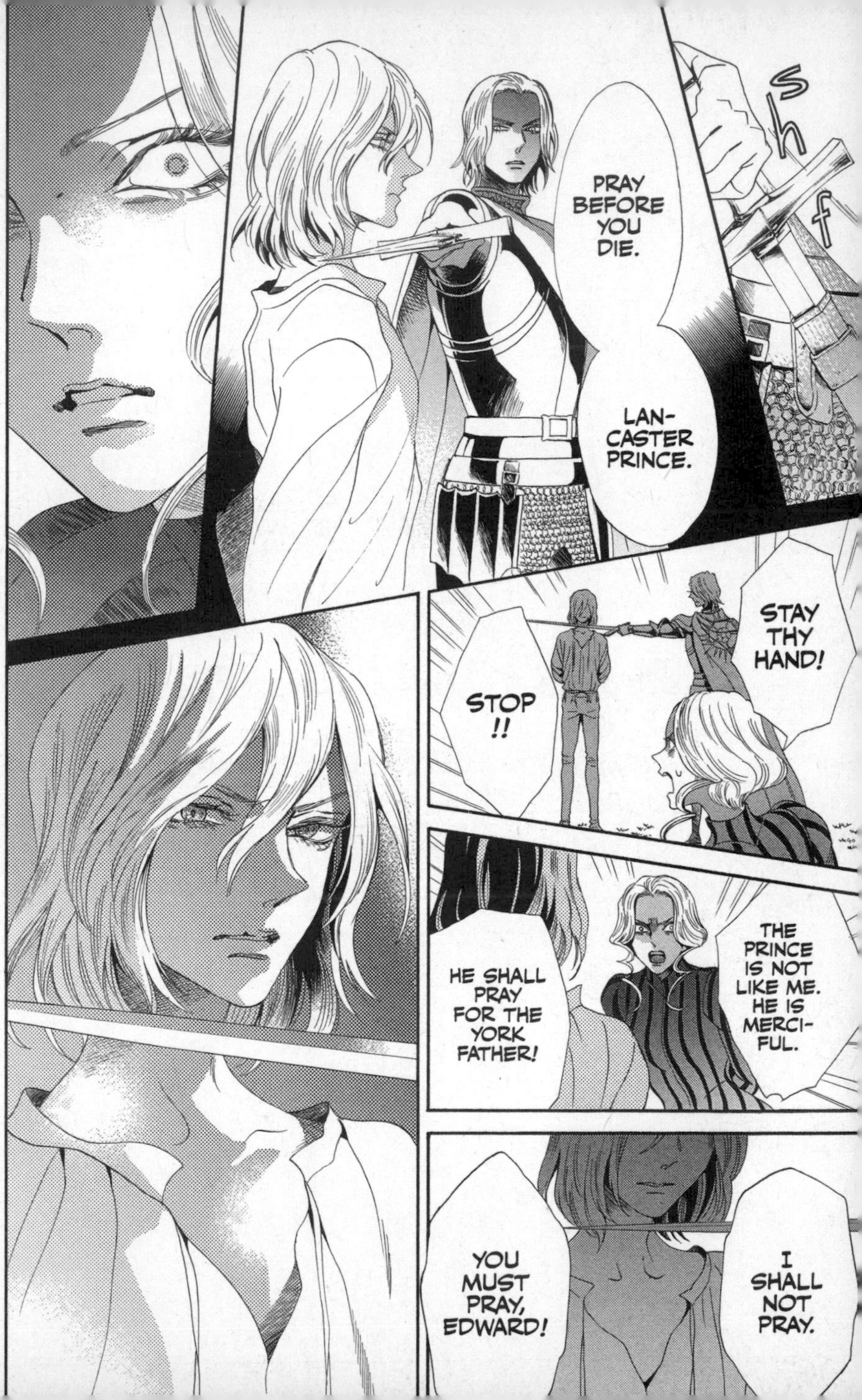

shf
PRAY BEFORE YOU DIE.
LAN-CASTER PRINCE.
STAY THY HAND!
STOP!!
THE PRINCE IS NOT LIKE ME. HE IS MERCI-FUL.
HE SHALL PRAY FOR THE YORK FATHER!
I SHALL NOT PRAY.
YOU MUST PRAY, EDWARD!

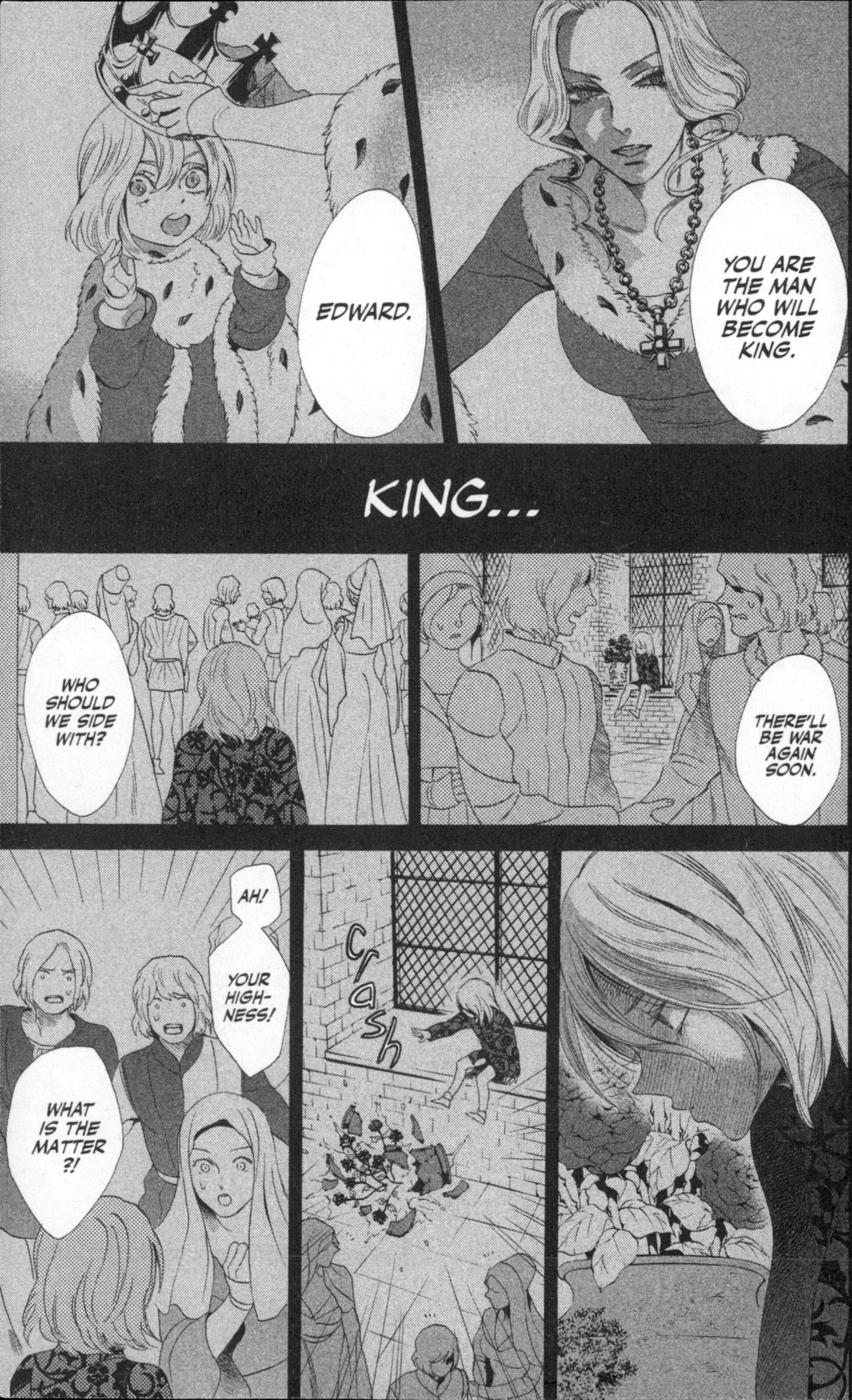
YOU ARE THE MAN WHO WILL BECOME KING.
EDWARD.
KING...
THERE'LL BE WAR AGAIN SOON.
WHO SHOULD WE SIDE WITH?
crash
AH!
YOUR HIGHNESS!
WHAT IS THE MATTER ?!

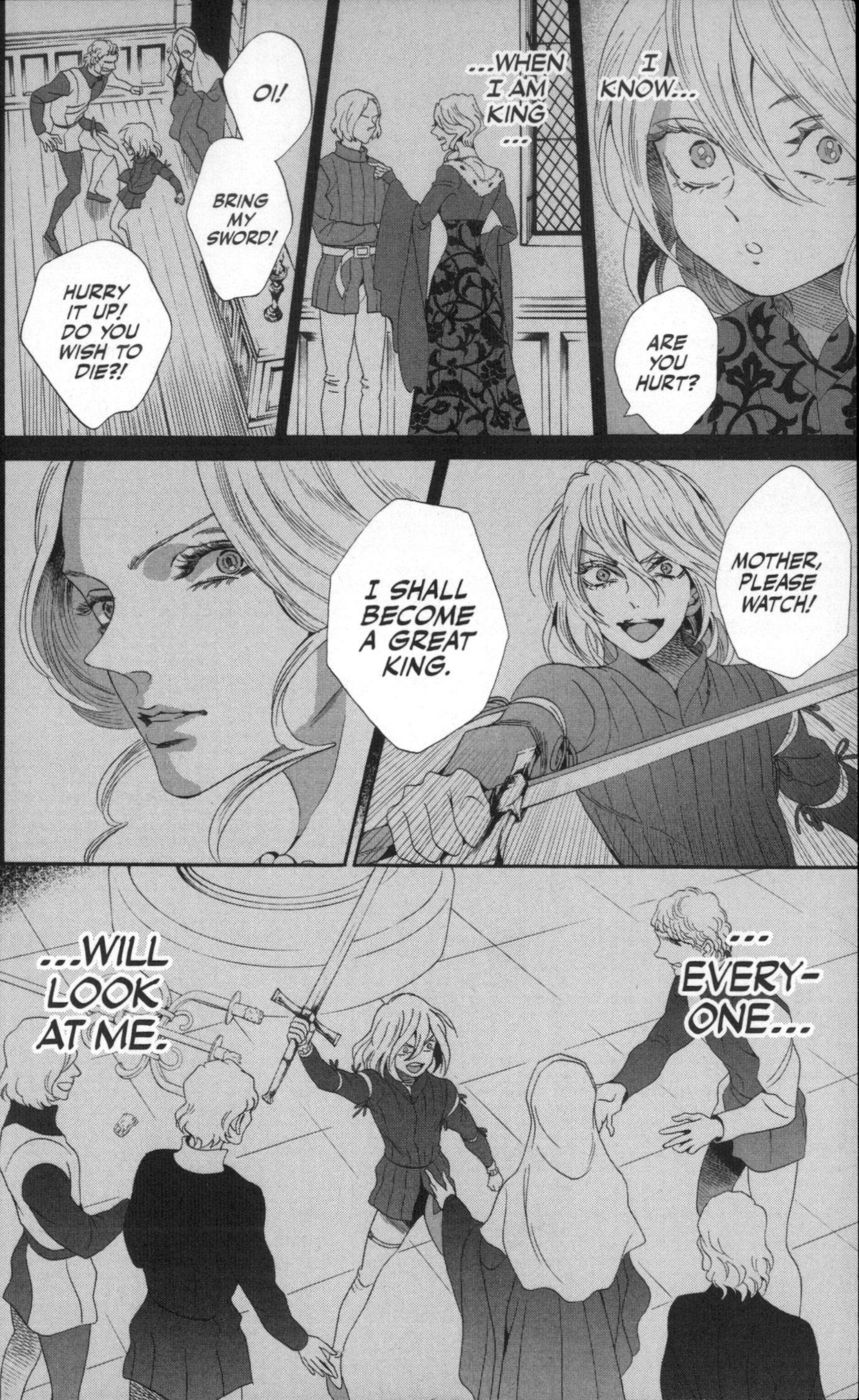
I KNOW...
ARE YOU HURT?
...WHEN I AM KING ...
OI!
BRING MY SWORD!
HURRY IT UP! DO YOU WISH TO DIE?!
MOTHER, PLEASE WATCH!
I SHALL BECOME A GREAT KING.
... EVERY-ONE...
...WILL LOOK AT ME.

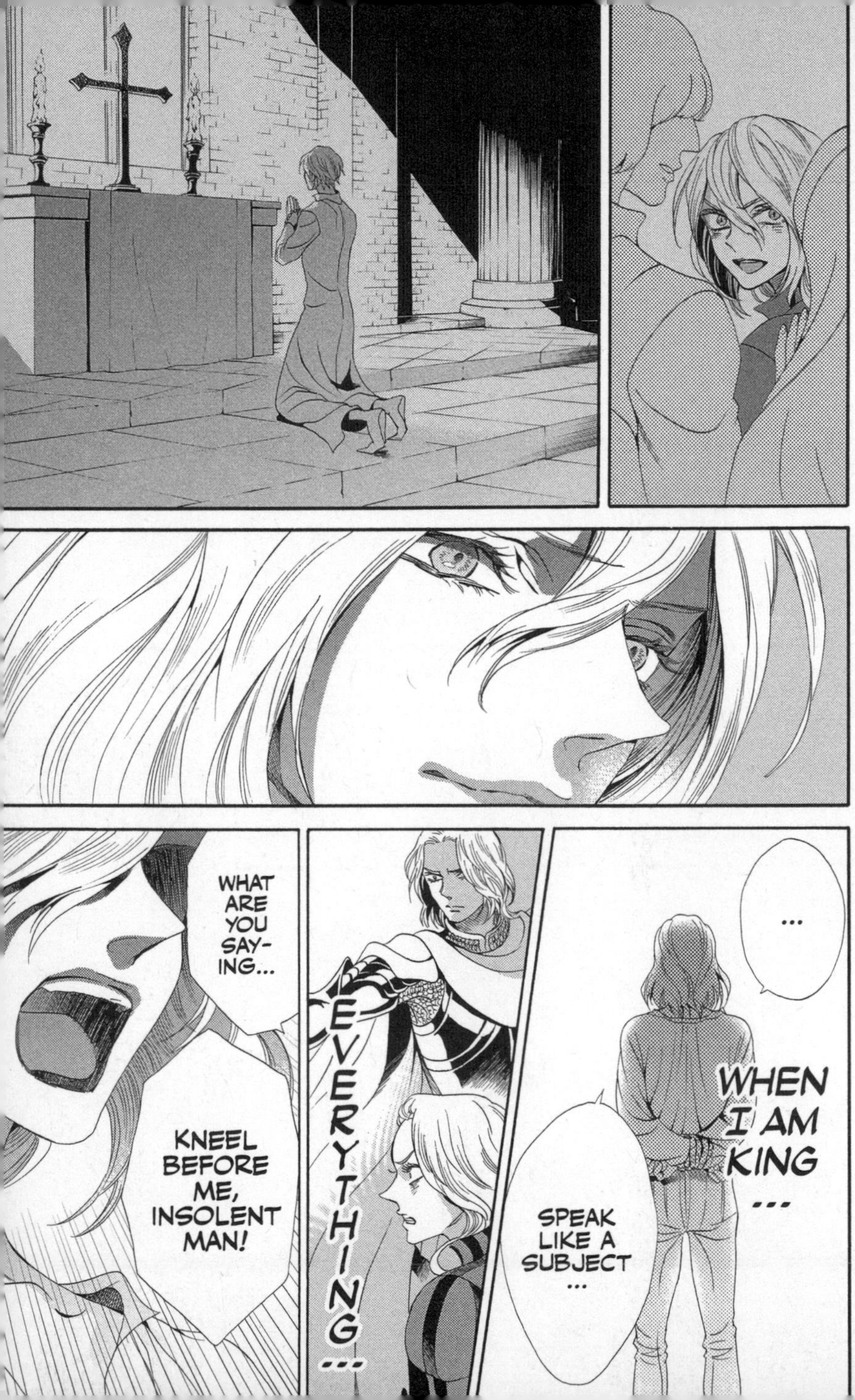
...
WHEN I AM KING ...
SPEAK LIKE A SUBJECT ...
EVERYTHING...
WHAT ARE YOU SAY-ING...
KNEEL BEFORE ME, INSOLENT MAN!

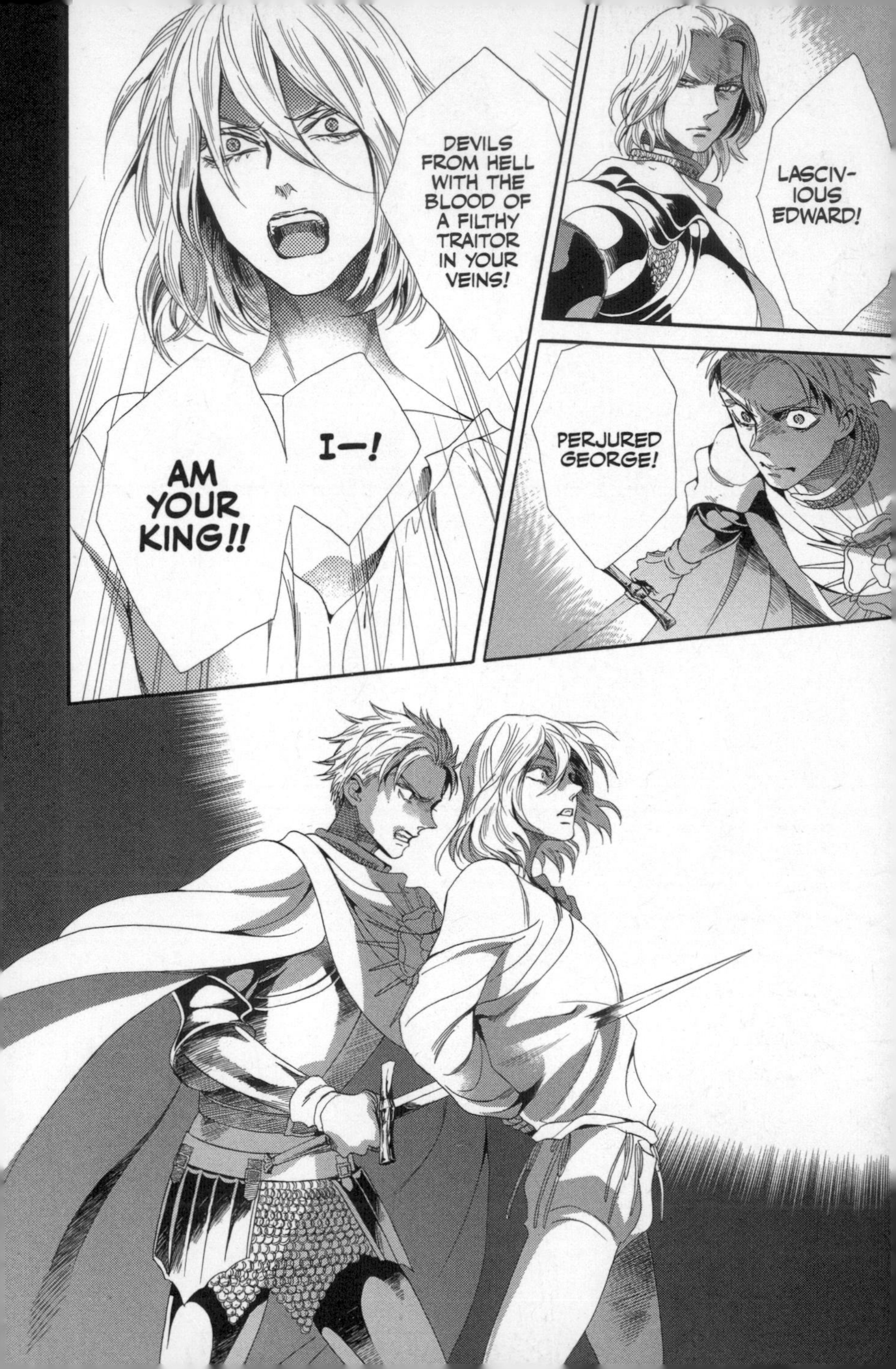
LASCIVIOUS EDWARD!
PERJURED GEORGE!
DEVILS FROM HELL WITH THE BLOOD OF A FILTHY TRAITOR IN YOUR VEINS!
I—!
AM YOUR KING!!

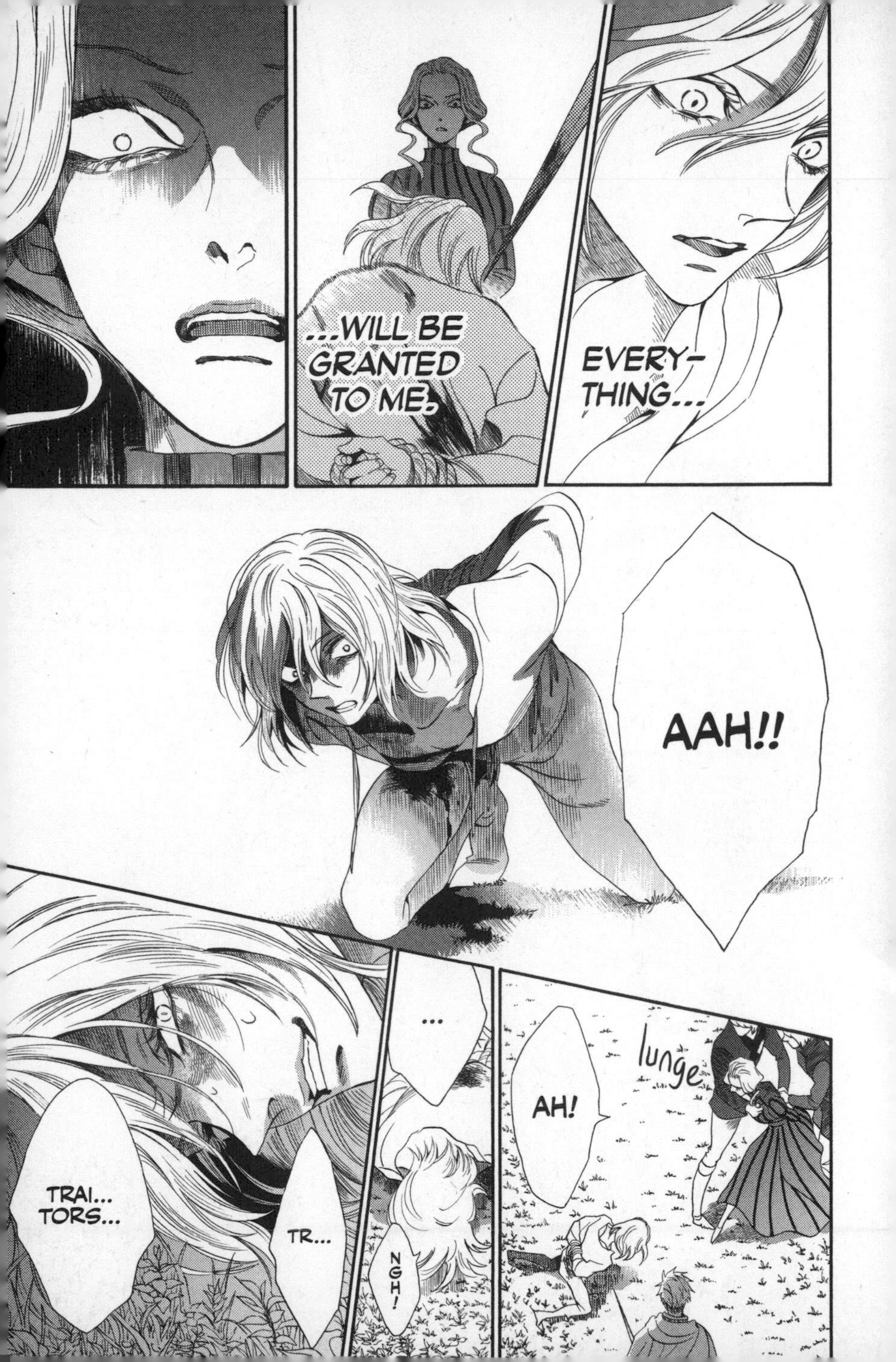
EVERY-THING...
...WILL BE GRANTED TO ME.
AAH!!
lunge
AH!
...
NGH!
TR...
TRAI... TORS...

EDWARD!

THWK

YOU...

EDWARD!!

AAAAH!

THUD

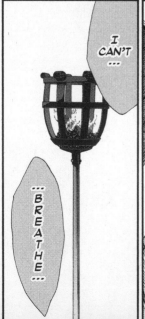

I CAN'T ...

...

...BREATHE...

NGH ...

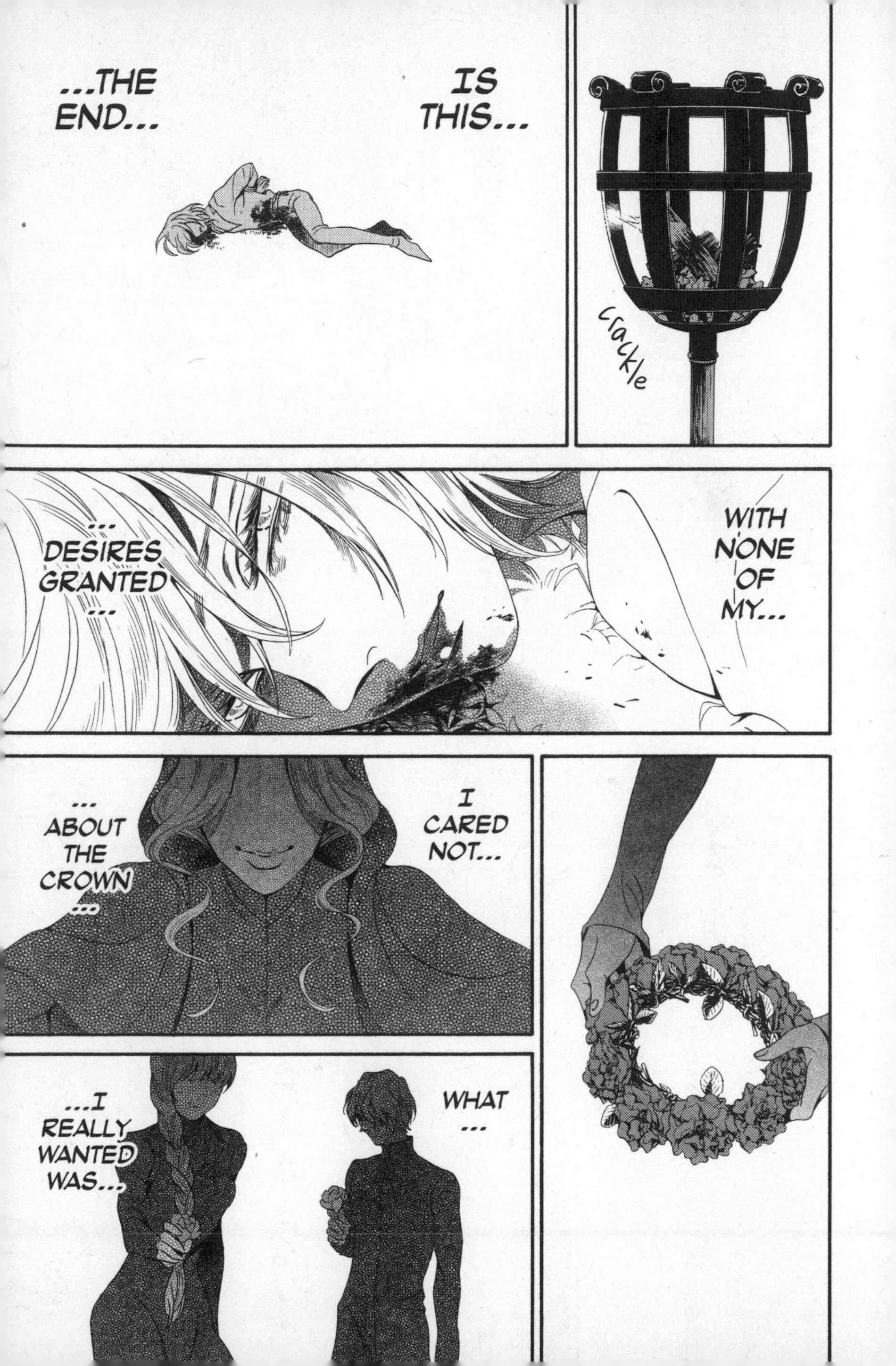
crackle
IS THIS...
...THE END...
WITH NONE OF MY...
...DESIRES GRANTED...
I CARED NOT...
...ABOUT THE CROWN...
WHAT...
...I REALLY WANTED WAS...

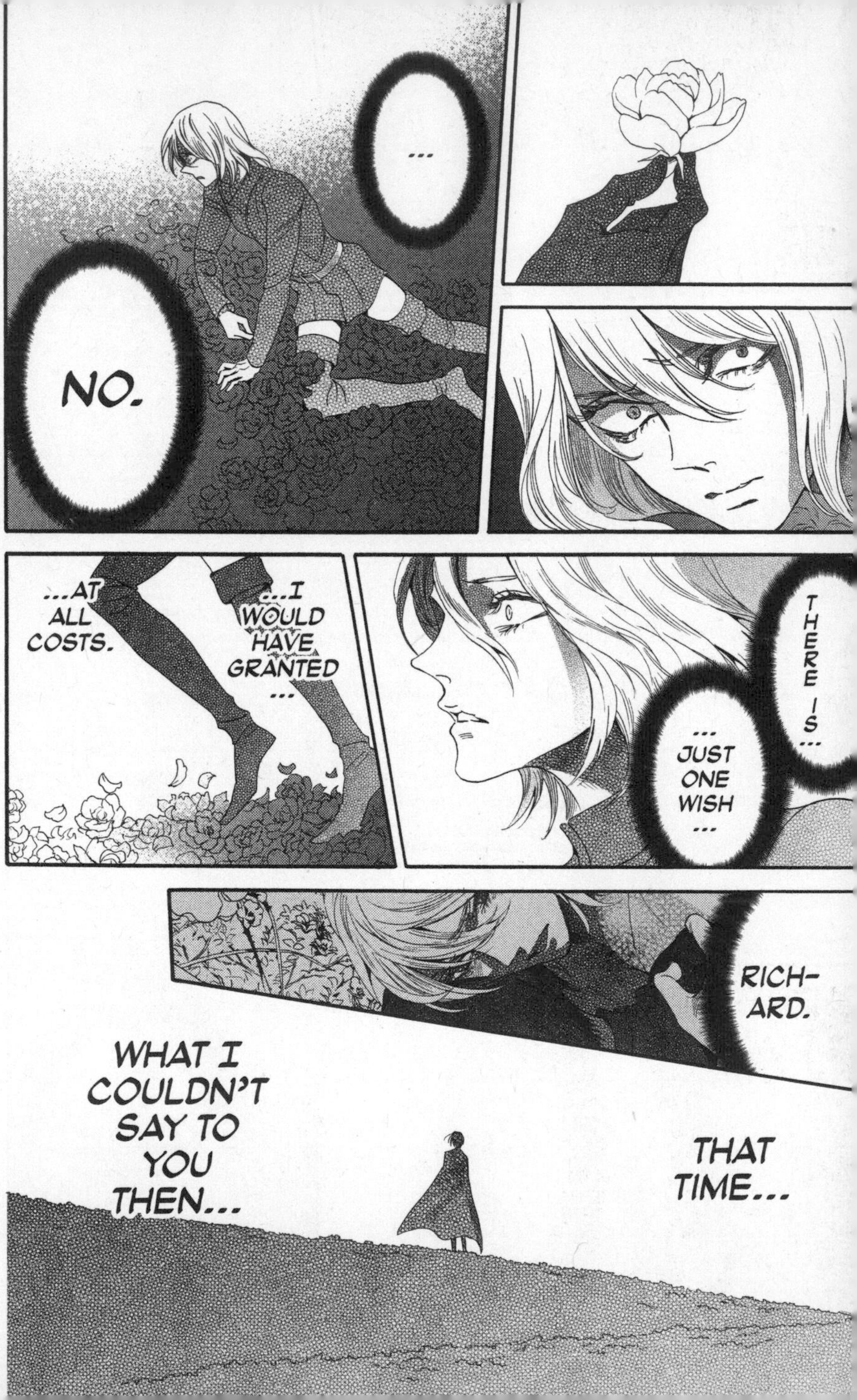
...
NO.
THERE IS...
...JUST ONE WISH...
...I WOULD HAVE GRANTED...
...AT ALL COSTS.
RICH-ARD.
THAT TIME...
WHAT I COULDN'T SAY TO YOU THEN...

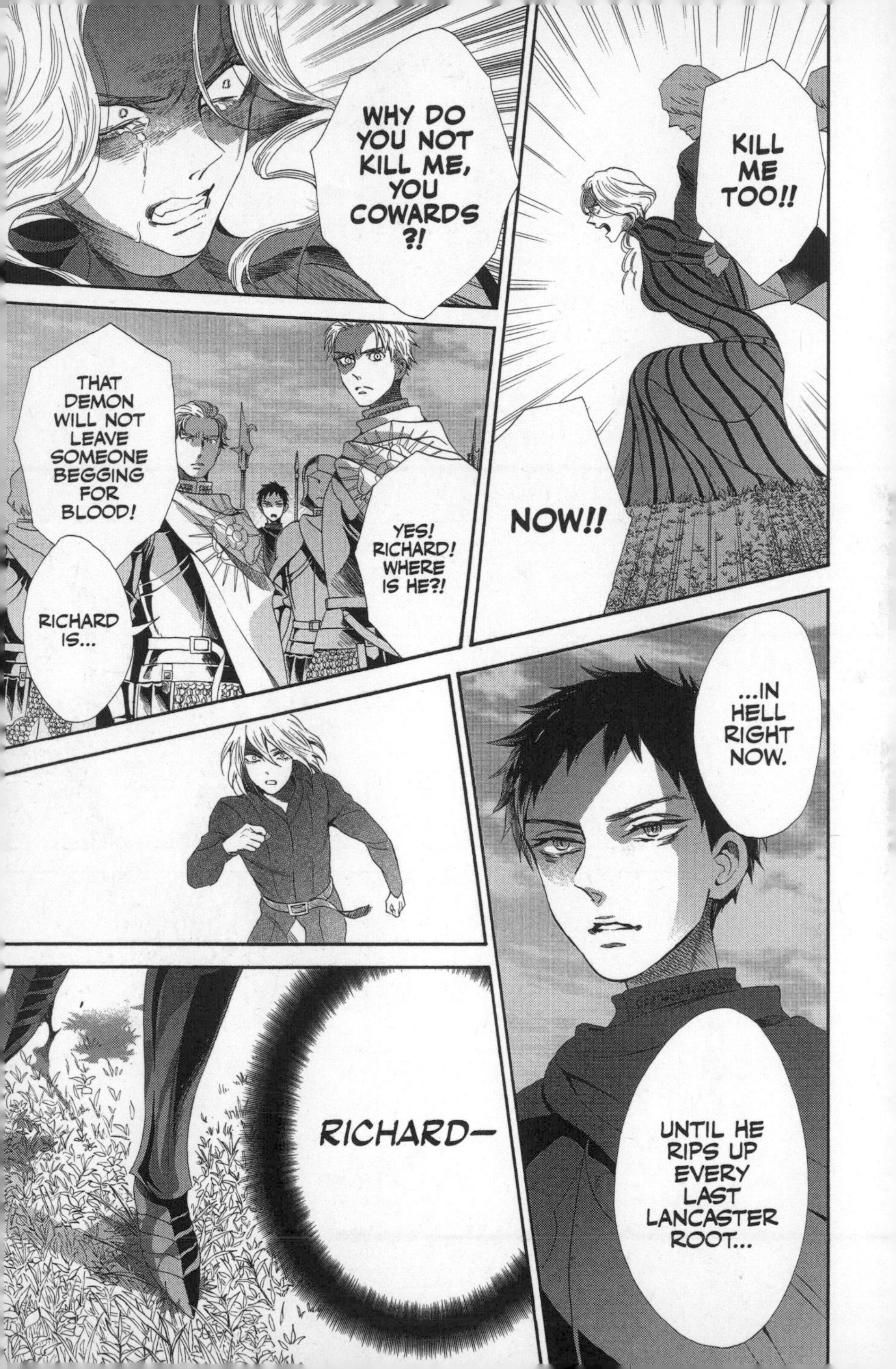
KILL ME TOO!!
NOW!!
WHY DO YOU NOT KILL ME, YOU COWARDS?!
YES! RICHARD! WHERE IS HE?!
THAT DEMON WILL NOT LEAVE SOMEONE BEGGING FOR BLOOD!
RICHARD IS...
...IN HELL RIGHT NOW.
UNTIL HE RIPS UP EVERY LAST LANCASTER ROOT...
RICHARD—

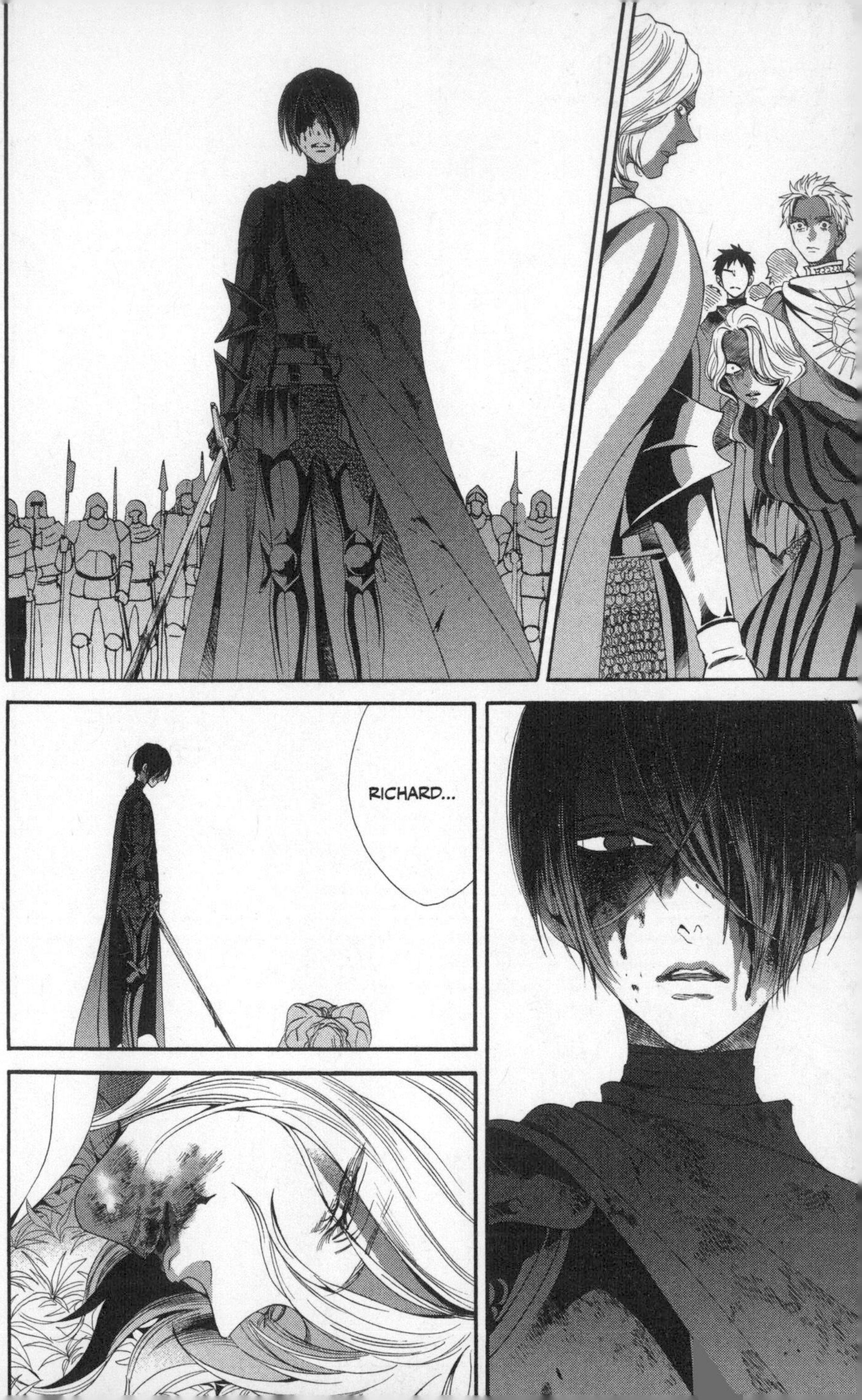
RICHARD...

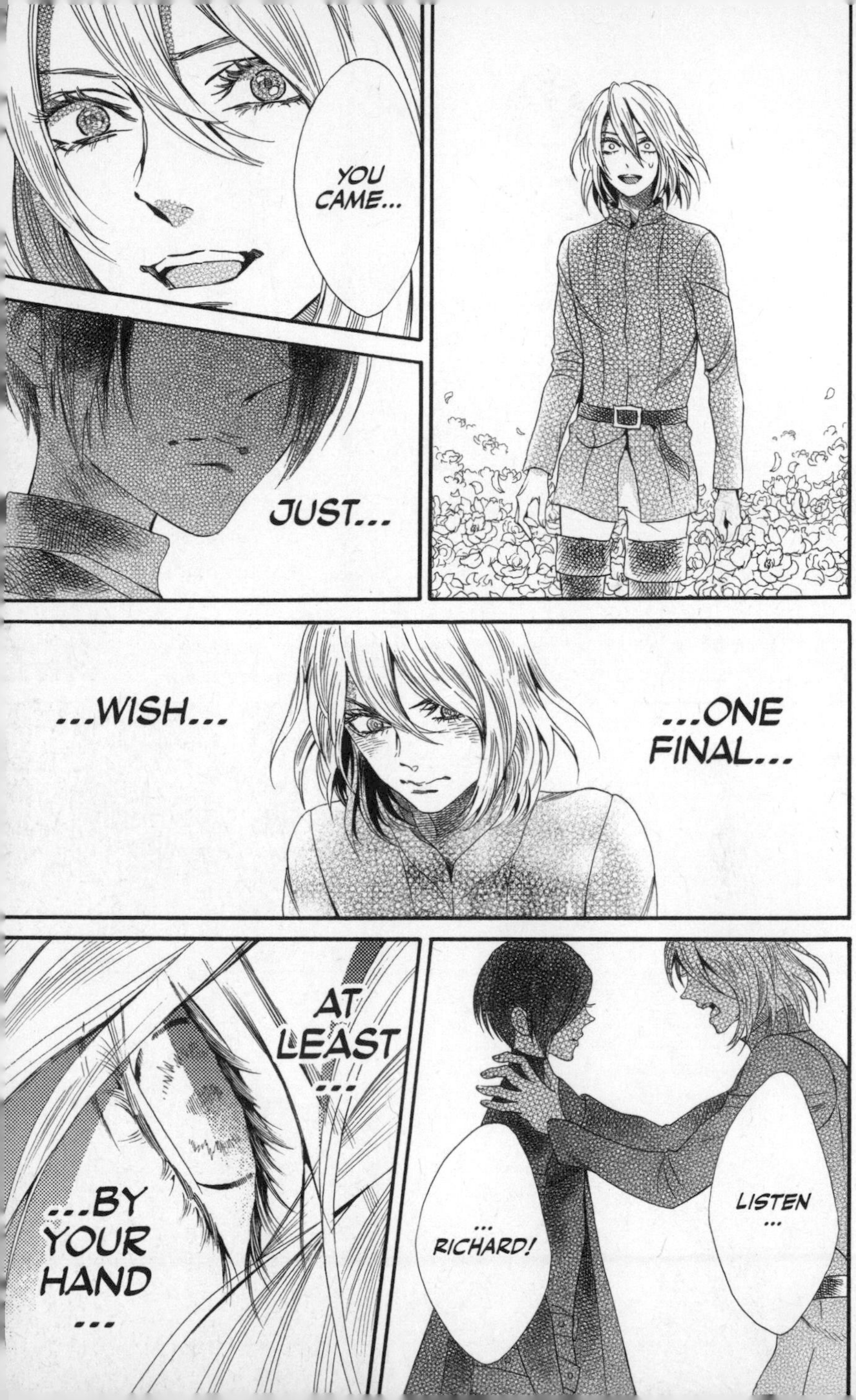
YOU CAME...
JUST...
...ONE FINAL...
...WISH...
LISTEN ...
... RICHARD!
AT LEAST ...
...BY YOUR HAND ...

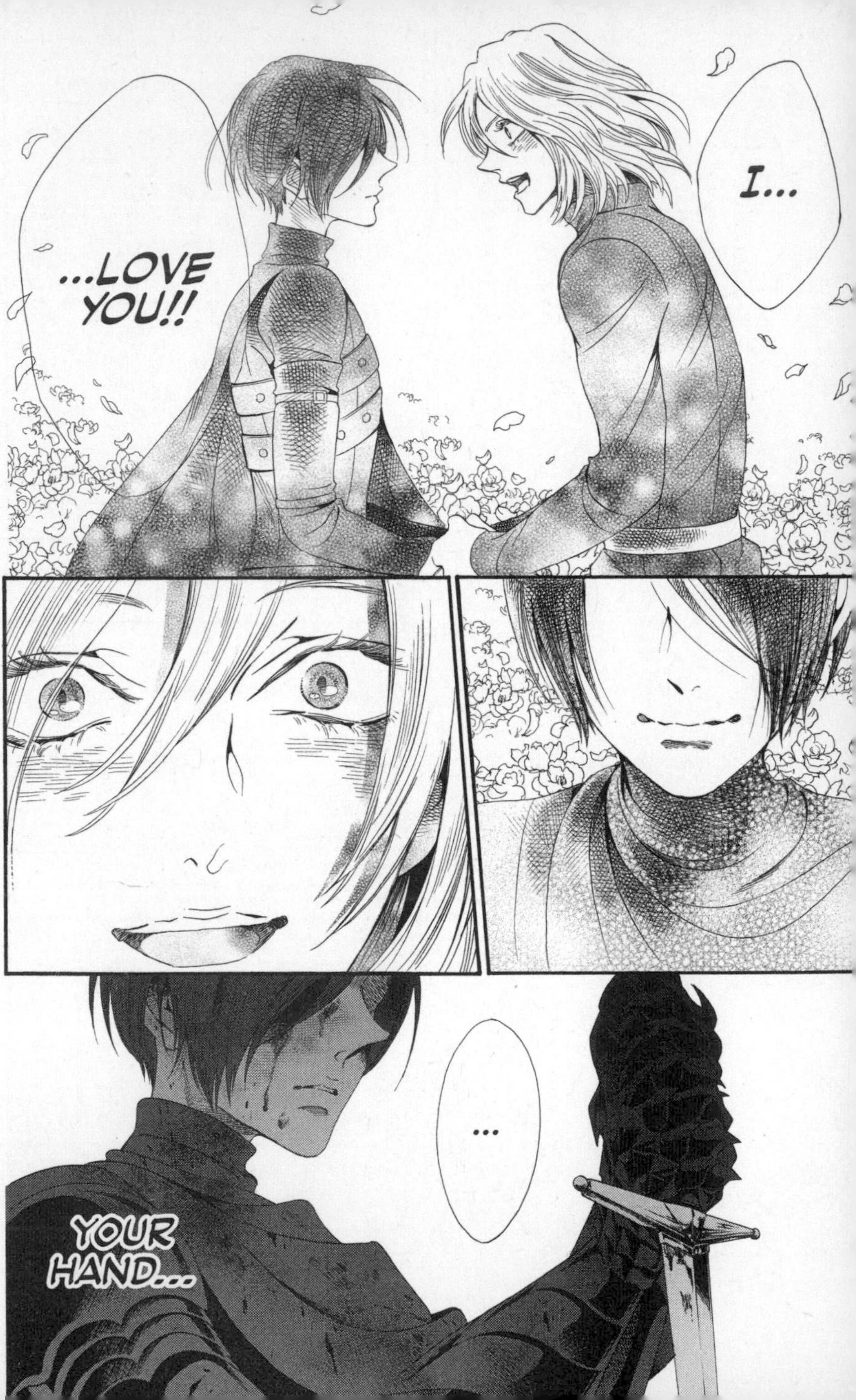
I...
...LOVE YOU!!
...
YOUR HAND...

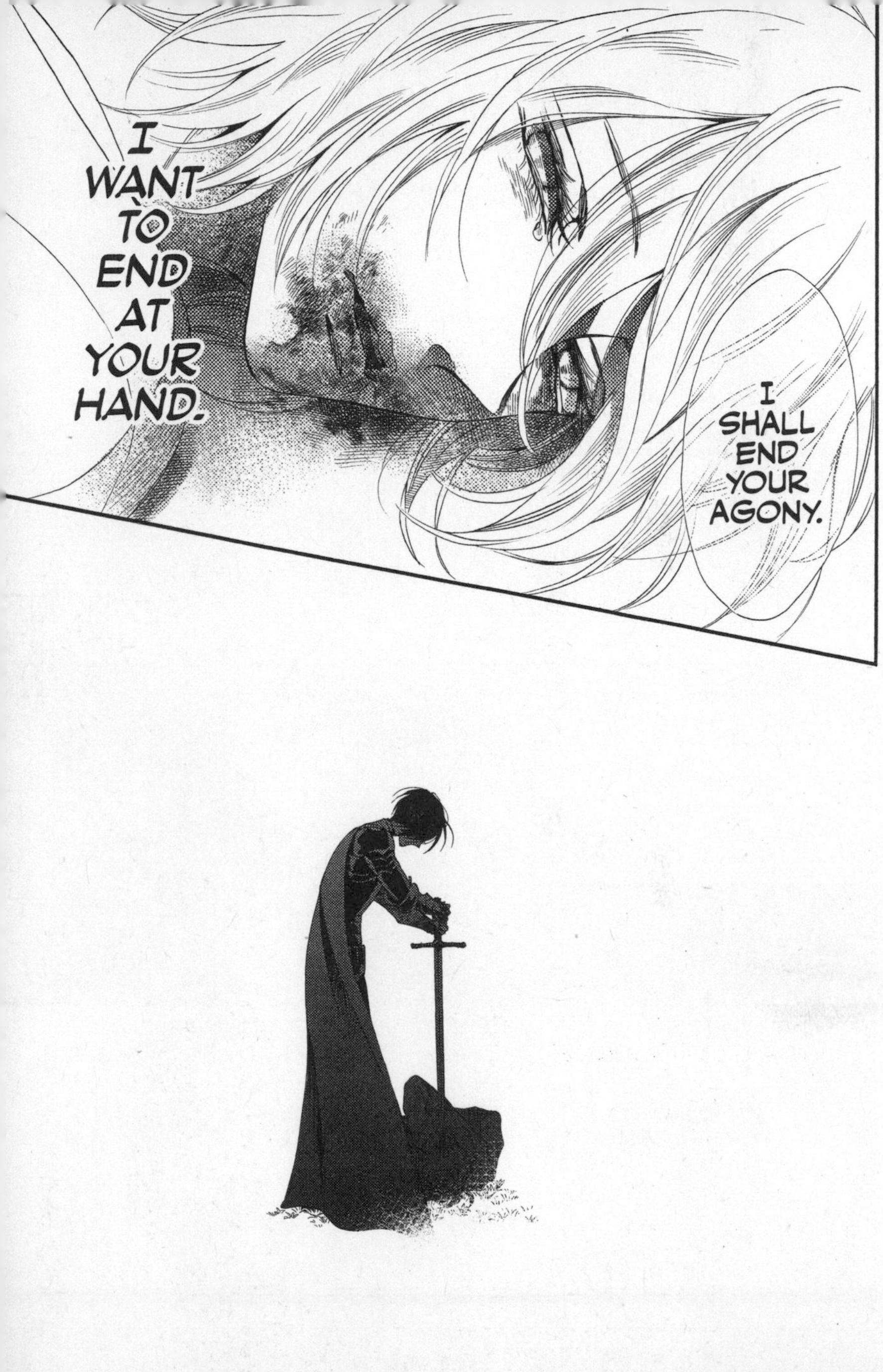
I SHALL END YOUR AGONY.
I WANT TO END AT YOUR HAND.

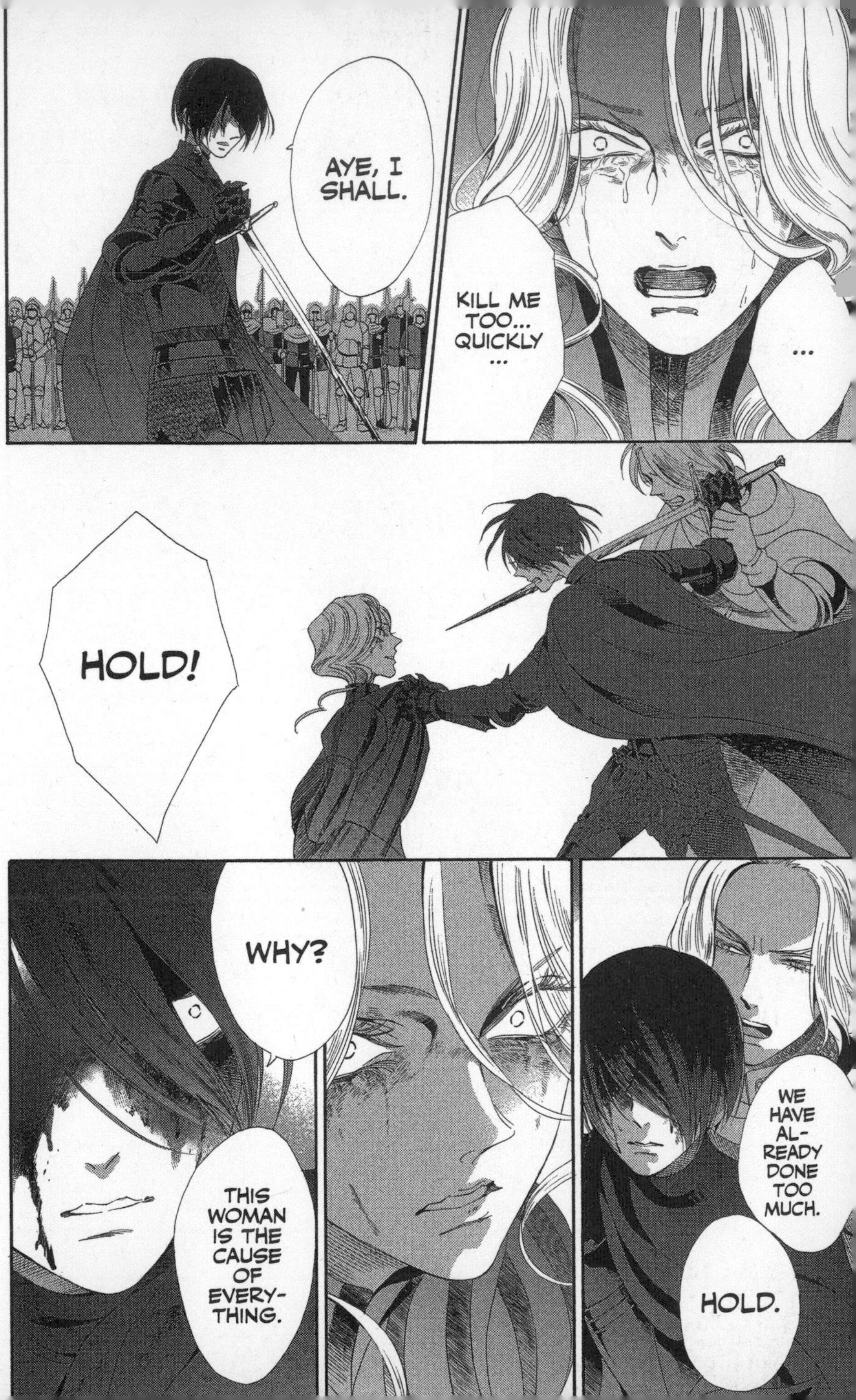
...
KILL ME TOO... QUICKLY ...
AYE, I SHALL.
HOLD!
WE HAVE AL-READY DONE TOO MUCH.
HOLD.
WHY?
THIS WOMAN IS THE CAUSE OF EVERY-THING.

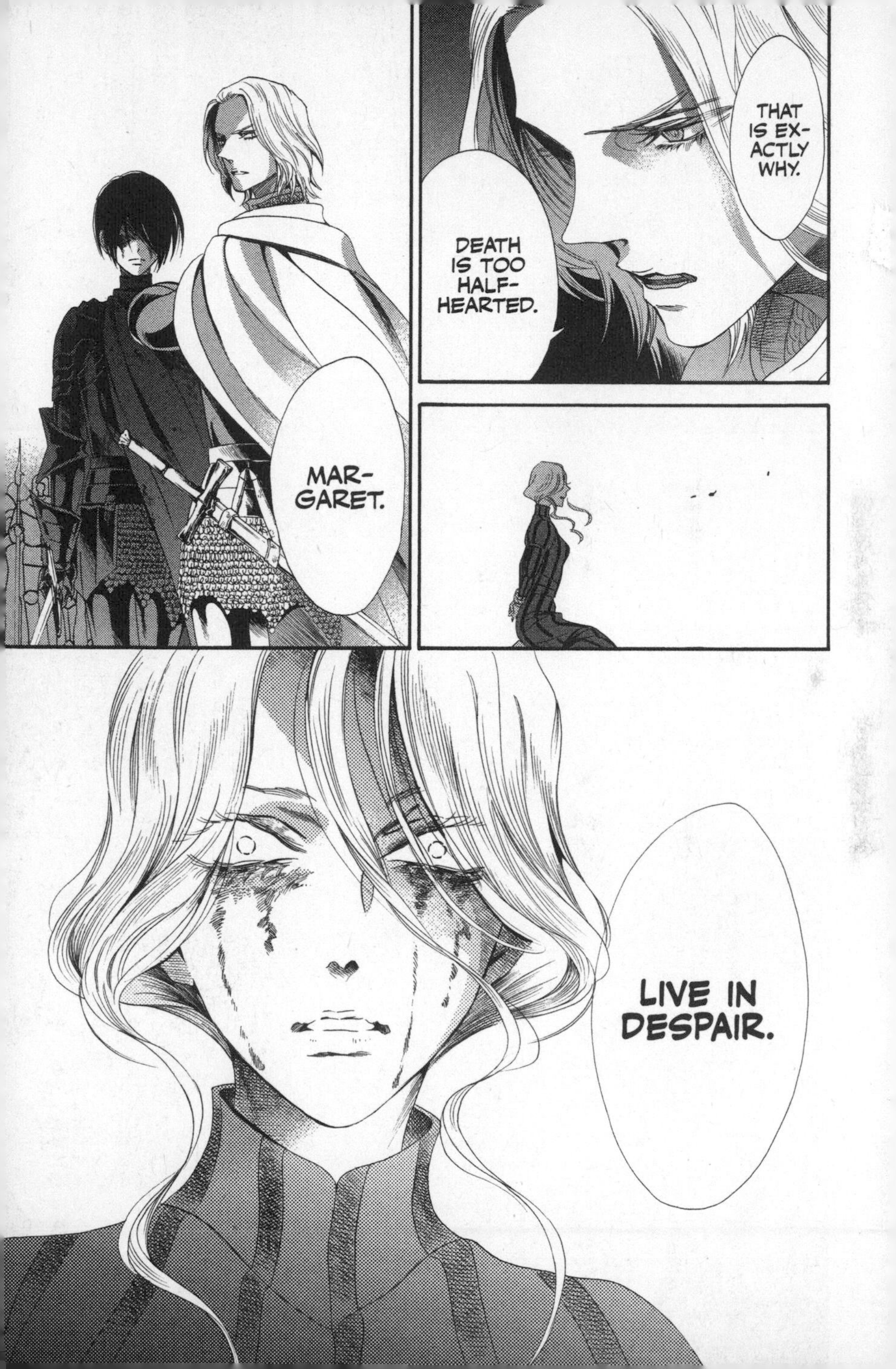
THAT IS EXACTLY WHY.
DEATH IS TOO HALF-HEARTED.
MARGARET.
LIVE IN DESPAIR.

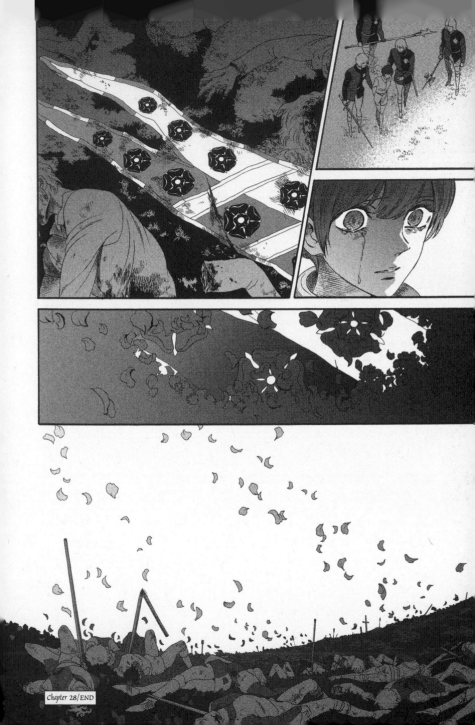

Chapter 28/END

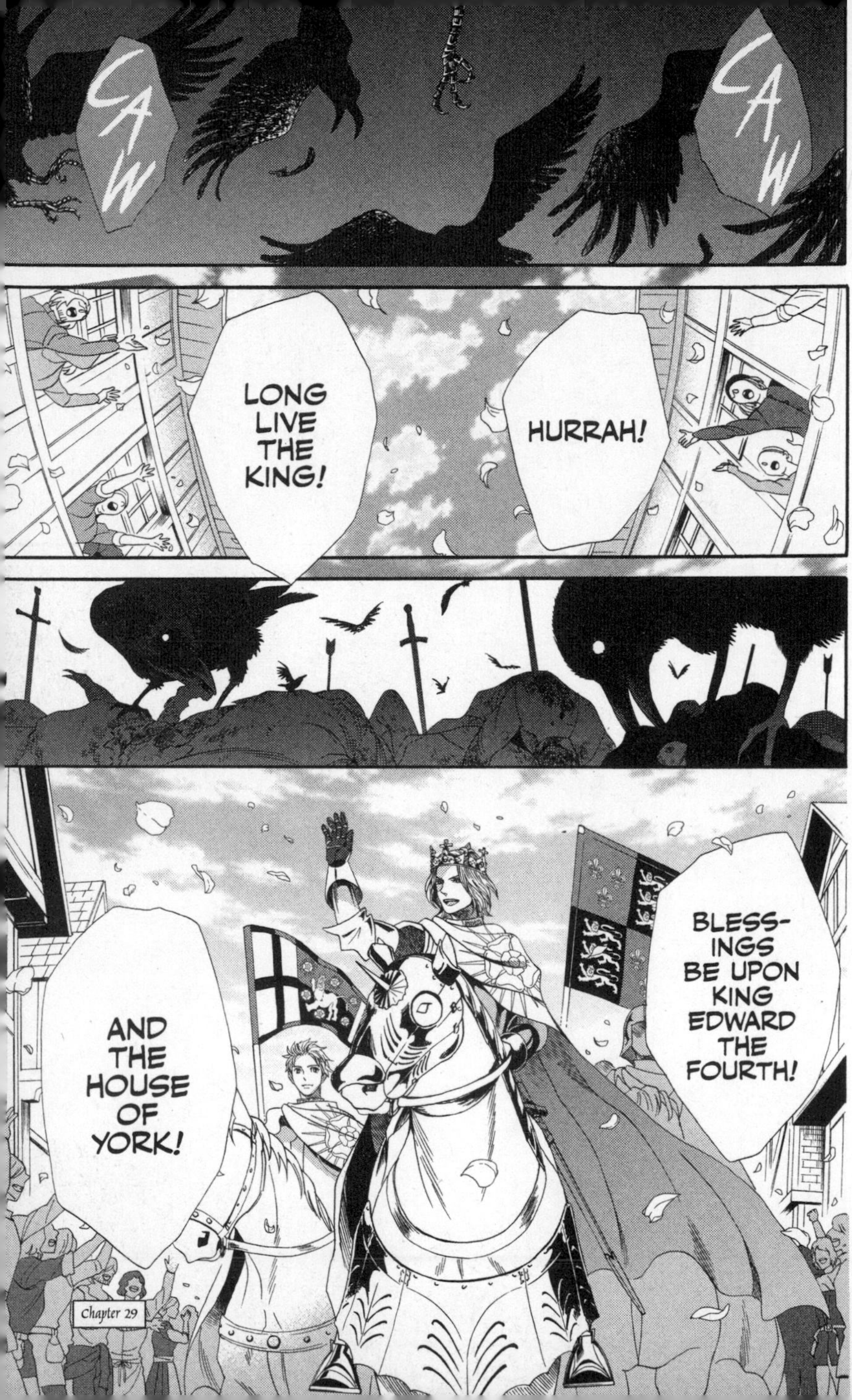
CAW
CAW
HURRAH!
LONG LIVE THE KING!
BLESS-INGS BE UPON KING EDWARD THE FOURTH!
AND THE HOUSE OF YORK!
Chapter 29

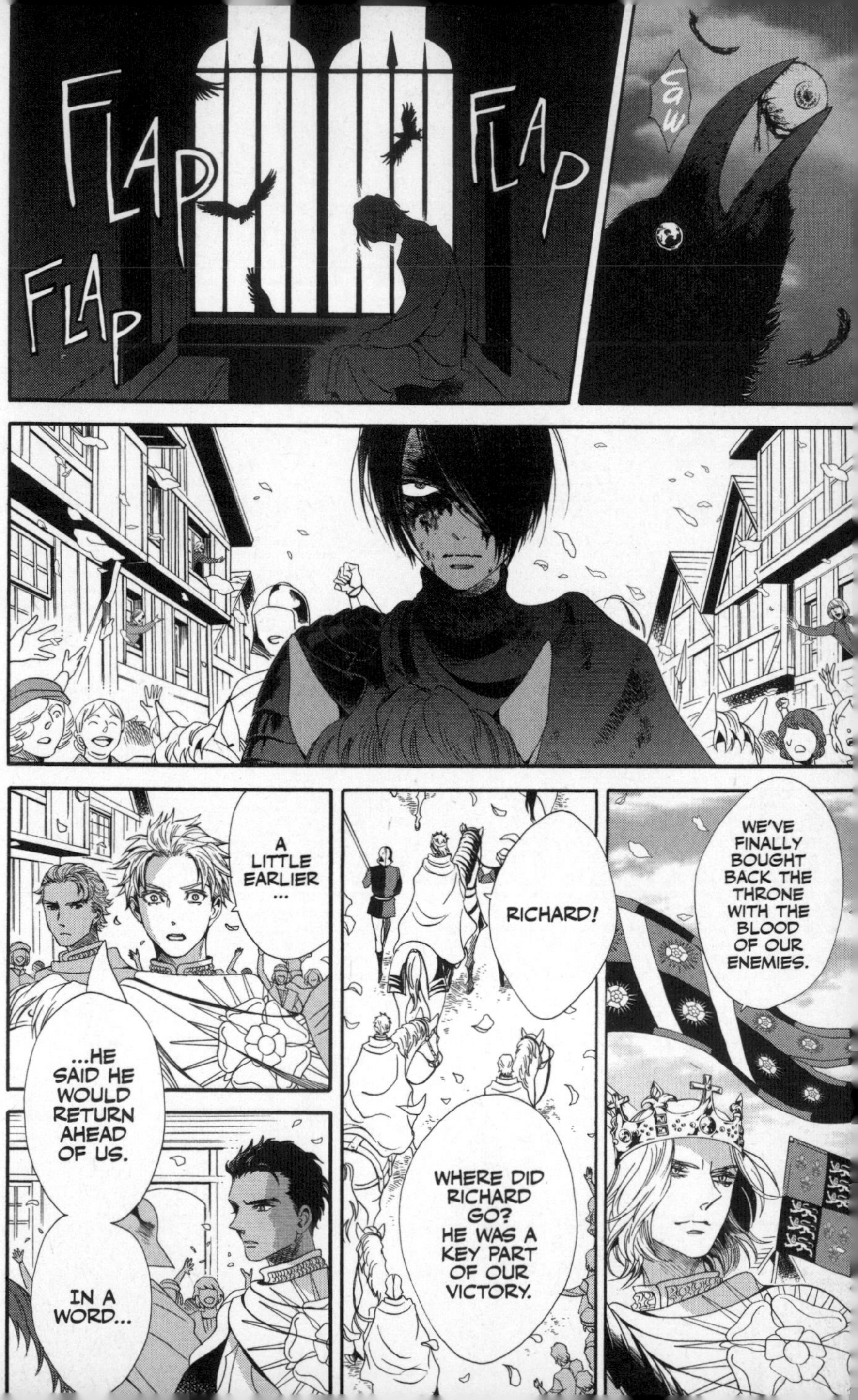
CAW
FLAP
FLAP
FLAP
WE'VE FINALLY BOUGHT BACK THE THRONE WITH THE BLOOD OF OUR ENEMIES.
RICHARD!
WHERE DID RICHARD GO? HE WAS A KEY PART OF OUR VICTORY.
A LITTLE EARLIER...
...HE SAID HE WOULD RETURN AHEAD OF US.
IN A WORD...

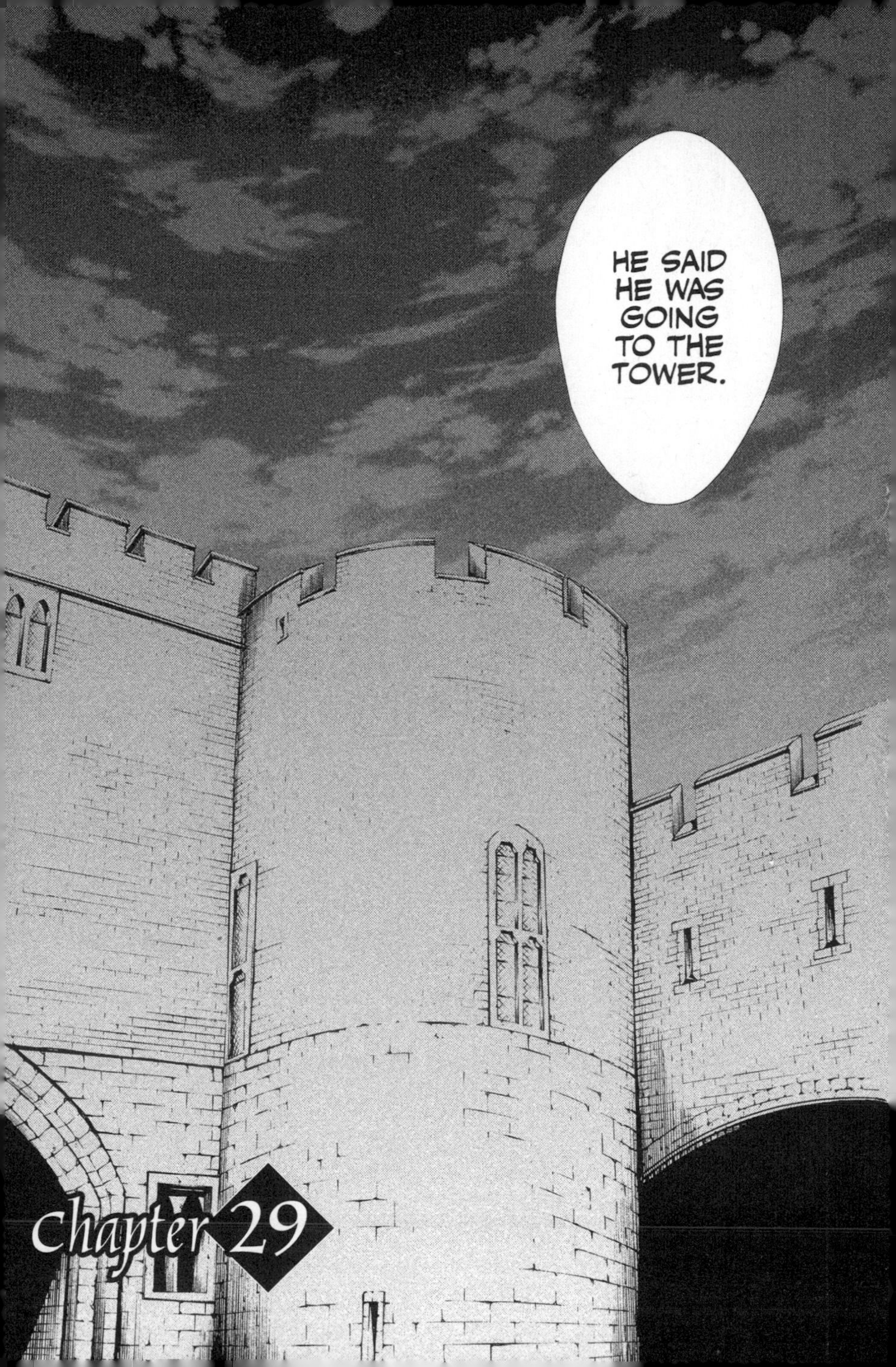
HE SAID HE WAS GOING TO THE TOWER.
Chapter 29

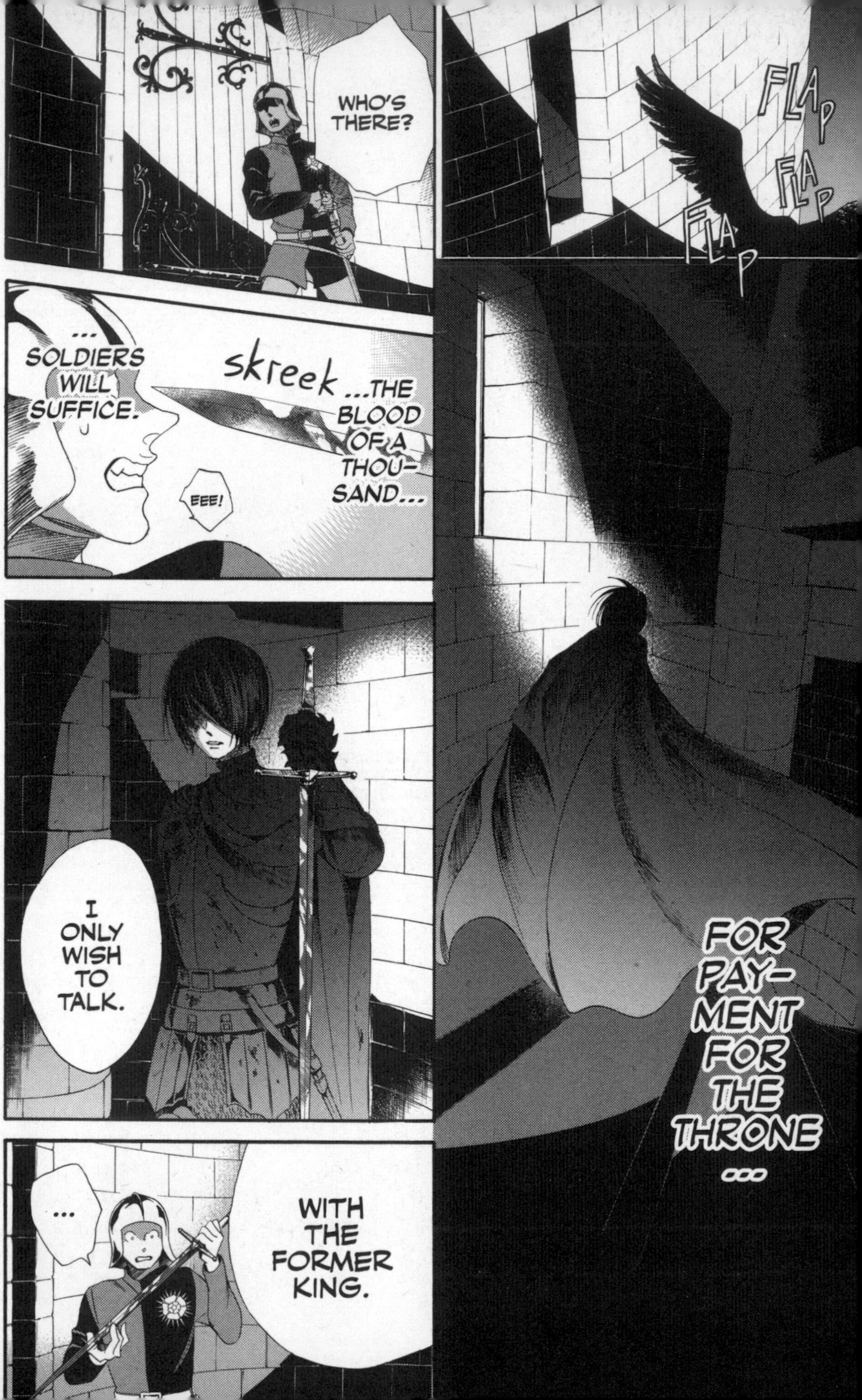
FLAP FLAP FLAP
WHO'S THERE?
FOR PAYMENT FOR THE THRONE...
...THE BLOOD OF A THOUSAND...
skreek
...SOLDIERS WILL SUFFICE.
EEE!
I ONLY WISH TO TALK.
WITH THE FORMER KING.
...

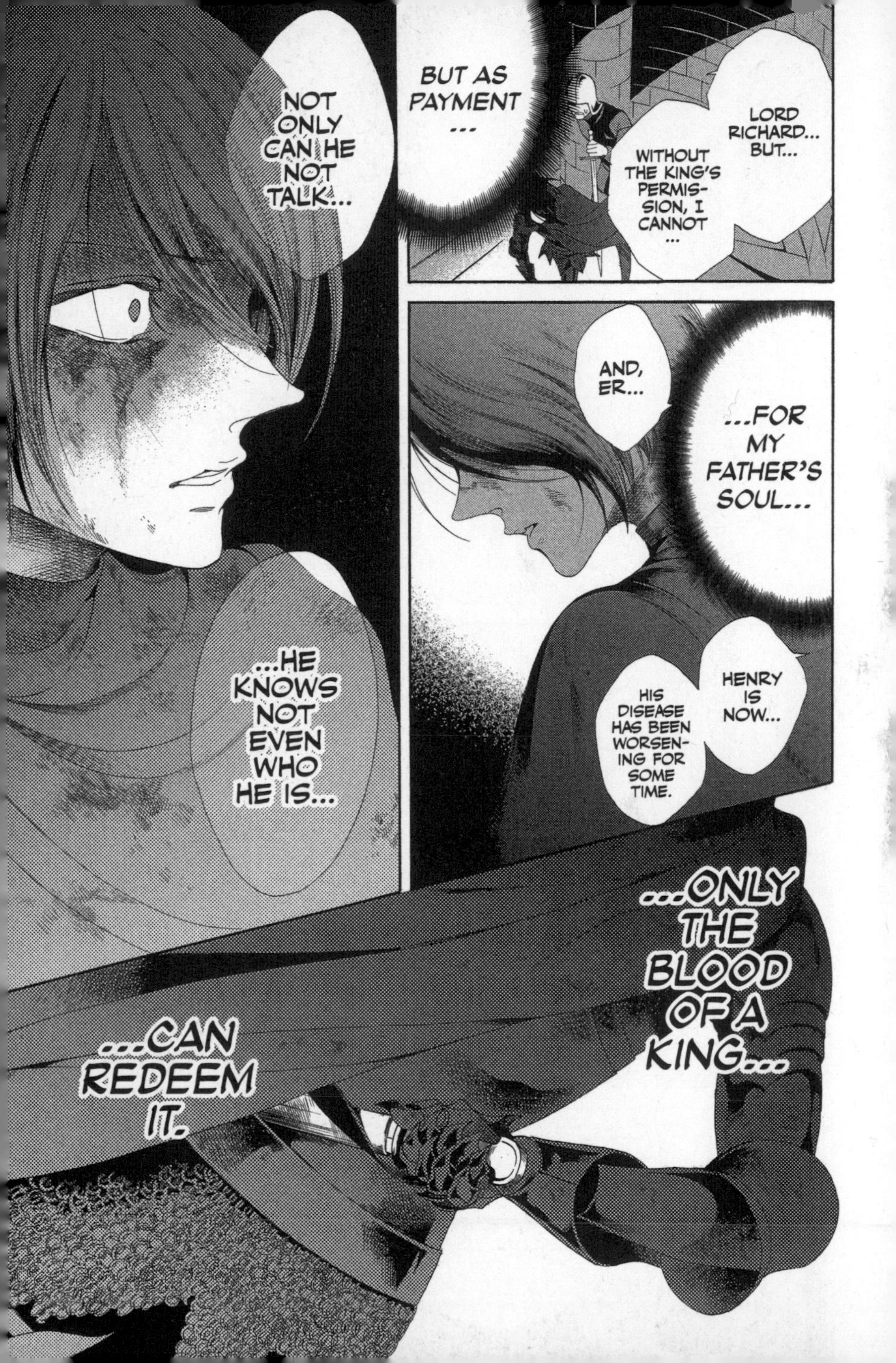
LORD RICHARD... BUT...
WITHOUT THE KING'S PERMIS-SION, I CANNOT ...
BUT AS PAYMENT ...
NOT ONLY CAN HE NOT TALK...
AND, ER...
...FOR MY FATHER'S SOUL...
HENRY IS NOW...
HIS DISEASE HAS BEEN WORSEN-ING FOR SOME TIME.
...HE KNOWS NOT EVEN WHO HE IS...
...ONLY THE BLOOD OF A KING...
...CAN REDEEM IT.

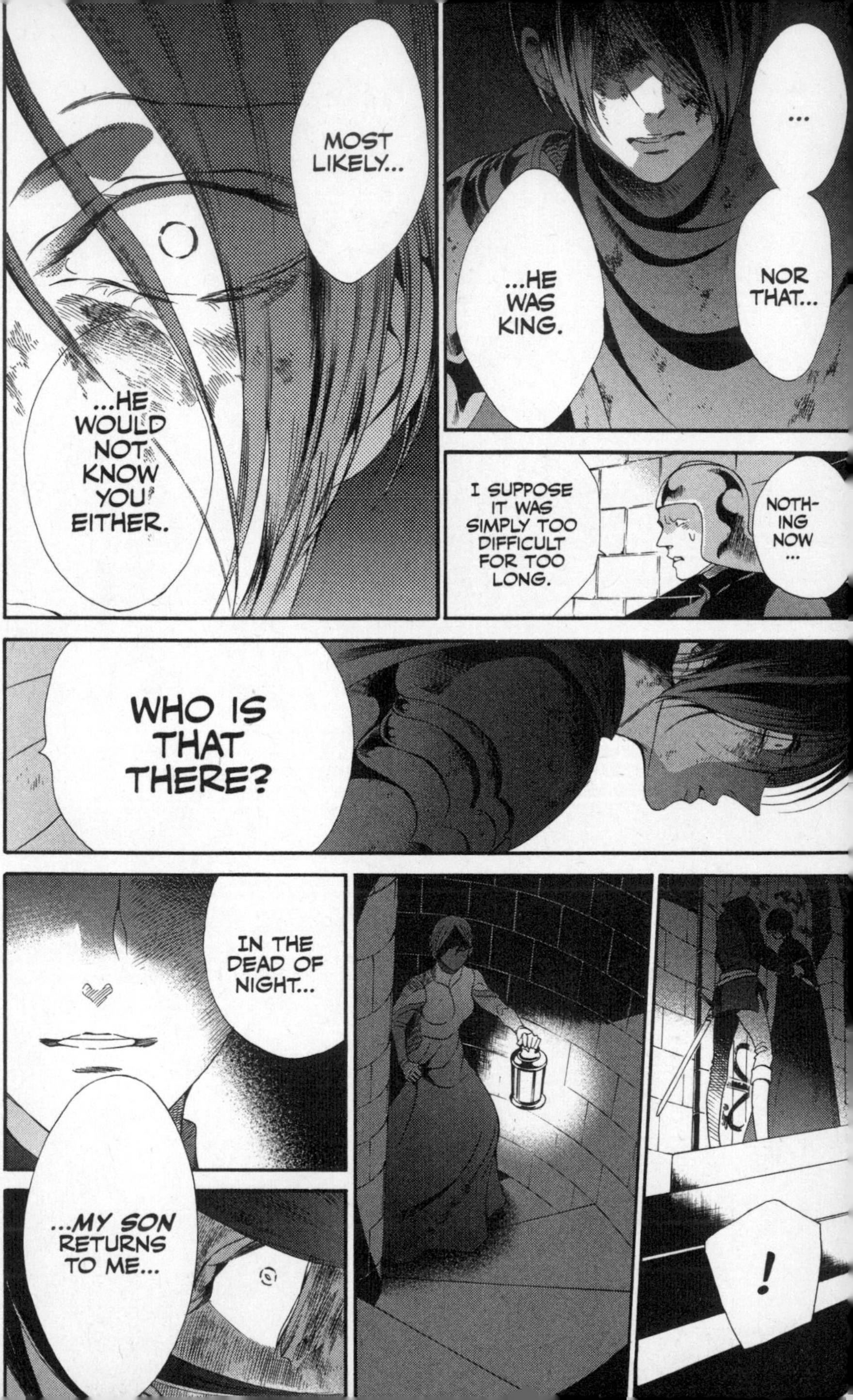
...
NOR THAT...
...HE WAS KING.
NOTHING NOW...
I SUPPOSE IT WAS SIMPLY TOO DIFFICULT FOR TOO LONG.
MOST LIKELY...
...HE WOULD NOT KNOW YOU EITHER.
WHO IS THAT THERE?
!
IN THE DEAD OF NIGHT...
...*MY SON* RETURNS TO ME...

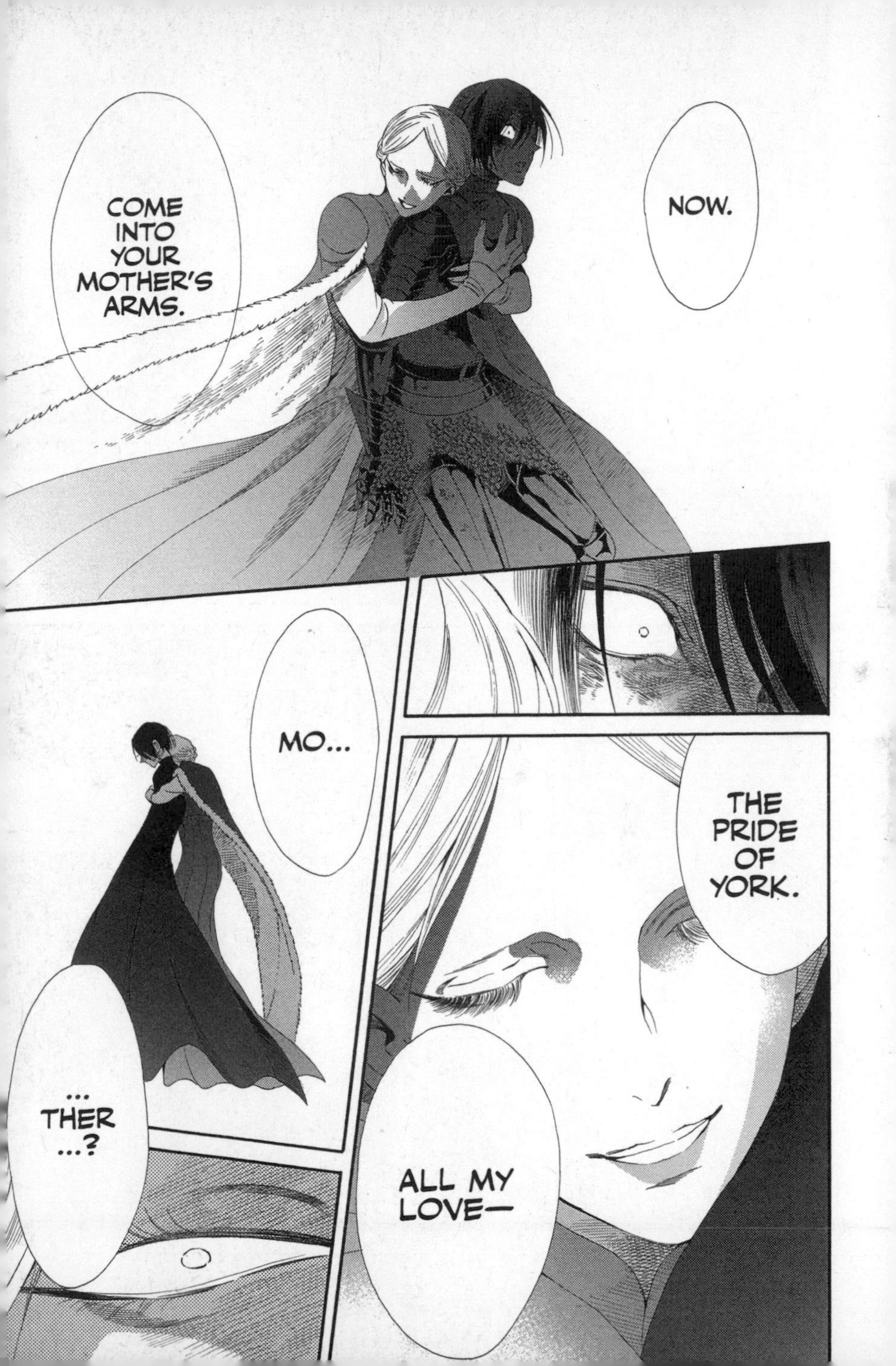
NOW.
COME INTO YOUR MOTHER'S ARMS.
THE PRIDE OF YORK.
ALL MY LOVE—
MO...
...THER...?

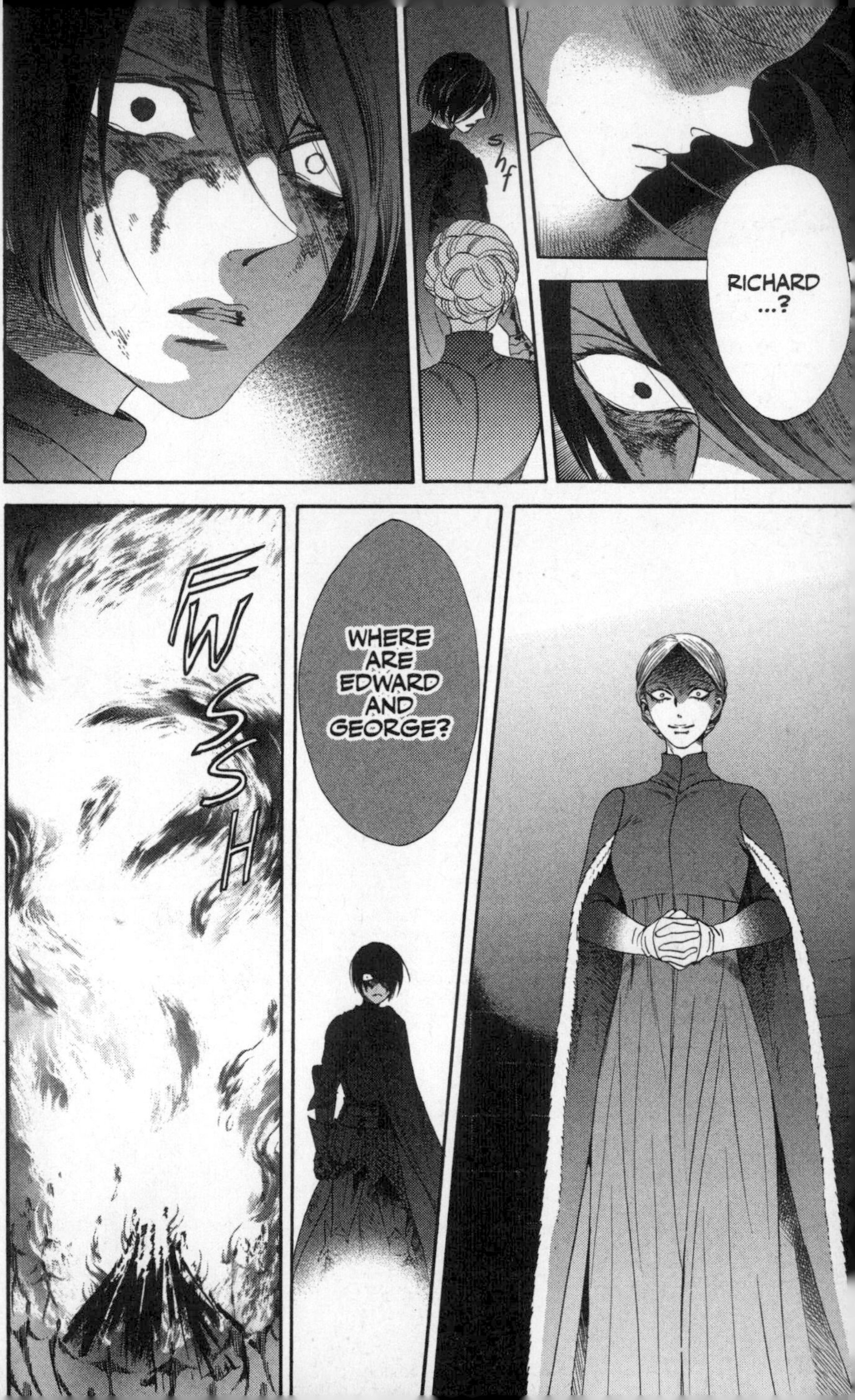
RICHARD ...?
shf
WHERE ARE EDWARD AND GEORGE?
FWSSH

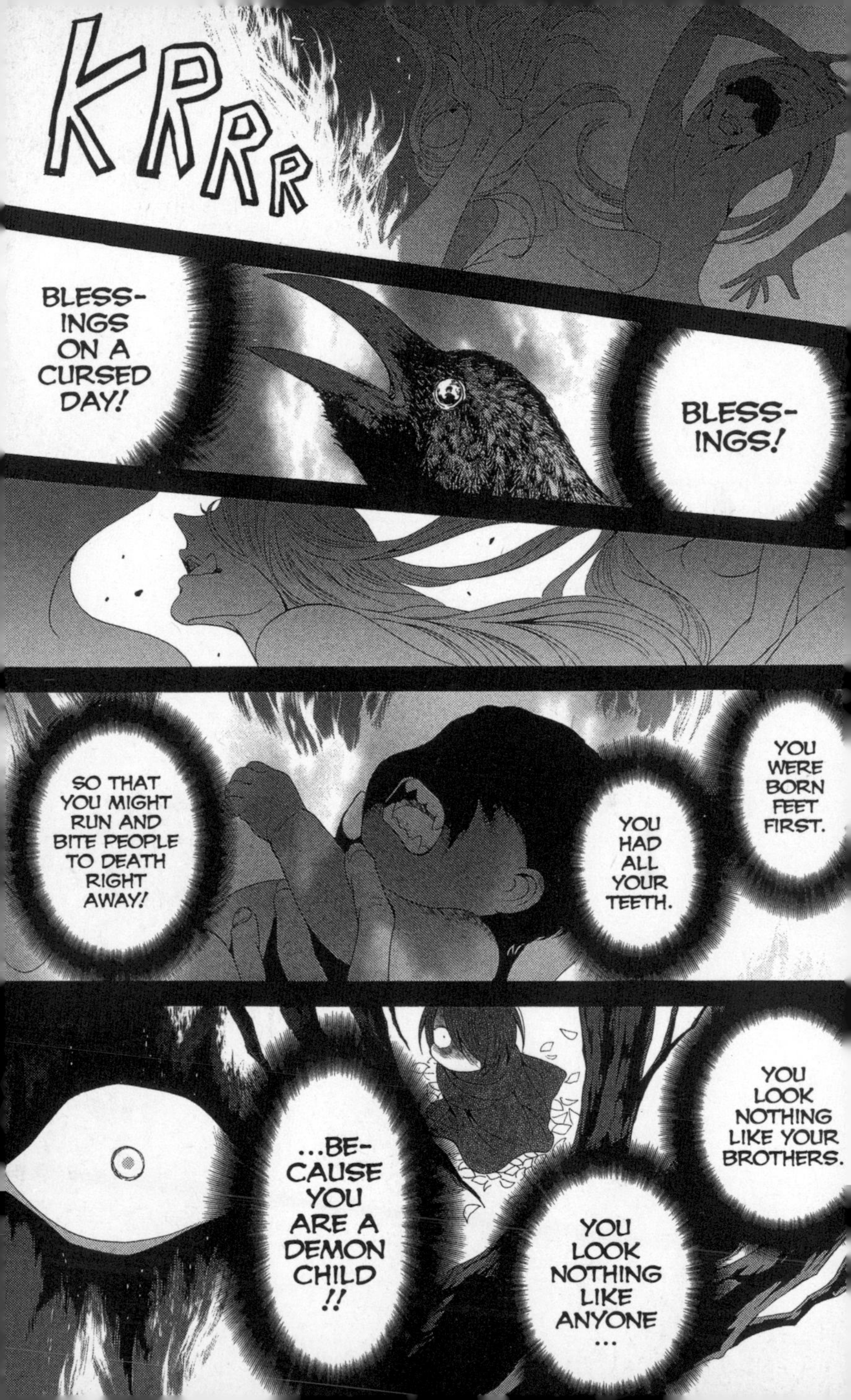
KRRR
BLESS-INGS!
BLESS-INGS ON A CURSED DAY!
YOU WERE BORN FEET FIRST.
YOU HAD ALL YOUR TEETH.
SO THAT YOU MIGHT RUN AND BITE PEOPLE TO DEATH RIGHT AWAY!
YOU LOOK NOTHING LIKE YOUR BROTHERS.
YOU LOOK NOTHING LIKE ANYONE ...
...BE-CAUSE YOU ARE A DEMON CHILD !!

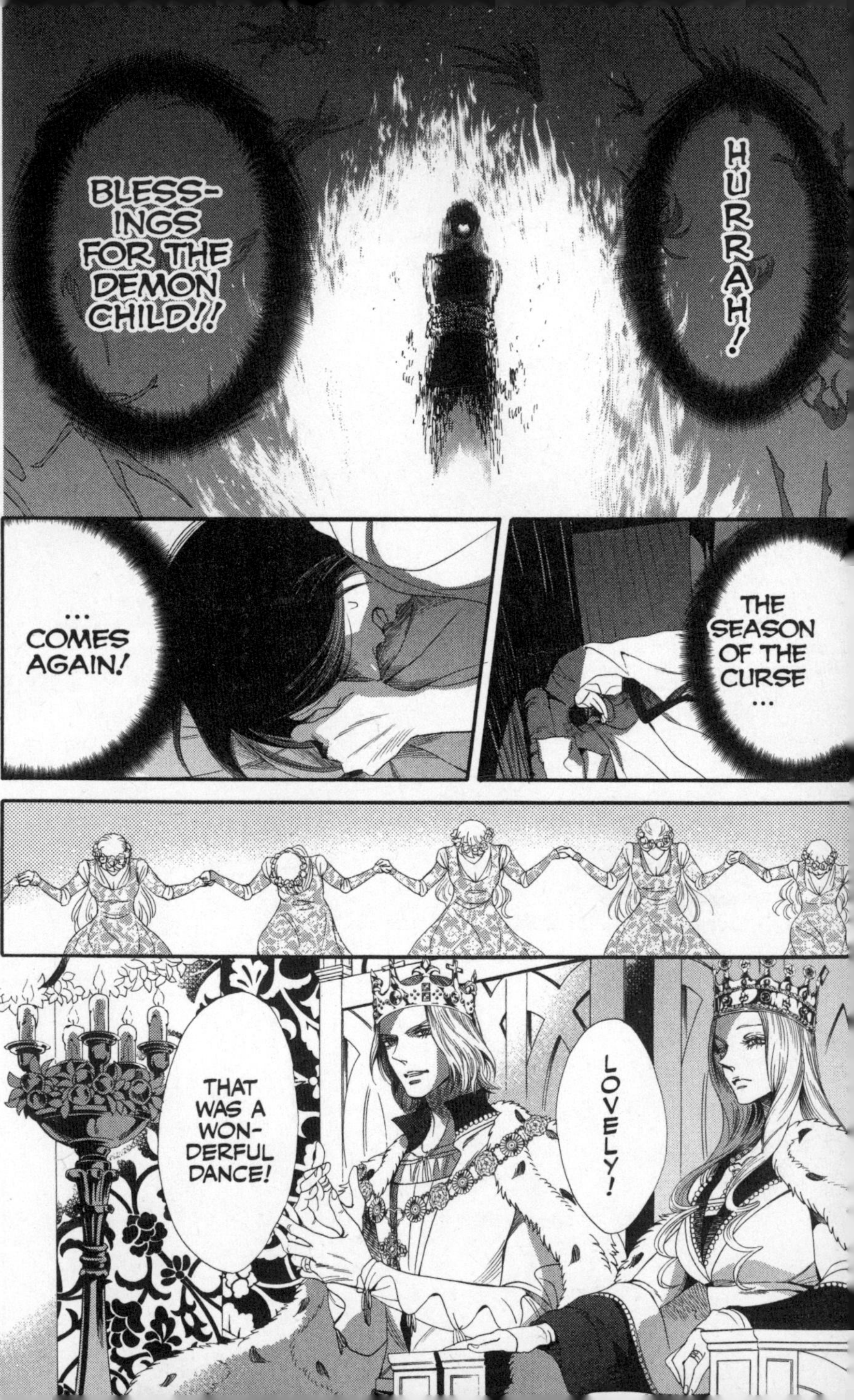
HURRAH!
BLESSINGS FOR THE DEMON CHILD!!
THE SEASON OF THE CURSE...
...COMES AGAIN!
LOVELY!
THAT WAS A WONDERFUL DANCE!

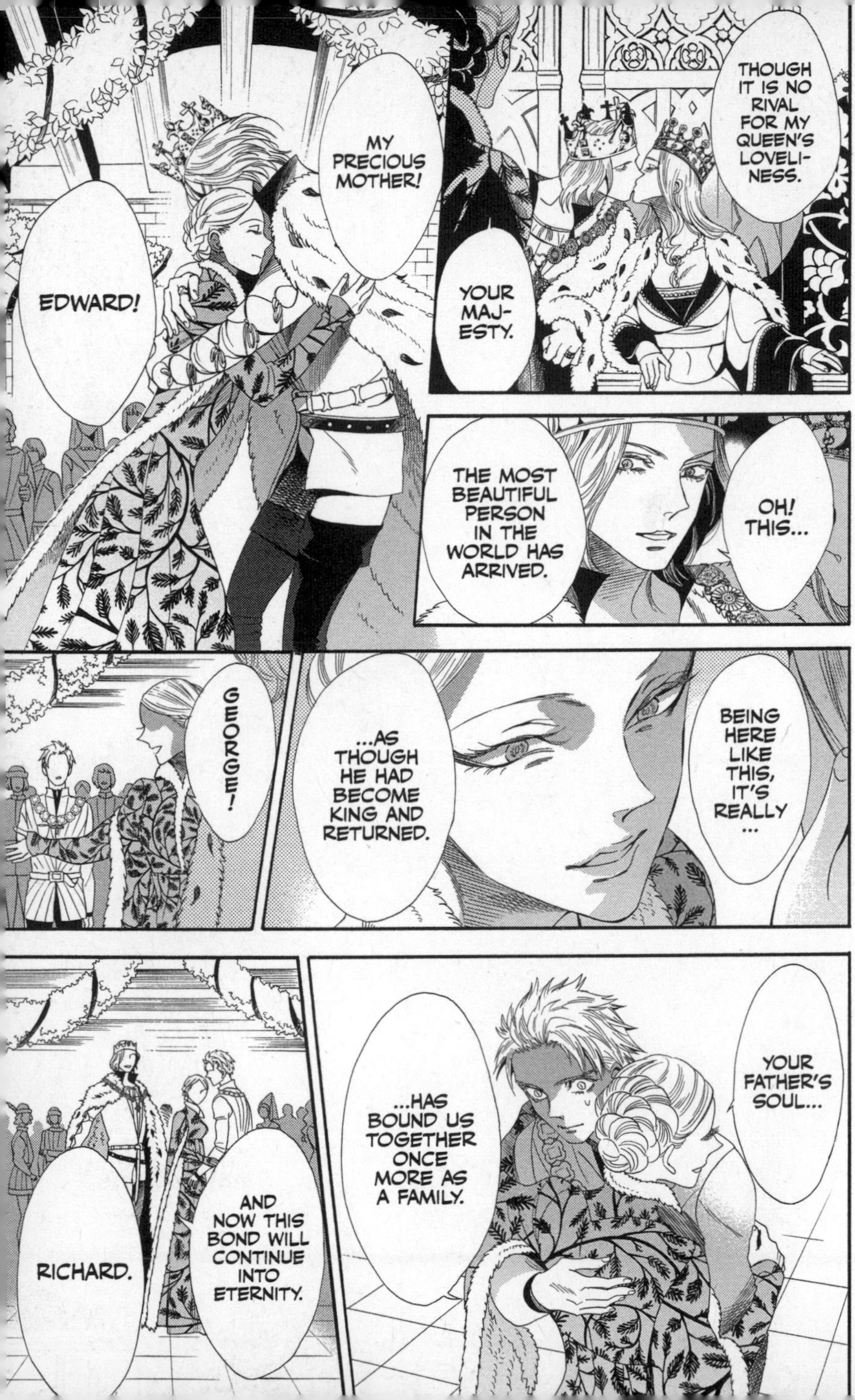
THOUGH IT IS NO RIVAL FOR MY QUEEN'S LOVELINESS.
YOUR MAJESTY.
OH! THIS...
THE MOST BEAUTIFUL PERSON IN THE WORLD HAS ARRIVED.
MY PRECIOUS MOTHER!
EDWARD!
BEING HERE LIKE THIS, IT'S REALLY ...
...AS THOUGH HE HAD BECOME KING AND RETURNED.
GEORGE!
YOUR FATHER'S SOUL...
...HAS BOUND US TOGETHER ONCE MORE AS A FAMILY.
AND NOW THIS BOND WILL CONTINUE INTO ETERNITY.
RICHARD.

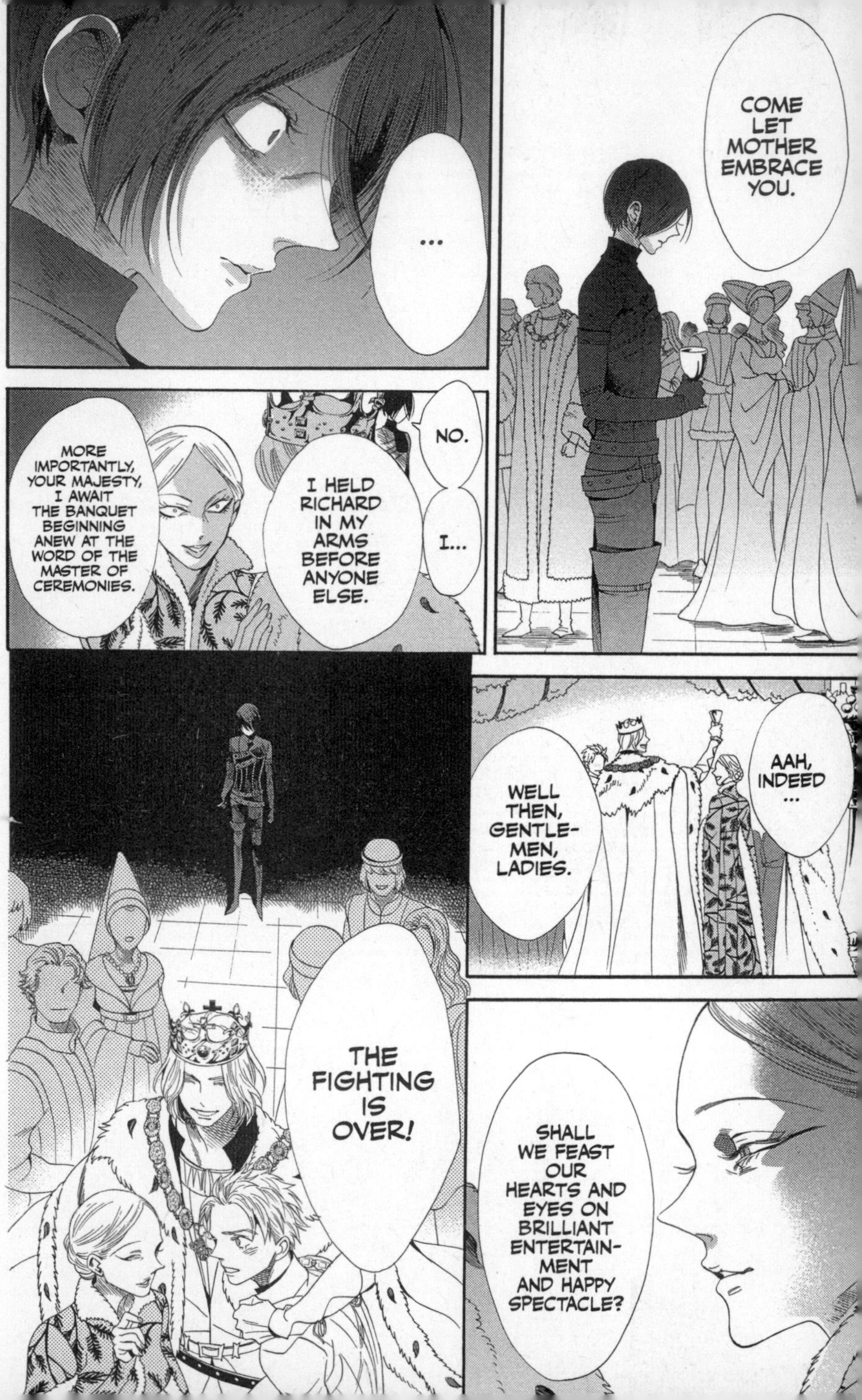
COME LET MOTHER EMBRACE YOU.
...
NO.
I...
I HELD RICHARD IN MY ARMS BEFORE ANYONE ELSE.
MORE IMPORTANTLY, YOUR MAJESTY, I AWAIT THE BANQUET BEGINNING ANEW AT THE WORD OF THE MASTER OF CEREMONIES.
AAH, INDEED ...
WELL THEN, GENTLE-MEN, LADIES.
SHALL WE FEAST OUR HEARTS AND EYES ON BRILLIANT ENTERTAIN-MENT AND HAPPY SPECTACLE?
THE FIGHTING IS OVER!

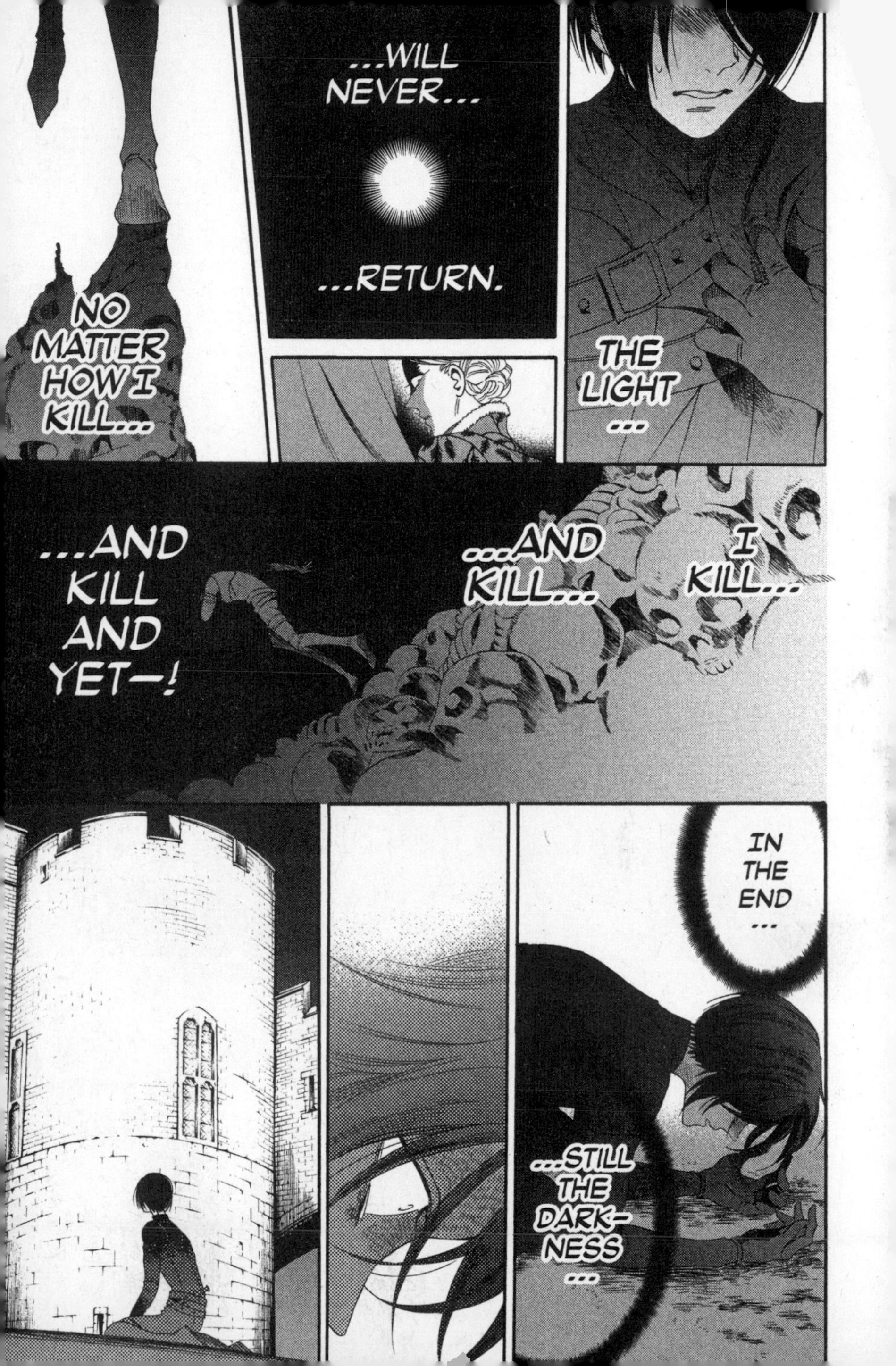
THE LIGHT ...
...WILL NEVER...
...RETURN.
NO MATTER HOW I KILL...
I KILL...
...AND KILL...
...AND KILL AND YET—!
IN THE END ...
...STILL THE DARK-NESS ...

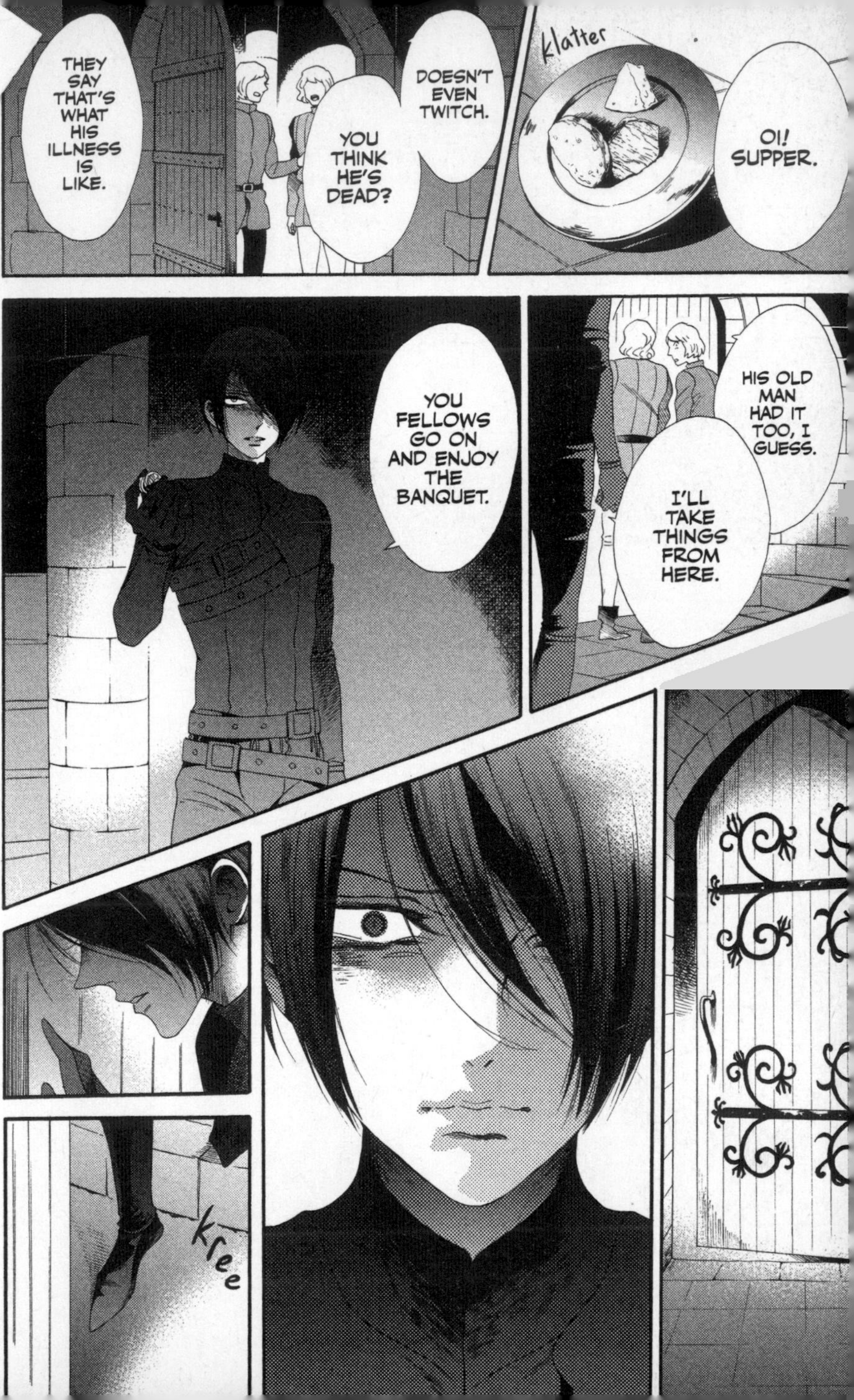
klatter
OI! SUPPER.
DOESN'T EVEN TWITCH.
YOU THINK HE'S DEAD?
THEY SAY THAT'S WHAT HIS ILLNESS IS LIKE.
HIS OLD MAN HAD IT TOO, I GUESS.
I'LL TAKE THINGS FROM HERE.
YOU FELLOWS GO ON AND ENJOY THE BANQUET.
kree

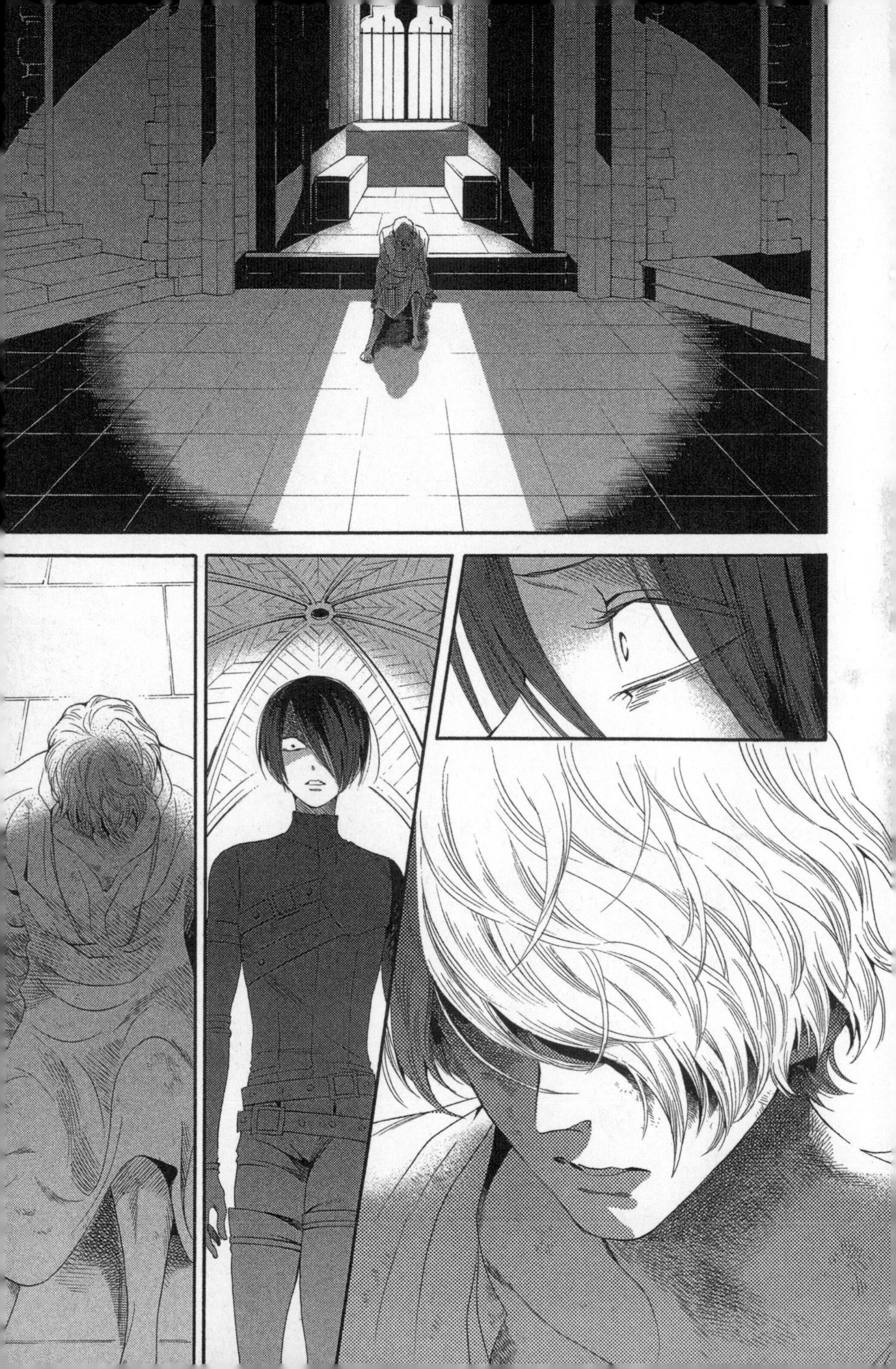

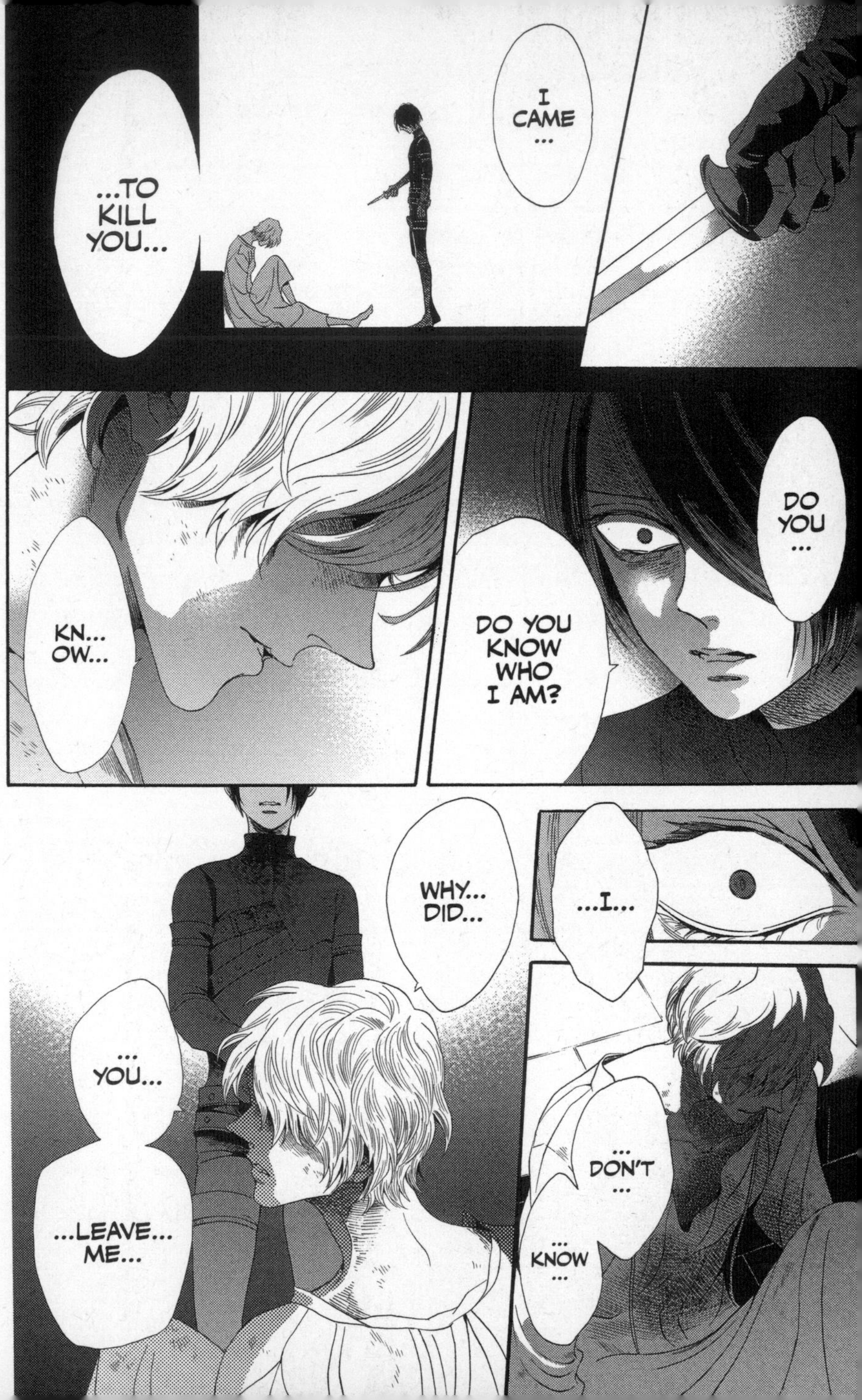
I CAME ...
...TO KILL YOU...
DO YOU ...
DO YOU KNOW WHO I AM?
KN... OW...
...I...
... DON'T ...
... KNOW ...
WHY... DID...
... YOU...
...LEAVE... ME...

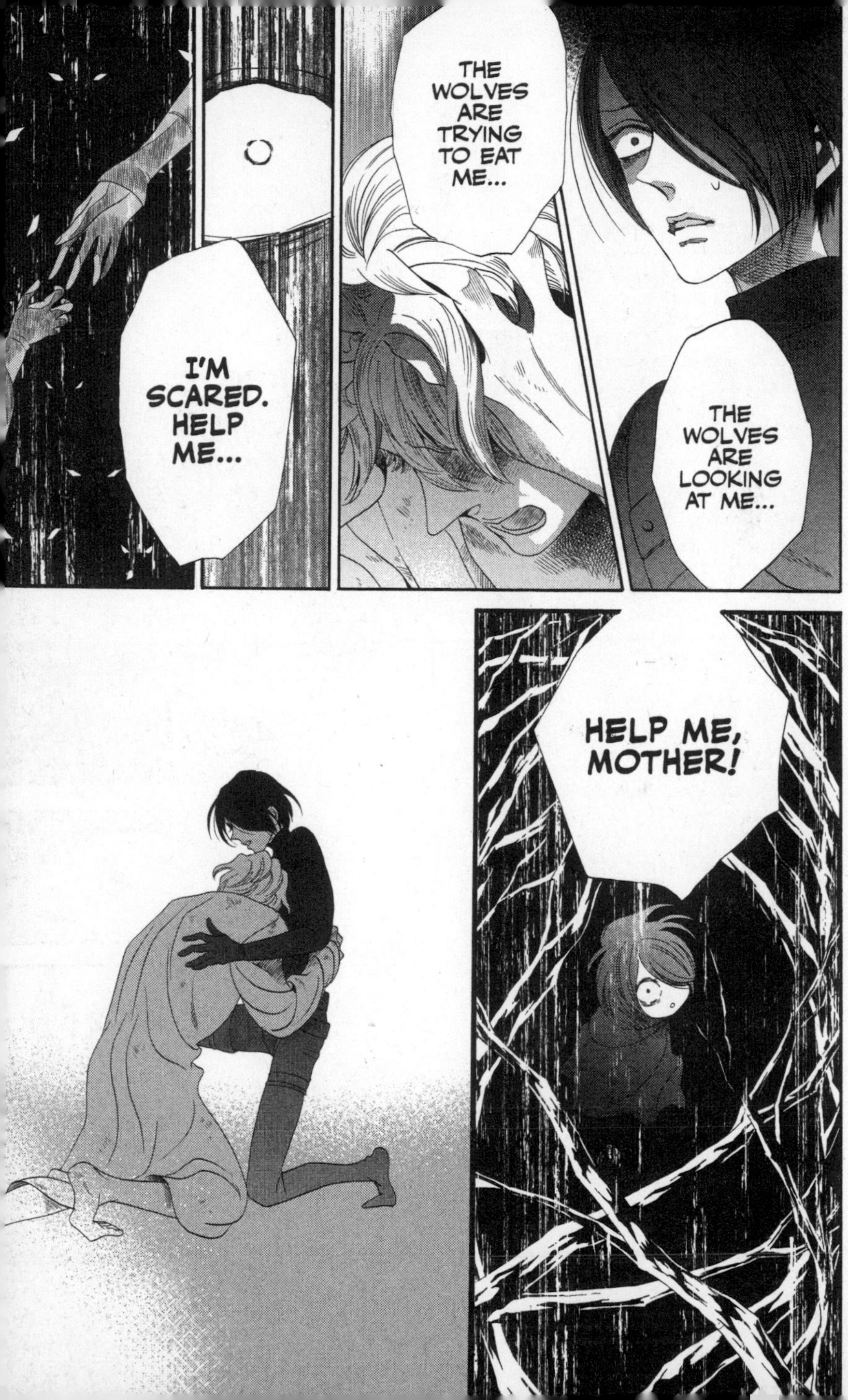
THE WOLVES ARE LOOKING AT ME...
THE WOLVES ARE TRYING TO EAT ME...
I'M SCARED. HELP ME...
HELP ME, MOTHER!

HENRY...

...

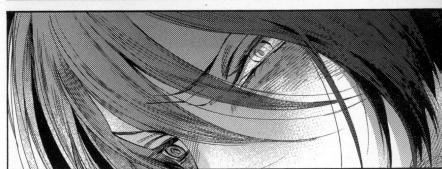

AT THE FACE OF THE MAN WHO WILL KILL YOU!

...AT ME...

HENRY...

SO THIS IS HOW... YOU RUN AWAY...

...

LOOK AT ME...

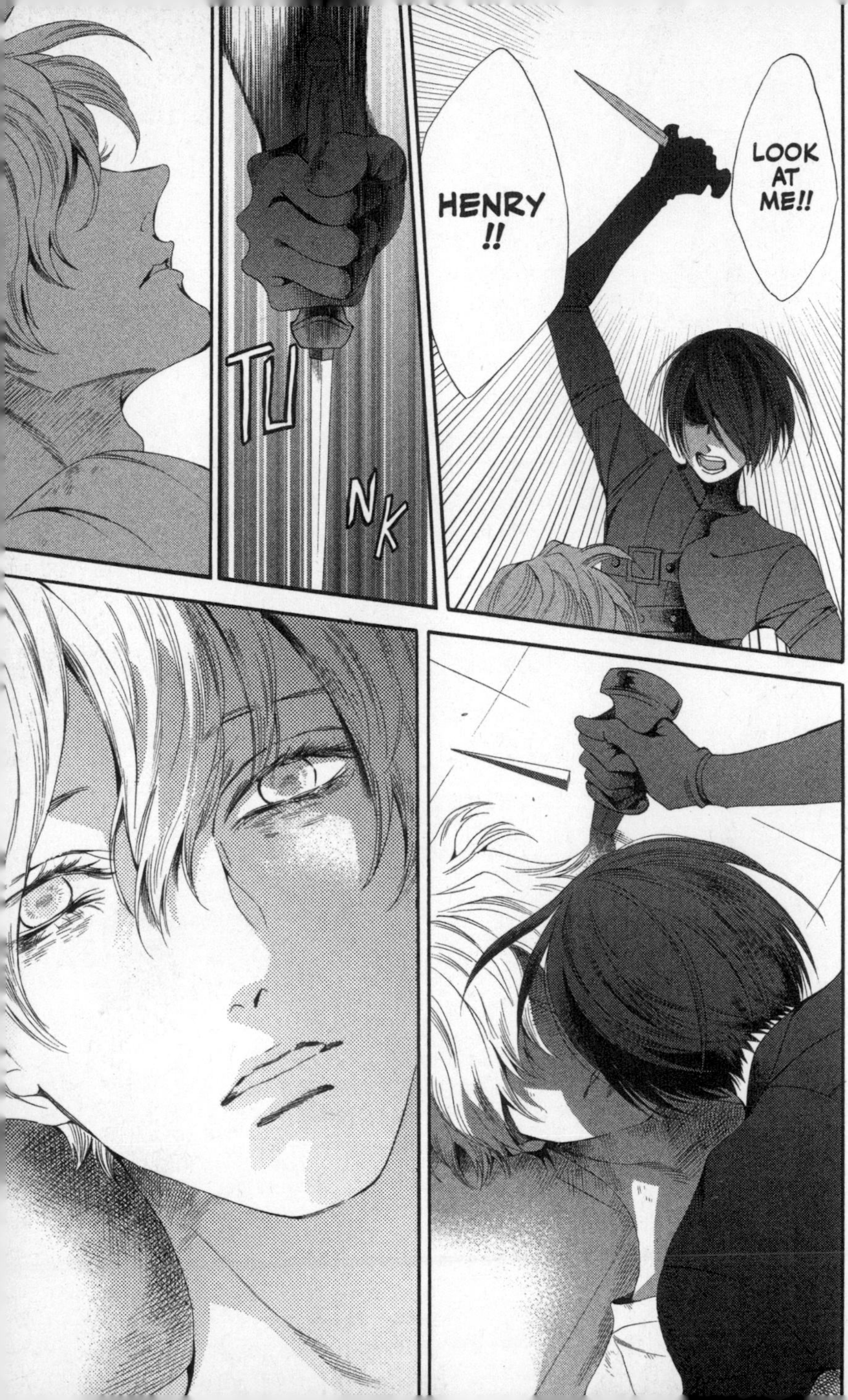
LOOK AT ME!!
HENRY !!
TUNK

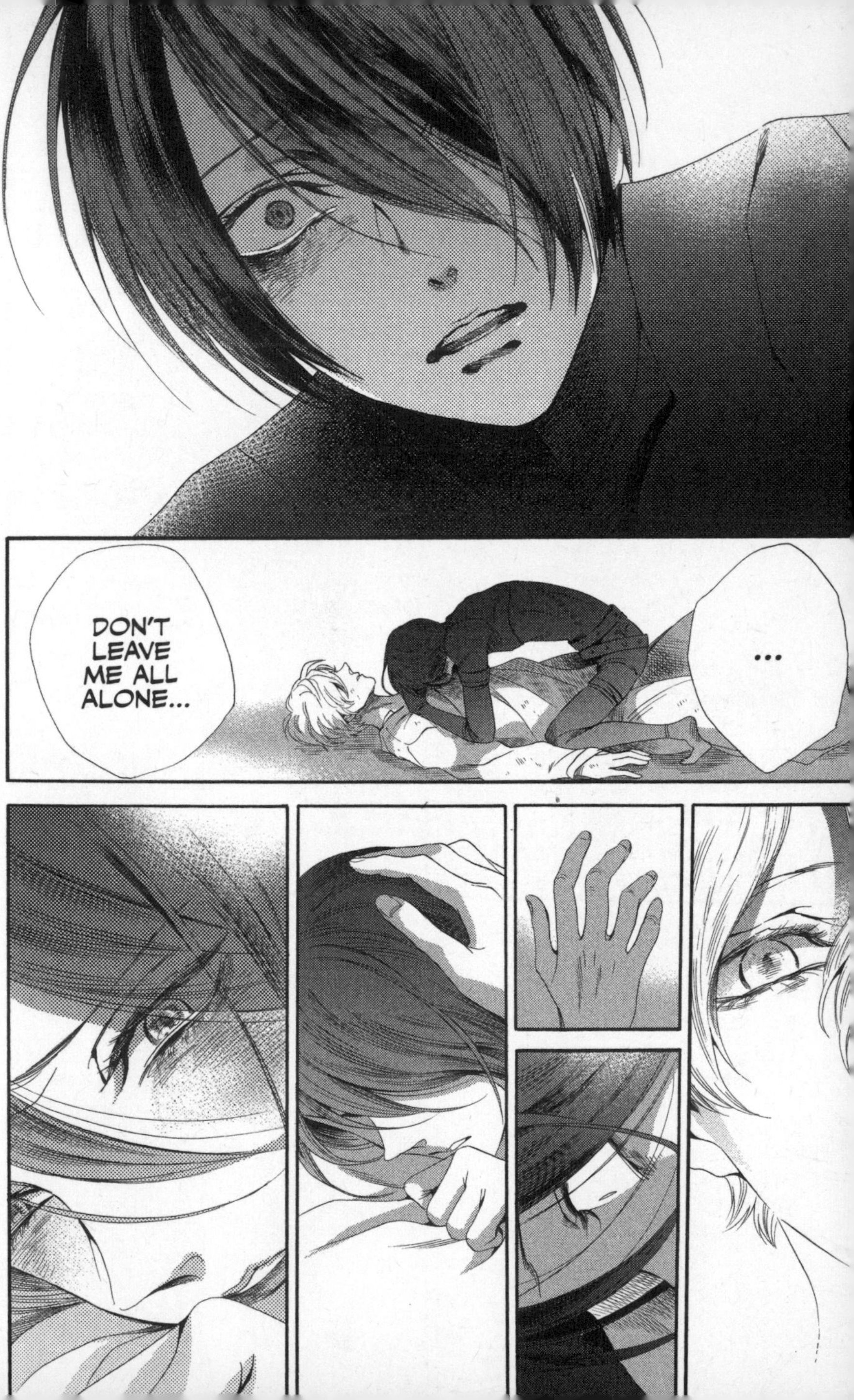
...
DON'T LEAVE ME ALL ALONE...

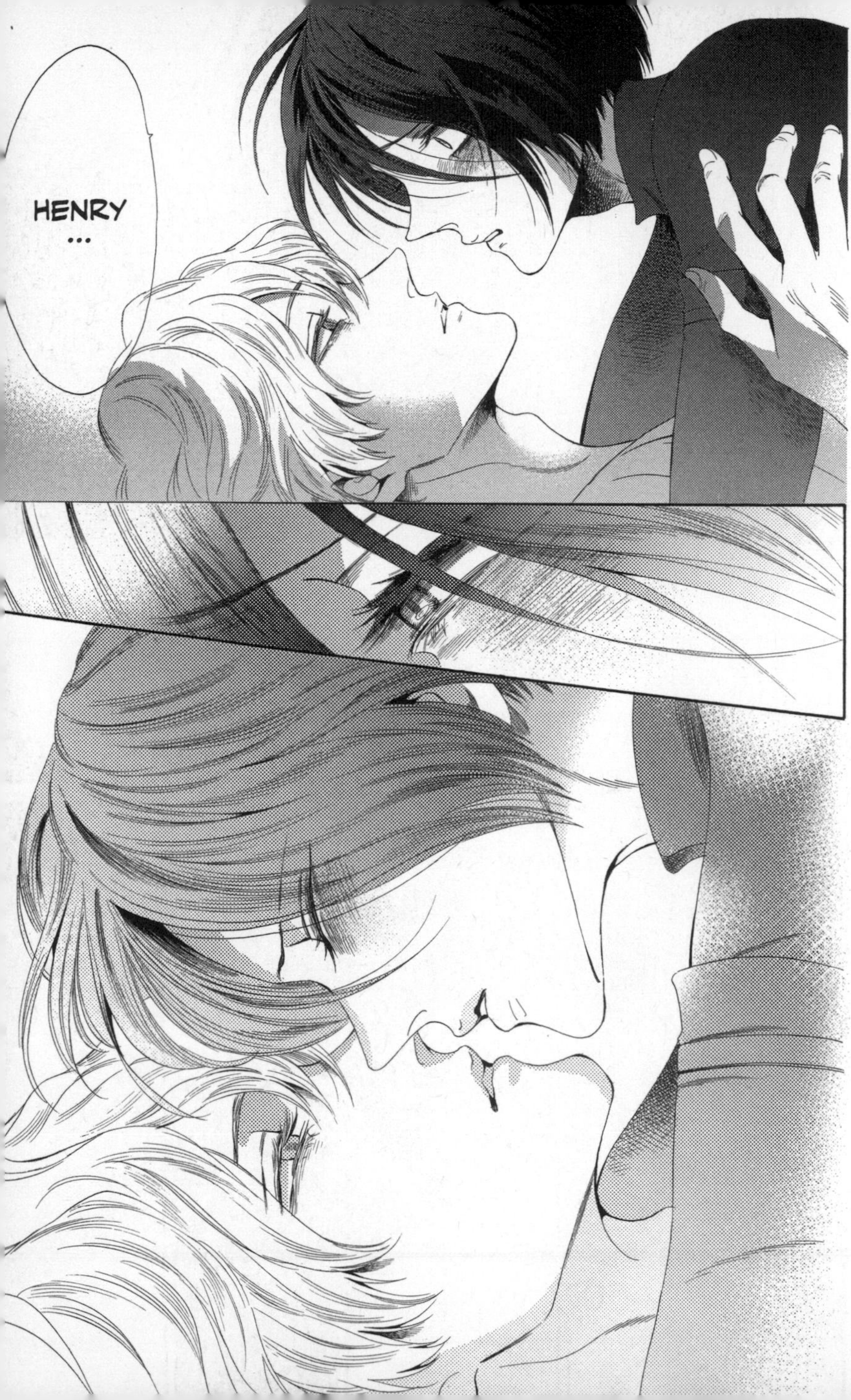
HENRY
...

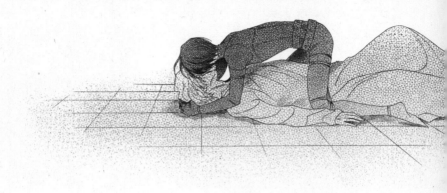

I...

...HATE
YOU...

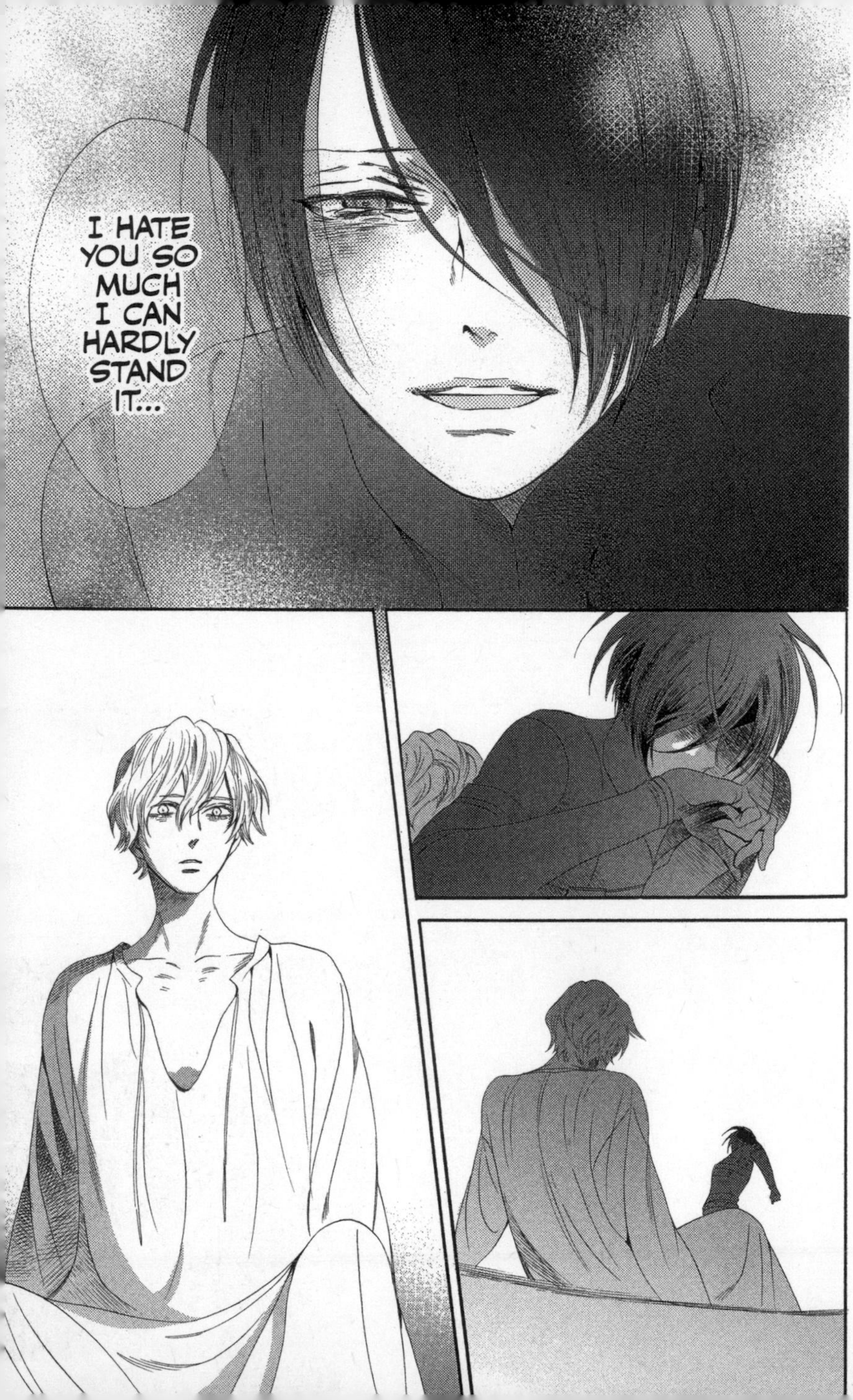
I HATE YOU SO MUCH I CAN HARDLY STAND IT...

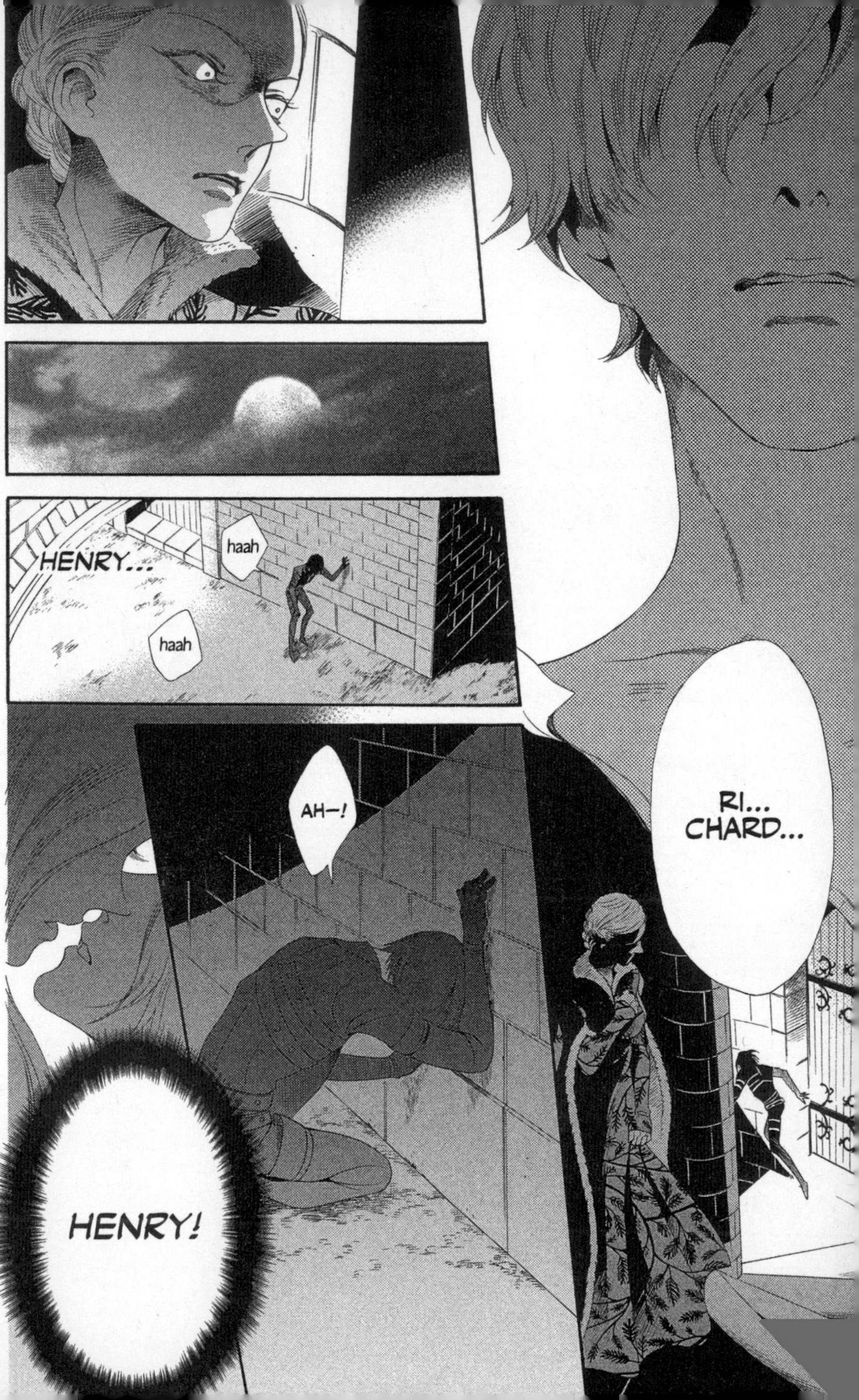
HENRY...
haah
haah
RI... CHARD...
AH—!
HENRY!

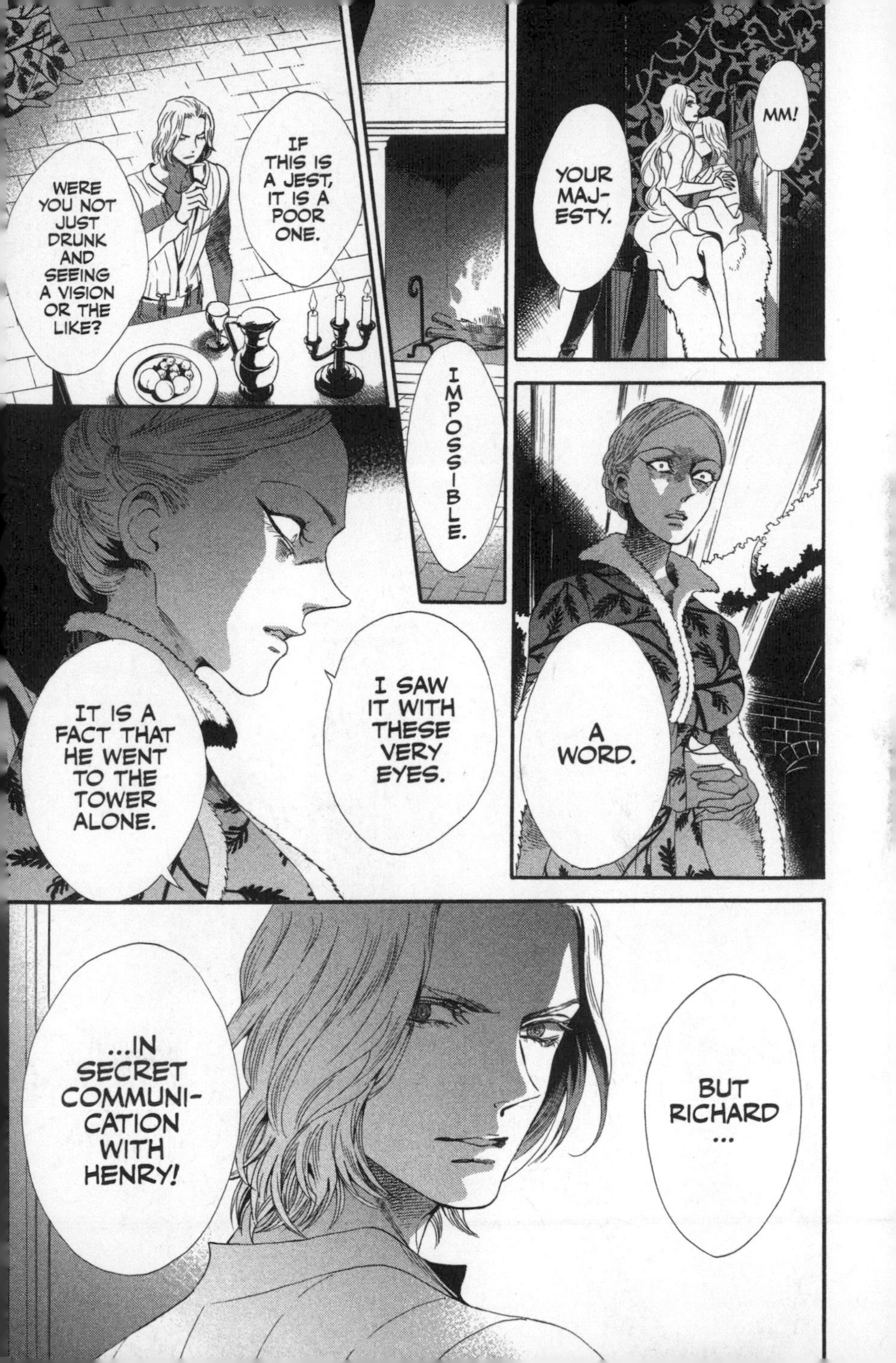
MM!
YOUR MAJESTY.
A WORD.
IMPOSSIBLE.
IF THIS IS A JEST, IT IS A POOR ONE.
WERE YOU NOT JUST DRUNK AND SEEING A VISION OR THE LIKE?
I SAW IT WITH THESE VERY EYES.
IT IS A FACT THAT HE WENT TO THE TOWER ALONE.
BUT RICHARD...
...IN SECRET COMMUNICATION WITH HENRY!

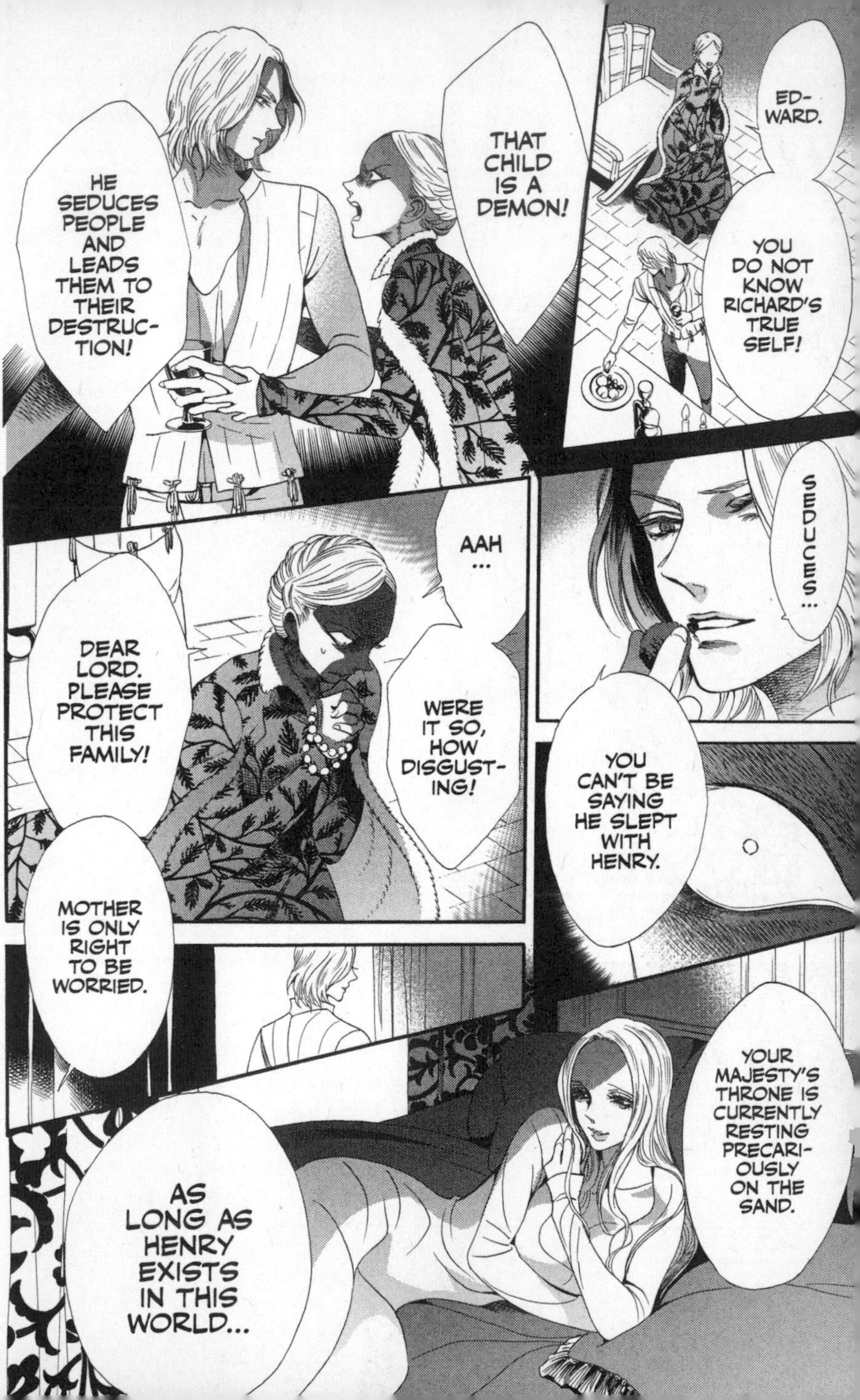
ED-WARD.
YOU DO NOT KNOW RICHARD'S TRUE SELF!
THAT CHILD IS A DEMON!
HE SEDUCES PEOPLE AND LEADS THEM TO THEIR DESTRUC-TION!
SEDUCES...
AAH...
WERE IT SO, HOW DISGUST-ING!
DEAR LORD. PLEASE PROTECT THIS FAMILY!
YOU CAN'T BE SAYING HE SLEPT WITH HENRY.
MOTHER IS ONLY RIGHT TO BE WORRIED.
YOUR MAJESTY'S THRONE IS CURRENTLY RESTING PRECARI-OUSLY ON THE SAND.
AS LONG AS HENRY EXISTS IN THIS WORLD...

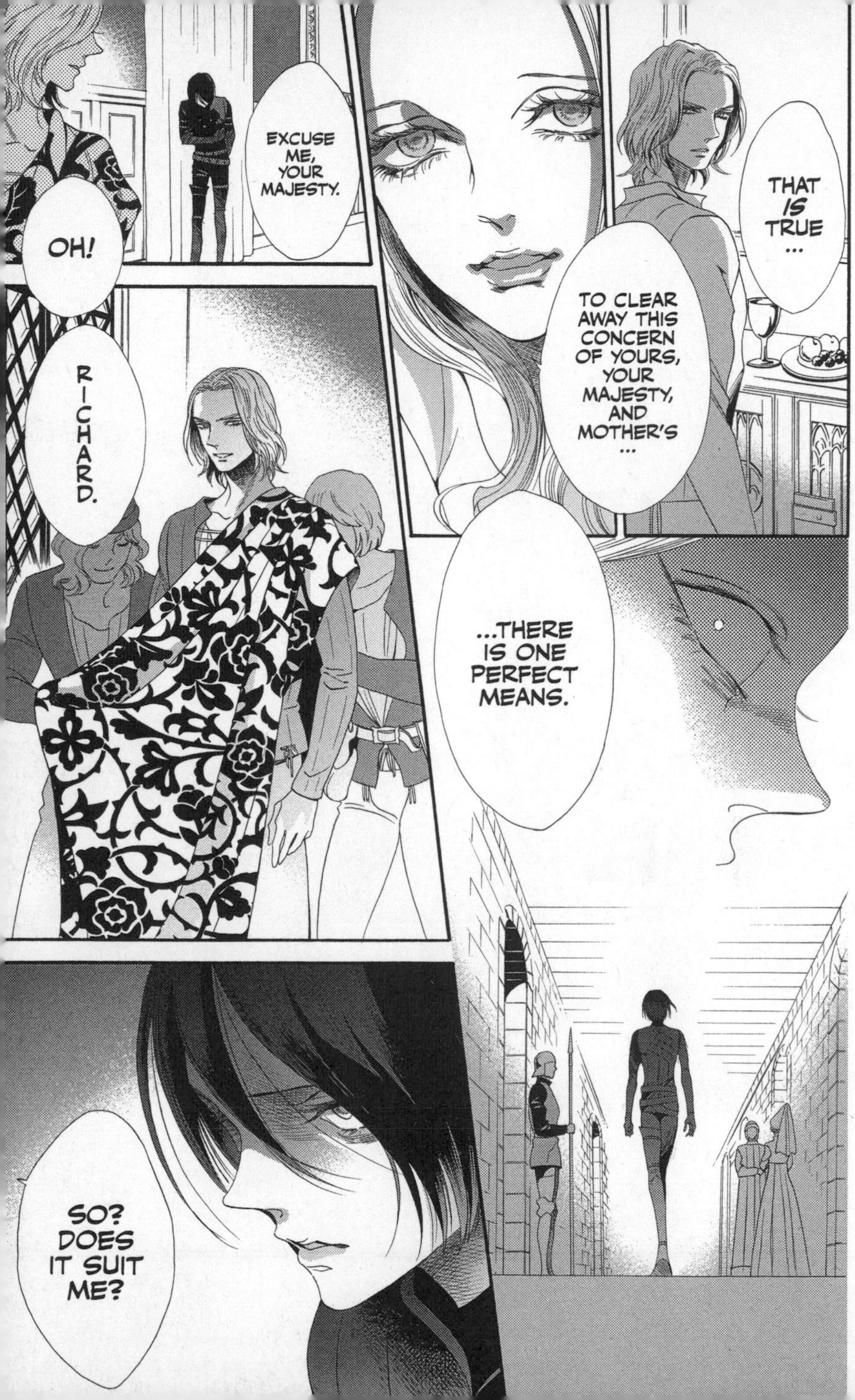
THAT *IS* TRUE ...
TO CLEAR AWAY THIS CONCERN OF YOURS, YOUR MAJESTY, AND MOTHER'S ...
...THERE IS ONE PERFECT MEANS.
EXCUSE ME, YOUR MAJESTY.
OH!
RICHARD.
SO? DOES IT SUIT ME?

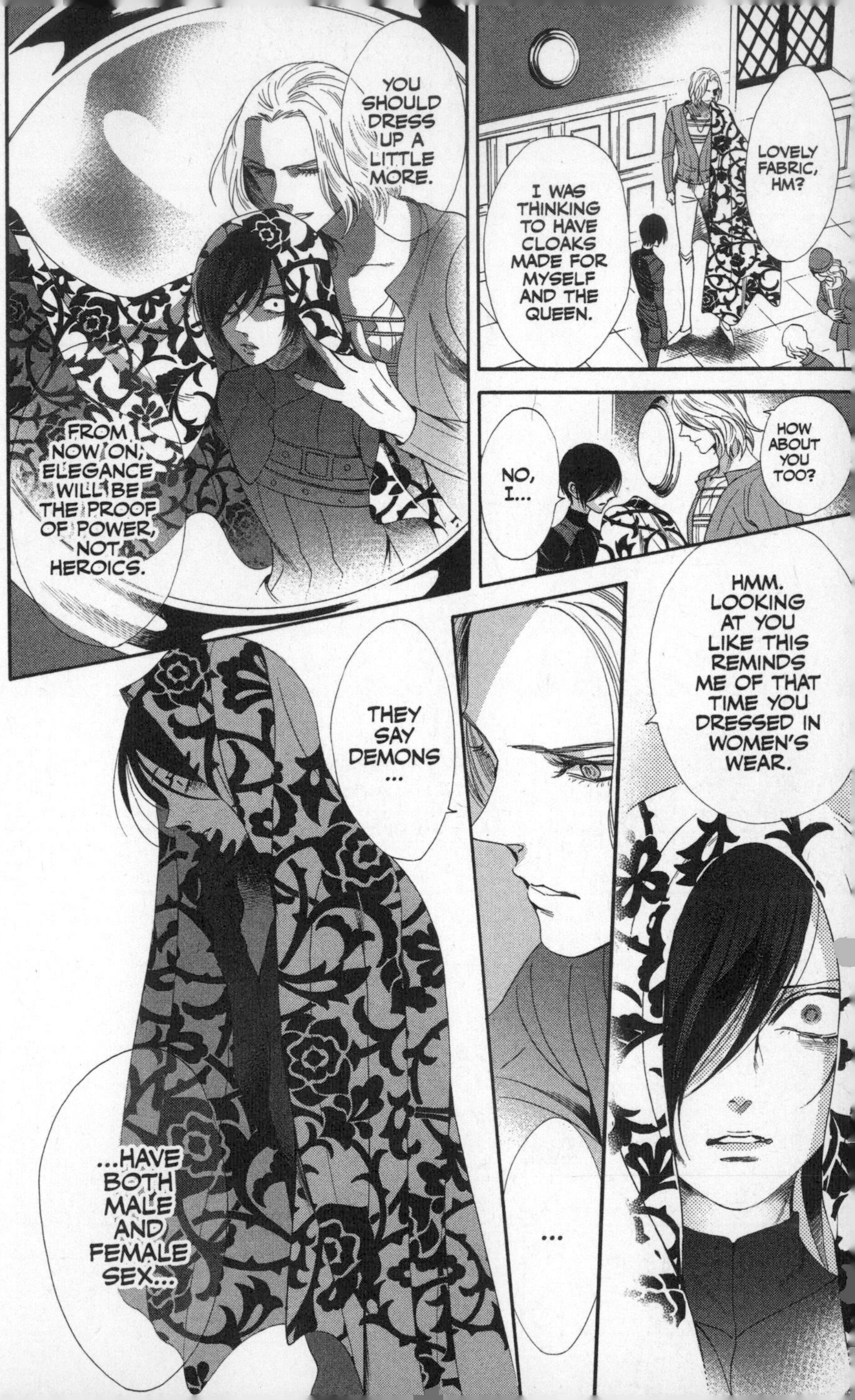
LOVELY FABRIC, HM?
I WAS THINKING TO HAVE CLOAKS MADE FOR MYSELF AND THE QUEEN.
HOW ABOUT YOU TOO?
NO, I...
YOU SHOULD DRESS UP A LITTLE MORE.
FROM NOW ON, ELEGANCE WILL BE THE PROOF OF POWER, NOT HEROICS.
HMM. LOOKING AT YOU LIKE THIS REMINDS ME OF THAT TIME YOU DRESSED IN WOMEN'S WEAR.
...
THEY SAY DEMONS ...
...HAVE BOTH MALE AND FEMALE SEX...

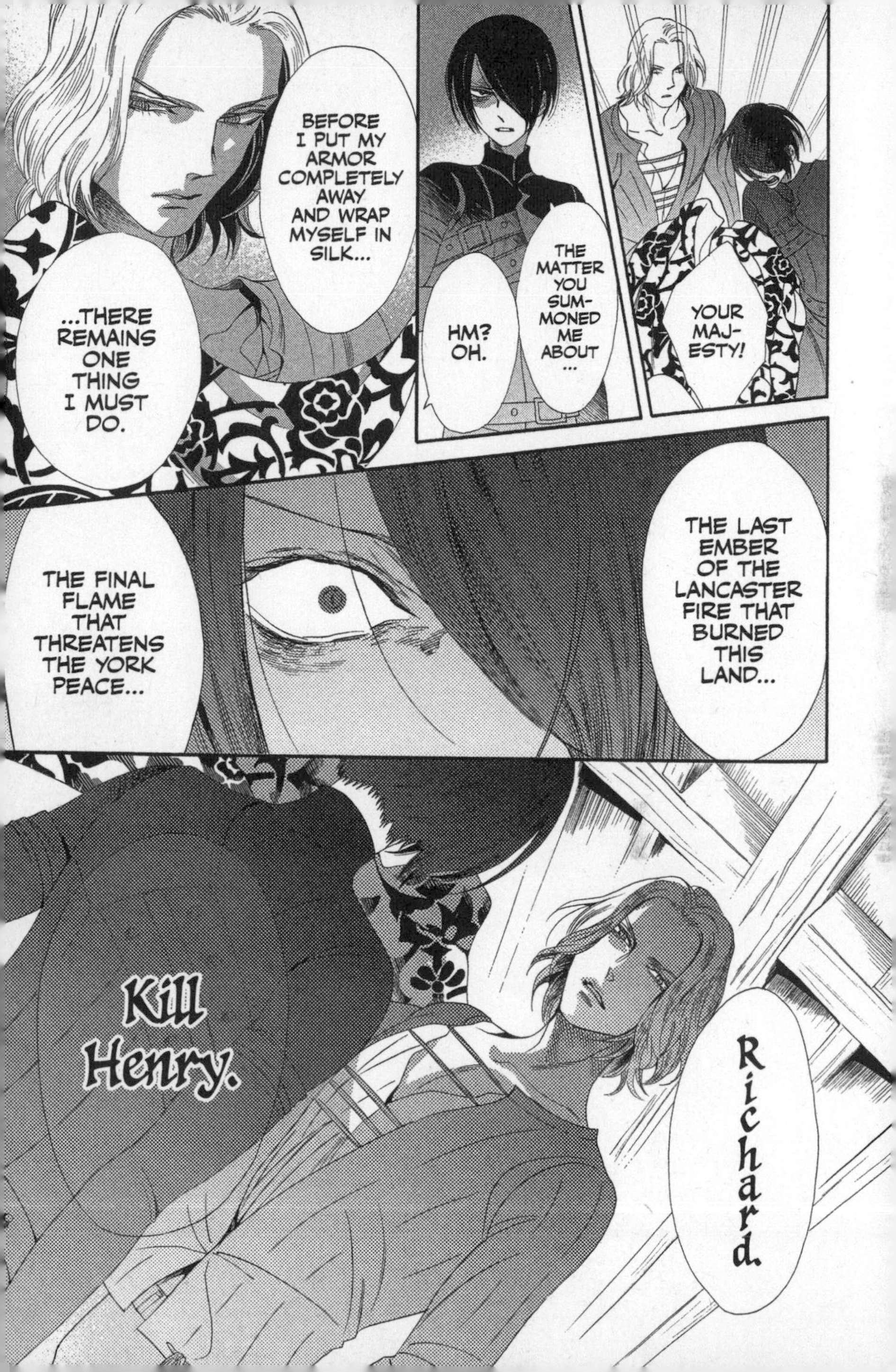
YOUR MAJESTY!
THE MATTER YOU SUMMONED ME ABOUT...
HM? OH.
BEFORE I PUT MY ARMOR COMPLETELY AWAY AND WRAP MYSELF IN SILK...
...THERE REMAINS ONE THING I MUST DO.
THE LAST EMBER OF THE LANCASTER FIRE THAT BURNED THIS LAND...
THE FINAL FLAME THAT THREATENS THE YORK PEACE...
Richard.
Kill Henry.

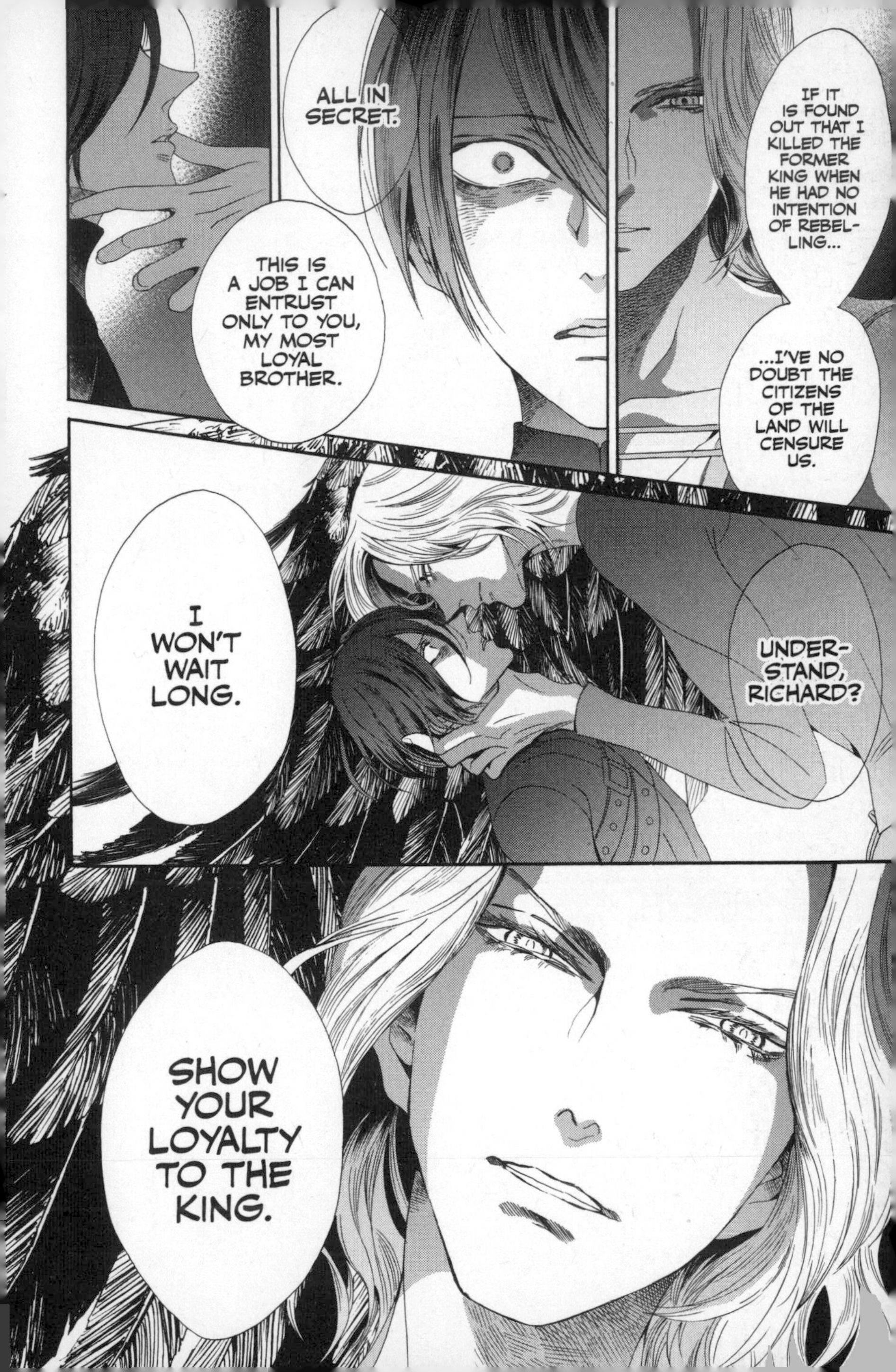
IF IT IS FOUND OUT THAT I KILLED THE FORMER KING WHEN HE HAD NO INTENTION OF REBEL-LING...
...I'VE NO DOUBT THE CITIZENS OF THE LAND WILL CENSURE US.
ALL IN SECRET.
THIS IS A JOB I CAN ENTRUST ONLY TO YOU, MY MOST LOYAL BROTHER.
UNDER-STAND, RICHARD?
I WON'T WAIT LONG.
SHOW YOUR LOYALTY TO THE KING.

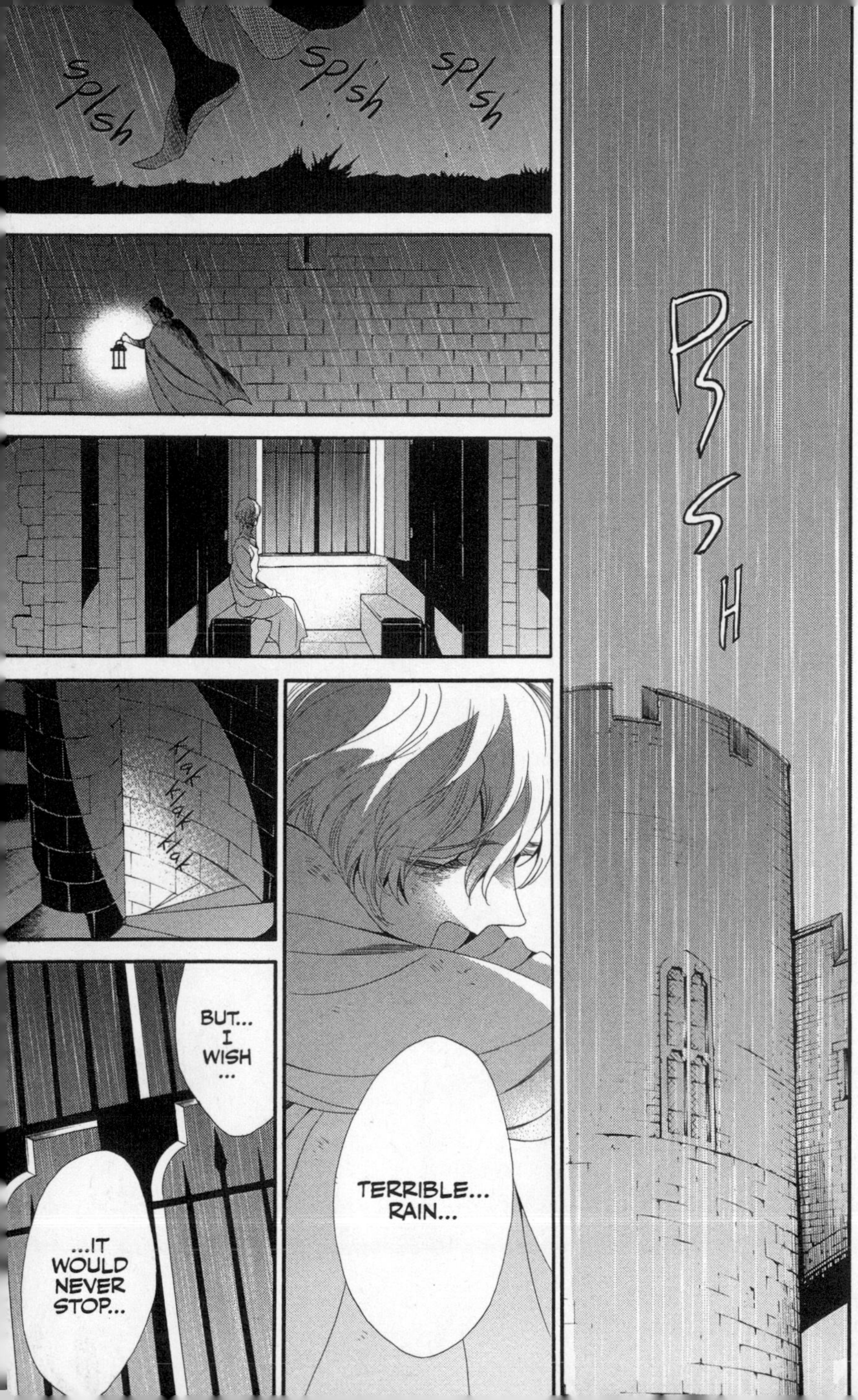
PSSH
splsh
splsh
splsh
TERRIBLE... RAIN...
klak klak klak klak
BUT... I WISH...
...IT WOULD NEVER STOP...

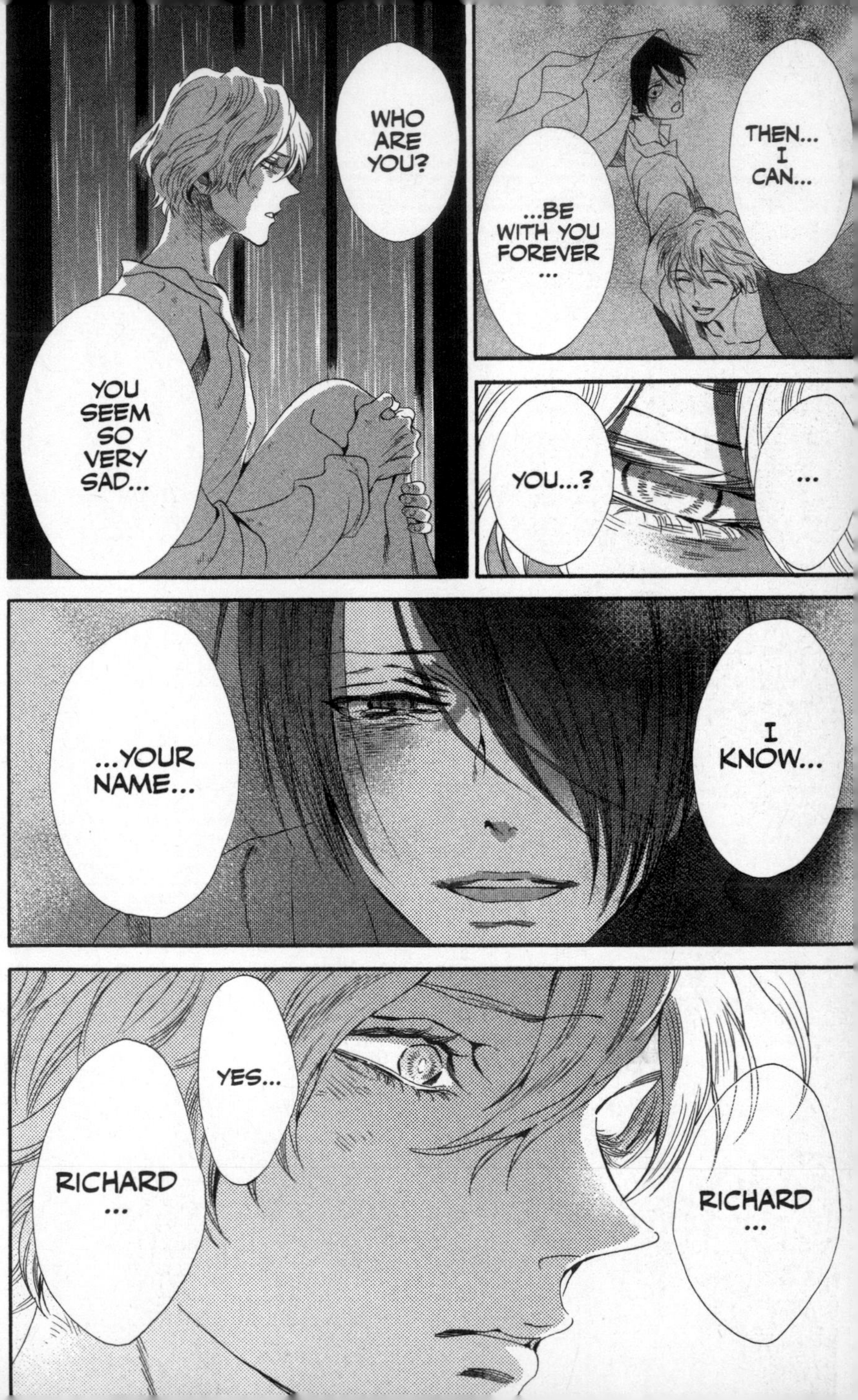
THEN... I CAN...
...BE WITH YOU FOREVER ...
...
YOU...?
WHO ARE YOU?
YOU SEEM SO VERY SAD...
I KNOW...
...YOUR NAME...
RICHARD ...
YES...
RICHARD ...

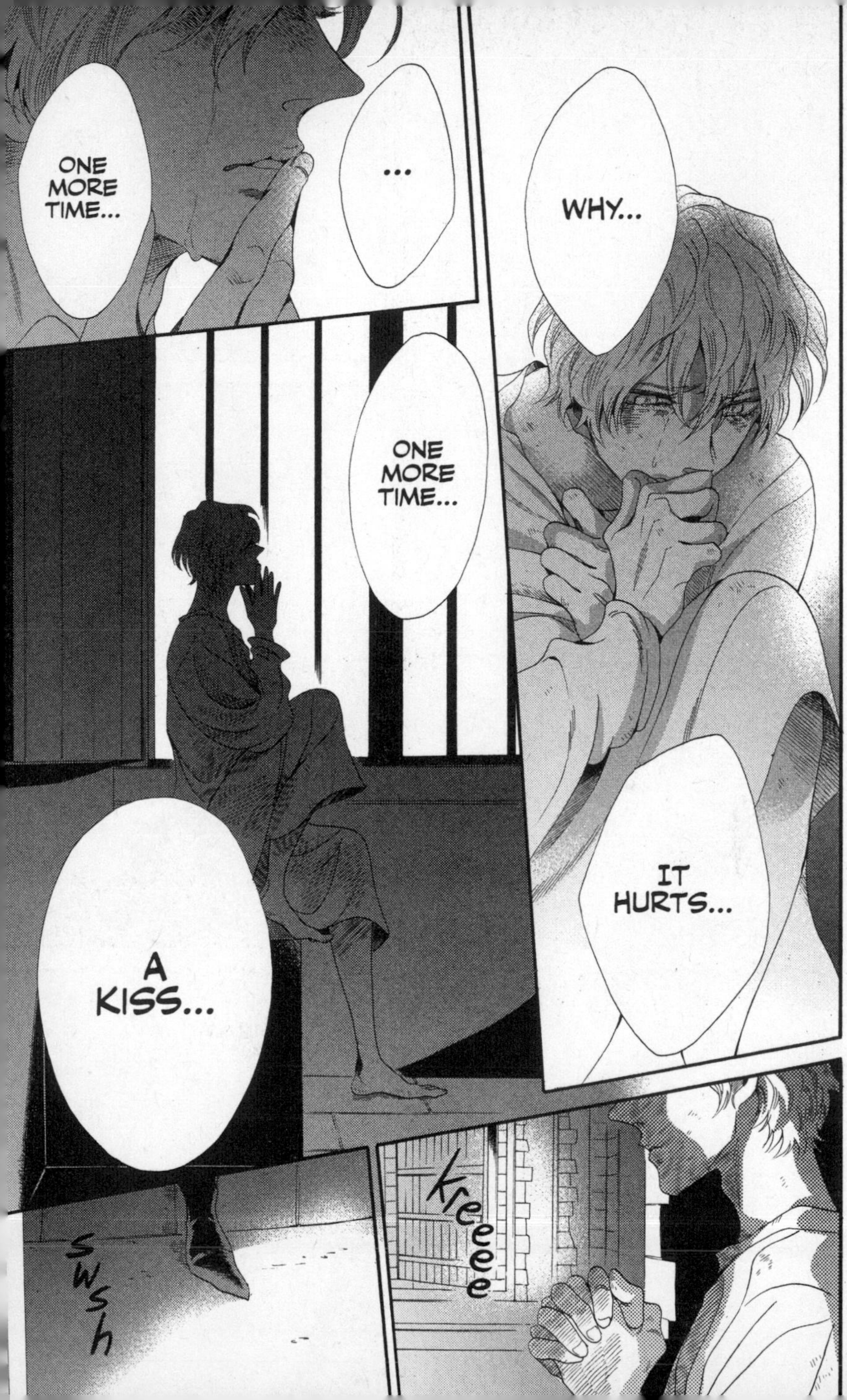
WHY...
IT HURTS...
...
ONE MORE TIME...
ONE MORE TIME...
A KISS...
kreeee
swsh

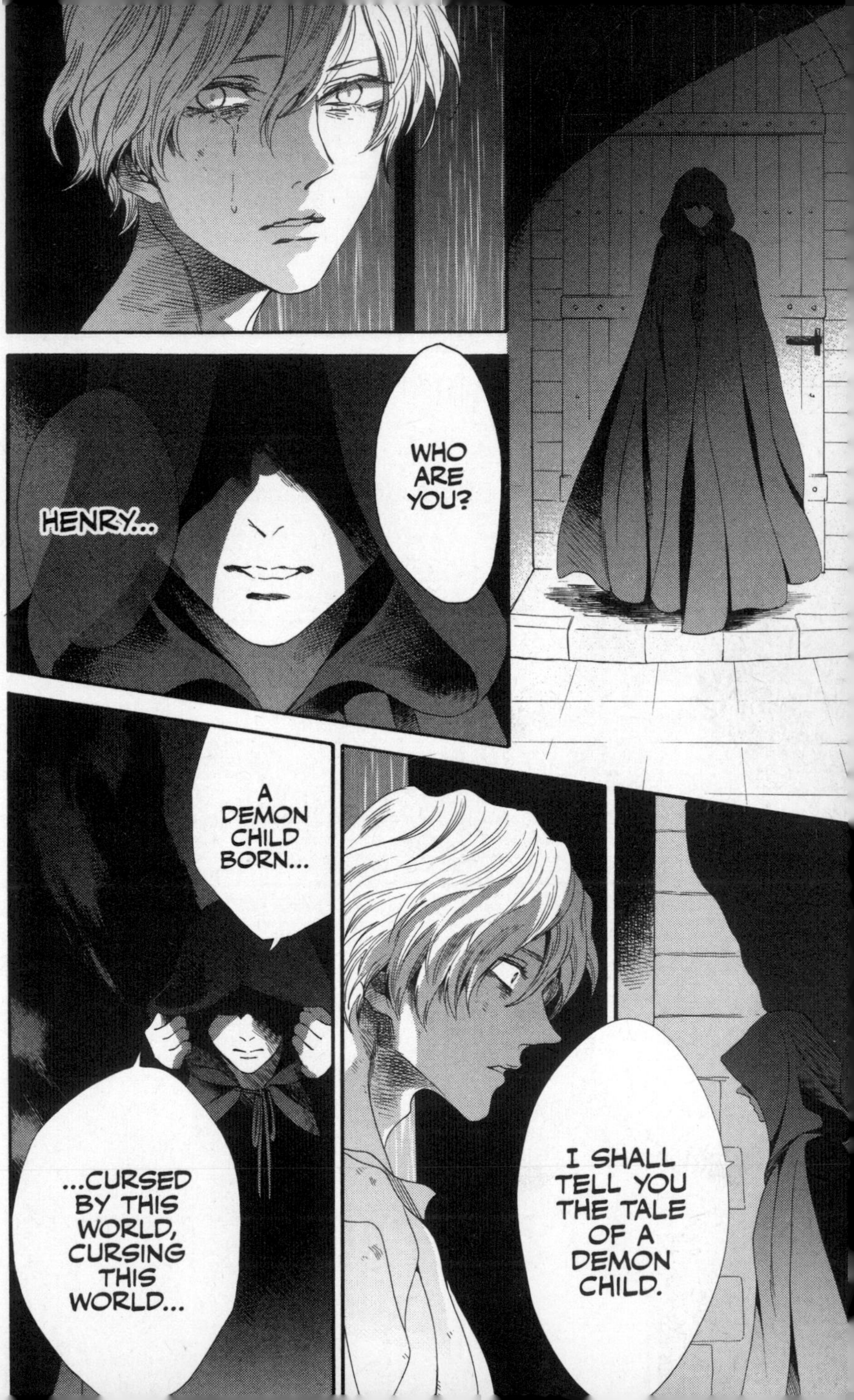
WHO ARE YOU?
HENRY...
I SHALL TELL YOU THE TALE OF A DEMON CHILD.
A DEMON CHILD BORN...
...CURSED BY THIS WORLD, CURSING THIS WORLD...

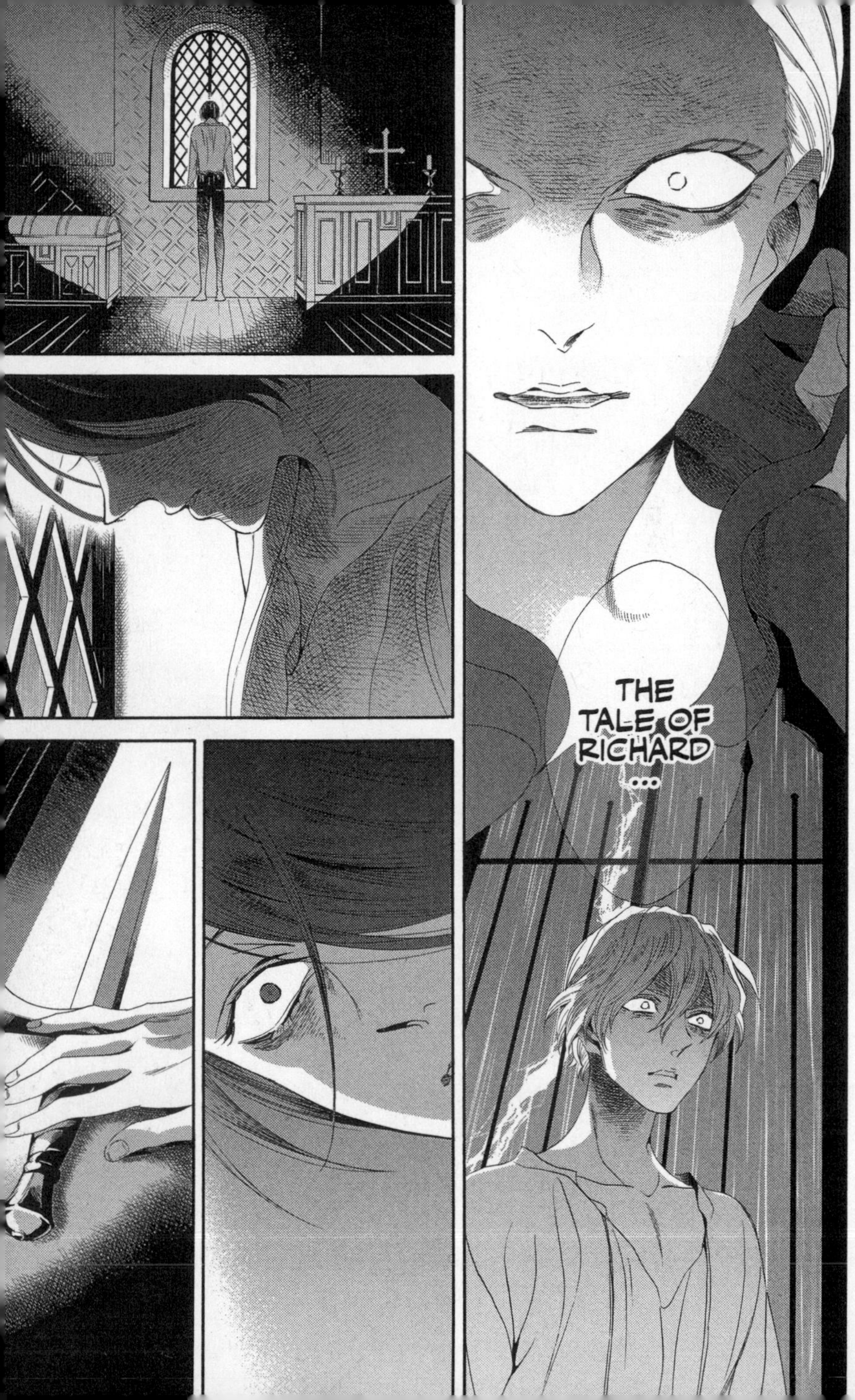
THE TALE OF RICHARD ...

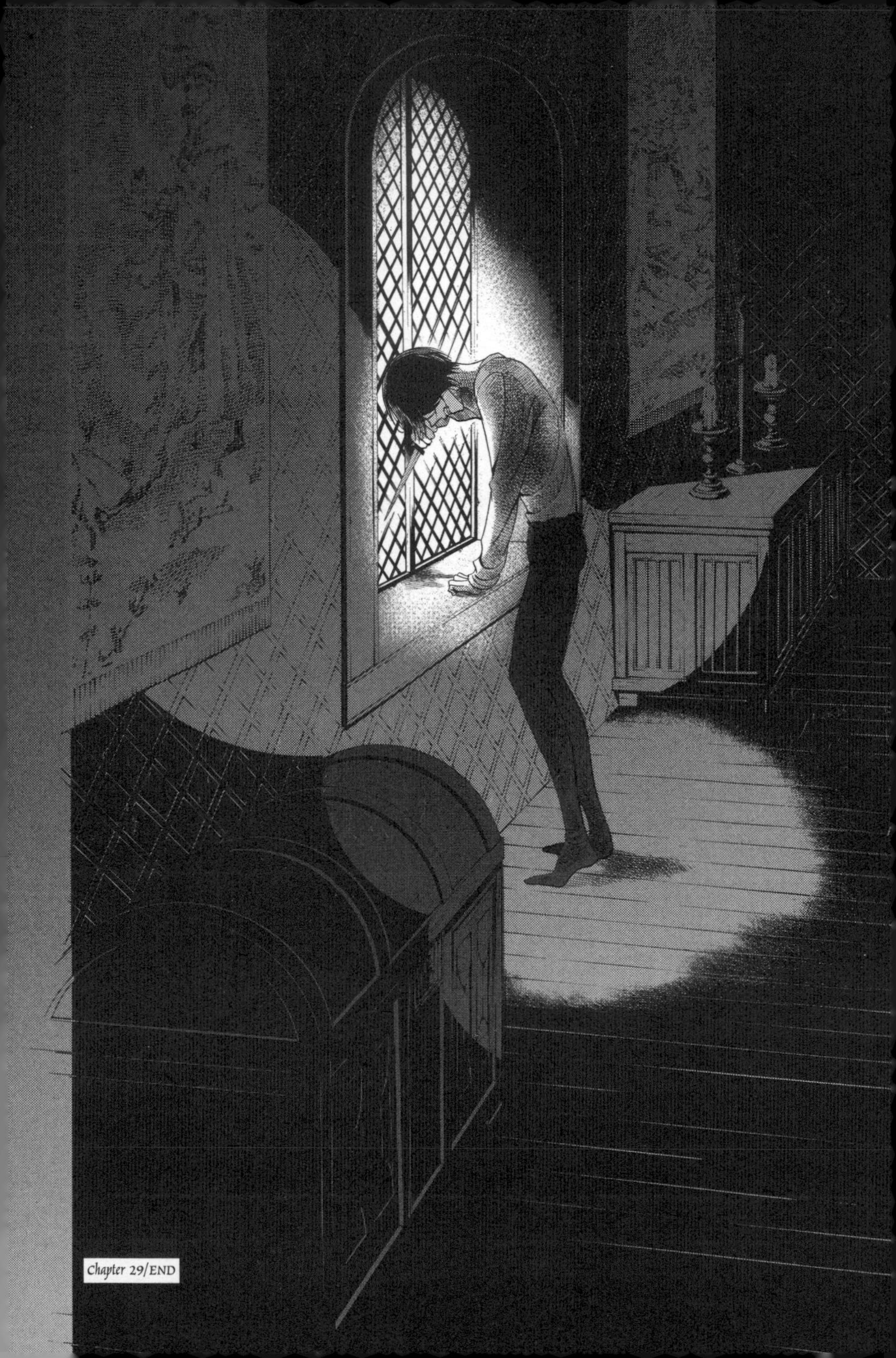
Chapter 29/END

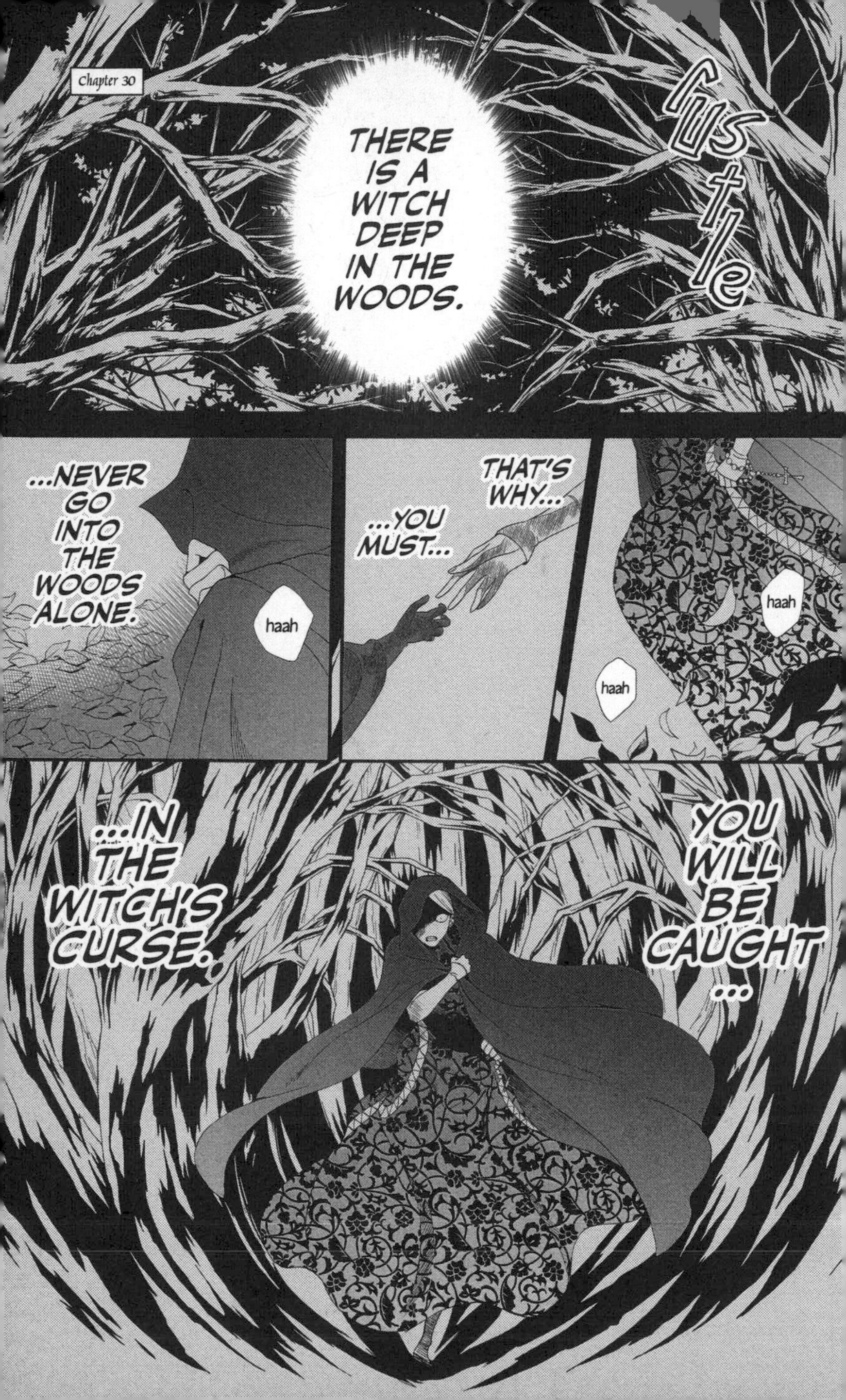
Chapter 30
Rustle
THERE IS A WITCH DEEP IN THE WOODS.
haah
haah
THAT'S WHY...
...YOU MUST...
...NEVER GO INTO THE WOODS ALONE.
haah
YOU WILL BE CAUGHT...
...IN THE WITCH'S CURSE.

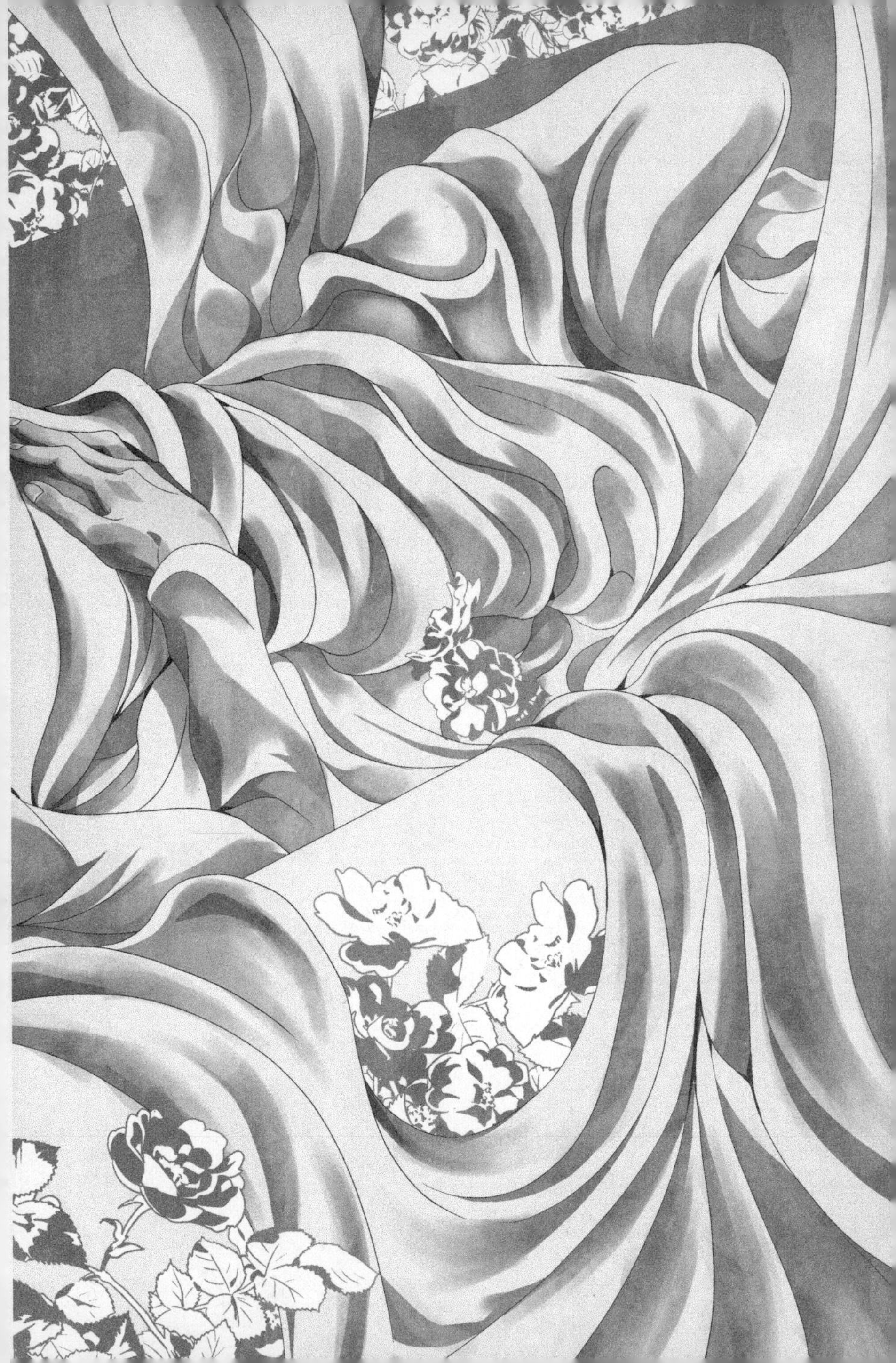

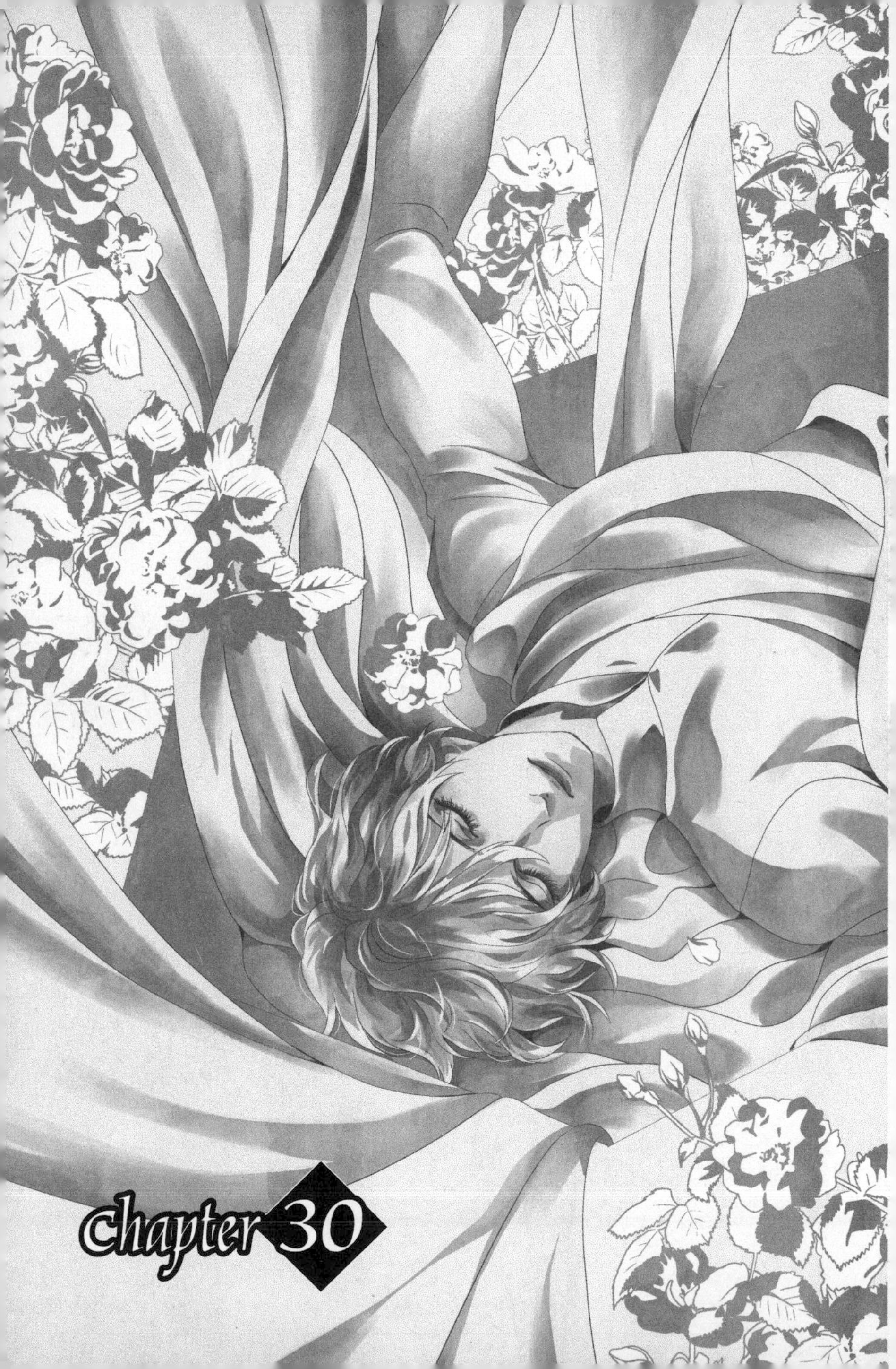
Chapter 30

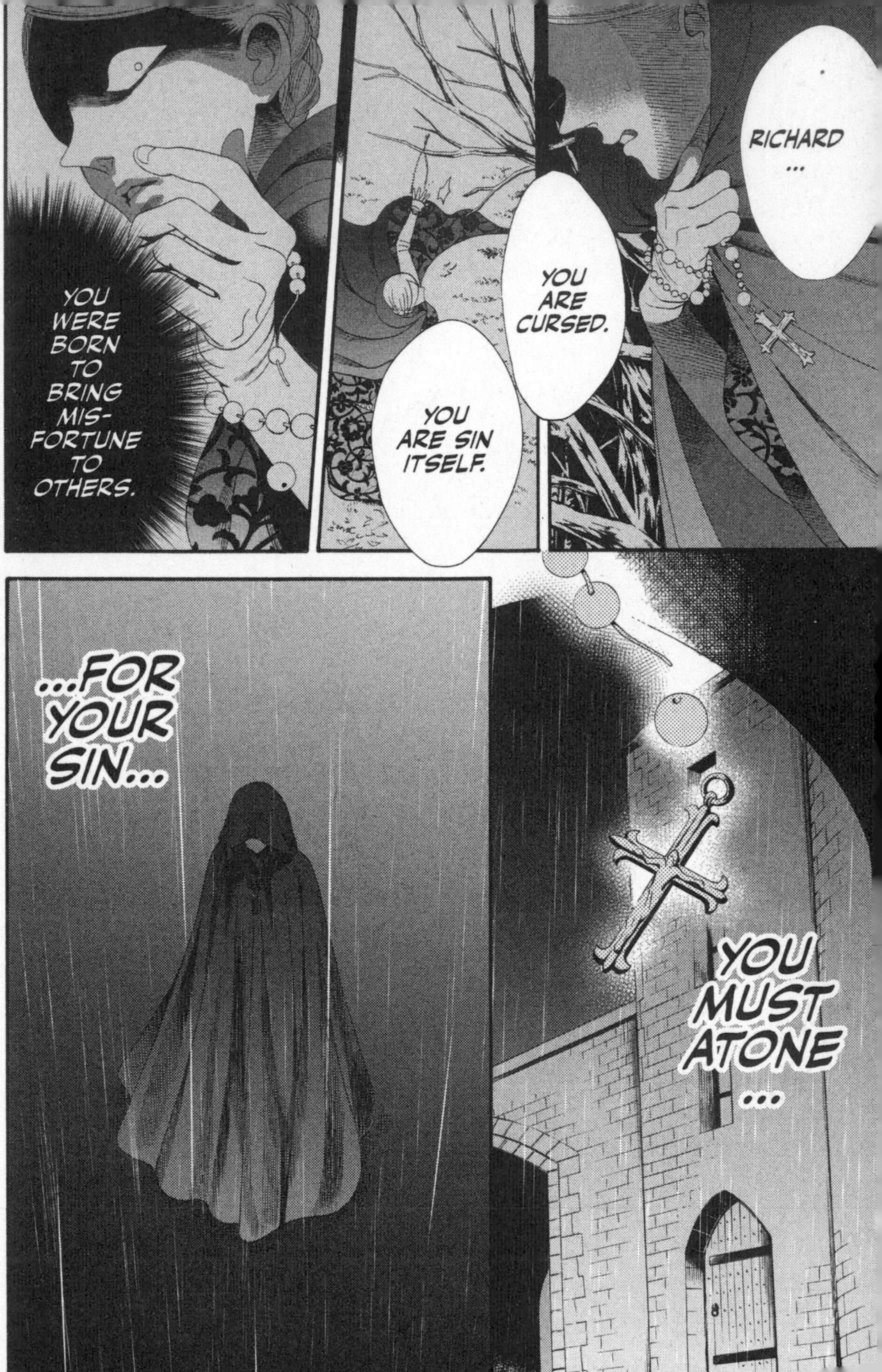
RICHARD ...
YOU ARE CURSED.
YOU ARE SIN ITSELF.
YOU WERE BORN TO BRING MIS-FORTUNE TO OTHERS.
YOU MUST ATONE ...
...FOR YOUR SIN...

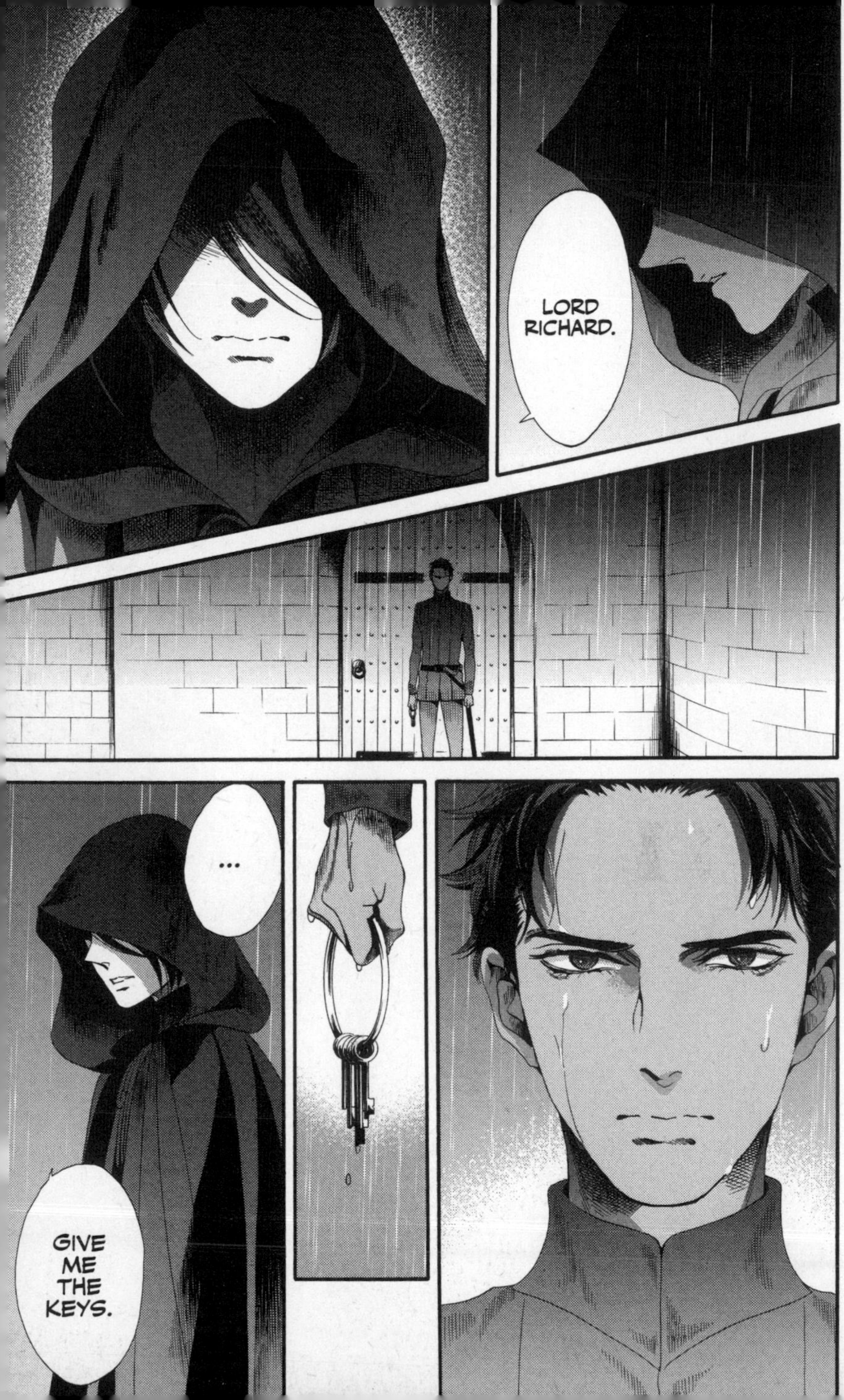
LORD RICHARD.
...
GIVE ME THE KEYS.

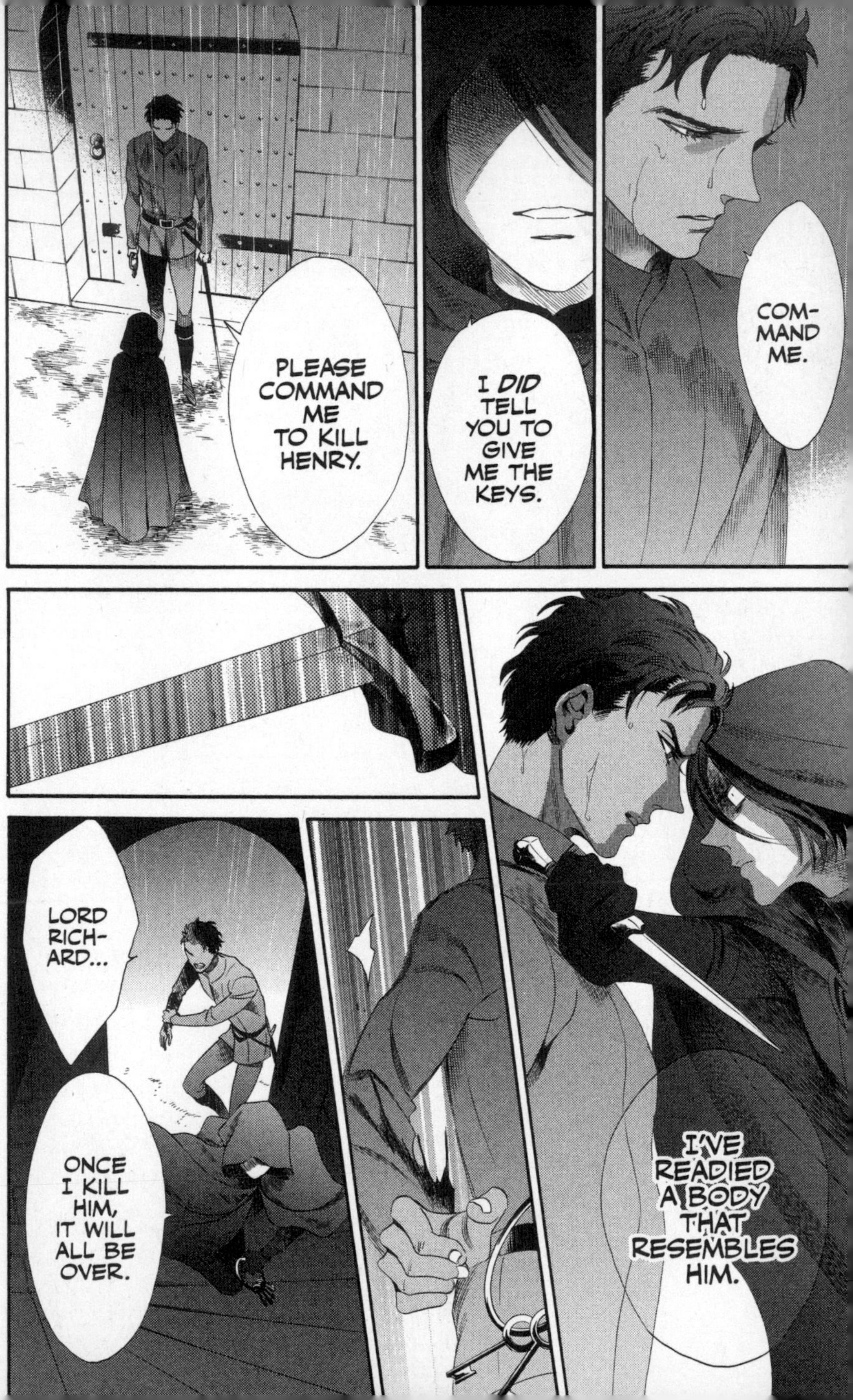
COM-MAND ME.
I *DID* TELL YOU TO GIVE ME THE KEYS.
PLEASE COMMAND ME TO KILL HENRY.
I'VE READIED A BODY THAT RESEMBLES HIM.
LORD RICHARD...
ONCE I KILL HIM, IT WILL ALL BE OVER.

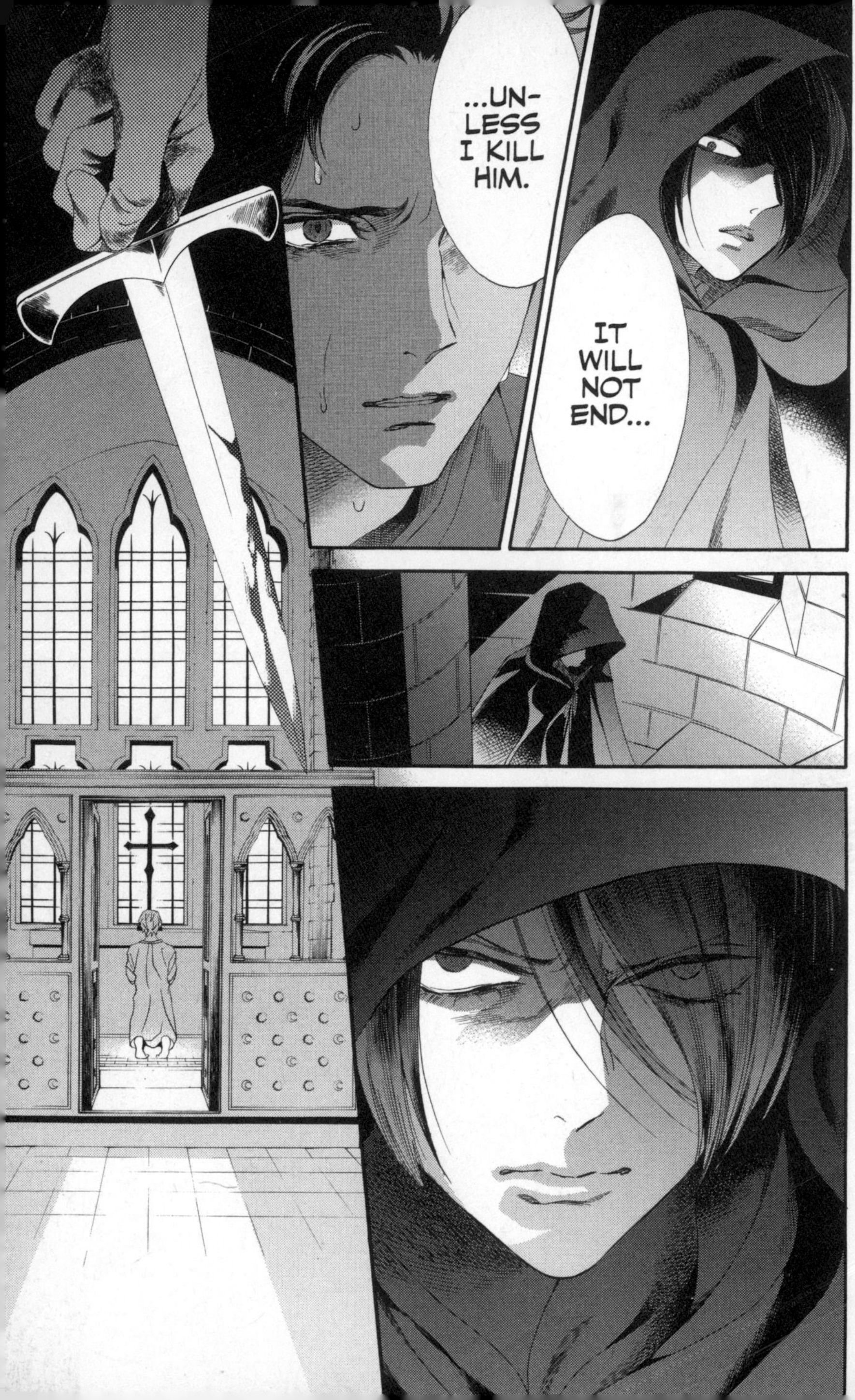
IT WILL NOT END...
...UNLESS I KILL HIM.

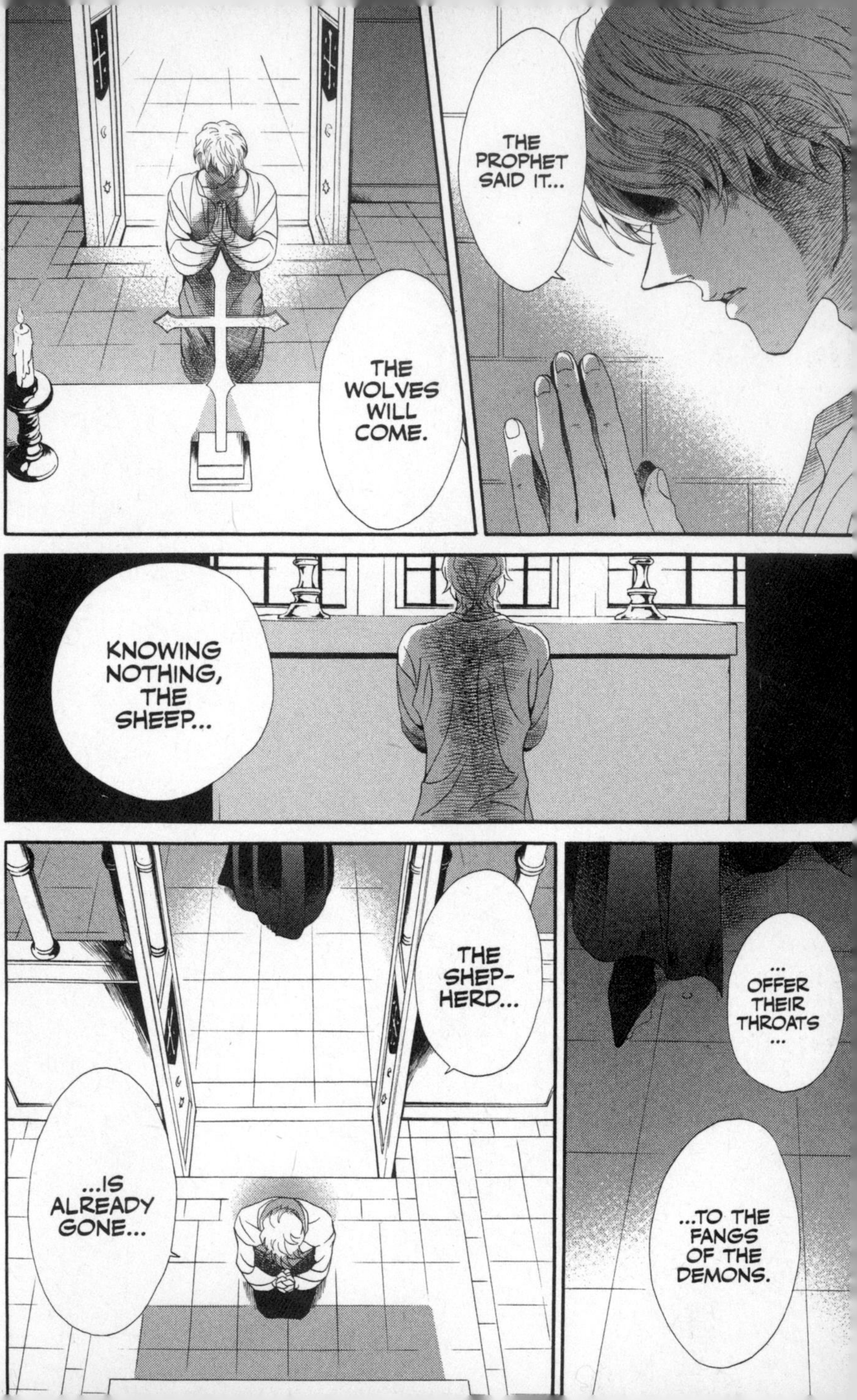
THE PROPHET SAID IT...
THE WOLVES WILL COME.
KNOWING NOTHING, THE SHEEP...
...OFFER THEIR THROATS...
...TO THE FANGS OF THE DEMONS.
THE SHEP-HERD...
...IS ALREADY GONE...

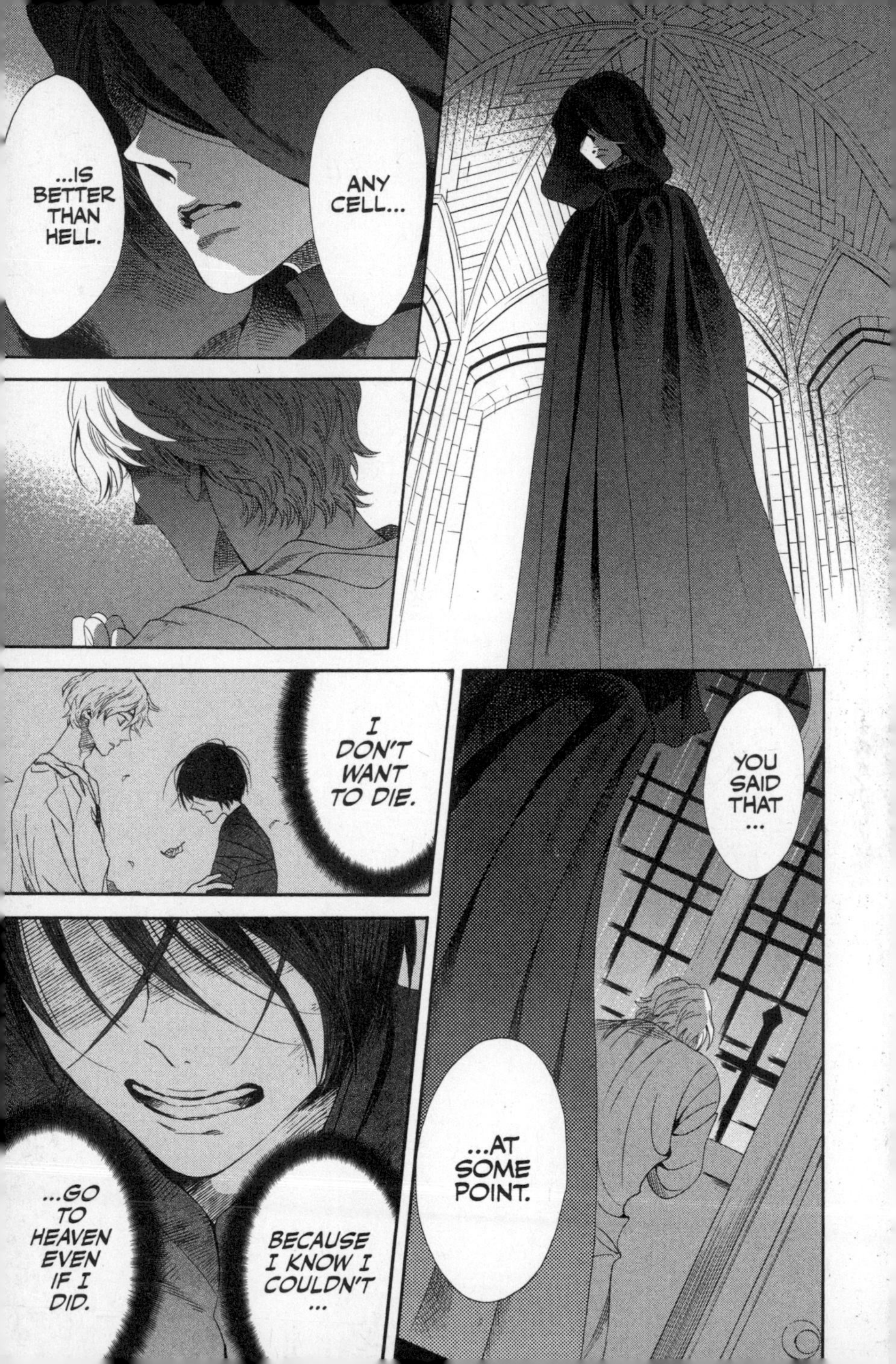
ANY CELL...
...IS BETTER THAN HELL.
YOU SAID THAT...
...AT SOME POINT.
I DON'T WANT TO DIE.
BECAUSE I KNOW I COULDN'T...
...GO TO HEAVEN EVEN IF I DID.

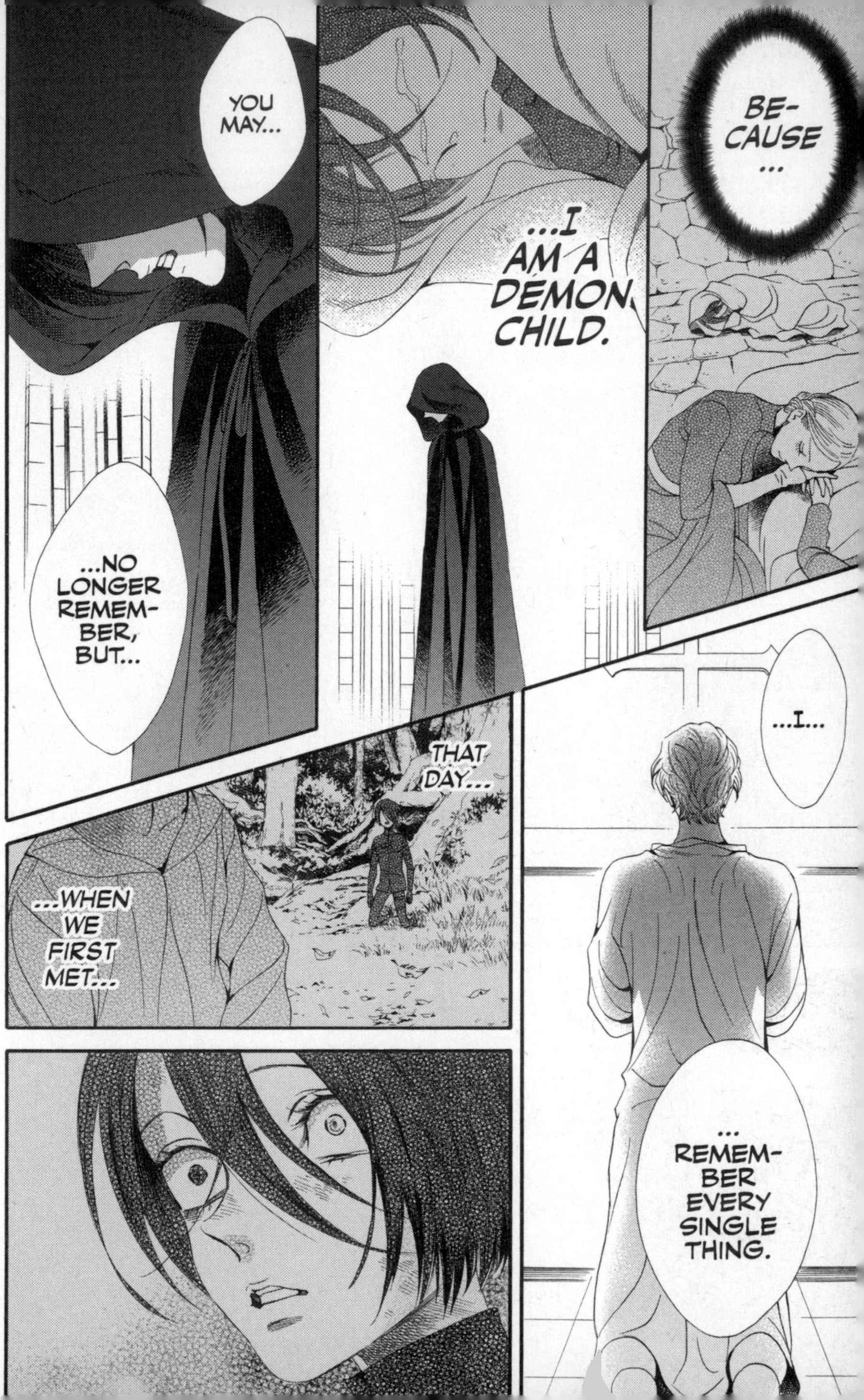
BE-CAUSE...
...I AM A DEMON CHILD.
YOU MAY...
...NO LONGER REMEMBER, BUT...
...I...
...REMEMBER EVERY SINGLE THING.
THAT DAY...
...WHEN WE FIRST MET...

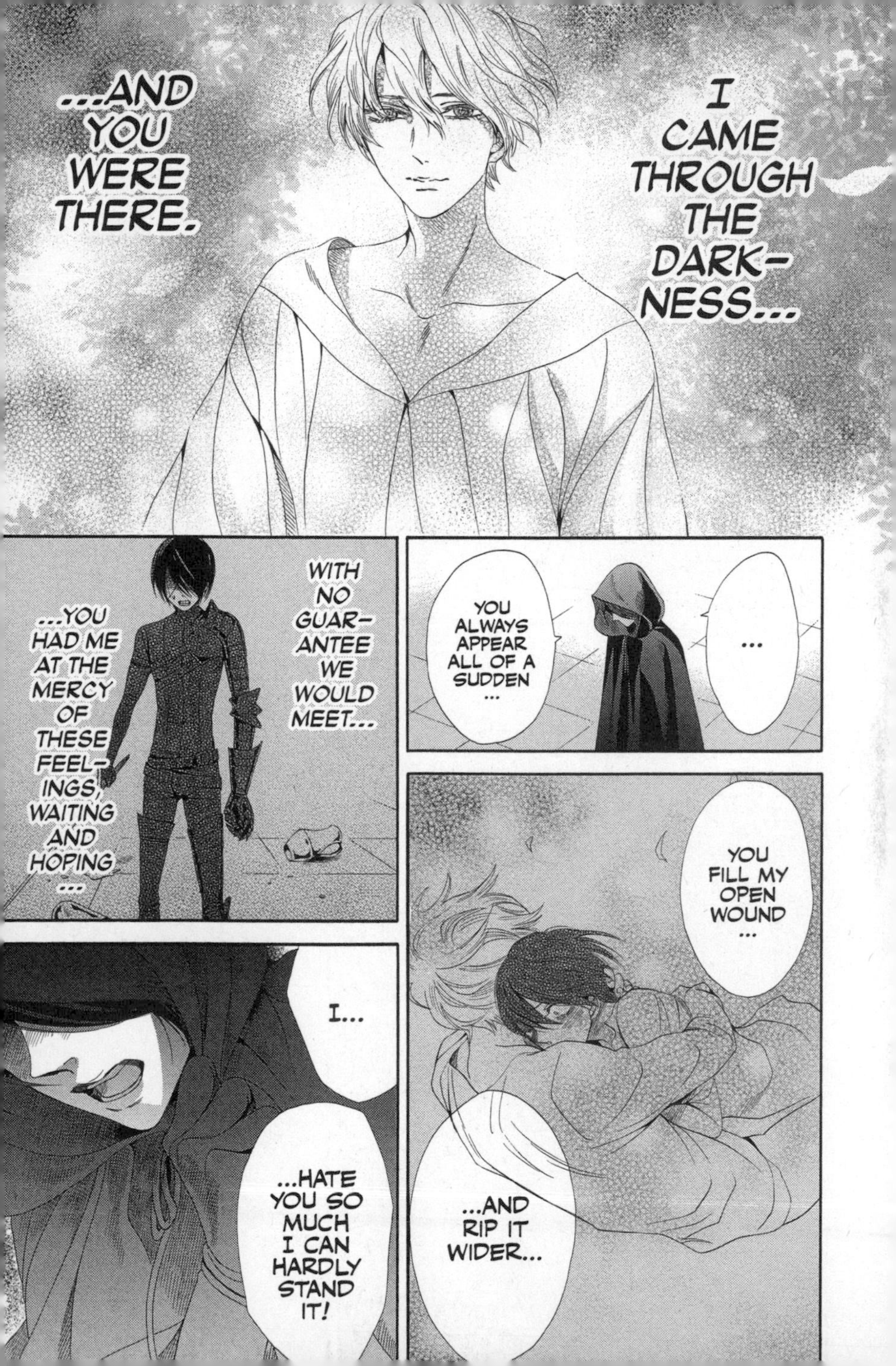
I CAME THROUGH THE DARKNESS...
...AND YOU WERE THERE.
...
YOU ALWAYS APPEAR ALL OF A SUDDEN ...
WITH NO GUARANTEE WE WOULD MEET...
...YOU HAD ME AT THE MERCY OF THESE FEELINGS, WAITING AND HOPING ...
YOU FILL MY OPEN WOUND ...
...AND RIP IT WIDER...
I...
...HATE YOU SO MUCH I CAN HARDLY STAND IT!

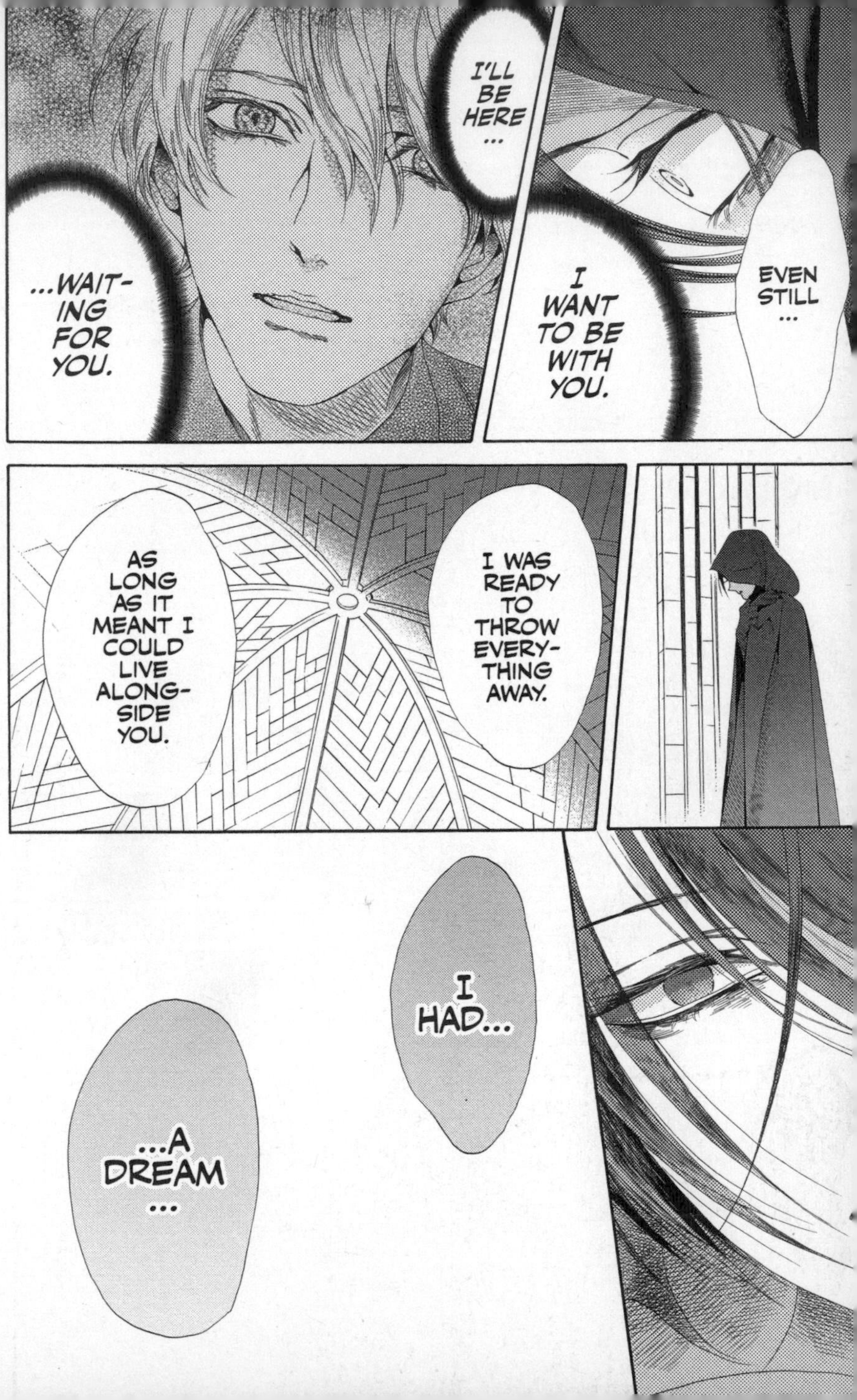
EVEN STILL...
I WANT TO BE WITH YOU.
I'LL BE HERE...
...WAITING FOR YOU.
I WAS READY TO THROW EVERYTHING AWAY.
AS LONG AS IT MEANT I COULD LIVE ALONGSIDE YOU.
I HAD...
...A DREAM...

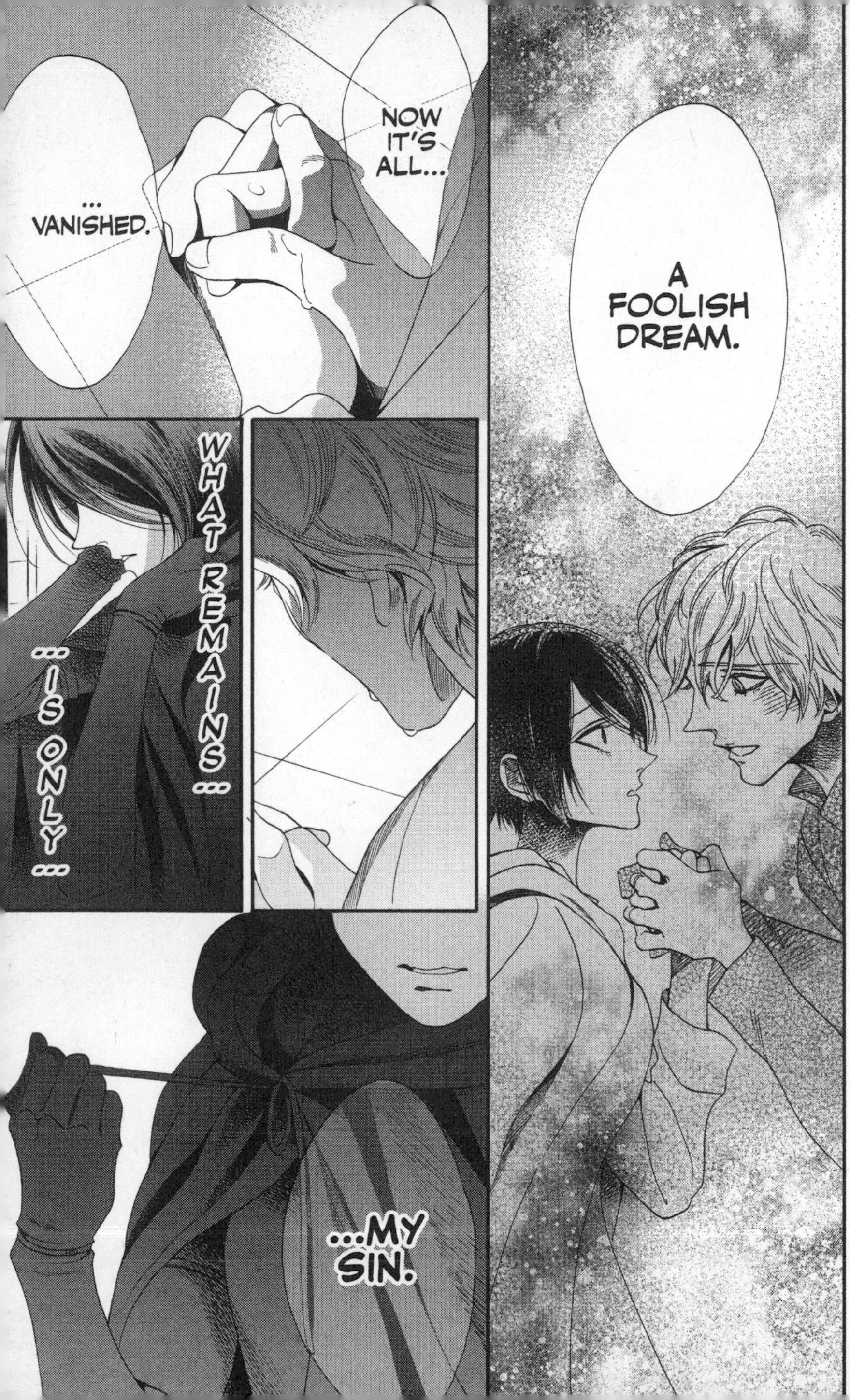
A FOOLISH DREAM.
NOW IT'S ALL...
... VANISHED.
WHAT REMAINS...
...IS ONLY...
...MY SIN.

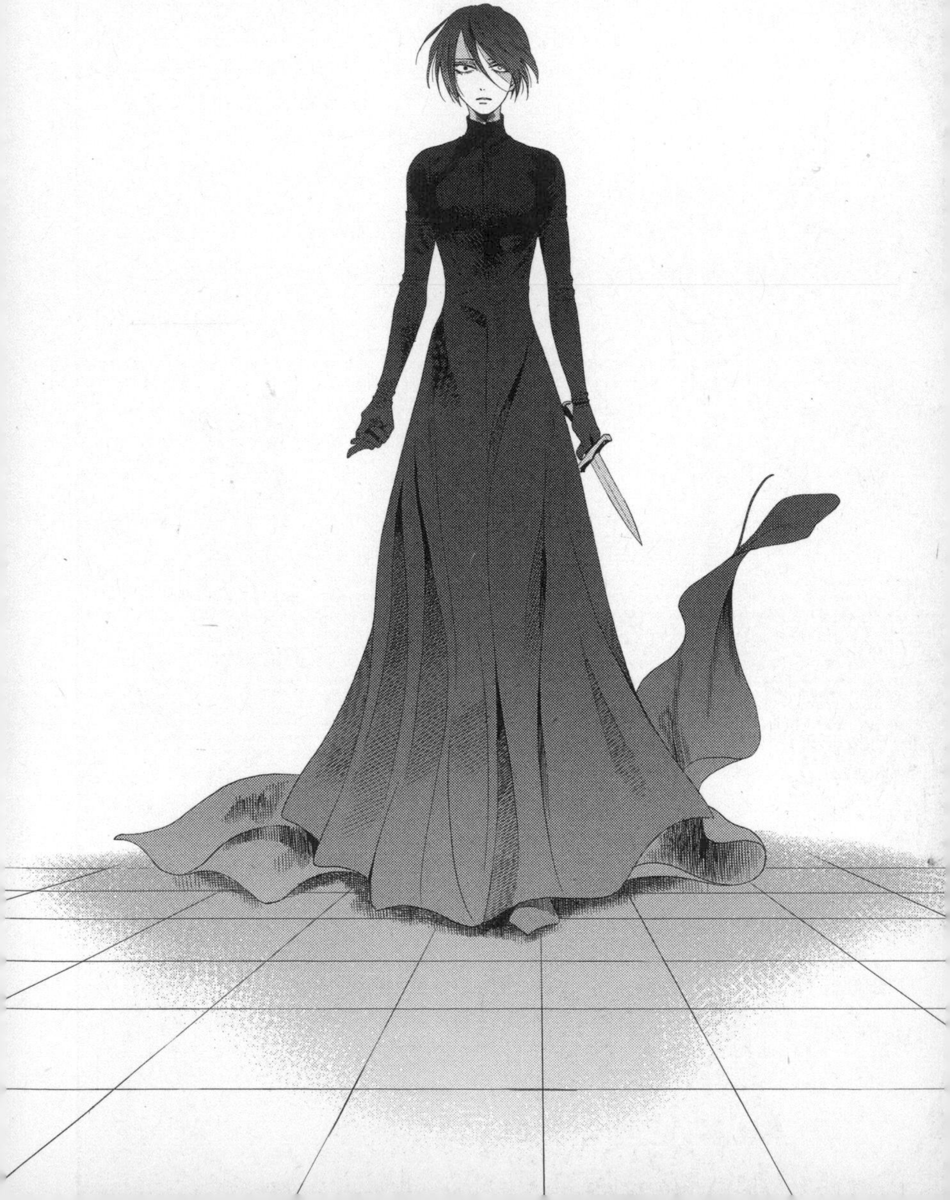

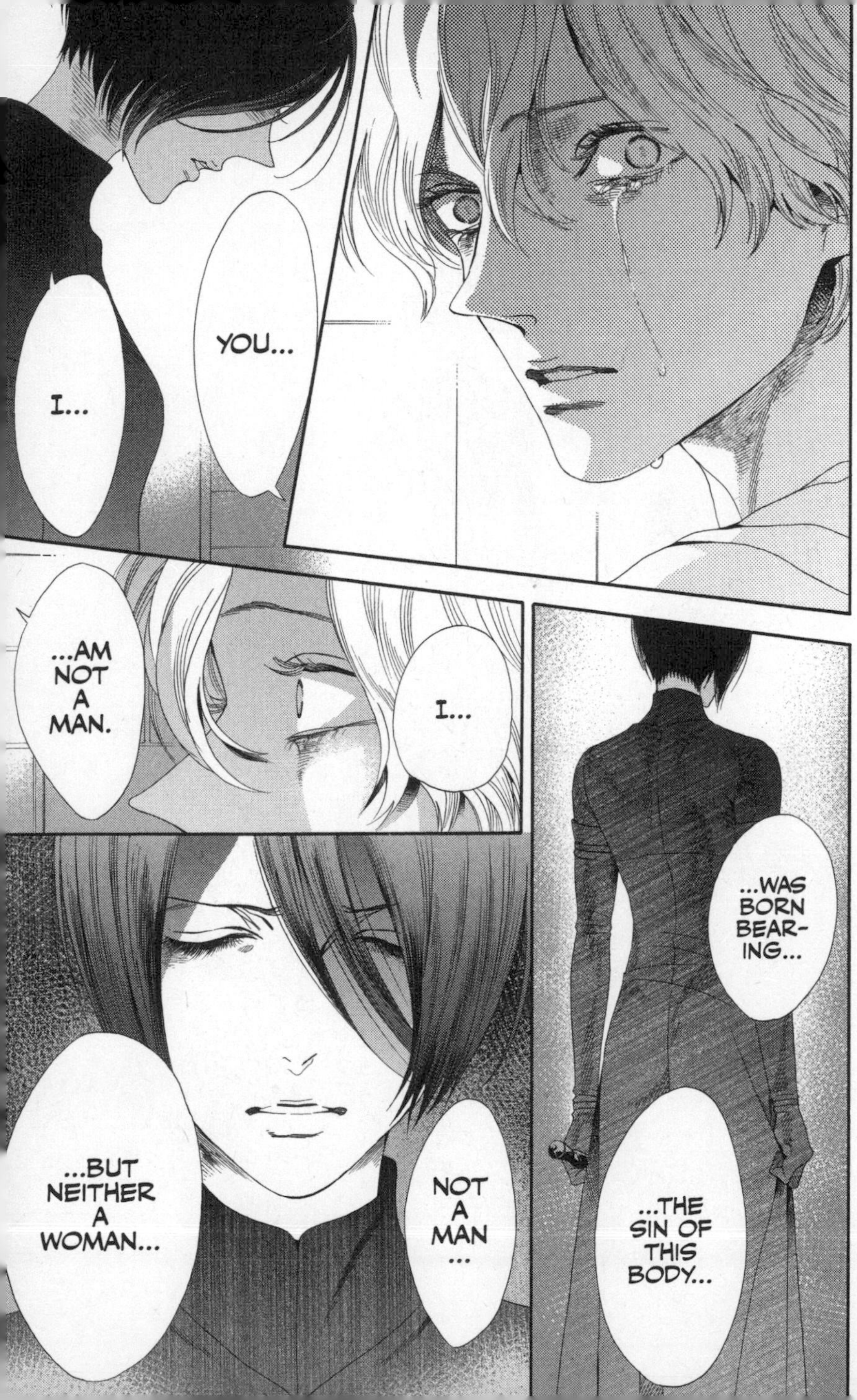
YOU...
I...
...WAS BORN BEARING...
...THE SIN OF THIS BODY...
I...
...AM NOT A MAN.
NOT A MAN ...
...BUT NEITHER A WOMAN...

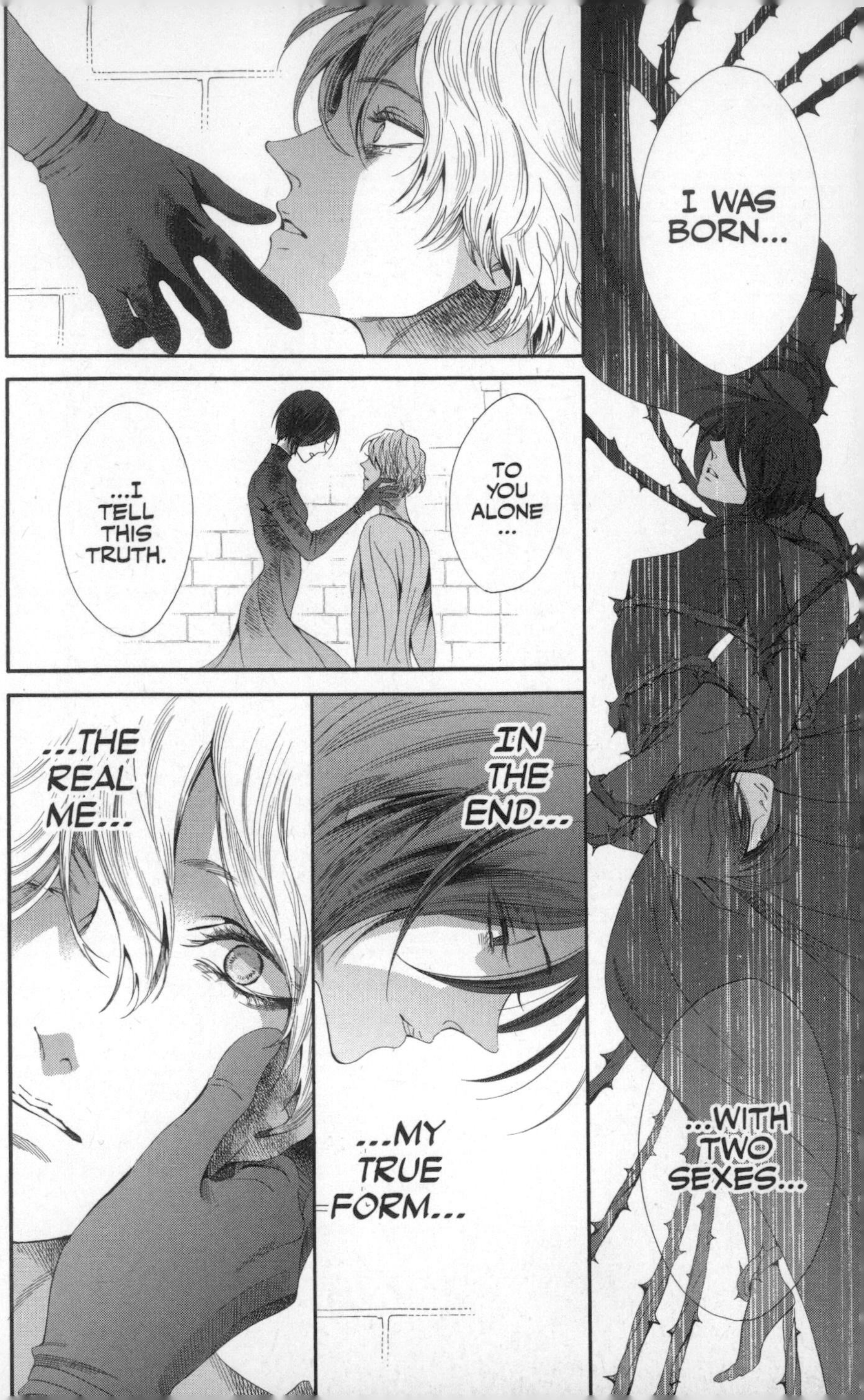
I WAS BORN...
...WITH TWO SEXES...
TO YOU ALONE ...
...I TELL THIS TRUTH.
IN THE END...
...MY TRUE FORM...
...THE REAL ME...

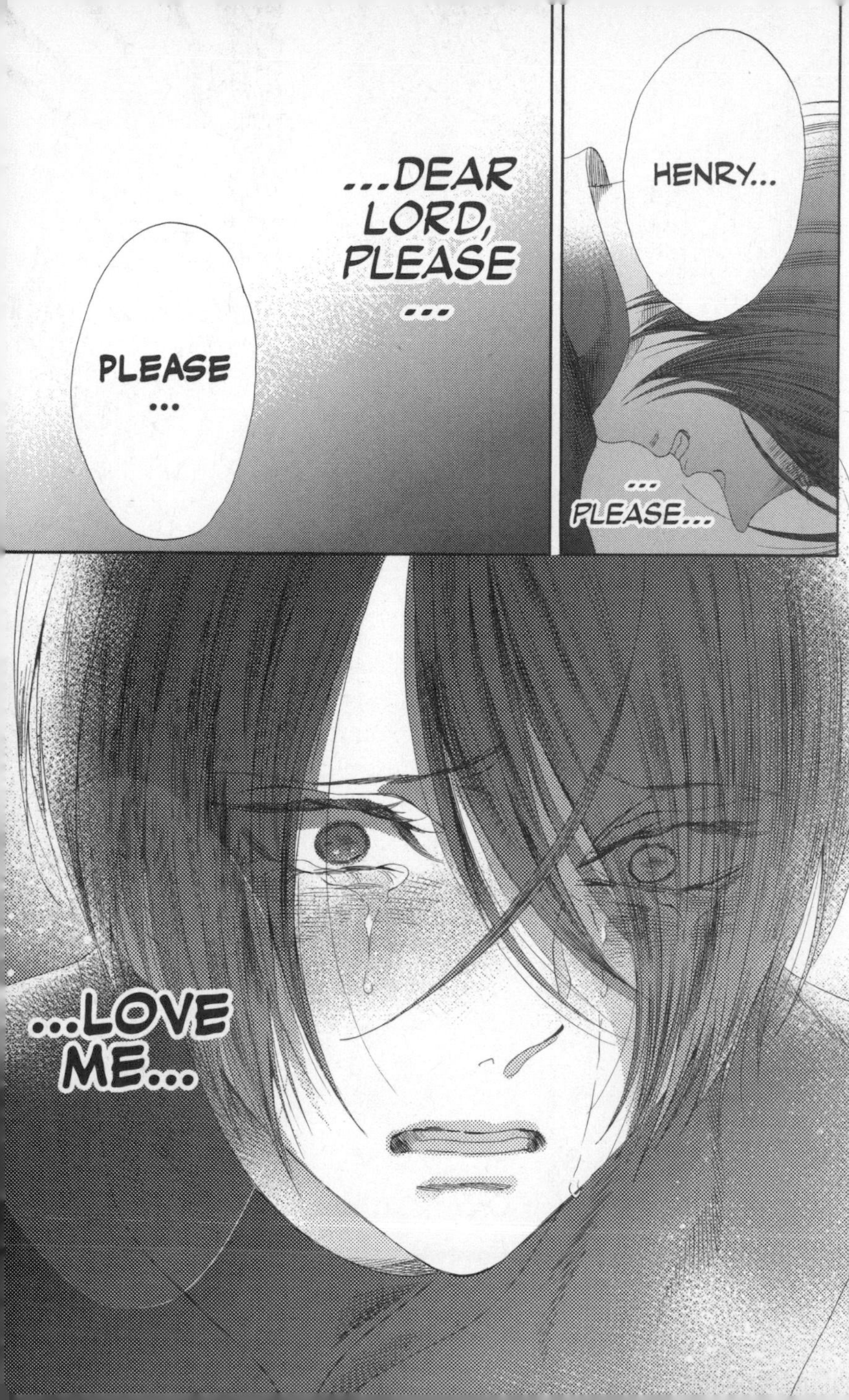
HENRY...
...PLEASE...
...DEAR LORD, PLEASE ...
PLEASE ...
...LOVE ME...

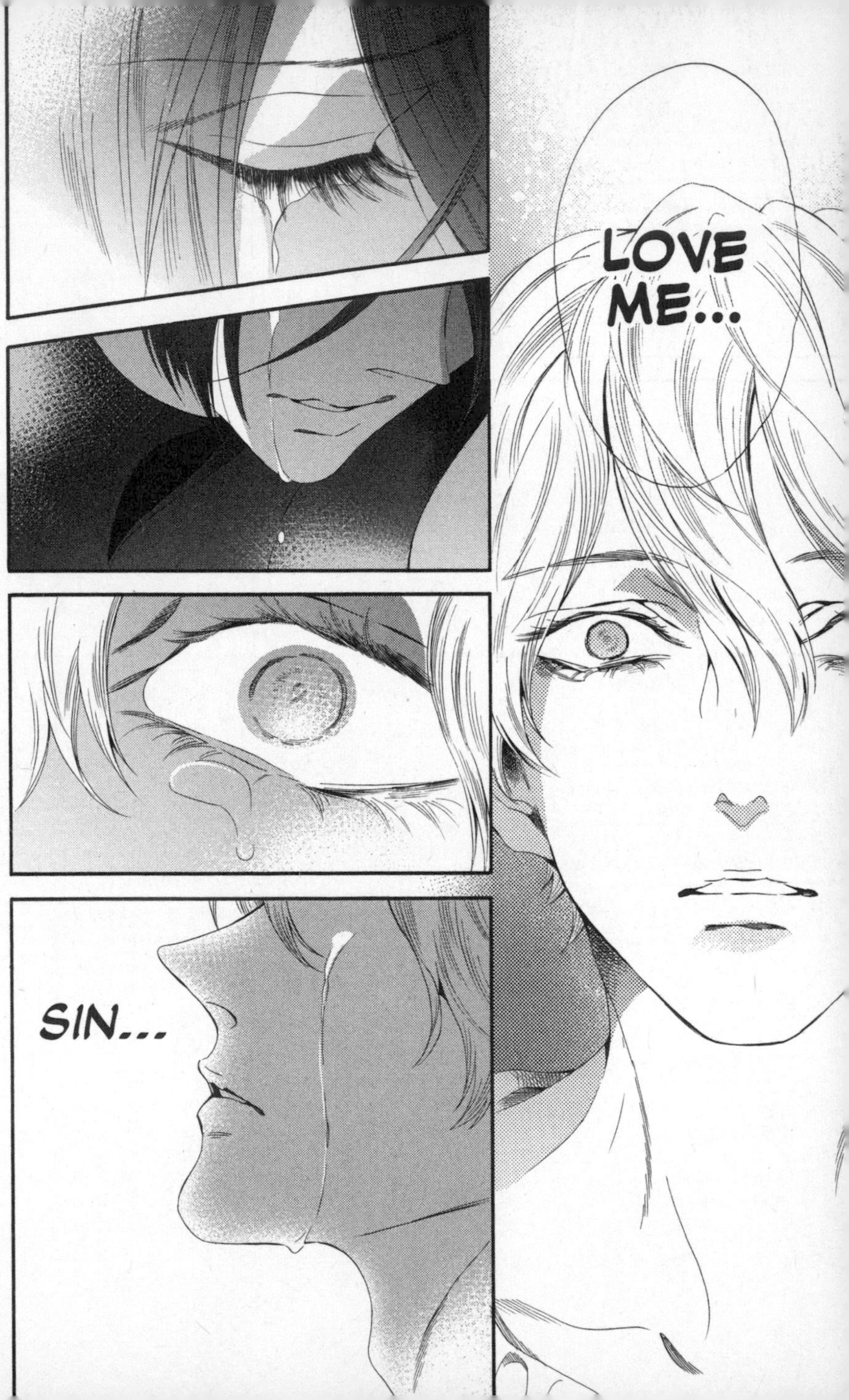
LOVE ME...
SIN...

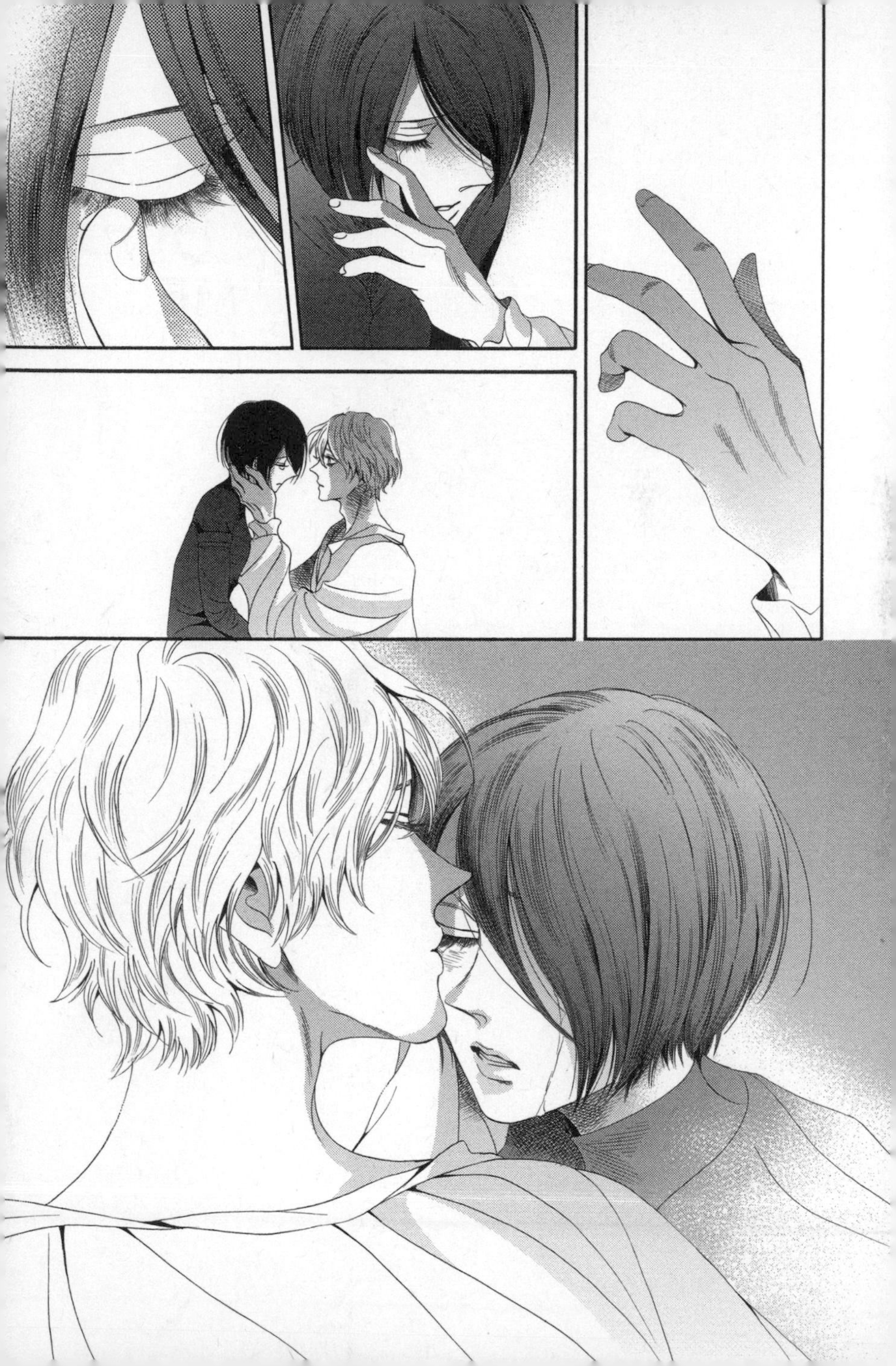

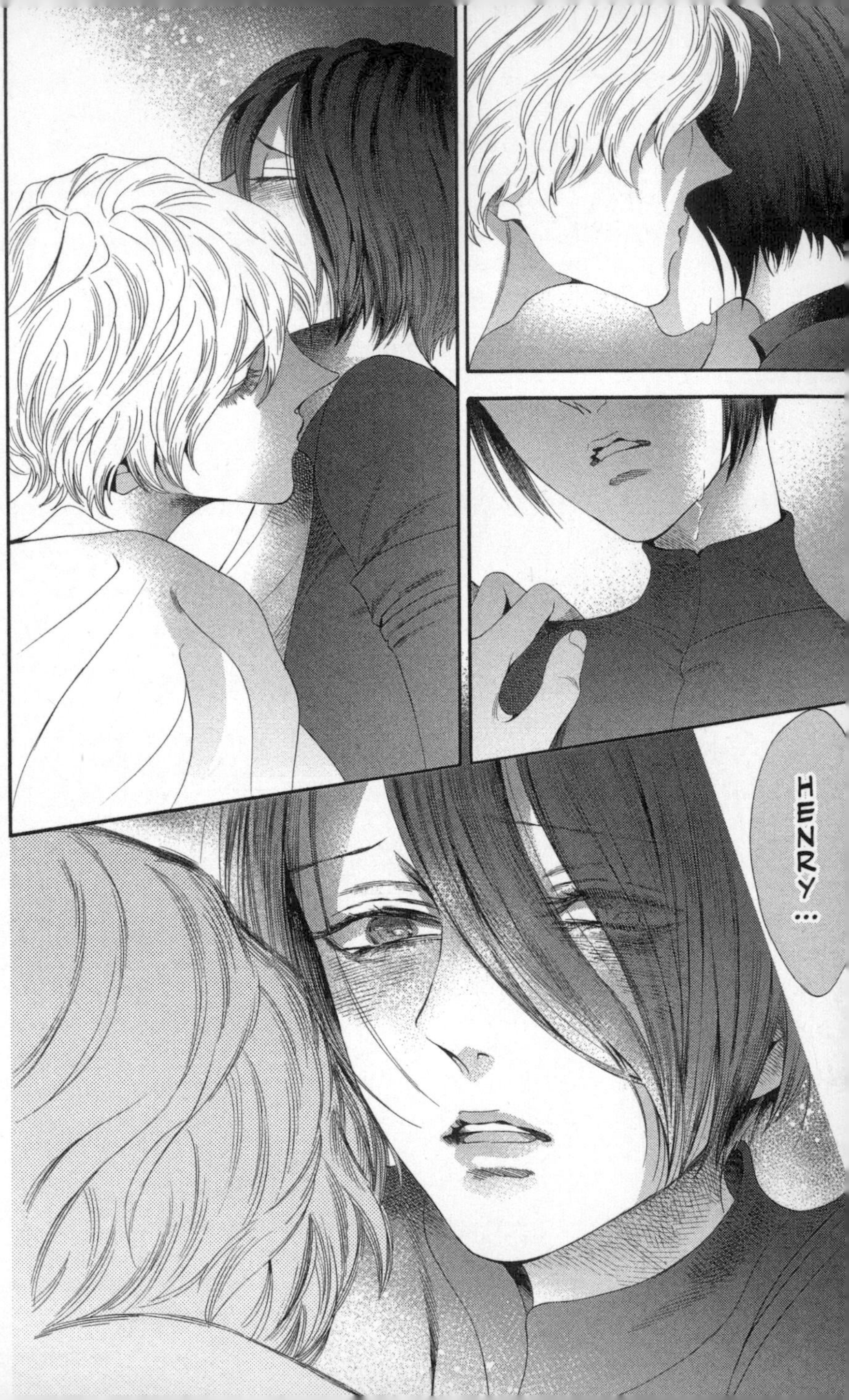
HENRY...

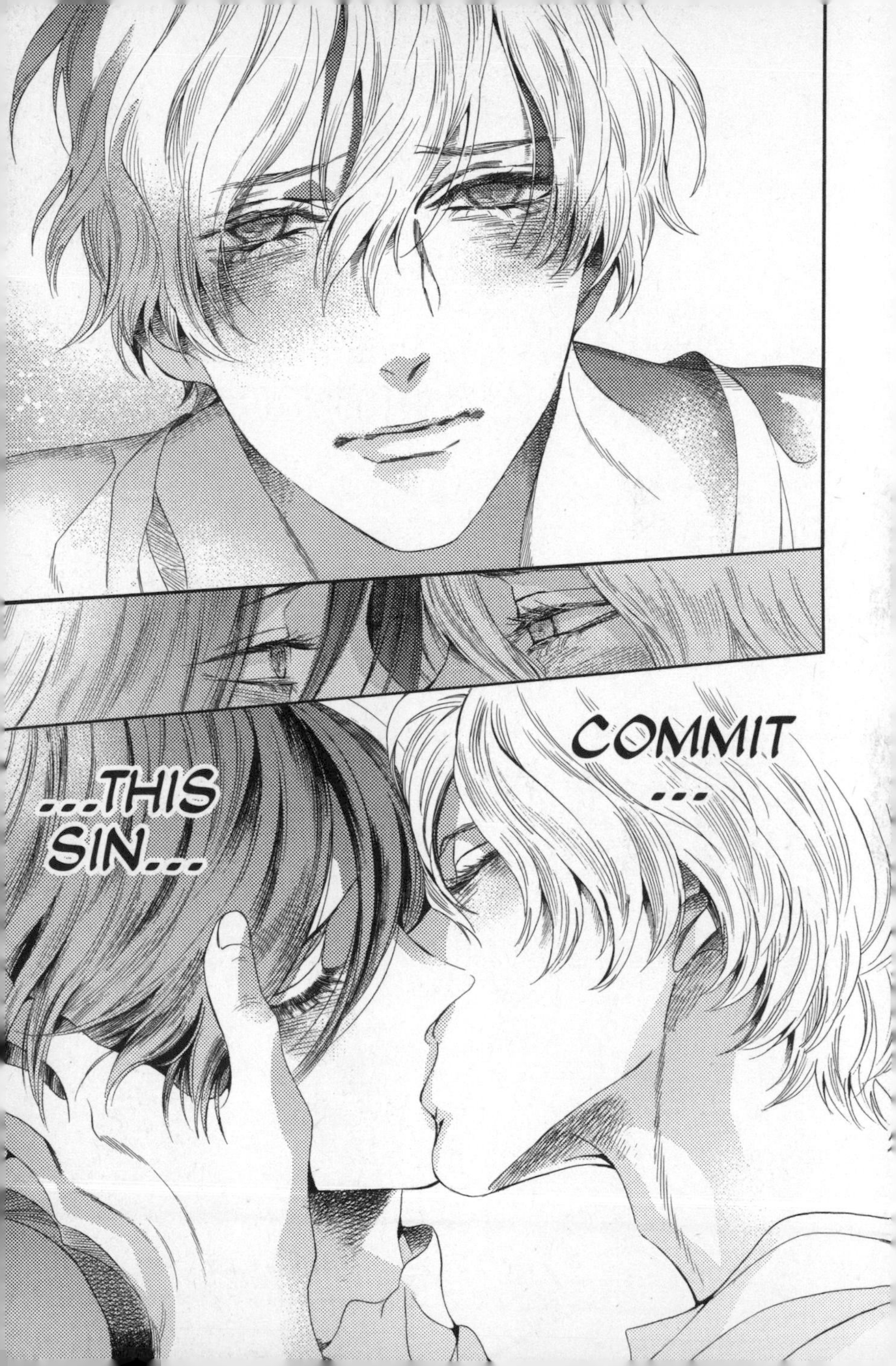
COMMIT ...
...THIS SIN...

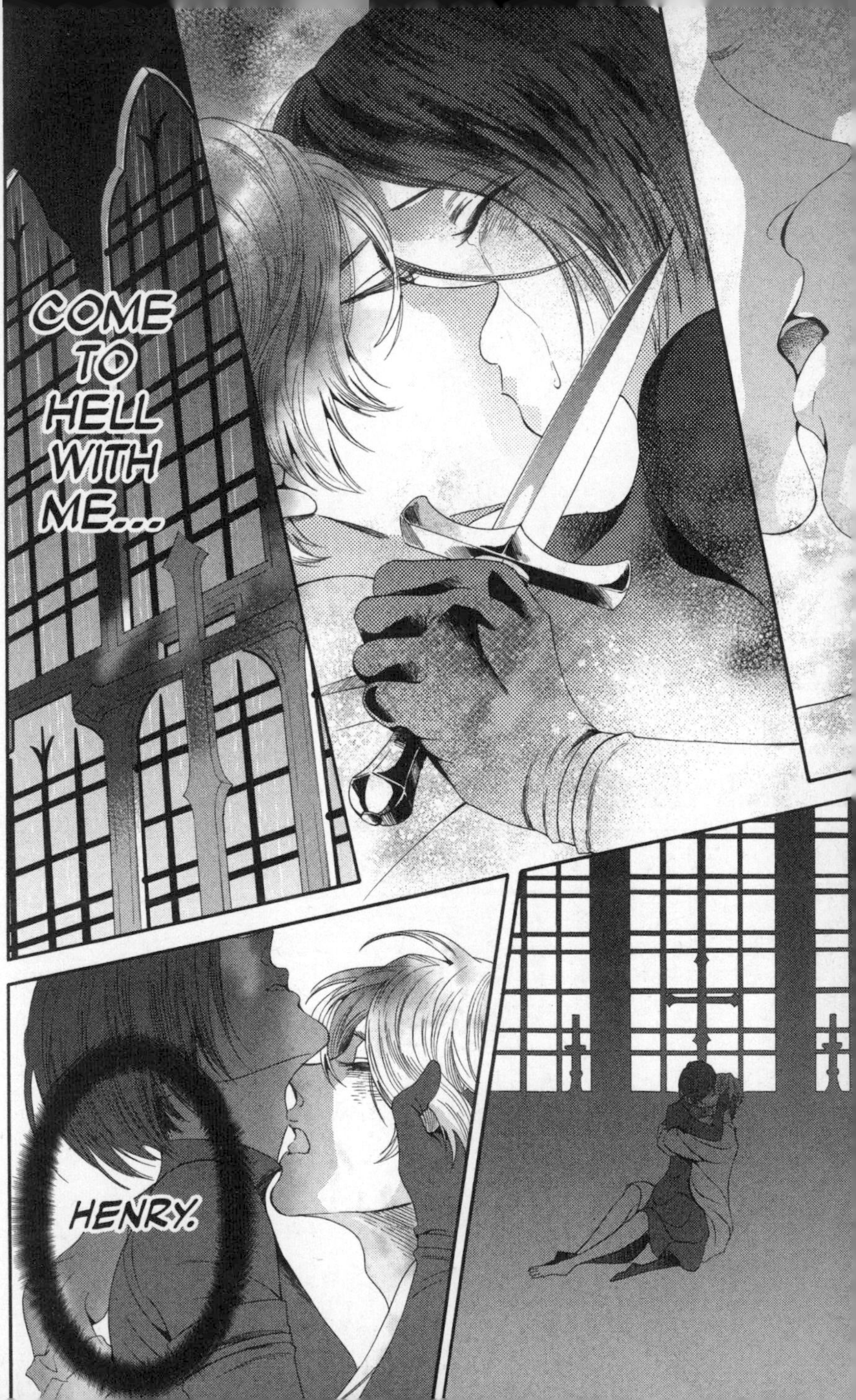
COME TO HELL WITH ME...
HENRY.

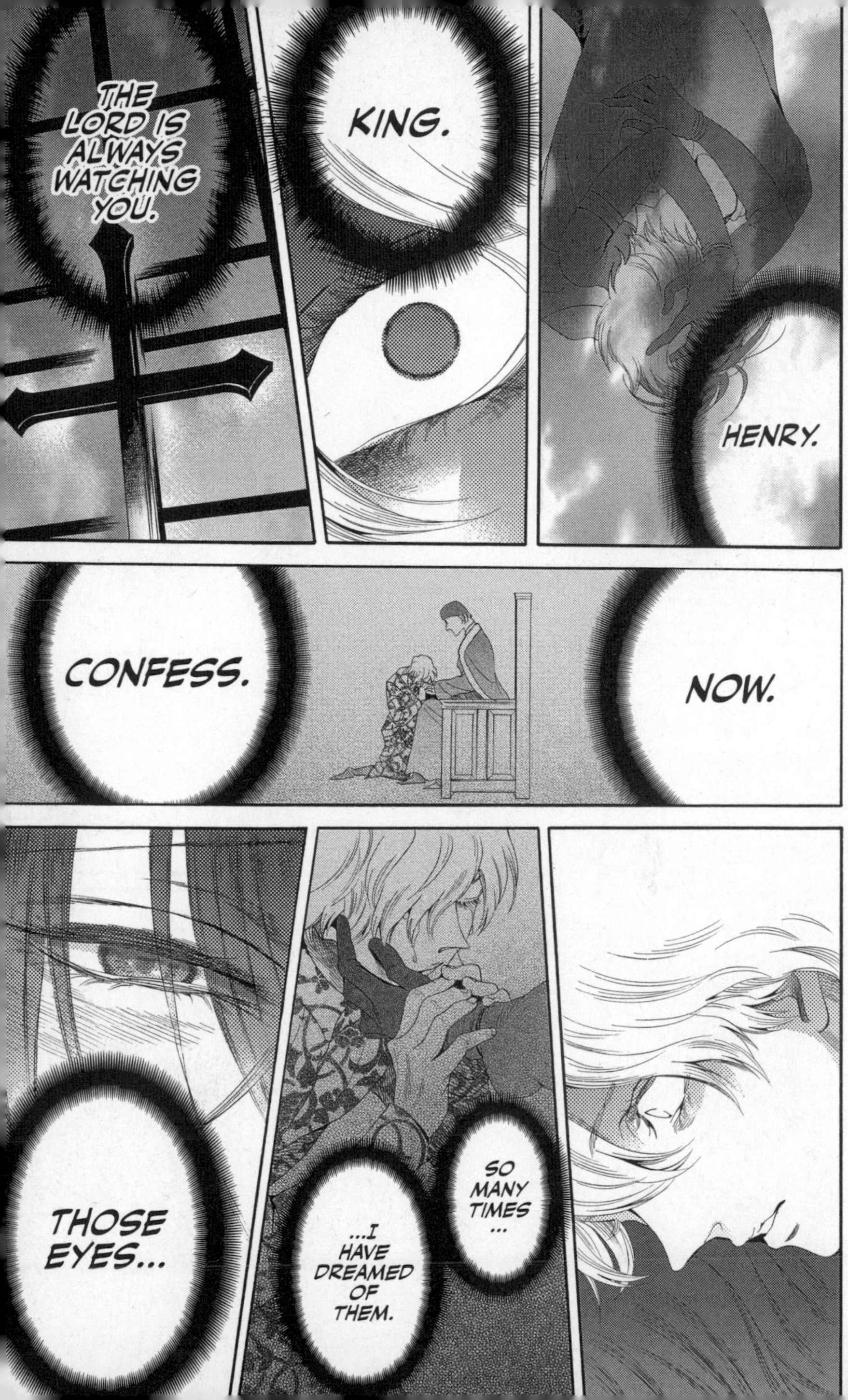
HENRY.
KING.
THE LORD IS ALWAYS WATCHING YOU.
NOW.
CONFESS.
SO MANY TIMES...
...I HAVE DREAMED OF THEM.
THOSE EYES...

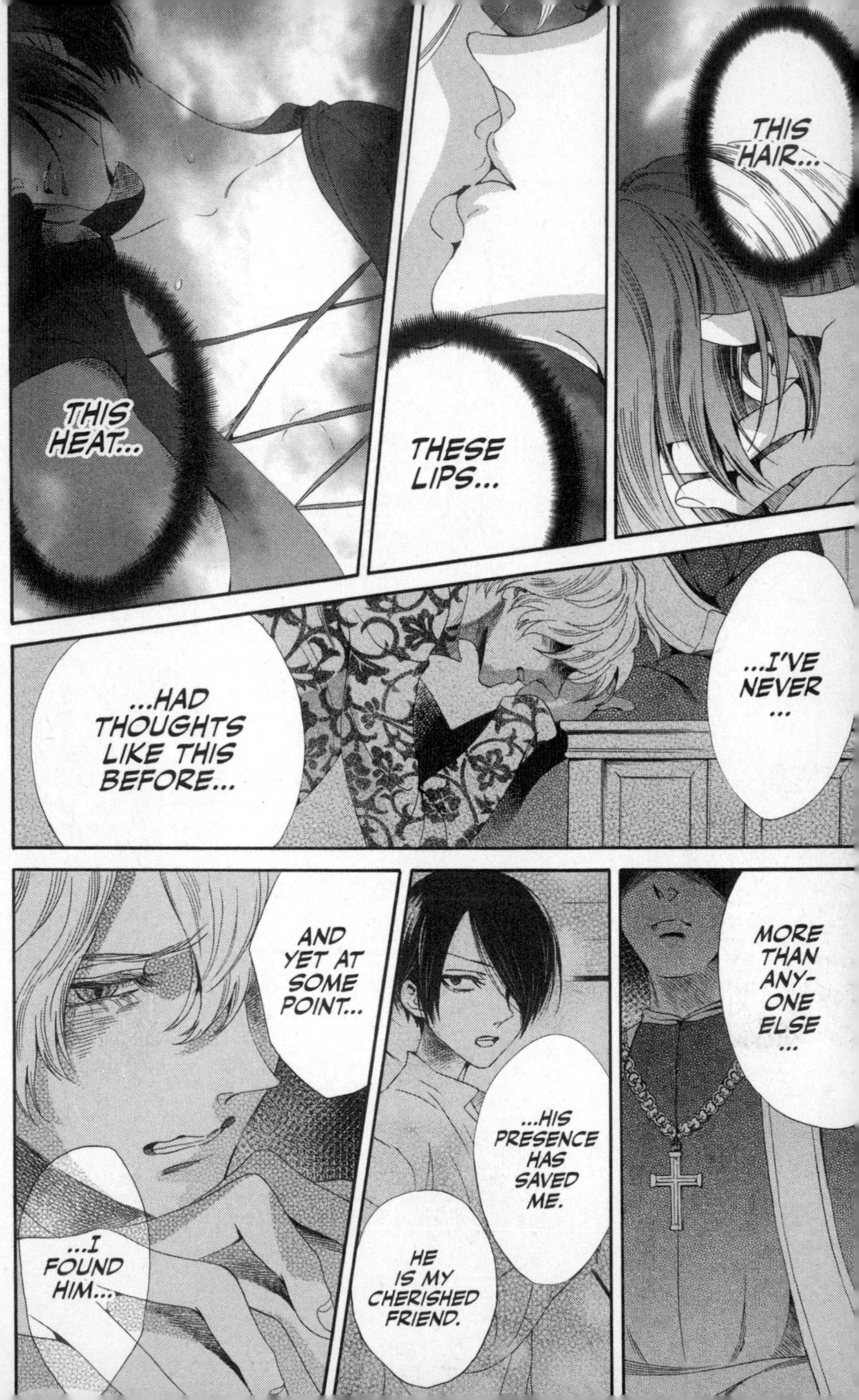
THIS HAIR...
THESE LIPS...
THIS HEAT...
...I'VE NEVER ...
...HAD THOUGHTS LIKE THIS BEFORE...
MORE THAN ANY-ONE ELSE ...
...HIS PRESENCE HAS SAVED ME.
HE IS MY CHERISHED FRIEND.
AND YET AT SOME POINT...
...I FOUND HIM...

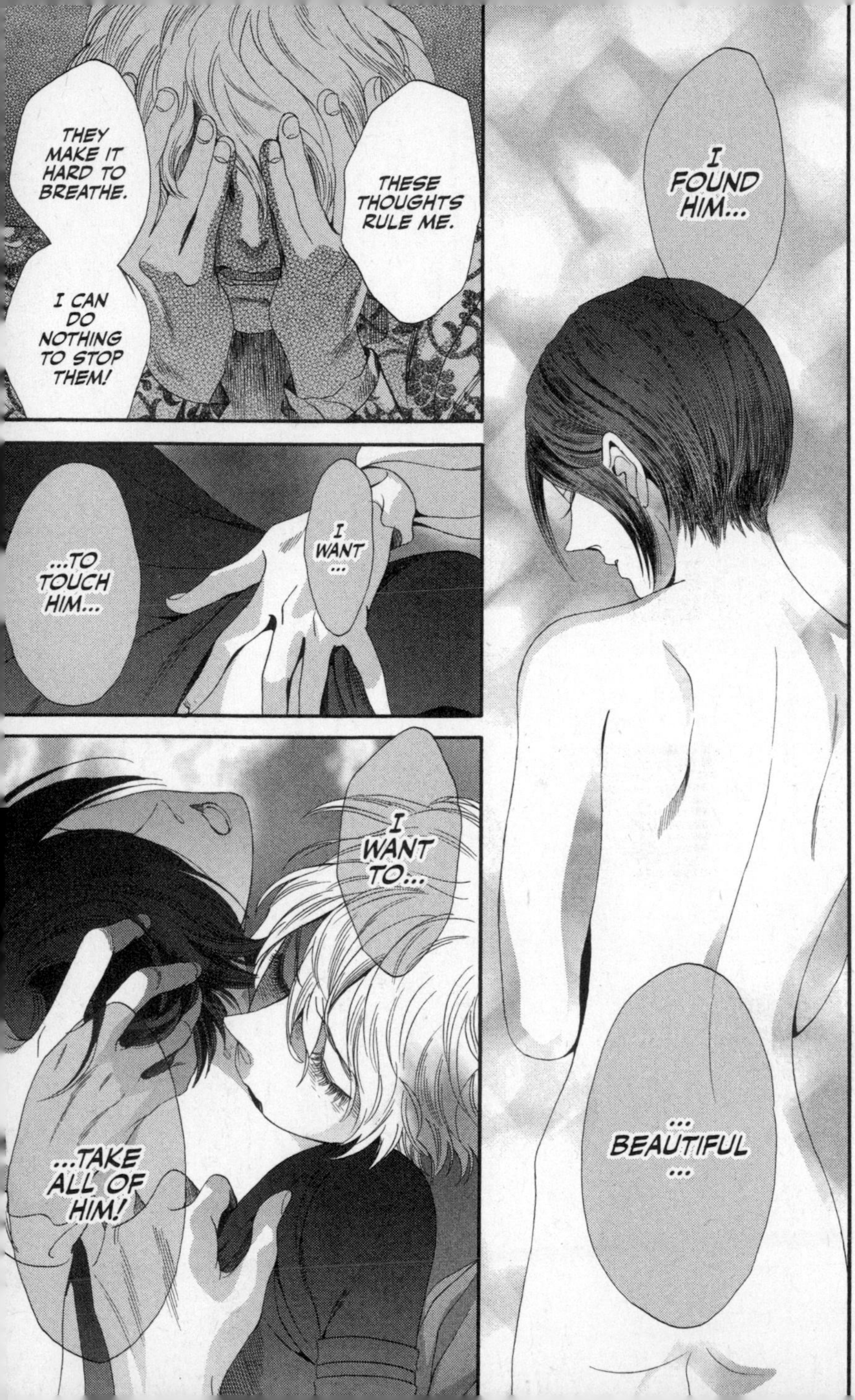
I FOUND HIM...
...BEAUTIFUL...
THESE THOUGHTS RULE ME.
THEY MAKE IT HARD TO BREATHE.
I CAN DO NOTHING TO STOP THEM!
I WANT...
...TO TOUCH HIM...
I WANT TO...
...TAKE ALL OF HIM!

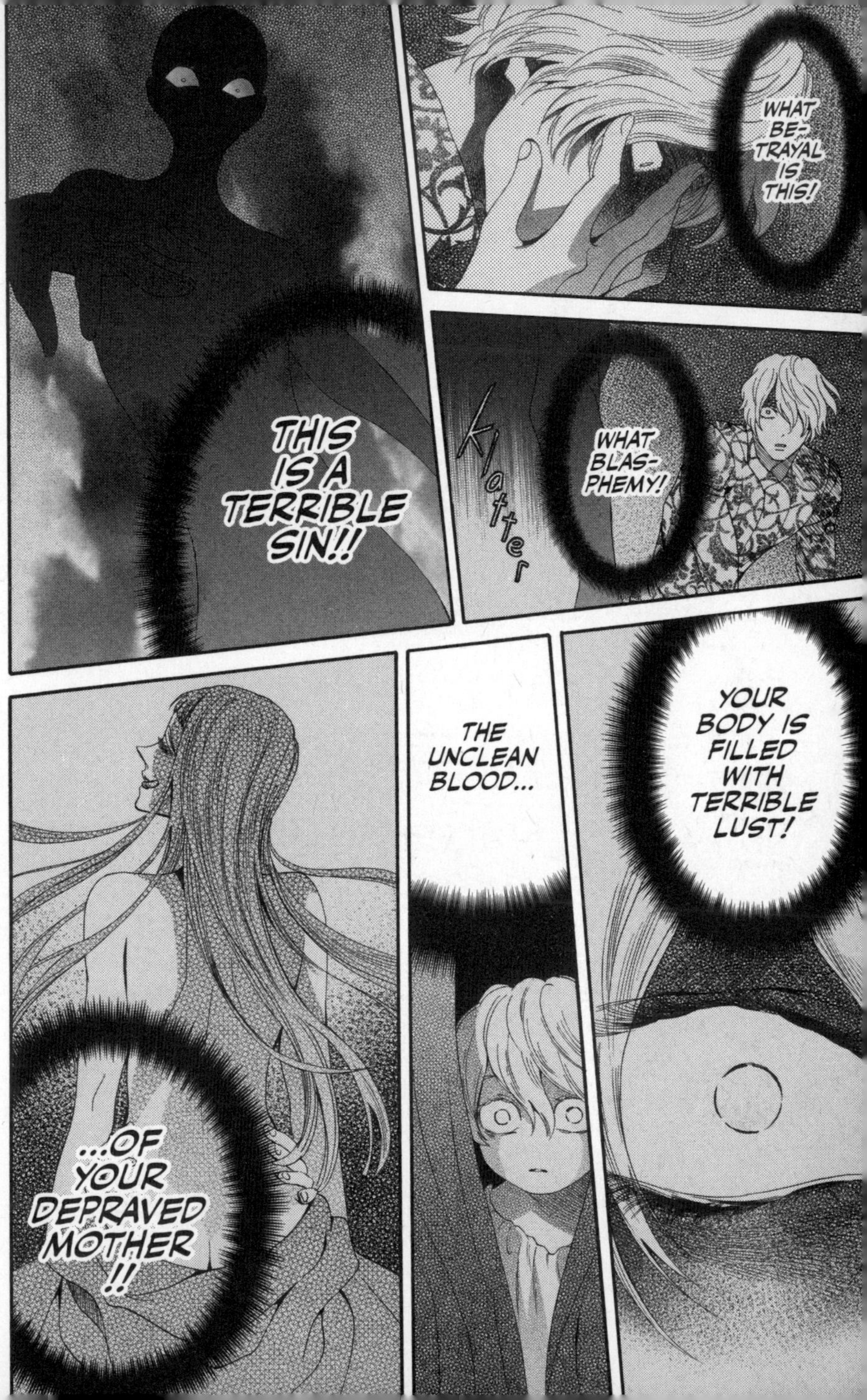
WHAT BE-TRAYAL IS THIS!
WHAT BLAS-PHEMY!
Klatter
THIS IS A TERRIBLE SIN!!
YOUR BODY IS FILLED WITH TERRIBLE LUST!
THE UNCLEAN BLOOD...
...OF YOUR DEPRAVED MOTHER!!

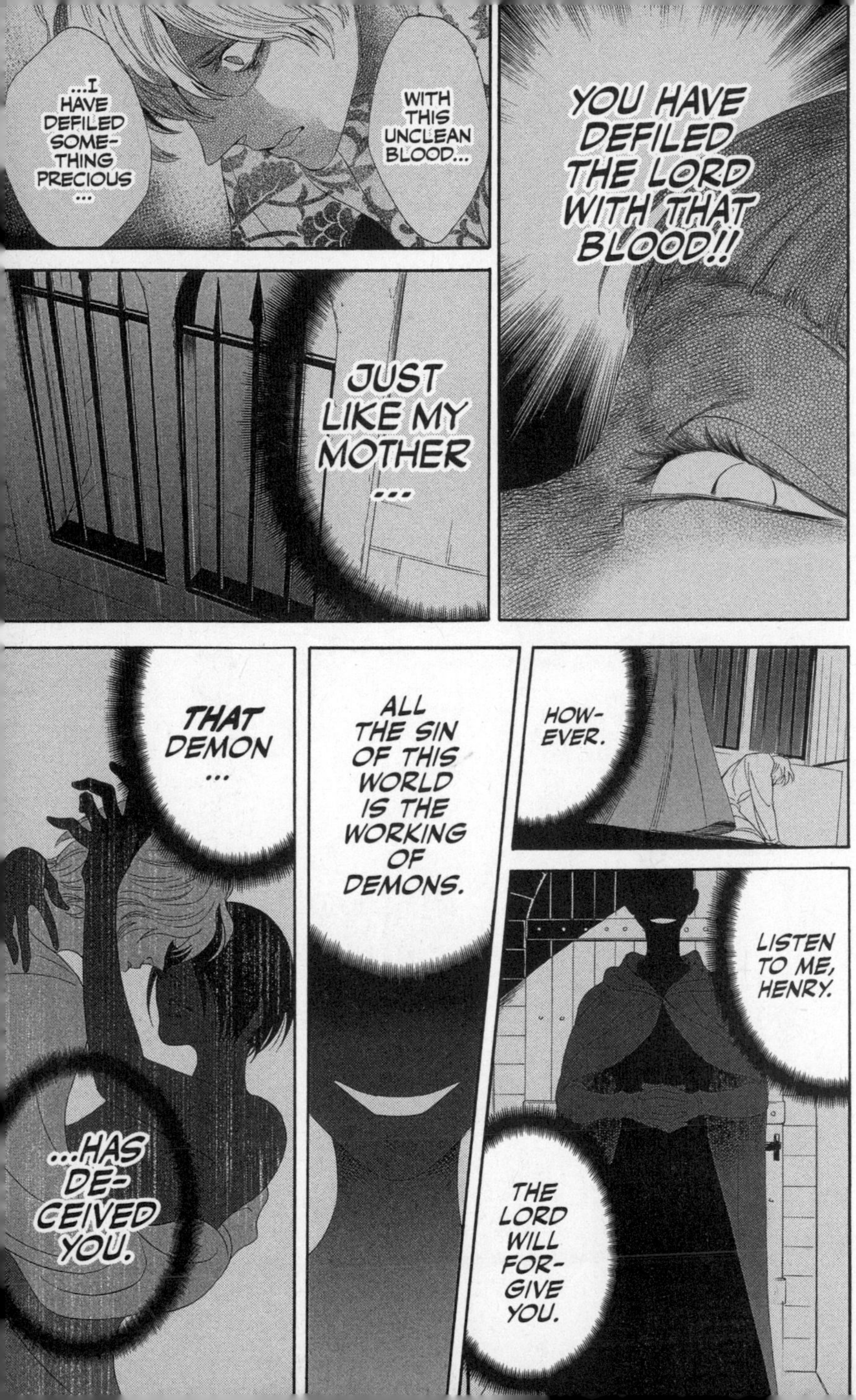
YOU HAVE DEFILED THE LORD WITH THAT BLOOD!!
WITH THIS UNCLEAN BLOOD...
...I HAVE DEFILED SOMETHING PRECIOUS...
JUST LIKE MY MOTHER...
HOWEVER.
LISTEN TO ME, HENRY.
THE LORD WILL FORGIVE YOU.
ALL THE SIN OF THIS WORLD IS THE WORKING OF DEMONS.
THAT DEMON...
...HAS DECEIVED YOU.

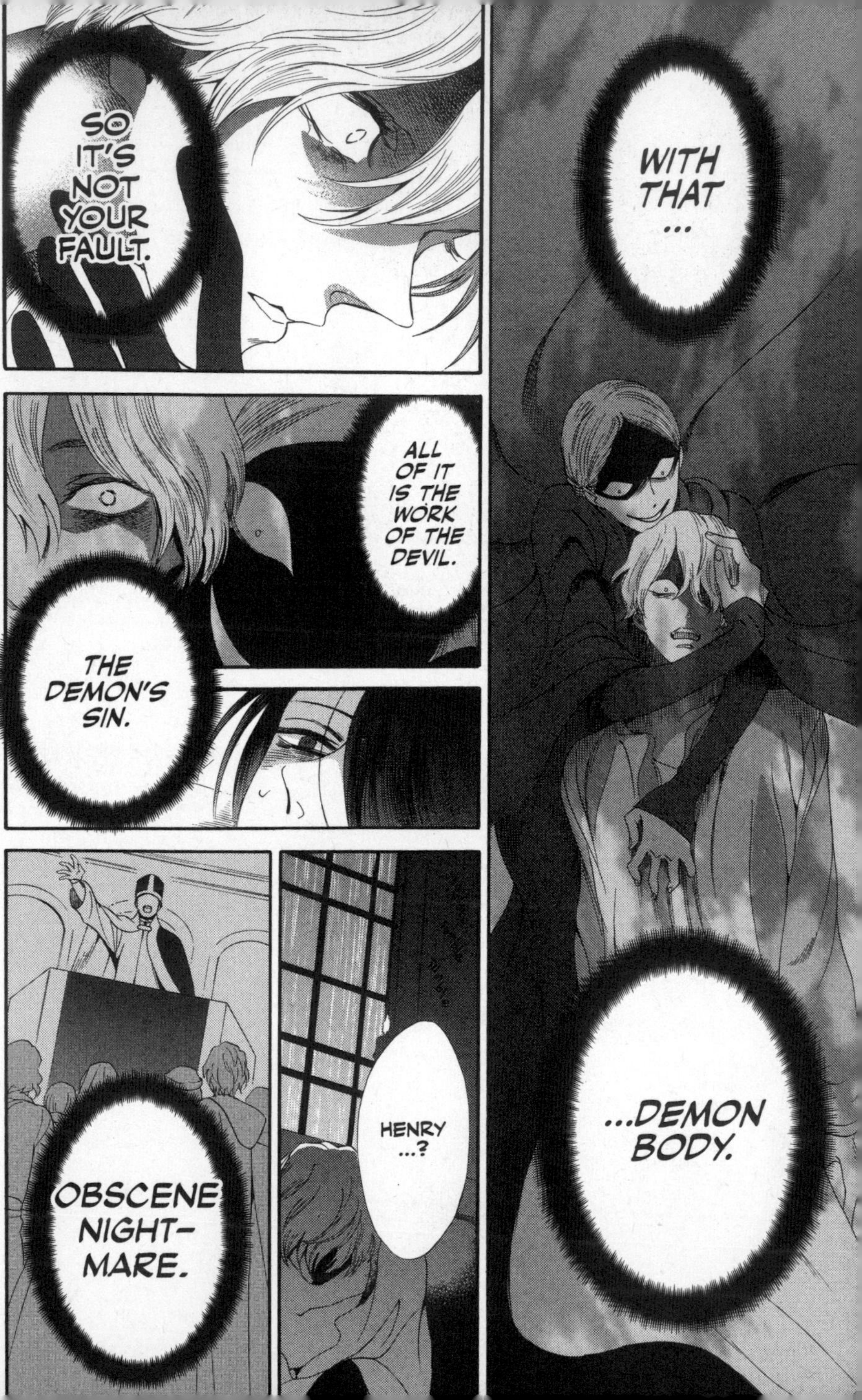
WITH THAT...
...DEMON BODY.
SO IT'S NOT YOUR FAULT.
ALL OF IT IS THE WORK OF THE DEVIL.
THE DEMON'S SIN.
HENRY...?
OBSCENE NIGHT-MARE.

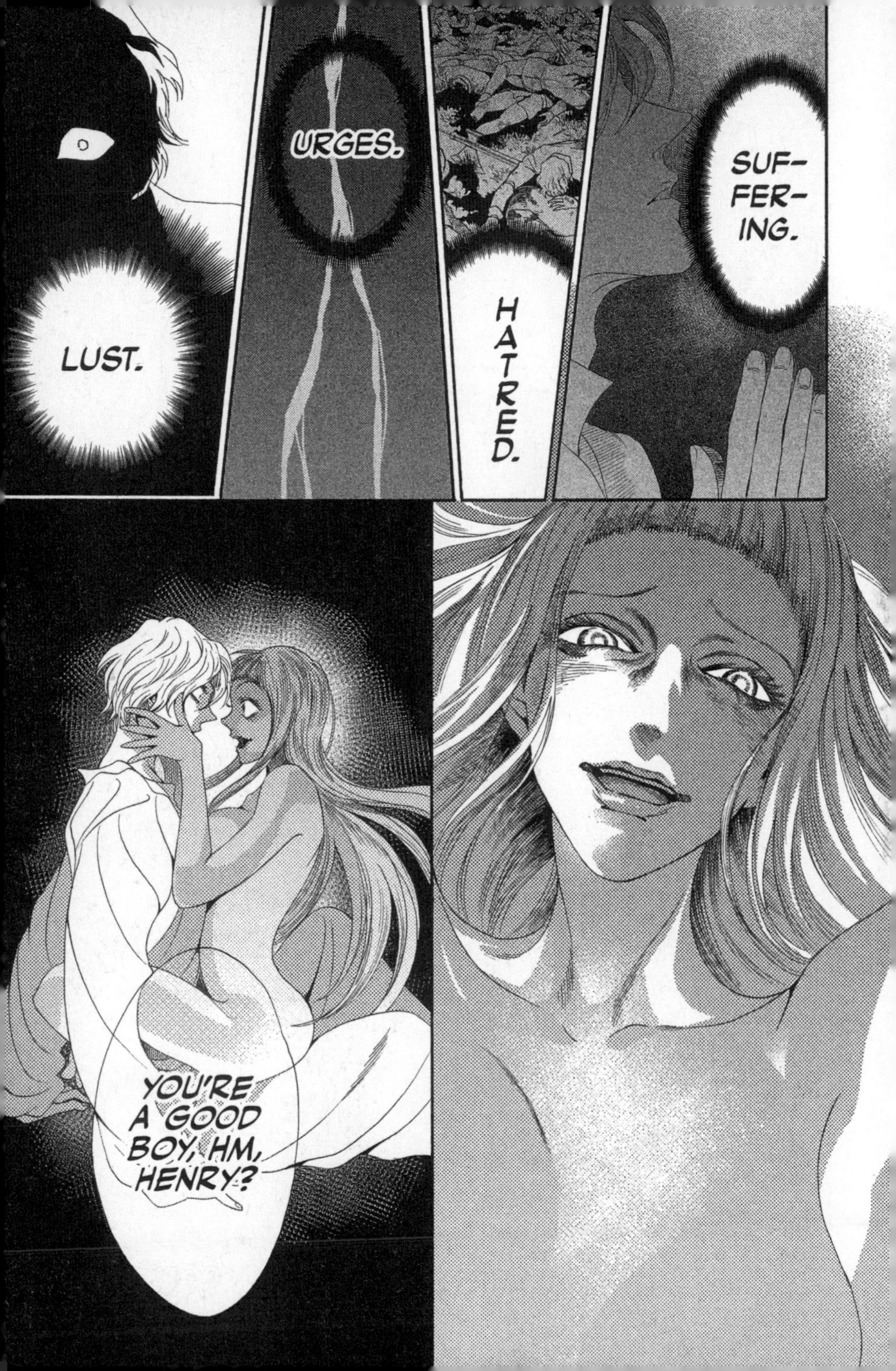
SUF-
FER-
ING.
HATRED.
URGES.
LUST.
YOU'RE A GOOD BOY, HM, HENRY?

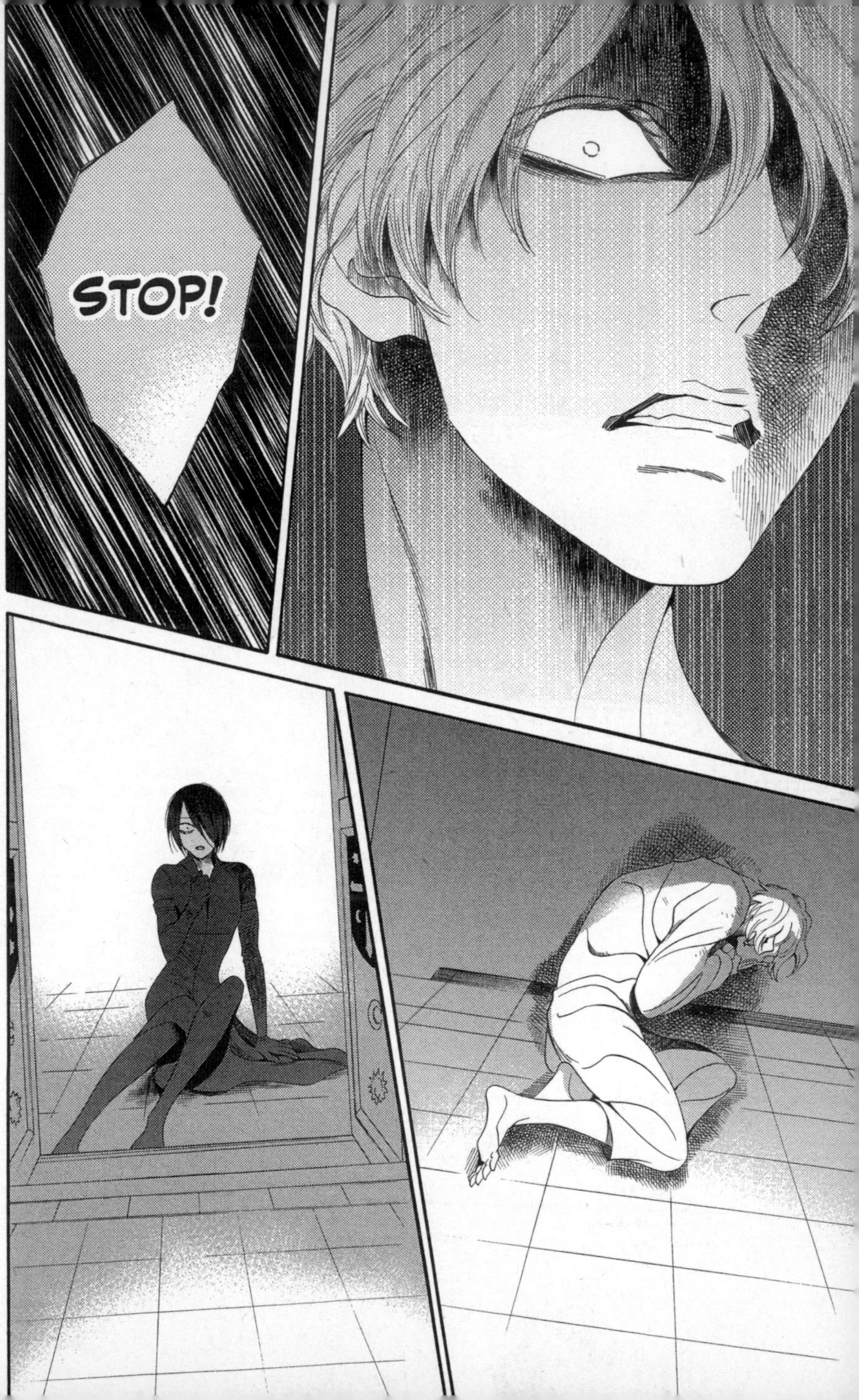
STOP!

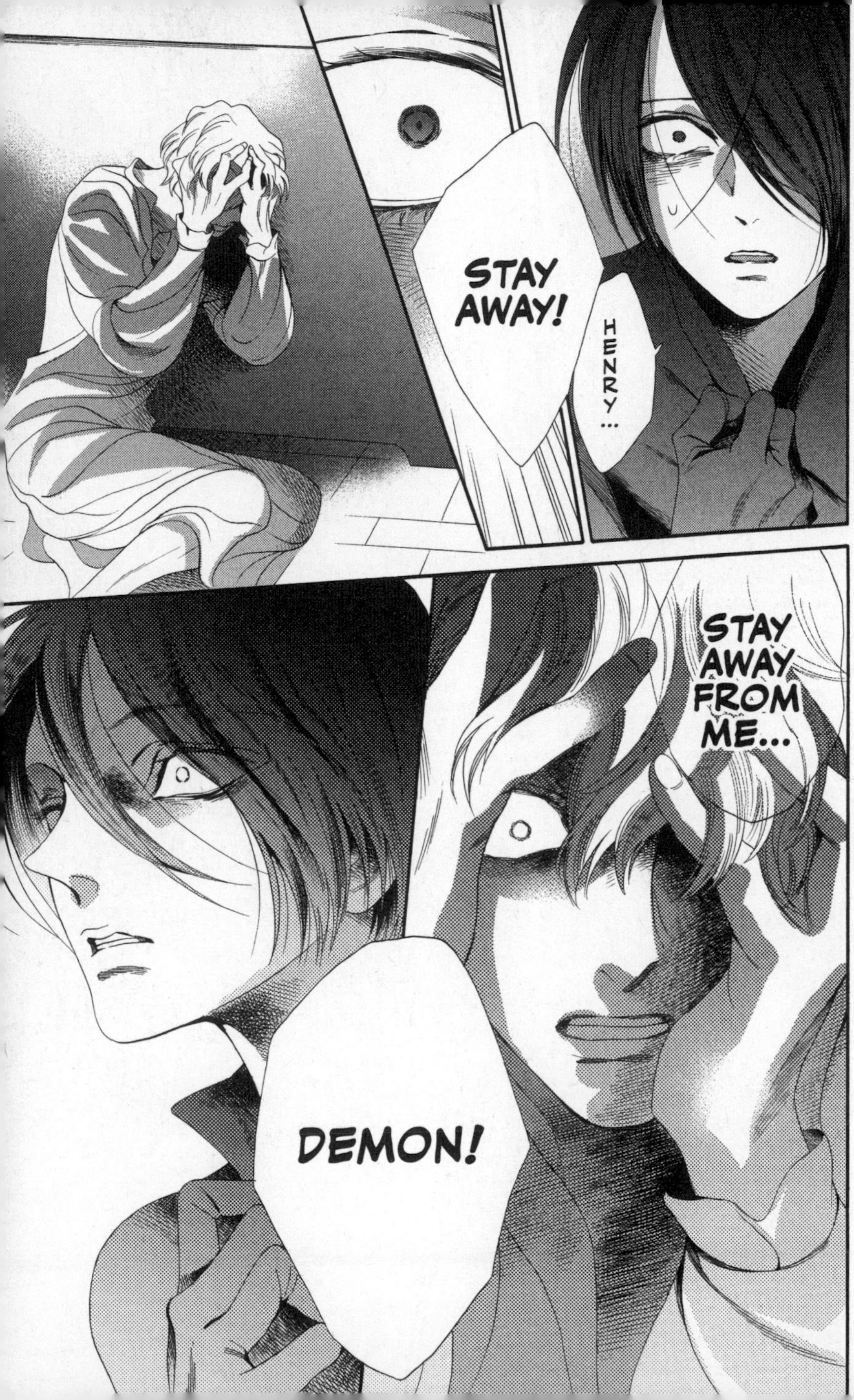
HENRY...
STAY AWAY!
STAY AWAY FROM ME...
DEMON!

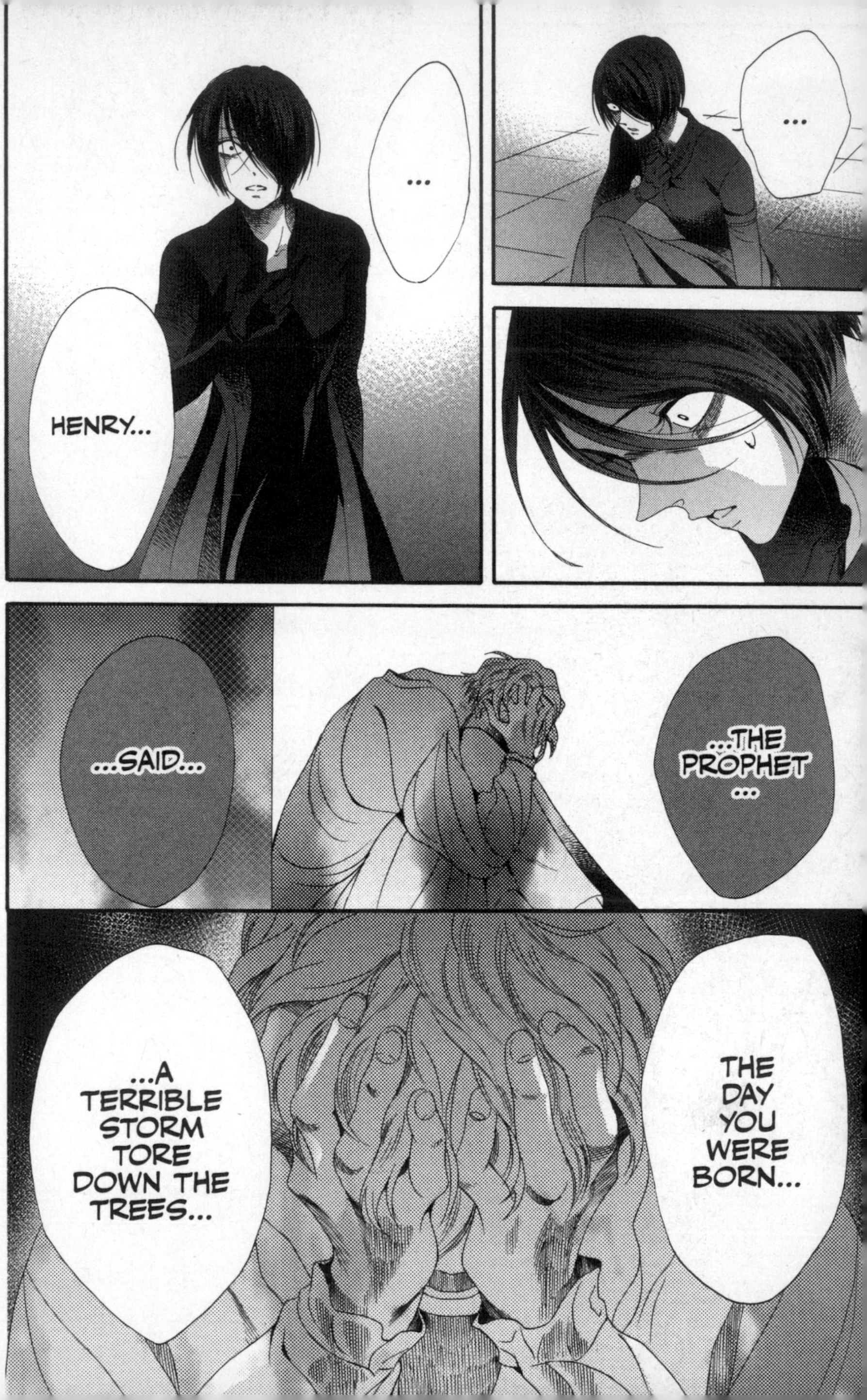
...
...
HENRY...
...THE PROPHET ...
...SAID...
THE DAY YOU WERE BORN...
...A TERRIBLE STORM TORE DOWN THE TREES...

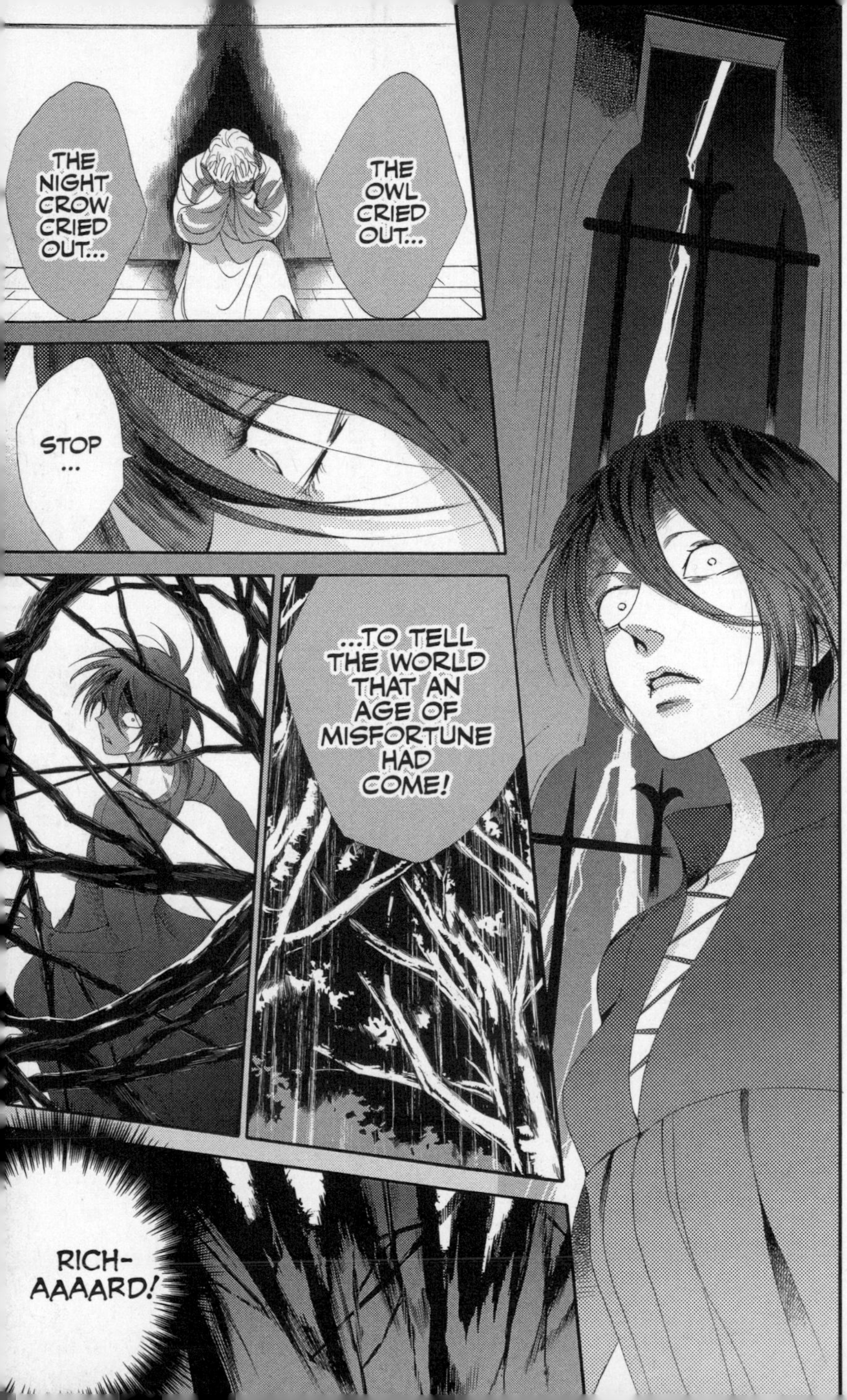
THE OWL CRIED OUT...
THE NIGHT CROW CRIED OUT...
STOP ...
...TO TELL THE WORLD THAT AN AGE OF MISFORTUNE HAD COME!
RICH-AAAARD!

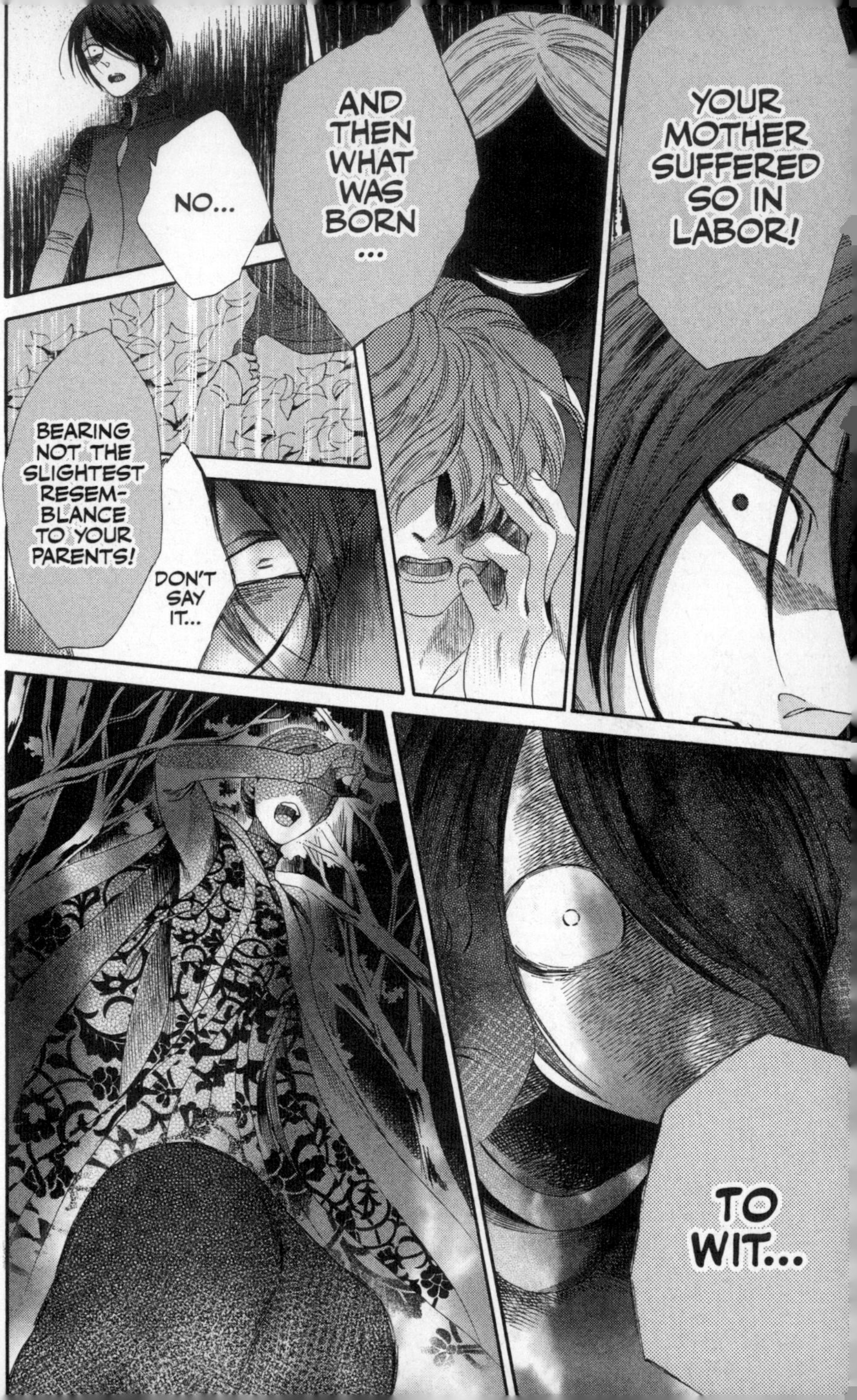
YOUR MOTHER SUFFERED SO IN LABOR!
AND THEN WHAT WAS BORN...
NO...
BEARING NOT THE SLIGHTEST RESEMBLANCE TO YOUR PARENTS!
DON'T SAY IT...
TO WIT...

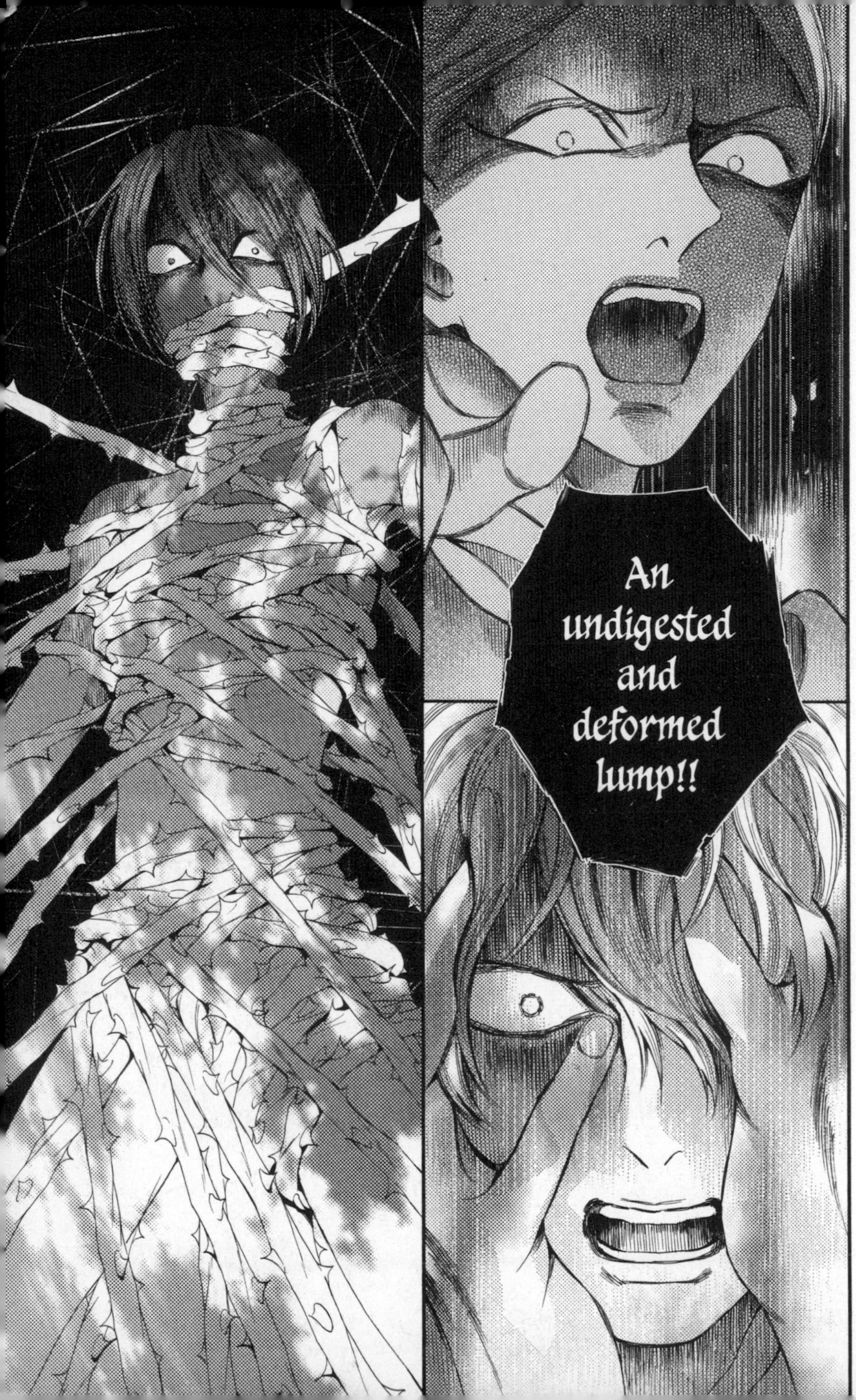
An undigested and deformed lump!!

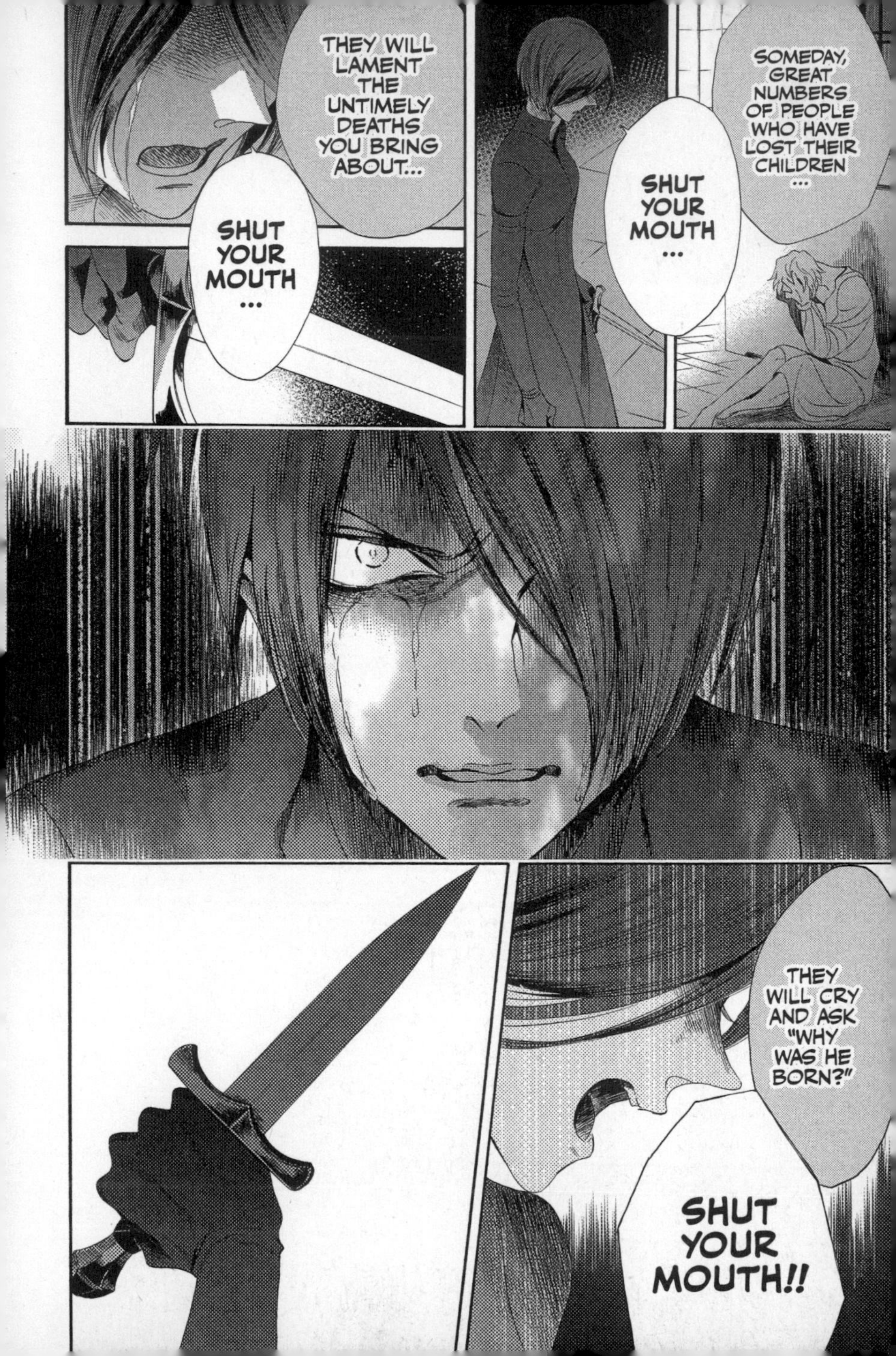
SOMEDAY, GREAT NUMBERS OF PEOPLE WHO HAVE LOST THEIR CHILDREN ...
SHUT YOUR MOUTH ...
THEY WILL LAMENT THE UNTIMELY DEATHS YOU BRING ABOUT...
SHUT YOUR MOUTH ...
THEY WILL CRY AND ASK "WHY WAS HE BORN?"
SHUT YOUR MOUTH!!

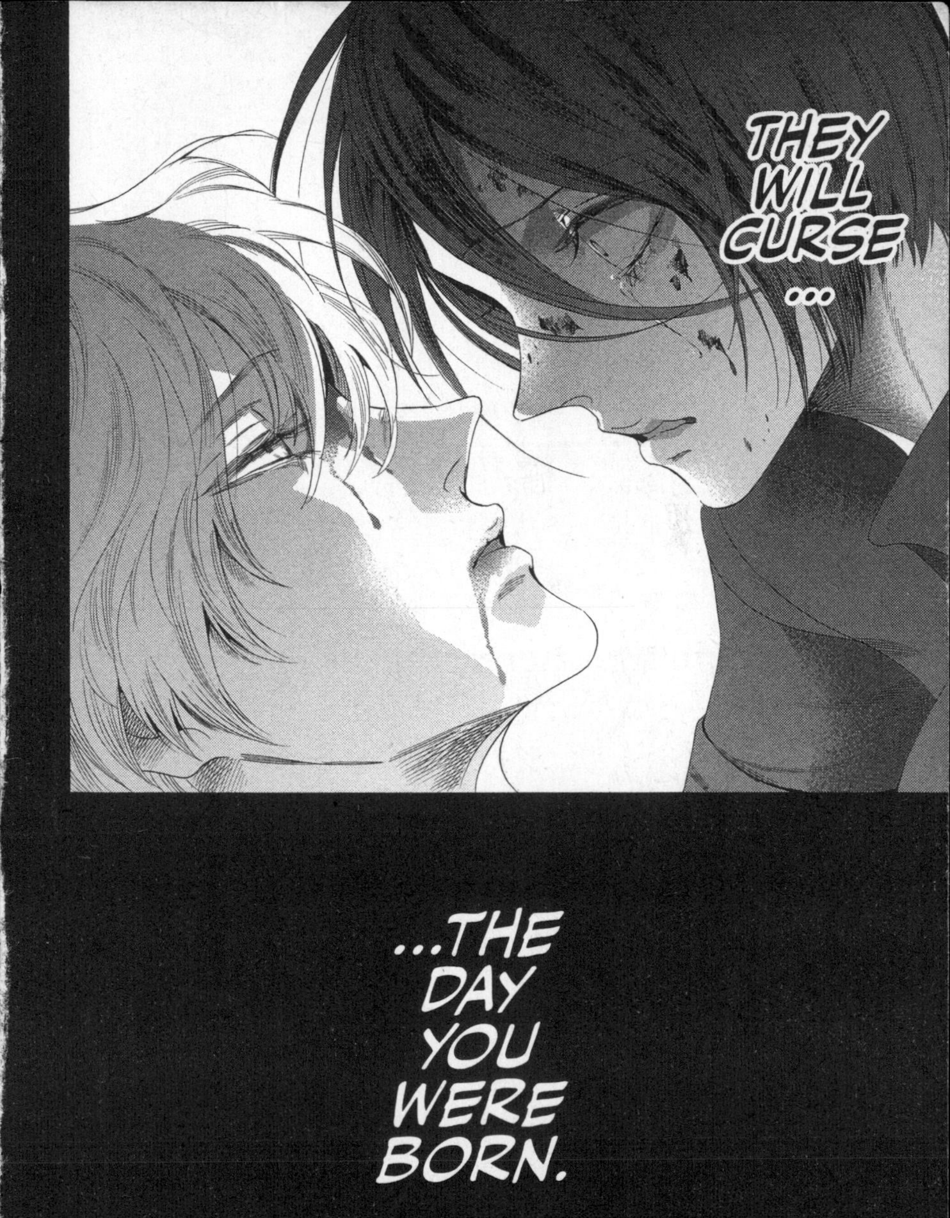
THEY WILL CURSE...
...THE DAY YOU WERE BORN.

Chapter 30/END

Requiem of the Rose King 7/END

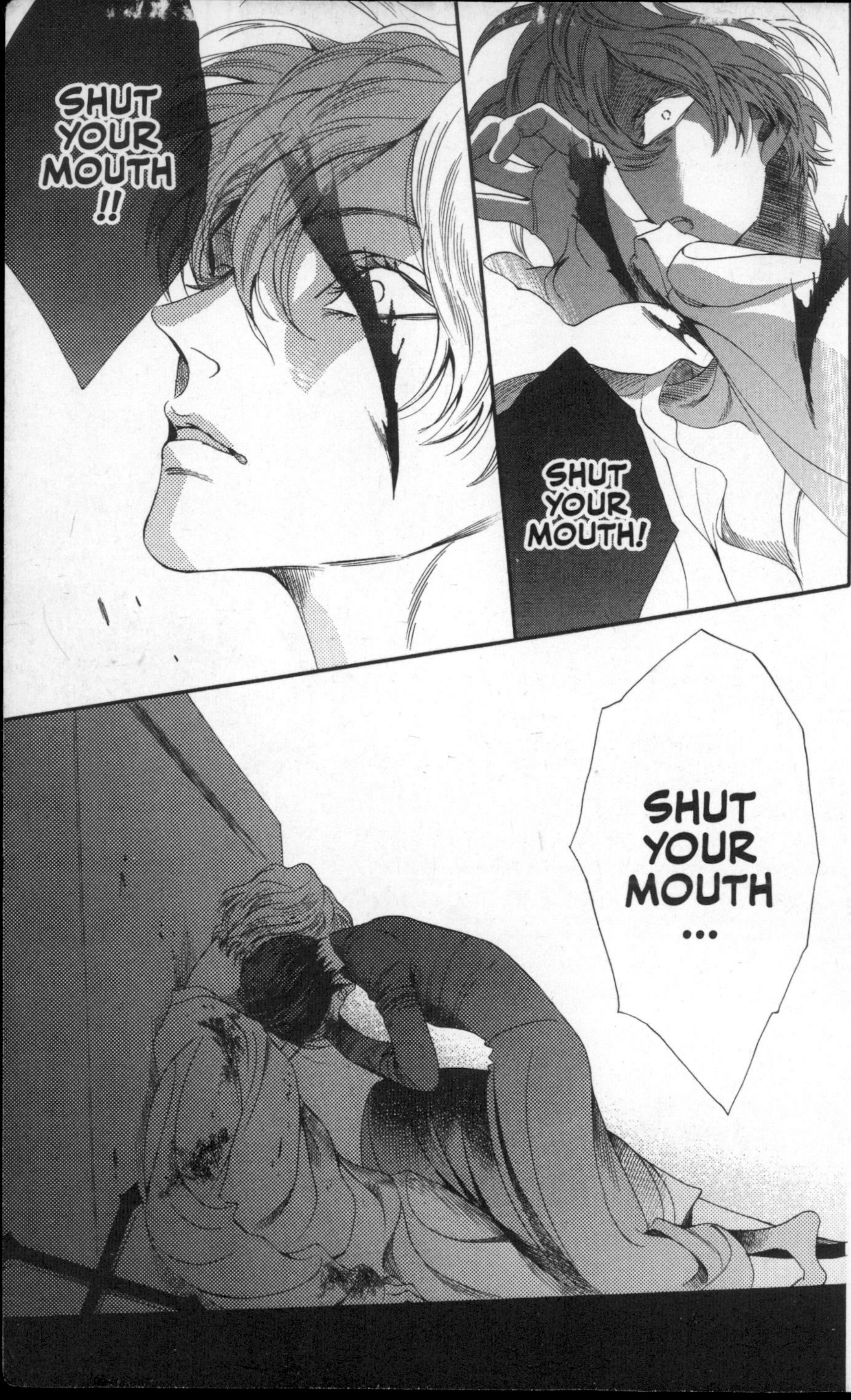
SHUT YOUR MOUTH!
SHUT YOUR MOUTH !!
SHUT YOUR MOUTH ...